*The
Fine Art
of
Italian
Cooking*

The Fine Art of Italian Cooking

GIULIANO BUGIALLI

Times
BOOKS

Library of Congress Cataloging in Publication Data

Bugialli, Giuliano.
  The fine art of Italian cooking.

  Includes index.
  1. Cookery, Italian.   I. Title.
TX723.B76   1977   641.5' 945   76–9699
ISBN 0-8129-0640-3

Manufactured in the United States of America

87   88   14   13   12   11

To my mother,
still the worst cook in the family,
but the best everything else.

I would like to thank Audrey Berman and Henry Weinberg, without whom the book could not have been written

and

Robert Nunnelley, whose painter's eye made the photographs much more than illustrations.

For individual recipes I thank Giovanni Minuccio Cappelli and Avv. Fabrizio Vitaletti of Florence, and, for advice on the Genoese recipes, Mrs. Carla Sanguineti Weinberg.

For permission to reproduce manuscript material, we are deeply grateful to Biblioteca Casanatense (#255), Biblioteca Universitaria di Bologna (#158), and the Library of Congress (Medieval #153).

Contents

Preface *xi*

Some Historical Background *3*

Some Basic Ingredients *13*

A Note on Equipment *26*

Breads and Pizzas *29*

Sauces *51*

BASIC SAUCES, *52*   SAUCES FOR MEAT OR CHICKEN, *57*

SAUCES FOR FISH, *65*   SAUCES FOR PASTA, RICE, AND SOUPS, *69*

Antipasti *83*

Soups *104*

BROTH AND CONSOMMÉ, *104*   PASSATI, *116*

MINESTRONI AND MINESTRE, *120*

Pasta *130*

FRESH PASTA, *131*   DRIED PASTA, *155*   STUFFED FRESH PASTA, *161*

LARGE STUFFED PASTA DISHES, *178*   TIMBALLO DISHES, *206*

ix

Rice First Courses   *2 1 3*

Miscellaneous First Courses   *2 2 4*

Fish   *2 3 7*

The Boiled Course   *2 6 6*

The Fried Course   *2 7 4*

Eggs   *2 8 5*

Poultry and Game   *2 9 0*

Veal and Beef   *3 3 1*

Pork and Pork Products   *3 4 5*

Variety Meats   *3 5 7*

Polenta   *3 6 7*

Composite Main Courses   *3 7 5*

Salads   *3 8 7*

Vegetables   *3 9 4*

Desserts   *4 2 9*

CUSTARDS AND CREAMS, *430*   PASTRY AND PASTRY DESSERTS, *438*

RICE DESSERTS, *482*   FRUIT DESSERTS, *492*

Afterword   *5 0 3*

Measurements Used in This Book   *5 0 4*

Recipes That Can Be Prepared in an Hour   *5 0 5*

Index   *5 0 7*

Preface

IF you have traveled in Italy or known Italians in America, you quickly realized that a Roman is different from a Florentine, a Neapolitan from a Milanese. These differences are even stronger in Italy than in most other countries, because each of its areas had both a long history and a developed culture before it became part of the unified Italy of recent times. In customs and in language, there are dialects—and there are dialects in food as well.

All the Italian cookbooks I have seen in America are written from the point of view of some "dialect," which then extends outward to include food from the other regions. Recently, there have been books written from the viewpoints of Naples, Sicily, and Emilia-Romagna. My book starts with a Tuscan, even a Florentine, point of view. But, just as one speaks dialect or vernacular in the home, with the family, so home cooking tends to exaggerate regional differences. And very rarely does one region restrict its cooking to those dishes which are "alla" that region. *Cotoletta alla milanese* is made all over Italy, as is *Pizza alla napoletana.*

In examining many Italian cookbooks in English, particularly those that stress northern Italian, one finds an inordinate number of Tuscan recipes. Probably the most immediate reason for this is that the most influential cookbook of modern times in Italy was that of Pellegrino Artusi, a Florentine of the last century. He established Tuscan cooking as the standard of *buona, sana cucina,* "good, healthy cooking." There is a further reason, however, of which most people are still unaware. Just as in the midst of a peninsula of different dialects the genius of Dante, Boccaccio, and Petrarch was able to establish Tuscan as the Italian language, so at the same time, in the fourteenth century,

Florentine cooks began to codify the cooking of the emerging Renaissance. The Florentine manuscript of the early 1300s was copied twenty-five years later by the Bolognese, fifty years later by the Venetians. By 1450 this tradition had expanded to and developed in the north of Italy and even France, and probably other countries influenced by the Italian Renaissance.

It is interesting to trace this tradition through the oldest extant manuscripts up to the early nineteenth century. They yield much valuable material that confirms the antiquity of many classic Italian dishes and help in arriving at authentic versions.

It must now be obvious that my attempt here is something more ambitious than telling you about the recipes I learned at my mother's knee. Aside from the fact that my mother hates to cook, I find that an inadequate approach for conveying the range and richness of Italian cooking.

If not in Mama's simple kitchen, where does one look for such cooking? Not in the *trattorie*. Essentially, *trattorie* are unpretentious places, generally of working-class origin, that produce dialect food, sometimes of very high quality but within a limited framework. In Florence and elsewhere in Italy, people of all walks of life enjoy the *trattoria* food for its honesty and simplicity, when it is genuine. The problem arises when *trattorie* attempt to become *ristoranti*, and they decide to add a touch of the "continental," or what they think is French cooking. Then they cease to be honest.

The fine cooking in Italy, that which indeed retains the old Italian gastronomy, takes place in the homes of certain old Florentine families, who have taken the trouble to preserve their traditions. One starts with these recipes. It is then very important to verify both the antiquity and the correctness of these recipes through ancient manuscripts and old printed books. By scrupulously comparing one's own experience with that of the old families, as well as with old manuscripts and early books, it is possible to arrive at generalizations about techniques, spicing, and so on, and to produce authentic recipes that remain gastronomically very valid indeed.

Dear reader, don't let me scare you off. This book is also a basic Italian cookbook, containing many recipes that are not too time consuming as well as some that are of more recent vintage. (I am not, for example, going to avoid dry pasta because it has formed a part of the Italian menu only for the last hundred and fifty years.) It is just that the book includes techniques, for sauces, aspics, pastry, breads, and so on, that truly belong to Italian cooking.

With the aid of photographs, I have attempted to help the reader acquire the basic culinary techniques that are necessary for the finer Italian *cucina*, techniques that go beyond the procedure for a single recipe. These include boning poultry and fish; tying and larding meats; making stuffings, forcemeats, and sausages, broths and aspics, pastries and breads; ways of chopping and cutting; something about presentation; and so on.

It was not possible to do everything in this book that one could in a more specialized one, but I hope at least to provide an introduction to the technical side of the art of Italian cooking.

I strongly feel that a northern Italian cookbook, from a Tuscan, even a Florentine, point of view is very much needed in English. As I previously mentioned, in northern Italian cookbooks quite a large percentage of the recipes are Tuscan. I hope my colleagues will forgive me if I now say, as a native Tuscan and Florentine, that for the most part their Tuscan recipes are unrecognizable to me. It would be pointless, even ungracious, for me to give specific examples of some of the gaffes in these recipes, for they could easily enough be traced to specific books and authors, some current ones justly held in high esteem for those areas closer to home in which they are indeed expert. In sum, while I don't want to criticize anyone, one simply cannot allow these completely inauthentic versions of Tuscan dishes to circulate with authority.

In closing this preface, I would like to discuss two books of the last century, one in English and the other in Italian but available in English translation. These are Janet Ross's *Leaves from My Tuscan Kitchen* from the 1890s and Artusi's own *The Art of Eating Well*.

Artusi's book, a classic and charming to read as well, is extremely valuable historically. It gave Italians in the last century the impetus to keep to their own cooking, and had a very positive influence. However, it still retains a lot of Austrian and French influence. (We must remember that when he wrote a Hapsburg was still sitting on the Tuscan throne.) For example, much as we all love sour cream, it just isn't Italian, and Artusi has recipes using it. Another problem is that Artusi's book, like most cookbooks in Italian, does not always give specific quantities and is vague on procedure. It is a book for those who already know the dishes.

The purpose of Janet Ross's book was probably to stimulate her fellow English to use more vegetables in their diet. But, while she took her recipes from the cooks in her Florentine villa, they must have been doing continental cuisine. Vegetables that are staples of the Tuscan repertory like rape and kale do not appear, while not really Italian vegetables such as Jerusalem artichokes and red cabbage do. And many of the recipes are overtly French. The book, then, is more an interesting historical document of what the international set who had Florentine villas ate in the late nineteenth century.

So now, after all this, perhaps you can understand why I feel that an Italian cookbook, in English, from a Tuscan point of view is necessary.

Page of an early fourteenth-century Florentine manuscript showing recipe for *savore per paparo*, a type of foie gras.

The
Fine Art
of
Italian
Cooking

Some Historical Background

VISITORS who spend a long time in Italy, especially those who come to know the language, often tell me that what they are most struck by is the uninterrupted historical continuity of Italian life and customs. The normal architecture of house and garden seems to be much the same as one sees in the paintings rescued from Pompeii and other places destroyed by the eruption of Vesuvius almost two thousand years ago.

There are also recipes that survive from that world of several thousand years ago. And why not? Many of the basic ingredients of Italian cooking were there—wine, olive oil, flour, and grains, most of the same species of game, meat, and fish, even some of the same cooking utensils in terra-cotta and copper. And today we find traces of two kinds of cooking. While Apicius' book gives us the elaborate dishes of the upper class of the Empire, there was a simpler cooking, which ordinary people ate every day, and this, like many aspects of Roman culture, came from the Etruscans, the people who inhabited Tuscany and whose descendants still live there.

We know that the upper classes in the Middle Ages ate in a way that was related to the way the ancient Romans did, and that a probable by-product of wars and campaigns of that period, such as the Crusades, was the protection of trade routes that brought back the important spices and other ingredients necessary for that elaborate cooking. (It seems probable that in these centuries the tradition of "high" gastronomy best survived at Constantinople, capital of the surviving Roman Empire until 1453, and possibly in Moorish Spain.) Polenta and fish-in-soup dishes survived from the food of the common man.

Modern gastronomy, like most of modern culture, begins in Italy about 1300. The first cookbook manuscripts, Florentine in origin, date from that period. (France's Taillevent was almost a century later.) And it is not merely the date of these manuscripts, but also the attitude contained in them, that is important, for they look toward the future rather than the past. The manuscripts are contemporary with Giotto, the founder of modern painting, with Boccaccio and Petrarch, and with Landini, the first great Renaissance composer, all of whom were Florentines who, we hope, ate the cooking of "Anonimo Toscano," the first modern cookbook writer. Butter, unknown in Roman times, had been discovered (ironic for those who think that Florentine cooking uses olive oil but no butter), and thickening with flour was known to "Toscano," while still unknown in France; so was a sauce quite close to the modern *maionese* and "milk pies" related to the modern quiche.

The English-speaking world tends to think that Italian cooking began with the mid-fifteenth-century writer Platina, and with the recipes of his friend, the great chef Maestro Martino. This is because Platina was lucky enough to benefit from the invention of printing and because his book, translated into French and German, was an important medium for carrying Italian cooking into those countries. But there were manuscripts long before Platina, manuscripts that have come to be studied only recently, and that I have studied for this book. (It was in one of the manuscripts, from the fourteenth century, that I found the term *quinquinelle* describing a sausage-shaped forcemeat, without skin or pastry covering—the origin of quenelles.) There is a tendency also to rely on *Larousse Gastronomique* for historical information, and this is not always accurate. For one thing, *Larousse*, I believe, relies completely on secondary sources, such as the books of Carême from the early nineteenth century, as well as histories that are not aware of manuscripts before Platina.

It is only when we realize the extent of Renaissance Italian influence on France, Germany, England, Poland, and other European countries in other cultural fields that it is possible to believe just how great was the gastronomic influence. There are many dishes we now do not consider Italian that probably originated there, or at least we can say they are present in sixteenth-century Italian cookbooks. These include cherry soup, which we now associate with Hungary; turtle soup, now thought of as English and American; fruit pies, again English and American; stuffed cabbage, Eastern European, and so many dishes now thought to be French that it is not possible to list them.*

In this vein, we can safely say that Italian gastronomic supremacy was not challenged until the time of Louis XIV, a ruler who, ironically, was grandson of a Medici, whose theater was called Theâtres des Italiens, and whose court composer and ballet master was the Florentine Lulli. It was a long time, however, before this challenge succeeded to any great extent. For one thing, while La Varenne's book was influential in Italy from about 1690 on, it was so principally because it listed actual amounts with the ingredients, not because its culinary approach was basically different from that of the Italians. Also, the *potacci* and fricassee found in La Varenne already existed in sixteenth-century Italian books. In the eighteenth century, some Italian dishes were given French names, but the dishes were basically the same. And as late as the second half of the eighteenth century, Catherine the Great of Russia still had an Italian rather than a French chef.

My purpose in giving this survey is to make the reader radically rethink what he regards as Italian cooking and its proper limits. And I can only conclude it by recounting a recent experience of my own. I was amused to see an advertisement for a cooking school in Paris that stated that it was including in its curriculum of classic French dishes pastas and *risotti*, because "after all, they are among the world's great dishes." If culinary history continues the way it has gone, a hundred years from now pasta and *risotti* will be considered French dishes, possibly with French names.

---

* It is worth noting just how the discovery of America affected first Italian and then other European food. The Spanish first brought back tomato and potato plants, but only for ornamental purposes. Again, it was the curious Florentines who started to eat them, in the sixteenth century. Tomatoes were eaten green, either breaded and fried or in *frittate*. Green tomatoes are eaten in both these ways to this day, and the recipes are included in this book. (The spread of the red, ripe tomato did not come until centuries later, going from Naples all over Italy.) Potatoes were widely eaten in Florence two centuries before Parmentier, and deep-fried potato strips, so-called French-fried potatoes, are doubly Florentine, since both the potato and deep-frying were taken to France from Florence. Cannellini beans, sometimes called Tuscan beans in modern times, are white kidney beans and come from America. It is doubly ironic when Italian cookbooks in America tell you to substitute Great Northern beans for Tuscan beans, since the latter are even more American than Tuscan. Turkey was quickly adopted by the Italians in the sixteenth century, to substitute for peacock, that most prestigious bird. Americans, who rightfully consider the turkey their own, are generally surprised to discover for how many centuries it has been an intrinsic part of the Italian menu.

"LA BUONA, SANA CUCINA"

DURING THE sixteenth and seventeenth centuries, Italian cooking reached an incredible degree of complication and elaborateness, not only in the cooking of the dishes, but also in their presentation, compared to which even nineteenth-century presentation is pale. That was the era in which butter, ice, and sugar sculpture, still enduring today as the acme of complex presentation, reached their height. Meat was served in such a way that the animal still appeared to be alive, and the feathers of birds were put back on after the birds were cooked. The supposed living creatures were then presented in a simulated natural environment, perhaps sculpted from sugar or marzipan. Fish were served on ice "brooks" or "rivers." Famous sculptors and architects were employed to do their work in sugar or butter for important banquets, and the sculptor Canova was discovered as a twelve-year-old cook's assistant—doing the butter sculpture.

But the sixteenth century was also the beginning of a revolt against unhealthy and complicated cooking. Good sense was not dead, even then. Many revolted against the excesses described above, just as many are today turning against all the overrichness—all the butter and cream, the foie gras, and so on—that flourished in the schools of chefs like Escoffier. In the sixteenth century the Florentines started their search for the lightest possible, the most healthy, the most elegantly simple cooking—a search that has continued to the present day.

This centuries-long search for a food that expressed the Florentine Renaissance point of view has arrived at a synthesis that stresses freshness, genuineness, and high quality of ingredients (in opposition to the view that covers up weak ingredients with spices and sauces); a classic simplification in approach to herbs and spices; and an abhorrence of heaviness, overrichness, and excessive use of fat. To this end, many spices, butter, cream, fat, and heavy sauces were removed from repertory dishes.

This is all in perfect accord with today's health preoccupations, and perhaps tells us why there is a new appreciation of Italian cooking and its natural attitude toward food.

A SIXTEENTH-CENTURY FLORENTINE DINNER

A FLORENTINE nobleman of the sixteenth century did us the great favor of writing down the menus of every meal eaten in one of the great houses during the year 1546. Some of the dishes eaten are still associated with international gastronomy, and it is a surprise to find that they were already established at that time in Florence. The renaissance of cooking that took place in Florence starting in the fourteenth century may have been given impetus by the arrival there of the Byzantines fleeing Constantinople when it fell to the Turks. Caviar was a standard item in this Florentine household, and while we know that sturgeon existed in northern Italy at that time, even in the Arno itself (it had been the favored fish even of the ancient Romans), caviar is referred to as a dish for which the Greeks (that is, the Byzantines) had a great taste. And it is possible, as we have suggested previously, that Constantinople was the center of gastronomy before Florence. It was at this time in Florence that the practice of dressing salad with oil and vinegar was established.

This listing of menus is particularly interesting because it shows that, for the first time in the modern West, there was a fixed order of courses and many defined conventions for formal dining. The strange thing to us is that fish and meat were never eaten on the same day. There were either many fish dishes or many meat dishes. (Eggs, mushrooms, cheese, of course, could be included with one or the other.) Indeed, the modern order of courses with fish before meat was established only relatively recently. La Varenne in 1650 and Brillat-Savarin in the early 1800s were still following the order of courses established in Florence in the sixteenth century.

The first course, called even then *antipasto*, was a series of appetizers quite different from what the term brings to most people's minds today. Since the pasta course was not introduced until the middle of the 1800s, the word *antipasto* could not have meant "before the pasta," but "before the *pasto*" (or meal).

The second course was the boiled course. This never varied, whether the third course was fried dishes or roasted dishes.

The fourth, or fruit, course included both fruit and vegetables and sometimes *frutta di mare*, like oysters.* (This may be how *frutti di*

---

* It was to the Florentines that we must give the credit for firmly including fruit, and especially vegetables, as a standard part of every meal. Other parts of Europe and America have lagged behind in this, even to the present day.

mare got its name, by being included in the fruit course.) If included, cheese was most generally eaten with this course. When, however, it was cooked in a special way, such as as fried or in a pastry, it could be served with the *antipasti*.

Pastries themselves could belong to any course, depending on what was in them. Again, it was the Florentines who tended to localize sweet dishes at the end of the meal. Honey and sugar had been used in many kinds of dishes before this time, and since cane sugar had been one of the sensational discoveries of the sixteenth century, it was not possible to localize sweet dishes totally; there was, however, a great push in that direction.

Let us start with a day in Lent, March 17, 1546. We can expect a fish day. But though some of the dishes eaten hardly connote sackcloth and ashes, the meal is still simpler and contains fewer courses than would a feast-day meal.

ANTIPASTI

Schiacciatine (little *schiacciate* or pizzas) with ground rosemary, olive oil, and pepper (see page 49)
White endive–dandelion salad
Tarts of *pesci ignudi* (a type of fish no longer available)
Fettunta with pignoli (see page 101)
Rombi (slices of turbot) fried with slices of glazed citron

THE BOILED COURSE

Poached sturgeon (using the whole large middle section)
Little sturgeon balls, *polpe,* poached in a spicy fish soup
Lentil soup served with caviar
Savor bianco di Amandole, spicy almond sauce (probably to accompany the poached sturgeon)
(A great variety of sauces and *savori* were used to accompany these boiled and poached dishes, some of the recipes for which are given later in this book.)

THE FRIED COURSE

Fried broccoli with bitter-orange sauce and pepper

Fried tench (the Bisenzio River near Florence was famous in that time for its fresh-water fish)

Deep-fried whole little fish from the Arno (*pesciolini*), squid, and little shrimp, garnished with lemon slices and olives

FRUIT

Tart or pie of pureed red chick-peas, with red apples (matching colors were important)

Ground almond pudding with sugar

Hearts of palm

Fennel

On the evening of the same day, everyone supped lightly:

Salad of mint, lettuce, field salad with flowers and capers

Spinach *alla fiorentina*, probably then as now with *balsamella* and Parmigiano (see page 422)

Little pastries, some each of artichokes, cardoons, and fennel

This really was a typical day. I did not choose one that had such rarified dishes as breasts of quail treated in some elaborate way, or peacock tongues, or sturgeon livers. The feast days included at least two more elaborate courses, as well as more dishes in each course. A roast could be substituted for the fried course, but it was not usual to have both. Game was widely used on the meat days, and since everything was eaten in what was regarded as its best season, there was no special single period for game.

A FORMAL DINNER IN ITALY

AMERICANS GENERALLY prefer to dine informally, but once in a while they like to "pull out all the stops." In serving a formal Italian dinner, it is fun to do it in the real Italian manner, which is different from that of England or France.

Before dinner, *aperitivi* are served. Among the best known are dry or sweet vermouths such as Martini, Cinzano or Punt e Mes, or non-vermouths such as Campari, Cynar, or Aperol. Food is not served with aperitifs, except for some light salted thing, like almonds.

An Italian table is set with the service plate and all the silver and glasses that will be used during the meal. Each course is brought on a plate, which is placed on the service dish and removed at the end of the course; the service plate is never removed during the meal. The silver used for a course is removed after that course, but since all the silver needed for the entire meal was already placed on the table at the beginning, no new silver is added during the meal. The same is true of glasses; a glass is removed when the wine changes, but new glasses are never added.

Bottles of wine are never kept on the table. If there are no waiters, the head of the house, if male, generally fills the glasses and keeps the bottles on a credenza until refilling is in order. If the head of the house is a woman, she either fills the glasses herself or asks her escort or the youngest male guest to do it for her.

When everyone is seated, the antipasto is served at the table. The kind of wine served depends on the dish, whether it is hot or cold. Generally, wines accompanying antipasti are on the light side, and the least serious wine of the evening.

It is with the so-called first course, or *primo piatto*, that true Italian convention departs from much overseas usage. Wine is *never* served with pasta at a fine dinner, a fact that never fails to shock my American friends. But so it is. With soups, there is more flexibility. If the soup contains wine, none is drunk to accompany it. If the soup does not contain wine, generally the wine of the antipasto course may be continued, but a serious new wine is not introduced. In an elaborate dinner, there is sometimes a course—the *piatto di mezzo*, or "in-between course"—between the first and second. This is usually an elaborate treatment of a vegetable, a *sformato* or some other complex dish. A typical example would be a *sformato* of vegetables with sweetbreads and brains in a sauce of *balsamella* and Parmigiano. The vegetable used should not be too closely related to the vegetable used to accompany the second course. The accompanying wine is usually the same as that of the second course, which follows.

The serious wine of the evening is usually served with the second course, *secondo piatto*. Usually one vegetable accompanies this course, served in a separate dish. The only exception to this is in those dishes of which the vegetable is an integral part, such as *arista* with *rape*, in which the vegetable should be served on the same dish as the meat.

Bread is always served with the second course, but is never accompanied by butter. The bread is brought in whole and then cut on the credenza, *not* on the table, in the presence of the guests. It is then passed around in a basket. The bread is not put on the plate with the main dish, but is usually left to rest on the table next to the dish. However, lately little silver bread dishes are being introduced, in imitation of usage in other countries. I repeat that butter is not eaten with the bread.

In general, Italians, not liking to confuse a dinner with a wine tasting, do not use more than three wines plus *aperitivo* in a single meal. In any case, more than one wine should never be served with the same course.

A salad may be served in lieu of the vegetable accompanying the second course. The dressing is always oil, salt, and either wine vinegar or lemon juice. Herbs, cheeses, croutons, and similar additions to a dressing are never used. If a cooked vegetable accompanies the second course, no salad is served. There is no separate salad course.

Next there is a fruit or cheese course—one or the other, not both. The well-known cheese-pear combination would not be used in a formal dinner. A mild cheese is served, such as Taleggio, a soft pecorino, or even a factory cheese such as Bel Paese. A strong cheese such as Gorgonzola, Parmigiano, provolone or even an aged pecorino would not be appropriate (these are all used for other purposes). If cheese is served, the wine of the previous course is continued. If fresh fruit—such as grapes, apples, pears, plums, or apricots—is served instead, it would not be accompanied by wine. If the fruit is cooked or embellished, as, for instance, strawberries or raspberries with whipped cream or in wine, it would be a combined fruit and dessert course. Except when the fruit is in wine, a fruit dessert may be accompanied by a sweet wine.

The dessert course is accompanied by a sweet wine or by a dry or sweet spumante or champagne. (Just as the French under English influence made champagne drier in the late nineteenth century, the Italians have now made some of their spumante dry.)

Espresso coffee, always black, is served after dinner, in another room. It is not served at the dinner table. Brandy and cordials are not really in order at a formal dinner in Italy.

Obviously, Italians do not dine formally every night. But it may amuse you to try it when you're planning a "big" night with an ambitious Italian menu.

Some Basic Ingredients

HERBS AND SPICES

THE BASIC herbs of Tuscan cooking are rosemary (*ramerino*), parsley (*prezzemolo*), sage (*salvia*), and basil (*basilico*). Tarragon (*dragoncello*) is a specialty of Siena, and marjoram and thyme are called for in special dishes. Oregano (*origano*) is rarely used in the north of Italy.

The omnipresent spices of Tuscany are nutmeg (*noce moscata*) and, of course, black pepper. White and red pepper are sometimes called for, and a great variety of spices is used in the older recipes—cinnamon, ginger, cardamom, coriander, and cumin. Saffron was once used as much as salt and pepper are today; fennel seed and aniseed are used in special dishes.

ROSEMARY

Dried rosemary leaves are perfectly fine to use, though they should not be so old that they have lost their flavor. (After about a year.) Even better, of course, is fresh rosemary. The plants grow well indoors in pots, as well as outside. The rosemary plant does most of its growing in the winter, so if it is kept indoors, it should be placed near a window that can be kept partially open in winter. The reason many indoor rosemary plants don't thrive is because they don't get enough air and light. Try to have enough plants to enable you to put an entire sprig inside a roast fish or fowl.

Quantities in the recipes which follow are for dried rosemary. If fresh is used, the amount should be increased a bit.

PARSLEY

Use the large-leaved, so-called Italian parsley. Fortunately, it is available throughout the year.

SAGE

Most dried sage sold in America seems to come from the Balkans and has a flavor that is not appropriate to Italian cooking. It is best to take the trouble to buy fresh sage in season and to preserve it in salt. American sage is the same as Italian. Preserve it the same way you preserve basil in salt (see below).

BASIL

Fresh basil is a joy and a necessity to many Italian dishes. Since it is not available all year, a number of ways have grown up over the centuries of preserving it. For me the least satisfactory of these are freezing and drying, since they both cause the essential flavor to be much diminished. The two better ways to preserve fresh basil are in coarse salt or under olive oil.

Preserving Basil in Salt

In a Mason jar with a lid that closes tightly, place a layer of coarse (kosher) salt. Make a layer of fresh basil leaves. Before using, wipe the basil leaves with paper towel, but do not wash them.

Alternate layers of salt and basil leaves until the jar is full. Cover the top layer of basil with a layer of salt.

Basil preserved in this way loses some of its green color, but preserves all of its flavor. Dishes based on really fresh basil such as *pasta alla puttanesca* (see page 159) would not be possible, but almost all others are with this substitution. Keep the jar in the refrigerator, tightly closed.

Basil leaves can also be preserved covered with olive oil. This type of preserved basil is best for making *pesto,* as it keeps its green color rather well. However, it is not useful for dishes that do not have an olive oil taste.

TARRAGON

Dried tarragon is usually imported from France for the American market. It is perfectly adequate, though fresh tarragon is of course preferable when it is in season. Be careful when you buy fresh tarragon when it is out of season in your area: some hothouse versions are completely flavorless and usually, to compound the insult, very expensive.

BAY LEAVES OR LAUREL

In this area I disagree with many of my colleagues, in that I prefer California bay laurel leaves, sold in jars still green and fresh-looking, to the completely dried imported bay leaves. (A brand such as Spice Islands sometimes has fresh-looking green leaves.) For me the true taste of laurel is better retained in those, and sometimes it is crucial to the dish (as in the chicken breast *tortellini* filling on page 176).

OLIVE OIL

EACH DECEMBER in Italy, olives are passed through a hot press to obtain their oil. The olives are pressed three times. The first produces extra-virgin oil, which—dark green and full of the taste of olive—is used for dishes that really depend upon olive oil. Tuscan olive oil is as famous as Chianti wine, and much of it comes from the same vineyards (see below). Its quality is deep and rich but light, countrified but not over refined. While lighter and finer than southern Italian and Sicilian oil, it is more genuine and less factory refined than the oil of Liguria or the Mediterranean coast that now belongs to France.

Remember, the best olive oil is produced in farms, often connected with vineyards, not by factories. Almost all of the Italian olive oil imported into America is factory produced and second or third pressing. The container will say *extra-vergine* if the oil is really first pressing. If it is not so labeled, you can be sure that it is not virgin oil. There is a little virgin oil imported from southern Italy, but it is too heavy for all but southern Italian food.

In Tuscany, the cult of oil and critical refinement about it equals the fanaticism of wine expertise. Some Americans who are aware of the difference visit the vineyard and bring oil back with them to America. But this is impractical for most people.

After considerable testing and comparing, I feel that the olive oil available in America that gets results closest to the Tuscan is the virgin Spanish imported by Goya products. Though a Spanish oil, it is closer to good Italian oil than the Italian oils available in the United States. Some say it is possible that California could produce something close to Tuscan oil, but my own experience has not confirmed this.

BUTTER AND "COOKING OIL"

Though renaissance cookbooks have sections on how to make different kinds of *butiro*, the old word for "butter," Italy does not produce outstanding butter compared to Denmark, France, or the United States. Italian butter is lower in fat content, which could be good, but it is also less tasty. Parma, the home of Parmigiano cheese, produces some of the best Italian butter.

Butter as a spread is almost unused in Italy, except with caviar; cooking with butter is characteristic of the regions north of Tuscany. Sauces based on butter, flour, and milk (as, for instance, *balsamella*) very probably originated in Florentine cooking of the Renaissance, but today it is Emilia-Romagna, with Bologna (which Italians call "Bologna the fat"), that stresses, and perhaps overuses, butter and cream, like some French cooking. In Bologna, a good festive meal could very well have a buttery and/or creamy base to every course. This is not typically Italian, not very healthy, and really just as limited as having a tomato base to every course. However, used with proper balance and sparingly, butter and cream-based dishes have an important place, and will probably taste even better made with American rather than Italian butter. And it is not out of the question to substitute a good margarine and get a good and authentic result.

The cooking oil most used in Italy—light and really completely tasteless—is a mixed-seed oil called, generically, *olio di semi*. None of the generally available seed oils in America get the same result. I have found that solid vegetable shortening (particularly Crisco) produces a result closer to Italian *olio di semi* than American seed oils, so for most purposes this is the best substitution. The recipes themselves specify if the dish requires olive oil or butter rather than cooking oil. In recipes not depending on the olive oil taste, in Italy I substitute *olio di semi* for a lighter result in many recipes which here specify olive oil. (*Note: Olio di semi* is only part corn oil.)

PROSCIUTTO, SALAMI, AND PANCETTA

ITALY PRODUCES a boiled ham (*prosciutto cotto*) quite similar to that produced in America, so when it is called for in a dish, there are no problems at all.

But it is the uncooked, unsmoked ham cured in salt that is the most characteristic kind of Italian ham. When we say "prosciutto" in America, we refer to this kind of ham, though properly it is *prosciutto crudo*, or uncooked ham.

Prosciutto varies a great deal in Italy according to region. The celebrated prosciutto of Parma from Langhirano is sweet, and if it is possible to say such a thing, it is almost like a "dessert" prosciutto. It is this prosciutto that goes so well with fresh figs or melon as an antipasto. (More salty prosciutti are less appropriate.) San Daniele prosciutto from the far north of Italy is equally celebrated and less sweet. Both of these types are, as far as I know, unavailable in America.

Tuscan prosciutto, salty and more countrified, is used with salami for antipasto, accompanied by good Tuscan bread without salt. This type is also unavailable here.

Most *prosciutto crudo* found in America is domestic and can be quite good indeed. Sometimes it is not really aged enough, but the flavor is fine. (Making your own prosciutto is not difficult if you have an unheated outdoor shed behind the house, but I am not suggesting it here.)

Caution: Be sure that the domestic prosciutto is *not smoked*. Italians do not smoke meats, and smoked prosciutto or *pancetta* (which would be bacon) would totally ruin an Italian dish.

Factory-made Genoese and Milanese salamis are available in the United States. Mortadella, the original bologna from Bologna, is also obtainable. Importers can get the original, shipped in cans, and there is also a domestic version. The Bolognese keep the recipe for real mortadella a secret, though it is made mainly from pork.

Tuscan salamis are celebrated in Italy, but again are made on farms and vineyards, rather uncommercially, and are not exported. The fennel-flavored *finocchiona*, also appropriate to eat with figs and melon as antipasto, is not exported either. When in Italy, be sure to try both of these.

Pancetta, the same cut of pork as bacon but salted rather than smoked, is very important to Italian cooking. It is generally found in a rolled-up form, resembling a salami. If *pancetta* is not available, substitute salt pork or a salt pork–boiled ham combination. Each recipe here specifies which to substitute if necessary. Since *pancetta* itself is salty, there is no need to blanch the salt pork before using it. (Fresh fatback is not used in Italy.)

WINE FOR COOKING

GOOD-QUALITY wine should be used for cooking. In fact, in dishes in which the wine is a main element, such as pears cooked in Chianti and port or fresh strawberries in wine, I would say that the right wine is essential to the dish.

Tuscan dishes taste more authentic when a Tuscan wine, such as imported Chianti, is used.

WINE VINEGAR

CHIANTI WINE vinegar is not widely available in the United States. For authenticity, check the label for Firenze as place of origin. It is probably more practical to think of obtaining a "mother" and making vinegar with Chianti wine.

In unpasteurized wine, a mother forms naturally, but wine imported into the United States generally is pasteurized. Therefore, it is necessary to obtain a mother from someone who already has homemade vinegar. Place the mother in a bottle of Chianti and allow it to stand, half open and unrefrigerated. The vinegar should be ready in a week to ten days. The better the quality of the wine, the better the vinegar.

COARSE SALT

THIS TYPE of salt, readily available in the United States as kosher salt, is much to be preferred for some purposes. In the recipes it is specifically called for when needed; otherwise use ordinary salt.

MUSHROOMS

WHITE, CULTIVATED mushrooms, so-called *champignons de Paris*, are not popular in Italy. There is still a wide acquaintanceship with wild mushrooms, of which the most popular is the large-capped brown *porcino* mushroom. *Porcini* grow best under the chestnut trees in Tuscany. They often reach great size, and the caps are broiled and eaten as a main dish. In season, they are widely available in markets there, along with several other species. The incredible flavor of *porcini* is preserved and in some ways even intensified by drying. Fortunately, *porcini* are available in Italian markets and some gourmet shops in the United States as "dried Italian wild mushrooms." Of the brands imported here, I have found the Folci one particularly fragrant. Though dried *porcini* are expensive, very small quantities go a long way, and they are worth the price.

TRUFFLES

THE MAIN truffle areas of Europe are Alba and Norcia in Italy and Périgord in France. The first produces white truffles and the last two black ones: the Italians prize the white ones above the black for their great fragrance and flavor. Though they are not commercially exploited, there are also white truffles in parts of Tuscany, generally gathered by local people who keep their location a well-guarded secret. No truffles have yet been discovered in the Western Hemisphere, though some knowledgeable people feel that parts of California should have them, as the countryside is similar in places to areas where they are found in Europe.

White truffles are available in cans, but are a poor substitute for fresh ones. They are sold in American gourmet shops.

Many feel the fall season, with its game and truffles, is the best time to see what Italian cooking is capable of.

ALMONDS

ONCE ALMONDS were to European cookery what butter and cream is to French today, or tomatoes to southern Italian. Almond trees grew (and still do, in lesser numbers) all over the lands and islands of the Mediterranean, and the trade in their nuts was a major industry. Ground up, they were used as the basic thickening and as the base of the dishes of the "white" category (remember the color categories of early cooking), such as *savor bianco* and *bianco mangiare*. Present research points to Catalonia in northern Spain as the key area for the origin of these dishes rather than France, as scholars used to automatically assume. Almond milk was also widely used, and effectively disappeared only recently.

The almond was for centuries one of the most important artistic and religious symbols of Europe. It was the symbol of fecundity. Tables for feasts were often almond shaped, and all of the paintings and early dramas about the Annunciation are full of almond shapes.

Almond trees are the first to bloom, usually in February, and to see a Mediterranean island covered with their white flowers and remarkable aroma is never to forget the experience.

Almonds are increasingly difficult to get in Italy. But in America, California almonds are fine, and easily available.

BITTER ALMONDS

ASIDE FROM the normal almond tree, there is another species that produces a nut of a totally different taste. These almonds, bitter almonds, are used extensively in Italian, Hungarian, and other types of cooking. The characteristic taste is that which predominates in the type of Italian cookie called *amaretti*, widely imported into America from Italy.

The real bitter almond is not imported, but the type sometimes available, and with a taste identical to that of bitter almonds, is the inside portion of apricot pits. However, even these are becoming scarce in Italy, which is their main place of origin. Hungarian stores in large American cities seem to be more conscientious about stocking them than Italian markets.

ANCHOVIES

ANCHOVIES ARE preserved in two ways: (1) in oil, filleted and lightly salted; (2) in salt, unfilleted. The first type is much more readily available and more convenient. However, the second type is preferred by good Italian cooks for their taste. They can be found occasionally in barrels, especially in Italy, but more often in large tins, canned in Italy but available in specialized Italian markets here in America. It is worth the extra trouble if you can find them.

Do not hesitate to open a large can, as the anchovies can still be preserved in their salt after the can is opened. The heads of the fish are already removed, but it is necessary to fillet them—that is, to open them and remove the central bone.

Anchovy paste is a commercial preparation sold in a tube. It is, of course, inferior to a freshly prepared paste, but is sometimes useful. It substitutes only for the anchovies; other ingredients must be added to it, depending on the recipe.

CHEESE FOR COOKING

PARMIGIANO

What can one say in praise of Parmigiano? Not only Italian cooking, but French cooking as well could not exist without it. It comes from the zone of Parma, as the name suggests, and of Reggio Emilia. Made from cow's milk, it is aged for about two years. The existence of Parmigiano has been documented for about two thousand years.

Caution: Be sure that the rind has *Parmigiano-Reggiano* printed all over it. The word *"grana"* is not enough, as this is merely a generic term for that kind of cheese. Lately an inferior substitute called *grana padano* has been appearing all over. Do not let your shopkeeper pass it off on you. It is a perfectly good cheese, but let them sell it for what it is, not pretend that it is Parmigiano.

The drier outer part of the cheese is best for grating. If the inside is still rather soft, it is better for eating. The already grated cheeses sold under the name of Parmigiano should not be considered, unless you have no other choice. In cooking, remember that Parmigiano should not be allowed to brown, as it becomes bitter. This is dealt with in the individual recipes.

PECORINO (Sheep's Cheese)

Italy produces a wide variety of sheep's cheeses. Some, aged a few months, are eaten as a dessert or as snacks. When aged longer, they are used for grating. Tuscany is famous for its pecorinos, the most celebrated being those of the Siena area. Every Chianti vineyard produces its own pecorino cheese for local consumption. These cheeses, aged a relatively short time, are unavailable in America, but should be tried when you visit Italy.

The Italian pecorinos which are known here are the aged ones used for grating, such as *Romano* and *Sardo*, from the areas of Rome and Sardinia. These usually play the same role as Parmigiano in the dishes of their areas, and are sometimes used in combination with Parmigiano. Sardo has come to be increasingly used for Genoese dishes as the local pecorinos of that area are disappearing. Romano is of course most suitable for Roman dishes. For those Tuscan dishes which specifically call for pecorino, I have made appropriate substitutions; such as *ricotta salata* of sheep's milk.

When buying Romano or Sardo, be careful to see that it comes from a large form of imported cheese. Local imitations should not be used unless there is no alternative.

GROVIERA

There is a border area of Switzerland, Italy, and France in which is produced a cheese (of the type we call in America "Swiss cheese") called in Switzerland and France "Gruyère" and in Italy "Groviera," the name coming from the Swiss town of Gruyère. The French and Italian versions are not imitations since they really come from the same area. Groviera is widely used in Italy, both for eating and, grated, for cooking. Though Groviera is not available here, this is no problem, since so-called Switzerland Swiss cheese is widely sold.

GORGONZOLA

Italians don't generally like moldy cheeses with a strong smell, but Gorgonzola is the exception. It comes from Lombardy, outside of Milan. Try to get the *dolce*, or sweet, type rather than the salty. Only substitute blue cheese if you absolutely must; Gorgonzola is sweeter and milder.

MOZZARELLA

The best mozzarella comes from the *bufaline* (water buffaloes) of Italy, not from cows. But it doesn't travel, so we must substitute the cow's milk form found domestically. In cooking, this is not a problem, since the *bufalina* cheese is too fine, in any case, to use in cooking and is reserved for eating. Part-skim mozzarella is available and produces a lighter result, closer to the Italian.

RICOTTA

Ricotta is not considered a cheese in Italy, any more than yogurt would be. Americans tend to class it with cheeses because it outwardly resembles cottage cheese. For eating, American ricotta is probably superior to that of Italy, because it is creamier and has a richer flavor. But it is more difficult to use for cooking because it is more watery. In the recipes I have compensated for this in various ways (though not by adding flour when it is not called for). If you like, squeeze out the ricotta in a cheesecloth to make it drier. Part-skim ricotta also produces a result closer to the original.

BEANS (see pages 119 and 400)

RICE (see page 213)

TOMATOES (POMODORI)

IN ITALY, plum tomatoes are used for sauces. Cherry tomatoes, never eaten in salad as in America, are preserved through the winter by keeping them on a layer of straw in a cool, high place; a few are added to cook in the broth. The larger tomatoes are used for salad, and are generally eaten greener than they are here.

Tomatoes were brought to Europe from South America by the Spanish, who used them for decoration, never to eat. It was the Florentines who, in the sixteenth century, first ate them, as we have already mentioned, but the real spread of the tomato in Italy and France began only in the late 1700s.

One must join in the tragic chorus of those complaining about the decline of tomato quality due to mass marketing. Mealy tomatoes with thick, difficult-to-bruise skin are promoted because they can travel cross country; the tender-skinned varieties, such as those from New Jersey (close in quality and texture to the San Marzano type), are less available. Also, like other fruit, tomatoes are picked unripened in order to make them last longer; they ripen artificially and lose their flavor. The great advantage is supposed to be that we can have fresh tomatoes all year long if they can travel long distances.*

* It is unjust to pretend that fresh tomatoes are always available in Italy. They are, in fact, available for a shorter period than in America, which has California and other regions to draw upon. Winter tomatoes for salad have become available only recently in Italy, because they are imported mainly from Spain.

For sauces, fresh, very ripe plum tomatoes are best. But, because of their sporadic availability, the quality of canned tomatoes becomes an important matter. We recommend, in the following order of preference:

1. San Marzano tomatoes (from the Naples area). The can should say "imported from Italy." Among the brands are Cirio, Vitelli, and some Progresso (be particularly careful with this last brand to check that the label says "imported from *Italy*").

2. American plum tomatoes. The American plum tomatoes are good, but they are often less ripe when canned, so they must be cooked at least fifteen minutes longer than the Italian ones. They also tend to be more watery, but the extra cooking will also take care of that, since it reduces the liquid. Do not add sugar in an attempt to duplicate the taste of the sweeter San Marzanos. It creates an artificial, unpleasant taste. Better less sweet but natural.

3. Imported (not Italian). Some brands, such as Progresso, distribute some cans that say "imported," but in small print you can read that it is from Argentina or another country, not Italy. For our purposes, the American tomatoes are preferable to these.

TOMATO PASTE

Tomato paste should not be overused. Some imported brands are packaged in tubes, so you can use a little at a time and not waste what remains. Encourage your stores to stock these tubes.

A Note on Equipment

---◆---

SEASONING NEW POTS

To INITIATE aluminum or stainless steel pots, the only thing you have to do is carefully clean them. But you must be very careful to season other types of pots in the right way.

FOR TERRA-COTTA POTS (glazed or unglazed)

Place the pots in cold water for 24 hours. Remove the pots from the water, fill them with more cold water, and let stand for 24 hours more.

Remove the water from the pot and carefully rub it, to be sure that any remaining surface dust is removed. The terra-cotta pot is now ready to be used, with the following cautions: Always put the pot on a "flame tamer." Start with a low flame until the pot is well warmed, then turn up the flame.

Terra-cotta pots are used a lot, not only because they retain heat evenly but because they give the food a particular "soft" taste that it is not possible to reproduce with a different pot. In Italy I think there is no family without a very old terra-cotta casserole or saucepan in which meat sauce is made year after year.

In the old times, terra-cotta pots were seasoned not only by placing them in water but also by rubbing them with garlic cloves afterward. This was done to avoid the formation of mold on unglazed terra-cotta, which can happen with seasonal changes. The garlic-seasoned pot, called *la pentola all' aglio*, could be used to make meat sauce adding little or no garlic.

FOR IRON FRYING PANS OR SKILLETS

Iron pots are the most difficult to maintain because they must be kept well seasoned to prevent rust from forming.

Quickly wash in cold water, then dry with paper towels. Freely oil the inside of the pan, all over. Sprinkle the inside part of the pan with salt, then place the pan on a low flame, and with some paper towels rub the salt-oil mixture all over inside. Keep doing this until the salt becomes dark in color and the pan very hot.

Remove the pan from the flame, discard the salt, and wipe the pan off with paper towels.

Repeat procedure with the oil and salt. In order to have a very well-seasoned pan you must repeat the procedure at least three times.

Copper pots do not have to be seasoned.

BAGNO MARIA AND DOUBLE-BOILER TECHNIQUE

THESE TECHNIQUES were invented by a Florentine lady, Maria de Cleofa, in the sixteenth century. The French term *bain-marie* is simply a translation of *bagno maria*, "*maria*" referring to the lady mentioned above.

In both *bagno maria* and double-boiler, you are using gentle, *moist* heat to cook slowly. In the *bagno maria*, which in Italy is used to cook, not merely to keep things warm, the large pot or container that holds the food is put into a large pot of water. The flame heats the water, which then transmits its heat to what is cooking. (*Fagioli in fiasco*, see page 400, is a special form of *bagno maria* cooking.)

In the double-boiler, one pot fits atop the other. The water in the bottom pot does not actually touch the upper pot; its steam, strong because enclosed, produces the necessary heat. (See page 431 for a photo of a double-boiler.)

Pastry creams and cream custards are among the things which require the double-boiler technique. When egg yolks are mixed with sugar and heated, a slight chemical change, as well as a change in color, takes place at a critical moment. The heat must be of the special sort produced by a double-boiler technique so the eggs heat but do not cook.

These devices involving a scientific principle, however modest, were typical of the Florentine mind when the *bagno maria* was invented, roughly the period of Leonardo da Vinci.

CHOPPING WITH THE MEZZALUNA

THE MEZZALUNA or half-moon is the usual implement for hand chopping in Italy. Cleavers and large knives are used in France but not in Italy. The rolling back-and-forth motion of the mezzaluna is perhaps less tiring because the implement does not have to be lifted off with each stroke. And when mastered it is also quicker for the same reason. If you are used to other implements, they may be substituted, but do get acquainted with the mezzaluna and see if you prefer it as do almost all Italians. It is particularly less tiring than the American wooden bowl and chopper combination.

Basic utensils for chopping: blender, mortar and pestle, food processor, chopping board and *mezzaluna*.

Breads and Pizzas

BREAD

TUSCAN "COUNTRY" bread is one of the main accomplishments of Tuscan cooking. It is extremely light and yeasty, having three rather than two risings, and it contains no fat. It ranges from almost white to slightly dark and even very dark, almost completely whole wheat. Its extreme versatility comes not only from its lightness and crustiness, but also from the fact that it contains virtually no salt. For this reason, it is easier at first to appreciate the superiority of this bread when it is accompanied by olive oil and condiments, such as in the dish called *fettunta*; or when covered by a game spread, such as in the dish called *crostini*; or when it is used in hearty soups or as the basis for home-made bread crumbs. Florentines say that the Tuscan bread is not meant to be eaten alone, but rather as an accompaniment to food or as an ingredient in a dish. But eventually addiction sets in; non-Tuscans adjust to the saltlessness and go on to appreciate the bread for its own sake. For this reason, local versions of it are sold in many parts of Italy. In Bologna or Milan, one can find what the natives call "Tuscan" bread in the stores. Once attuned to it, one finds some other breads, previously admired, now too heavy or too greasy. Forgive my paean, but I am trying to convey just how passionate even the most sophisticated and traveled Florentines are about their bread.

It is possible to make completely authentic Tuscan bread in America. First of all, a brick oven can be improvised in your own oven (to be explained later). Then for the white bread, all-purpose unbleached flour is perfectly adequate. For darker bread, however, even *pane integrale*, a little more "elbow grease" is necessary, since a small amount of whole-wheat flour must be ground by hand, American whole-wheat flour being ground differently from Italian. But the result is worth the 10 minutes or so of extra work.

Tuscan cooking includes a goodly number of dishes made with bread, more than any other Italian region, many of them dating back to a time before dry pasta was used in central Italy as a standard part of the diet. One can jump to the conclusion that these bread dishes are "peasant," or country, food, but this would be incorrect. Bread was an expensive, even luxury item until recent centuries—probably because the flour for bread had to be ground very fine. More standard, inexpensive staples were made from coarsely ground meal, from the *puls* that was the standard staple of the ancient Roman populace to the polenta of modern times. These Tuscan bread dishes come from a period when bread was a food of the rich.

We include recipes for the standard light Tuscan country bread; the dark bread *pane scuro,* which has some chaff in it; and the real whole-wheat, or *pane integrale.* In addition, there are recipes for bread with olives, bread with sausage, and the famous ancient *pan di ramerino* (bread made with rosemary and olive oil), mentioned by Boccaccio. We include as well *pane co' Santi* made with nuts, and *buccellato,* the famous sweet bread of Lucca.

After breads, there are recipes for pizzas and their Tuscan relatives, *schiacciate.* Then we discuss how to make good homemade bread crumbs, so important in Italian cooking, and little fried *crostini* (croutons) for soup.

Throughout the book there are recipes for a few of the Tuscan standby dishes that are made from bread. This saltless bread is versatile enough to form the basis for both "salted" and "sweet" dishes.

YEAST

Fresh Compressed Yeast

Compressed yeast is found in cakes of just over ½ ounce, which are comparable to single packets of active dry yeast, or in 2-ounce cakes. With the resurgence of interest in home-baked bread in America, compressed yeast is found in more and more stores and supermarkets.

This yeast should be dissolved in lukewarm water (about 85 degrees). Watch the expiration date on the wrapper to be sure that the yeast is fresh.

Active Dry Yeast

Packets of active dry yeast are found almost everywhere. Each packet is comparable to a cake of compressed yeast just over ½ ounce in weight, but may take slightly longer than compressed yeast to rise to the desired lightness. Two packets are generally necessary for each of the loaves of bread described here. This yeast must be dissolved in hot water (about 115 degrees); be sure that you use it within the cut-off date on the packet.

Absolutely do *not* proof the active dry yeast with sugar. It will ruin the taste of Tuscan bread.

FLOUR AND WHEAT

White Flour

All-purpose unbleached flour works well for Tuscan bread; no special or imported flours are necessary. Do not sift the flour before using. One cup of flour weighs 4 ounces.

Dark Flour

To make both the dark bread and the whole-wheat bread, a little extra work is necessary, for it is not possible to use already ground American dark flour. Wheat is ground with a cylindrical grinder in Italy, instead of the rotary type used in America, and the result is a completely different type of dark flour, in which the chaff is not pulverized but remains in larger pieces. (Even American cracked-wheat flour is not the same.) There is, however, an easy solution to this. The old-fashioned wooden hand coffee-grinders are still used and widely available (see photo, page 38). Using the hand coffee-grinder and winter-wheat berries, widely available in health food stores and elsewhere, you can grind, in about 10 minutes, the small amount of dark flour necessary to mix with the white flour for *pane scuro*, the dark bread.

IMPROVISING A BRICK OVEN

The taste of bread varies a lot depending on how it is baked. The optimum for taste and for consistency of crust is obtained by baking bread in a brick oven, heated by burning oak branches mixed with a few walnut branches, and then swept out with a broom of olive branches dampened with rain water. This is the old way of baking bread, and the result is superb. The bread has a perfume that is impossible to forget, and the crust has a crispness obtainable only by baking in a brick oven. While we may not be able to duplicate the flavor produced by oak, walnut, and olive, we can easily produce a brick oven.

To improvise a brick oven in any stove, just cover the middle shelf of the oven with a layer of ovenproof unglazed terra-cotta bricks or tiles from ½ inch to 1 inch thick. It is only the bottom surface that must be of brick in order to get the effect of a brick oven.

Be sure to light the oven at least 10 minutes before the usual time, because bricks need extra time to warm up (see photo, page 37).

Pane Toscano
(Tuscan Country Bread)   (MAKES 1 LOAF)

To make the basic white bread, use all-purpose unbleached flour. First, the yeast is dissolved and mixed with a little flour and allowed to rise, then the risen "sponge" is mixed with the rest of the flour and the dough allowed to rise again. Finally, the dough, which is not placed in any pan or container, is put in the oven, directly upon the bricks. Though the dough is not actually punched down when carried to the oven, it does fall, and has to rise a third time in the oven. This third rising, once much used in America but now rare, produces a very light bread.

Begin to make the bread at least 6 hours before you need it, as it requires at least 2 hours for the two risings, 55 minutes in the oven, and 3 hours to cool. (A little leeway should be left in case the yeast rises more slowly than usual.) Remember, concentrated yeast should be dissolved in lukewarm water, active dry yeast in hot tap water. The latter may take a little longer to rise to the required lightness. (Photos 5–7 show what the two risings should look like, and the use of the hands and movements for kneading.)

Bread is always served with the second course in an Italian meal, and with cheese if there is a cheese course. As we have seen, it is also used for a good many other things. Tuscan white bread has no oil, but can still keep for some days wrapped in a cotton towel—not in plastic or foil, as it will become soggy. It can also be frozen.* Naturally, this bread has an affinity for Chiantis and other Tuscan wines. (Tuscan cheeses complete the trinity, but are unfortunately not available in America.)

Tuscan bread is not eaten with butter at meals. The main exception is in *crostini* with butter and caviar, as an antipasto. Bread and butter is sometimes eaten as a snack, particularly by children.

For the "sponge" (first rising)

> 1 ounce (2 cakes) compressed fresh yeast or 2 packages active dry yeast
> ½ cup lukewarm or hot water, depending on the yeast
> ½ cup plus 1 tablespoon unbleached all-purpose flour

For the dough (second rising)

> 5 cups unbleached all-purpose flour
> 1¾ cups lukewarm water
> Pinch of salt

Dissolve the yeast in the water in a small bowl, stirring with a wooden spoon (see photo 1).

Place the ½ cup flour in a larger bowl, add the dissolved yeast, and mix with the wooden spoon until all the flour is incorporated and a small ball of dough is formed. Sprinkle the additional tablespoon of flour over the ball of dough, then cover the bowl with a cotton dish-towel and put it in a warm place away from drafts. Let stand until the dough has doubled in size, about 1 hour (see photo 2).

Arrange the 5 cups of flour in a mound on a pasta board, then make a well (see photo 1). Place the sponge from the first rising in the well, along with the salt and ½ cup of the lukewarm water.

* Freezing does not affect the crust, but the inside becomes more crumbly. The bread works perfectly for cooking and toasting, but perhaps should not be served as is.

Pane toscano: 1. Dissolving the yeast.

2. The sponge doubled in size.

With a wooden spoon, carefully mix together all the ingredients in the well, then add the remaining water and start mixing with your hands, absorbing the flour from the inside rim of the well little by little (see photo 3).

Keep mixing until all but 4 or 5 tablespoons of the flour are incorporated (about 15 minutes), then knead the dough with the palms of your hands, in a folding motion, until it is homogenous and smooth (about 20 minutes), incorporating the remaining flour, if necessary, to keep the dough from being sticky (see photo 4).

3. Combining the flour and sponge.

4. Kneading the dough.

Give the dough the shape you prefer (a long or round loaf), then place in a floured cotton dishtowel (see photo 5). Wrap the dough in the towel and again put it in a warm place, away from drafts, and let stand until doubled in size, about 1 hour (see photo 6). The time varies a bit, depending on the weather.

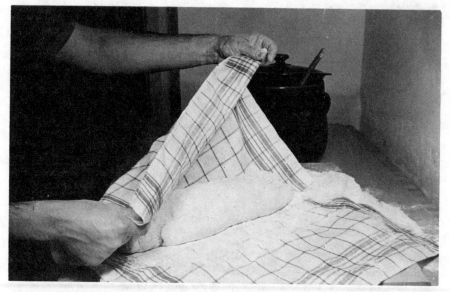

5. Covering the shaped dough with a towel for the second rising.

6. The shaped dough, doubled in size.

Preheat the oven to 400°. Be sure the bricks in your oven are free from dust. When the dough in the second rising has doubled in size, quickly remove from the towel and place immediately in the oven.

Bake the bread for about 55 minutes. Do not open the oven for 30 minutes after you have placed the dough in the oven. (See photo 7.)

7. The bread after being baked in the improvised brick oven.
The photo also shows a terra-cotta casserole of baked Tuscan beans (see page 403).

Cooling the Bread

When the bread is finished, remove it from the oven and place it on a pasta board, standing on one of its sides, not lying flat. The bread must cool for at least 3 hours before it is at its best for eating, and the room where the bread cools must be very airy.

Pane Scuro
(Tuscan Dark Bread)   (MAKES 1 LOAF)

Darker Tuscan breads are as common as ordinary "country" bread in Florence and the rest of Tuscany. They are made in the same way, with the three risings and the brick oven. The major difference is that the darker flour is coarser and requires more yeast in order to rise.

Tuscan dark bread, showing whole winter wheat berries and the hand coffee grinder used to grind them.

The darker breads last longer than the white bread, as they do not dry out as fast. For dishes such as the salad *panzanella* (see page 92) or the bread soup (see page 230), they are preferable to the lighter bread.

Using the hand coffee-grinder (see photo), grind ¼ pound of winter-wheat berries, and mix all of it, wheat and chaff, with 5 cups unbleached all-purpose flour. The ratio 1:5 dark to white flour gives a good dark bread.

Follow the directions for *pane toscano* on page 33, but using 1½ ounces (3 cakes) of compressed fresh yeast (or 3 packages active dry yeast) for the "sponge" and 1 cup (¼ pound) whole-wheat flour, ground as described above, plus 5 cups unbleached all-purpose flour, instead of all-white flour, for the second rising.

Pane Integrale
(Tuscan Whole-Wheat Bread)   (MAKES 1 LOAF)

Follow the directions for *pane toscano* on pages 33–37, but using 2 ounces (4 cakes) compressed fresh yeast (or 4 packages active dry yeast) for the "sponge" and 2 cups (½ pound) whole-wheat flour, ground as described on page 31, plus 4 cups unbleached all-purpose flour, instead of the all-white flour, for the second rising.

Pane con Salsicce
(Sausage Bread)   (MAKES 1 LOAF)

The sausage bread described below and the bread with olives on page 40 are both snacks rather than bread to be eaten with a meal. In the country, especially in the vineyards and villas, bread was usually baked in large quantities, and one of each of these would be included for *merenda,* or "snack." Because the sausages or olives make the dough heavier, and more difficult to rise, extra yeast is added.

The sausage bread is also deliciously flavored with sage.

    ½ pound sweet sausage (preferably Tuscan, see page 350)
    2 tablespoons olive oil

For the "sponge" (first rising)

    1½ ounces (3 cakes) of compressed fresh yeast or 3 packages
          dry active yeast
    ¼ cup of lukewarm or hot water, depending on yeast
    ½ cup plus 1 tablespoon unbleached all-purpose flour

For the dough (second rising)

    6 cups unbleached all-purpose flour
    1¾ cups lukewarm water
       Pinch of salt
    4 or 5 sage leaves, fresh or under salt (see page 14)
    2 teaspoons olive oil

Cut the sausages into 1-inch pieces, then put, along with the olive oil, into a saucepan and sauté very gently for 10 minutes. Remove from the flame and set aside until needed.

Using the ingredients listed, make the "sponge" and dough according to the directions for *pane toscano* on pages 33–35, through the kneading of the dough.

Add the sausage pieces to the dough and knead gently for 5 minutes more.

Lightly oil a 10-inch springform. Place the dough in the springform, cover with a cotton dishtowel and put in a warm place, away from drafts. Let the dough stand until doubled in size (about 1 hour); the time will vary a bit, depending on the weather.

Preheat the oven to 400°.

When the dough has doubled in size, remove the towel and immediately place the springform in the oven. Bake the bread for about 60 minutes; do not open the oven for 30 minutes after you have placed the springform in the oven.

Remove the springform from oven, allow to cool for 5 minutes, then open it and transfer the bread to a pasta board.

To cool the bread, follow the directions on page 37.

Pane con Olive
(Bread with Olives)   (MAKES 1 LOAF)

Large olives are used in olive bread. In Tuscany, small olives are used to make the marvelous oil, but large ones were cultivated for eating. This type, so-called Greek olives, are now even being imported into Tuscany, as the cultivation of olives for eating is disappearing there, along with the ancient agriculture. The olives are usually baked into the bread with their pits, but since Americans are not used to this, I advise you to pit the olives first—since someone might just bite too hard and lose a tooth.

Pane con olive is made exactly the same as *pane con salsicce*, except that ½ pound pitted black olives are kneaded into the dough instead of the sautéed sausages, and the sage is left out of the ingredients for the second rising. See pages 39–40 for instructions.

Pan di Ramerino
(Rosemary Bread)   (MAKES 1 LOAF)

The earliest known source for the *pan di ramerino* recipe is a sixteenth-century manuscript that belonged to the Medici family, but the dish is even older. In certain earlier periods it was associated with Thursday of Easter week, when it was customary to visit seven churches. During the period of these visits, vendors at stands outside the churches would sell little *panini di ramerino* with crosses on top, much like the English hot cross buns. The hawkers would shout one of the best-known Florentine street cries, "*Pan di ramerino all'olio*." Our recipe is for the older version, the large single *pane*, without religious association, and said to have been used to place food on, in lieu of dishes, before such conveniences were common. Nowadays, *pan di ramerino* is eaten all year round, and is one of the favorite snacks of Florentine schoolchildren.

Despite its additional ingredients—rosemary, olive oil, and raisins—the technique of making *pan di ramerino* is the same as that of making Tuscan bread. The same can also be said for the following recipes with special ingredients, *buccellato* (see page 42) and *pane co' santi* (see page 44).

For the "sponge" (first rising)

> 1 ounce (2 cakes) compressed fresh yeast or 2 packages active dry yeast
> ½ cup lukewarm or hot water, depending on the yeast
> 1 cup unbleached all-purpose flour

For the dough (second rising)

> 4½ ounces raisins
> ½ cup plus 2 tablespoons olive oil
> 2 heaping tablespoons rosemary leaves
> Pinch of salt
> ½ cup lukewarm water
> 3 cups less 2 tablespoons unbleached all-purpose flour

Dissolve the yeast in the ½ cup lukewarm or hot water. Put the cup of flour in a bowl and add the dissolved yeast. Mix until thoroughly combined, then cover the bowl with a cotton dishtowel and let stand in a warm, draft-free place until doubled in size (35 minutes to 1 hour, depending on the freshness of the yeast).

Meanwhile, in another bowl, soak the raisins in lukewarm water to cover for 15 to 20 minutes.

Place the ½ cup olive oil in a saucepan with 1 heaping tablespoon of the rosemary and sauté very lightly, until the rosemary turns light brown. Allow to cool (about 15 minutes). When the "sponge" is ready, mix the olive oil containing the rosemary into it with a wooden spoon.

Drain the raisins and add to the "sponge"-rosemary mixture, along with a pinch of salt and ½ cup lukewarm water. Mix everything together with a wooden spoon, and then, when thoroughly combined, add the remaining rosemary, uncooked. Incorporate 1 cup of flour, little by little, continuously mixing with the wooden spoon.

Sprinkle the remaining flour (almost 2 cups) on a pasta board and place the dough on it. Knead the dough until all the flour is incorporated, then oil your hands and continue to knead for 8 or 9 minutes more. Repeat, oiling your hands again and kneading for a final 8 or 9 minutes.

Oil an 8½-inch springform. Place the dough in springform and let rise in a warm, draft-free place until doubled in size (about 40 to 55 minutes), covered with a cotton dishtowel.

Preheat the oven to 425°.

Bake the bread for 40 to 50 minutes, until the crust is brown and the bottom sounds hollow when rapped with the knuckles.

Pan di ramerino may be eaten warm after 15 or 20 minutes, or cold.

Buccellato
(Luccan Sweet Bread)   (MAKES 1 LOAF)

A sweet bread from the old walled town of Lucca, it is eaten as a snack or with strawberries as a dessert (see page 470), and can be made in a regular loaf shape or as a ring. Because of the glacéed fruit, raisins, and other extra ingredients, it requires more yeast than ordinary bread.

You can't stroll through Lucca's marvelous old piazzas without seeing someone eating *buccellato*.

For the "sponge" (first rising)

>   1 cup milk
>   2 ounces (4 cakes) compressed fresh yeast or 4 packages active
>   dry yeast
>   2 cups unbleached all-purpose flour
>   Pinch of salt

For the dough (second rising)

>   5 ounces raisins and mixed glacéed fruit, combined
>   1 cup lukewarm milk
>   1 large, thick-skinned orange
>   10 tablespoons (1¼ sticks) butter

5 ¾ cups unbleached all-purpose flour
   1 cup less 1 tablespoon granulated sugar
   2 tablespoons rum
   5 eggs
  ⅓ cup dry Marsala
1 ½ tablespoons aniseed

To make the "sponge," heat the milk in a saucepan to lukewarm or hot, depending on the yeast you are using. Dissolve the yeast in the milk in a small bowl.

Place the 2 cups flour in a large bowl and make a well in it. Pour the dissolved yeast into the well, along with a pinch of salt. With a wooden spoon, gradually incorporate all the flour into the liquid yeast. When all the flour is incorporated, cover the bowl with a cotton dishtowel and leave to rise in a warm place, away from drafts, until the yeast has doubled in size (about 1 to 1 ½ hours).

Soak the raisins and glacéed fruit in a bowl with the lukewarm milk for 20 to 25 minutes. Grate the peel off the orange and let stand until needed. Melt 1 stick of the butter in a small saucepan and set aside.

When the "sponge" has risen, place the 5 ¾ cups flour on a pasta board. Make a well in it and place the "sponge" in the well. Add the sugar and mix well with a wooden spoon, and when all the sugar is incorporated, add the warm melted butter, rum, 4 of the eggs, the Marsala, and aniseed. Mix with the wooden spoon until all the ingredients are well combined.

Start adding the warm milk, little by little, incorporating some of the flour from the inside rim of the well. Keep mixing until three-fourths of the flour is incorporated, then add the grated orange peel and start kneading the dough. Knead until all but 2 tablespoons of the flour are incorporated and the dough is smooth (about 20 minutes).

Add the soaked, drained raisins and glacéed fruits to the dough and knead for 5 minutes more incorporating the leftover flour. Shape the dough into a circle.

Butter and flour an aluminum baking sheet. Place the dough on it, cover with a cotton dishtowel, and leave to rise in a warm place, away from drafts, until it has doubled in size (from 1 to 1 ½ hours).

Preheat the oven to 400°.

Place baking sheet in the oven for 35 minutes, then beat the remaining egg in a bowl and quickly remove the baking sheet from the oven.

Paint the top of the *buccellato* with the beaten egg and replace it in the oven for 20 to 25 minutes more.

Remove the *buccellato* from the oven and let stand until cold (2 to 3 hours) before serving.

Pane co' Santi
(Nut Bread for All Saints' Day)   (MAKES 1 LOAF)

Pane co' santi or *dei santi* is, as the name suggests, originally for All Saints' Day, November 1 (our Halloween is All Saints' Eve). This bread exists in a nonsweet version, given here, but is also made with sugar as a dessert. Made with both walnuts and almonds, its fascinating combination of ingredients, combining flavors associated with sweets such as anise, with a shocker like black pepper, reveals the medieval palate. *Pane co' santi* is, however, still very much alive.

Pane co' santi: The nut bread for All Saints Day, shown after baking in my family's old Tuscan terra-cotta oven. Traditionally it was placed on a wood or charcoal fire. In America, I use it on a modern gas stove with good results.

For the "sponge" (first rising)

> 2 ounces (4 cakes) compressed fresh yeast or 4 packages active dry yeast
> 1 cup lukewarm or hot water, depending on the yeast
> 1½ cups unbleached all-purpose flour

For the dough (second rising)

> 4 ounces raisins
> 4 ounces shelled, blanched walnuts
> 1 cup olive oil
> 2 tablespoons lard
> 2 ounces blanched almonds
> 6 cups unbleached all-purpose flour
> Pinch of salt
> Grated peel of ½ orange
> 1 teaspoon aniseed
> 1 teaspoon freshly ground black pepper
> ¾ cup lukewarm water

Prepare *pane co' santi* with the ingredients listed, according to the directions for sweet bread for All Saints' Day on page 471.

Pangrattato
(Homemade Bread Crumbs)

When you have some Tuscan bread left over, allow it to become hard and make it into bread crumbs. You will see what a difference there is in flavor when you use bread crumbs made from good homemade bread.

Cut leftover Tuscan bread (see page 32) into small pieces and place on a sheet of aluminum foil. Put the sheet into an oven preheated to 175° and bake the bread pieces for about 45 minutes, until golden brown and very crisp.

Remove the sheet with the toasted bread from oven and let stand until completely cool (about 2 hours), then transfer the bread pieces to a food processor or blender and grind until very fine.

Remove the bread crumbs from the food processor and place them in a jar. Close the jar tightly and store it in a place that gets a good bit of light; do not refrigerate.

These bread crumbs may last, without losing their flavor, for as long as 6 months.

Piccoli Crostini Fritti

(Italian Croutons)   (S E R V E S   4)

With soups of the *passati* and *minestre* types, homemade croutons are often served. A few float on top with the grated Parmigiano. Versatile Tuscan bread, left over, even some days old, is cut into little squares, which are then fried in olive oil until quite crisp. These add their own delicious flavor and crispness to the soup.

> 2 large slices Tuscan bread, several days old
> ½ cup olive oil
>   Salt

The bread should be some days old, but not completely hard. Cut the bread into pieces about ½ inch square. Prepare a serving dish with paper towels on bottom.

Heat the olive oil on a medium flame in a frying pan. When the oil is hot, put in the bread pieces and let them fry until golden brown all over (about 6 minutes), then remove from the pan with a strainer-skimmer and place on the prepared serving dish. Sprinkle with a little salt.

Place about 1 heaping tablespoon of *crostini* in each individual bowl and pour the *passato* or *minestra* over them just before serving.

Pizza alla Napoletana

(Pizza, Neapolitan Style)   (S E R V E S   4)

This is the classic pizza, made with a yeast dough.

For the dough

> ½ ounce (1 cake) compressed fresh yeast or 1 package active
>   dry yeast
>   Slightly less than 1 cup lukewarm or hot water
> 2 cups unbleached all-purpose flour

Pinch of salt
1 tablespoon olive oil

For the topping (*alla napoletana*)
2½ tablespoons olive oil
6 canned plum tomatoes, approximately (to make 10 table-spoons pureed tomatoes)
4 ounces mozzarella
6 anchovy fillets
1 heaping tablespoon capers in wine vinegar
Salt, freshly ground pepper, and oregano to taste

Dissolve the yeast in the lukewarm or hot water.

Arrange the flour in a mound on a pasta board and make a well in it, then pour the dissolved yeast, salt, and the olive oil into the well.

With a fork, slowly work the flour from the inside wall of the well into the liquid.

When the mixture becomes solid enough to resemble a dough, work in the rest of the flour with a folding motion of your hands, leaving about 1 tablespoon of flour unincorporated. Place the dough in a bowl, sprinkle with the leftover flour, and cover with a cotton dishtowel. Let rest until doubled in size (about 1 hour at warm room temperature, away from drafts).

Meanwhile, using 6 whole tomatoes from the can, but none of the liquid, pass the tomatoes through a food mill into a small bowl. Using the large holes of a cheese grater, coarsely grate the mozzarella; set aside. If whole salted anchovies are used, clean them, removing the bones under cold running water; place the fillets in a small dish.

Preheat the oven to 450°.

When the dough is ready, place a sheet of heavy aluminum foil (about 16 x 18 inches) on a board. Oil it with 1 tablespoon of olive oil, then place the dough on the foil. Spread the dough (using the tips of your fingers, not a rolling pin) until you have a sheet of dough about 16½ x 14 inches.

Spread the pureed tomatoes over the surface of the dough. Distribute the grated mozzarella evenly over the tomatoes, then the anchovy fillets and capers. Add salt, pepper, and oregano to taste and pour the remaining 1½ tablespoons olive oil over everything.

Slide the pizza and the foil directly onto the middle shelf of the oven and bake in the preheated oven for about 35 minutes, or until crisp. Remove, slice, and serve.

Pizza con Cipolle
(Pizza with Onions)   (SERVES 4)

This pizza is made exactly the same as the pizza in the previous recipe, but 3 large red onions, cut up and sautéed in 1 tablespoon of butter until soft (about 30 minutes), are spread over the pizza instead of the tomatoes, mozzarella, anchovies, and capers. The seasonings remain the same, but the amount of oil poured over before baking is increased to 2 tablespoons. Bake as previously directed.

Special Pizza   (SERVES 4)

This is a pizza dough that substitutes potato for yeast as a fermenting agent. It takes a longer time to rise, but the results are well worth it; the pastry can be made thinner, for a finer, crisper pizza. Also, because of the potato content, the pizza will keep longer and when reheated become completely fresh again.

The pastry probably represents the influence of the southern Italian *torta di patate* upon the Neapolitan pizza.

For the dough

          1 potato
         ½ cup cold milk
         ½ cup cold water
       2 ½ cups unbleached all-purpose flour
          1 tablespoon olive oil
         ½ level teaspoon salt

For the topping

          Either of the toppings (*alla napoletana* or *con cipolle*) on
          pages 46–48

Boil the potato for about 25 minutes, then cool, peel, and put through a ricer. Measure ½ cup of riced potatoes and set aside.

Combine the milk and water and set aside.

Arrange the flour in a mound on a pasta board and make a well in it. Place the riced potato in the well and add the olive oil and salt. With your left hand, slowly pour the watered milk into the well; at the same time, with a fork, slowly work the flour from the inside rim of the well into the potato. Take care always to leave some flour under the potato-flour mixture so it does not stick to the board.

When the mixture becomes solid enough to resemble a dough, work in the rest of the flour with a folding motion of your hands, leaving about 1 tablespoon of flour unincorporated. Flour the ball of dough with the remaining flour and place it in small bowl. Cover the bowl with a cotton dishtowel and set aside for 3 hours at warm room temperature, away from drafts. (Do not expect the dough to double in size; it will rise only a little.)

When the rising time for the dough is almost up, preheat the oven to 450° and prepare the filling of your choice. Proceed with forming and baking the pizza as directed on page 47.

Schiacciata con Ramerino
("Pizza" with Rosemary)   (SERVES 6)

The pizza-like *schiacciate* of yeast dough have been made in Florence at least since the sixteenth century and are mentioned in the 1546 dinner discussed on page 8. In the most famous Neapolitan cookbook of the eighteenth century the only reference to pizza is to *pizzette alla fiorentina*. The typical Florentine *schiacciata* is flavored with rosemary or sage and olive oil on top, and does not use tomatoes like the various Neapolitan *pizze*.

    ½ ounce (1 cake) compressed fresh yeast or 1 package active
        dry yeast
    1 cup lukewarm or hot water, depending on the yeast
    2¼ cups unbleached all-purpose flour
        Salt
    3 tablespoon olive oil
    1 heaping tablespoon of rosemary leaves, preferably fresh
        Freshly ground black pepper

In a small bowl, dissolve the yeast in the lukewarm or hot water.

Place the flour in a mound on a pasta board. Make a well in the flour and pour in the dissolved yeast and a pinch of salt, and then, using a fork, slowly incorporate all but 3 or 4 tablespoons of the flour from the inside rim of the well. At that point the dough should be firm. Knead it for 15 minutes more.

Sprinkle the dough with the remaining flour and cover it with a cotton dishtowel; let stand in a warm place until doubled in size (about 1 ½ to 2 hours).

When the dough has risen, oil a 15-x-10½-x-1-inch jelly-roll pan with a tablespoon of the oil. Place dough in the pan and spread it out with your fingers until it covers the bottom. Sprinkle on the rosemary, salt, lots of freshly ground pepper, and the remaining oil, then cover with a cotton dishtowel and let stand until the dough has risen again to almost double in size (about 1 hour).

Preheat the oven to 450°.

Bake the *schiacciata* for about 40 to 45 minutes, until crisp, then remove from the oven and serve immediately from the pan, cutting it across into slices.

Sauces

GOOD Italian cooking avoids the overuse of sauces. If one or two courses have a sauce, usually the others do not. Meats and vegetables are often cooked to bring out only their own flavors, and these flavors are not covered with sauces.

A new school of French cooking has recently adopted this attitude in reaction to what many now consider the overuse of sauces in that cuisine in recent centuries. This same reaction took place in Italian cooking some centuries ago, for sixteenth-century Italian cooking had many, many sauces, some called "savors," of which a number served as bases for later French sauces. However, it would be a mistake to think that present-day Italian cooking does not retain a great variety of sauces, though they may be used sparingly.

In the Renaissance, sauces were often placed in categories according to color: *ginestrate*, or yellow sauces, the color of broom flower, often containing saffron; white sauces based on ground almonds and dried bread; green sauces based on herbs, and red sauces on wine or kermes. The substances that created these colors were often the same that produced vegetable dyes for fresco painting or fabric dyeing; it is no accident that chefs belonged to the same guild as painters and pharmacists, the latter using spices for medicines. Many of these sauces remain. The egg- and oil-based sauces, mayonnaises and so forth, likely emerged within the same Florentine guild, as the techniques are not unrelated to those of making paints from vegetable dyes for fresco and oil painting (see *savore di gamberi* page 66). Those sauces based on hot oil or butter thickened with flour and mixed with milk or broth, such as *balsamella* (béchamel) or *salsa bianca* (white sauce), probably originated in Italy, as thickening with flour was known in Italy for some time before it was known in France.

The best-known Italian sauces are those used with pasta, some including tomatoes and some without them. We have included about an equal number of each. A sauce such as *carbonara* really exists only in the context of its pasta dish and is included under pasta. We have attempted to clarify some misconceptions about the three basic types of meatless tomato sauce, and to give a variety of types containing meat and fish. However, as we feel that in American Italian food tomato sauces are overused, we offer an equal number of sauces for pasta that do not contain tomatoes.

Aside from pasta, Italians use sauces mainly on meat, fowl, and fish. Deep-fried dishes, with or without batter, are almost never served with sauce, and sautéed meats most often have their own sauces, already part of the dish. Roasted and poached or boiled meat dishes are most often accompanied by a sauce, but by no means always. A Florentine would never adulterate the purity of the Chianina steer meat in a *bistecca alla fiorentina*. (A châteaubriand with béarnaise sauce would probably shock him.) The most he might add is a few drops of lemon juice after the steak is cooked.

In sum, when sauces are used on freshly cooked or cold roasted and boiled meats and fish, by far the majority will be uncooked and based on fresh herbs, garlic, olive oil, nuts, wine vinegar or lemon or *maionese*. There is quite a goodly variety of these, and we include a large sampling. Most fulfill the requirements of our health-conscious age. Even the cooked ones are rather light.

There are a few vegetables that are sometimes served with sauce, such as cauliflower with anchovy sauce or with shrimp sauce.

Some of the sauces we include have such an interesting and surprisingly long history that we have added some historical notes. We hope you will find them entertaining; we are sure you will be surprised about the origins of some.

BASIC SAUCES

Balsamella
(Béchamel)   (MAKES 2 TO 2 ½ CUPS)

Though this sauce was given the name *béchamel* by the French in the eighteenth century, it probably existed long before that in Italy.

The fifteenth-century recipe for *crema di miglio fritta* starts with a technique very close to this.

Balsamella is a basic sauce used in making many dishes. It is placed on top in some, used as a base inside of others, and ties together the ingredients of still others. It also serves as the base for several other sauces.

> 4 tablespoons butter
> ¼ cup flour
> 1½ to 2 cups milk, depending on thickness desired
> Salt to taste

Melt the butter in a heavy saucepan over a low, steady flame. (It is important to use a heavy pan and a low flame so the sauce will thicken without burning.) When the butter has reached the frothing point, add the flour. Mix very well with a wooden spoon, then let cook until the color is golden brown. Remove the pan from the flame and let rest for 10 to 15 minutes.

While the butter-flour mixture is resting, heat the milk in another pan until it is very close to the boiling point. Put the first saucepan back on the flame and very quickly add all of the hot milk. Be careful not to pour the milk in slowly; that can create lumps in the sauce. Begin mixing with a wooden spoon while you pour and keep mixing, always stirring in the same direction, to prevent lumps from forming.

When the sauce reaches the boiling point, add the salt and continue to stir gently while the sauce cooks slowly for 12 to 14 minutes more. Remove from the flame; the sauce is ready to use.

Salsa Bianca
(White Sauce)

Italian cooking shares with French not only *balsamella*, called *béchamel* in France, but also the basic sauce called *salsa bianca*, in which broth substitutes for the milk of *balsamella*. Florentine scholars count these sauces among the simple *colle*, or binders, that Caterina de Medici's cooks took to France. Certainly Pantanelli, one of Caterina's cooks who arrived in France in 1533, knew the technique of what the French call the *roux*, because he brought it with him in the *pasta soffiata* (page 440) or as the French later called it, *pâte à chaud*.

Page of a fifteenth-century manuscript, including the recipe for *crema di miglio fritta*, showing the early Italian use of flour for thickening and the technique of roux and *balsamella*.

In any case, *salsa bianca* is the base for three sauces included here: *salsa di capperi* (caper sauce; see page 68), *salsa di funghi* (mushroom sauce; see page 68), and *savore di gamberi* (shrimp sauce; see page 66). If the butter is left light, the *salsa bianca* is called *bionda*; if the butter is allowed to turn brown, *salsa scura*.

There is no need to give a separate recipe for *salsa bianca*, as the technique is incorporated into the three recipes mentioned above.

Maionese
(Mayonnaise, the "Good Old Way")
(MAKES MORE THAN 2 CUPS)

Italian *maionese* differs from some other types. It employs green virgin olive oil and egg yolks rather than whole egg, and is flavored only with lemon juice. Good virgin olive oil is basic to the sauce; therefore the color of the sauce will be a rich green, not a light yellow. And all the other ingredients must be of top quality—very fresh eggs, freshly squeezed lemon juice—as they have no place to hide. The *maionese* should have an almost solid texture.

Maionese can be made with a blender or electric beater, but the result is not the texture of the typical Italian *maionese* and the taste is a bit metallic. Making it by hand is a little more work, but with some practice it can be done in 10 or 15 minutes.

Regions of Italy that do not have good olive oil, such as Emilia-Romagna, sometimes substitute vegetable oil, but we do not recommend it.

It is not the Italian practice to keep *maionese* very long. In Italy it is almost always made just a few hours in advance. We do not recommend keeping it in the refrigerator for several days.

The written sources for *maionese* and mayonnaise are both quite late ones, and the French one is a little older. The name is probably of French origin. However, let us put forward some reasons supporting a probable Italian origin for the technique itself: (1) the fourteenth-century Italian recipe for *savore di gamberi* (see page 67) uses a mixture of egg yolk, oil, and lemon juice, though it is flavored with other things and perhaps was lightly cooked; (2) the Italian recipe is simpler and more basic; (3) much of the olive oil region of France belonged to Italy until quite recently; (4) egg yolk emulsion in oil is related to Florentine painting techniques. Remember, painters and chefs in Florence belonged to the same guild.

2 egg yolks, very fresh, at room temperature
Scant 2 cups virgin olive oil
1 tablespoon freshly squeezed lemon juice
Salt to taste

The egg yolks must be at room temperature; if the eggs are refrigerated remove them 1 hour in advance. Squeeze the lemon juice.

Place the egg yolks in a crockery bowl. Mix them slowly, using a wooden spoon and always stirring in the same direction.

When the yolks are well mixed, add the first drop of olive oil and stir slowly until it is absorbed. Continuing to stir slowly, always in the same direction, add more oil, a drop at a time, only adding new oil when that already present is well absorbed.

As the emulsion begins to thicken, add several drops of oil at a time, but be careful not to add too much oil too soon. At this point it should begin to resist as you stir.

In the later stage, when the emulsion begins to resemble *maionese* in thickness, the oil may be added in slightly larger amounts. *This can be a danger point.* Be sure not to add too much oil before that already present is well absorbed, or the emulsion can separate—in Italian *impazzire*, "go crazy." Don't get overconfident.

Be sure to mix in the last oil thoroughly, then place the lemon juice and salt in a tablespoon, mixing with a fork until the salt is somewhat dissolved. Cautiously add 1 drop of juice to the *maionese* (this is the danger point for curdling). When the danger of curdling is past, put in the rest of the lemon juice and salt, mixing well.

Making *maionese* by hand.

SAUCES FOR MEAT OR CHICKEN

Maionese
(Mayonnaise)

Plain *maionese* is the most basic sauce for meat or chicken. For the recipe, see page 55.

Salsa Verde
(Green Sauce)   (MAKES 1 ½ TO 2 CUPS)

Green sauces were an entire category centuries ago. They could be based on many types of green herbs, which were ground together with other ingredients in the all-purpose grinder of that time, the mortar and pestle. Thyme, marjoram, and tarragon were among the herbs that could be used. The modern *pesto*, now associated with Genoa, could be considered a type of *salsa verde*.

These green sauces are generally uncooked, and are piquant accompaniments to boiled and poached dishes. The basic, most usual type used today is given below. It can be varied by adding anchovies and/ or capers to taste.

    1 slice Tuscan bread (see page 32) or white bread, if Tuscan
        bread is not available
        Wine vinegar to cover
    1 bunch Italian parsley (about 25 sprigs), stems removed
    2 medium cloves garlic, peeled
    1 hard-boiled egg yolk, cold
    1 cup olive oil, approximately (enough for a creamy texture)
        Salt and freshly ground pepper to taste

Soak the bread in wine vinegar for 20 minutes.

Place the parsley leaves and garlic on a chopping board and chop very, very fine; then transfer to a crockery bowl, add the cold egg yolk, and mix very well with a wooden spoon. Squeeze the soaked bread dry and place it in the bowl.

Little by little add the olive oil, always stirring; mix thoroughly until the sauce has a creamy texture. Add salt and pepper, then stir again until the salt and pepper are very well incorporated.

Place the sauce, covered, in the refrigerator for 1 hour before serving.

Salsa Verde del Chianti
(Green Sauce with Walnuts) (MAKES 1½ TO 2 CUPS)

I would like to thank Giovanni Minuccio Cappelli, whose estates produce Cappelli Chianti wines, for this recipe and the following one. They have been in his family for centuries, and I have been able to verify their antiquity in Renaissance cookbooks. They are among the many uncooked, piquant sauces that are used with boiled meats and fowl or poached fish.

This differs from *salsa verde* in its use of ground walnuts.

> 6 ounces shelled walnuts
> ½ bunch Italian parsley (10 to 12 sprigs, stems removed)
> 3 to 4 leaves of basil, fresh or under salt (see page 14)
> 2 cloves garlic
>   Salt, freshly ground black pepper, and cayenne pepper to taste
> 2 hard-boiled egg yolks
> 1 cup olive oil

Place the shelled walnuts on a chopping board and chop them very fine. Transfer to a crockery bowl.

Place the parsley, basil, and garlic on the board and chop very fine, then transfer to the crockery bowl with the walnuts. Season with salt, freshly ground black pepper, and cayenne pepper and mix very well with a wooden spoon.

Continuously stirring, add the first egg yolk, then the second, and finally the olive oil, tablespoon by tablespoon. Keep stirring until the sauce is smooth and homogenous.

Taste for salt and pepper, then cover the bowl with lid or aluminum foil and place it in the refrigerator for 1 hour before serving.

Salsa Rossa del Chianti
(Red Sauce) (MAKES ABOUT 1 ½ CUPS)

This sauce is found among the old families of the Chianti. Though the tomato paste was added in recent centuries, it was probably a substitution for some other ingredient that intensified the red color of the Chianti vinegar; we know that color was very important in Renaissance food.

The inside of the bread, mashed with mortar and pestle, was a very characteristic binding element in sauces and soups of that time. (It is interesting that in English we don't even have a word for the inside of the bread to correspond with the Italian *mollica di pane*.) Probably bread crumbs, which are widely used in modern times, at some point substituted for *mollica* in many recipes.

 2 large slices Tuscan bread (see page 32)
 1 cup wine vinegar
 8 to 9 sprigs Italian parsley
15 leaves fresh basil, approximately
 2 tablespoons tomato paste
 ½ cup olive oil, approximately (enough for a smooth texture)
    Salt and freshly ground pepper

Remove the crust from the bread slices and soak the slices in the wine vinegar for 20 minutes.

Meanwhile, chop the basil and parsley leaves very fine and place in a crockery bowl.

Squeeze the liquid out of the bread and put it in the bowl with the herbs, then add the tomato paste and start stirring with a wooden spoon. Add, little by little and stirring constantly, enough olive oil to make a smooth cream.

Taste for salt and pepper. Let the sauce rest, covered, in the refrigerator for 1 hour before serving.

Salsa d'Agresto
(*Agresto* Sauce) (MAKES 1 ½ TO 2 CUPS)

Although this sauce has disappeared from regular use, it is delicious. I discovered it in a Renaissance cookbook, and much to my surprise my mother remembered eating it in a country village before the First World War. It survived until that recently.

Agresto is the juice of grapes that are not yet ripe, and in olden times it was used more often than vinegar or lemon juice.

Since unripe grapes are available for only about one month a year, it was a very special seasonal dish. My mother remembers that in that village, with its little tenth-century Romanesque church, the inhabitants would peel each grape by hand before crushing them in the mortar. The *agresto* could also be preserved by cooking it with herbs and spices to make an aromatic vinegar. (A fourteenth-century cookbook gives a recipe for making *agresto* from the sediment in the wine kegs. This was also cooked to preserve it.)

Unless you have a grape arbor and the month is July or August, substitute lemon juice for the *agresto* in this sauce. It is still very good.

    2 handfuls *agresto*, or juice of 1 lemon and peel of ½ lemon
    9 walnuts, shelled
    2 ounces blanched almonds
    ½ small red onion
    6 to 8 sprigs Italian parsley, stems removed
    1 clove garlic
    2 slices white bread, crust removed
    1 teaspoon granulated sugar
      Salt and freshly ground pepper to taste
    ½ cup lukewarm chicken or meat broth, approximately (enough
        for a smooth sauce)

Grind the *agresto* (or lemon juice and peel), shelled walnuts, and blanched almonds in a mortar or blend in the blender.

Chop up the onion, parsley, and garlic. Add to the contents of the mortar or blender, along with the bread. Blend until very thoroughly mixed, then season with sugar, salt, and pepper. Add enough lukewarm broth to obtain a smooth sauce.

Put the sauce through a food mill, then heat on a low flame for 2 minutes; do not allow it to boil. Transfer the sauce to a sauceboat and allow it to cool before serving.

Note: This sauce can be preserved in a jar by covering over with a thin layer of olive oil.

Savore di Noci
(Walnut Sauce) (MAKES ABOUT 1 ½ CUPS)

Another Renaissance herb sauce, based, like *salsa verde del Chianti*, on crushed walnuts, but flavored with parsley and *agresto* or lemon juice. It contains no garlic. Use on boiled and unspiced roasted meats and fowl.

    2 ounces shelled walnuts
    5 to 6 sprigs Italian parsley, stems removed
    3 tablespoons *agresto* (see page 60), or juice of ½ lemon and
        peel of ¼ lemon
    Salt and freshly ground pepper
    Scant ½ cup olive oil, approximately (enough to obtain a
        smooth sauce)

Put the walnuts and parsley in a mortar, along with the *agresto* (or lemon juice and lemon peel), and grind very fine. Taste for salt and pepper, then add olive oil, little by little and stirring constantly with a wooden spoon (always in the same direction, as when you make *maionese*).

When you have obtained a smooth and homogeneous sauce, transfer it to a crockery bowl, cover, and refrigerate for 1 hour before serving.

Note: You can also make this sauce using a blender. If you do so, put all the ingredients except half the olive oil into the blender container and blend until smooth and homogeneous. Remove from the blender, pour into a crockery bowl, then add the remaining olive oil, little by little and stirrring as described above.

Salsa Rossa Forte
(Spicy Red Sauce) (MAKES ABOUT 1 CUP)

This colorful sauce gets its color and its name from the fresh sweet red peppers that are so easy to find in Italy. In America, if they cannot be found, fresh pimentos or, as a last resort, sweet green peppers may be substituted. The flavor remains excellent, but the color changes and gives lie to the sauce's name.

    1 slice white bread
    ½ cup wine vinegar, approximately
    2 large fresh sweet red peppers, pimentos, or sweet green pep-
        pers
    1 large clove garlic
    ½ teaspoon hot red pepper flakes or cayenne pepper
        Scant ½ cup olive oil, approximately (enough to obtain a
        smooth sauce)
        Salt and freshly ground black pepper

Soak the white bread in the wine vinegar for 20 minutes.

Place a pot of boiling water on a burner; next to that burner place the peppers, so they get singed by the flame. (The singeing makes it easy to peel the skin from the peppers; the steam from the boiling water keeps the singed peppers from drying out.) Keep turning the peppers in order to singe them all over. Remove the peppers from the flame and place them in cold water, then remove the skin, seeds, stems, and hard top sections.

Squeeze the soaked bread dry, then combine with the peppers and garlic and either chop very fine or blend in the blender.

Transfer everything to a crockery bowl and add the olive oil, little by little, stirring constantly with a wooden spoon, until all the oil is incorporated and the sauce is very smooth. Add red pepper, taste for salt and pepper, then refrigerate for 1 hour before serving.

Salsa Primavera di Magro
(Spring Vegetable Sauce)   (MAKES ABOUT 1 ½ CUPS)

A red sauce for the season when the vegetables, especially tomatoes, are fresh. It comes from Grosseto, near the Tuscany seaside. The name evokes the springtime quality of fresh uncooked vegetables newly in season. *Salsa primavera* is used mainly with roasted and boiled meats and fowl, not with fish.

    1 small red onion
    1 large, ripe tomato or 2 canned tomatoes
    1 large clove garlic
    2 or 3 fresh basil leaves or ½ teaspoon dried basil

½ slice white bread, crust removed
   Pinch of red pepper or cayenne pepper
1 tablespoon red wine vinegar
¼ cup olive oil
   Salt and freshly ground black pepper

Cut up the onion and tomato, then place in a mortar with the garlic, basil leaves, bread, and red pepper. Grind very well, until homogeneous, then transfer to a crockery bowl and add the olive oil, little by little and stirring very well with a wooden spoon. Taste for salt and pepper (the sauce should be very peppery), then add the wine vinegar, stirring until very well incorporated.

Transfer the sauce to a sauceboat and refrigerate for 1 hour before serving.

Salsa al Dragoncello
(Tarragon Sauce from Siena)   (MAKES ABOUT 1 CUP)

The old city of Siena, sitting proudly on its hill, is full of ancient dwellings, each with window boxes full of flowers—and tarragon. This herb is still called there by its antique name, *dragoncello*, and its flavor fills many of its old dishes—including this sauce, which is still very much alive in its native city.

The combination of the tarragon and red wine vinegar, best when made from old Chianti, makes this a pungent sauce for roasted or boiled meats and fowl. Naturally, fresh tarragon works best, but good dried tarragon that has retained its flavor also works well. The vinegar should be from a good-quality wine, if Chianti vinegar is not available.

2 slices white bread, crusts removed
¼ cup wine vinegar
3 cloves garlic
1 heaping tablespoon fresh tarragon leaves or 1 scant tablespoon dried tarragon leaves
2 to 3 tablespoons olive oil
   Salt and freshly ground pepper to taste

Soak the bread in ¼ cup of wine vinegar for 20 minutes.

Chop the garlic and tarragon leaves finely, or else grind finely in a mortar. Transfer to the bowl containing the bread and wine vinegar and mix very well with a wooden spoon, so that the bread comes apart and combines smoothly with the other ingredients.

Using the wooden spoon, stir continuously for 10 to 12 minutes, adding the olive oil in the process. Years ago, a type of ridged wooden spoon called a *frullino,* which had the effect of a wooden hand blender, was used at this point. Alas, it has almost disappeared. Taste for salt and pepper, then stir for 10 minutes longer.

Cover the bowl and refrigerate for 1 hour before serving.

Acciugata
(Anchovy Sauce)   (MAKES ABOUT 1 CUP)

A very simple sauce in which the anchovies are crushed and mixed into hot olive oil, this is also widely versatile, being equally at home with dried pasta, a vegetable such as cauliflower, or with leftover cold veal cutlets *alla milanese* or *braciole fritte.*

(See the recipes for *spaghetti all' acciugata* on page 159, *cavolfiore con acciugata* on page 411, and *braciole fritte con acciugata* on page 281.)

> 5 anchovies in salt or 10 anchovy fillets in oil
> 1 cup olive oil
>   Freshly ground pepper
>   Salt, if necessary

If anchovies under salt are available, fillet them while holding them under cold running water to remove excess salt. Drain on paper towels.

Put the olive oil in a heavy aluminum saucepan and heat on a low flame. When the oil is very hot, almost sizzling, remove the pan from the flame. Immediately add the filleted anchovies and mash them into the oil, using a fork, until they make a paste.

Sprinkle with pepper, then taste for salt and add it if necessary. (If the anchovies have been preserved in salt, it probably will not be.) Serve very hot.

SAUCES FOR FISH

Maionese
(Mayonnaise)

Plain *maionese* is the most basic sauce for poached fish. For the recipe, see page 55.

Maionese con Gamberetti
(Shrimp Mayonnaise)   (SERVES 6)

A variant of *maionese* used for poached or deep-fried fish.

> *Maionese* (see page 55)
> 5 medium-sized shrimps, unshelled
> 3 or 4 drops wine vinegar
>   Salt to taste

Make the *maionese*. Leave it in the crockery bowl in which it was made.

Cook the unshelled shrimps for 6 to 7 minutes in boiling water to which the wine vinegar and salt have been added, then shell and chop coarsely.

Wait until just before serving to mix the chopped shrimp into the *maionese*.

Maionese al Prezzemolo
(Parsley Mayonnaise)   (SERVES 6)

Another variant of mayonnaise used for poached or deep-fried fish.

> *Maionese* (see page 55)
> 8 or 9 sprigs Italian parsley, stems removed
> 1½ teaspoons very finely chopped, cooked spinach (optional)

Make the *maionese* mixing it a little longer at the end so that it will be even more solid (the parsley will liquify it somewhat).

Chop the parsley very fine. Wait until a few minutes before you serve the sauce before adding the chopped parsley to mayonnaise. Combine thoroughly. (If you prefer a very green color, add the optional cooked spinach.) Taste for salt, as the addition of the parsley may require a little more.

Note: The mayonnaise may be made several hours before and kept in the refrigerator, but the parsley must be added only immediately before serving.

Savore di Gamberi
(Shrimp Sauce)

(SERVES 6)

Certain Florentine dishes of the fourteenth century were more highly spiced than most Italian cooking of the present day and relate more to various types of curry. Here is a spiced and creamy shrimp sauce that is really worth serving. Cooking the sauce is optional. I prefer it uncooked, both for taste and because the connection to later sauces is clearer that way.

The mixture of egg yolks, oil, and *agresto* (here, lemon juice) makes it an early version of *maionese*, one that works beautifully with a light fish, poached or roasted. For the sweet and strong spices, we have selected, with much historical justification, the ones used below.

    1 slice white bread, crusts removed
    ½ cup cold milk
    8 medium-sized shrimp, unshelled
    5 blanched almonds
    2 egg yolks
    ½ cup olive oil
    ½ teaspoon ground coriander
      Pinch of freshly grated nutmeg
      Pinch of ground ginger
      Pinch of cayenne pepper
      Salt and freshly ground black pepper to taste
    2 tablespoons lemon juice

Page of another fourteenth-century manuscript, a Venetian copy of the Florentine original, showing the recipe for *savore di gambari*, a shrimp *maionese*, the recipe for which appears opposite.

Soak the bread in the milk for 15 to 20 minutes.

Boil the shrimp for 8 minutes in salted water. Remove the shells; cut off the tails about ½ inch from the ends and save them.

Place the shrimp and almonds in a mortar or blender and grind or blend very thoroughly, then transfer to a crockery bowl. Squeeze the bread dry and add it to the contents of the bowl. Mix very well with a wooden spoon, so the bread comes apart and combines smoothly with the other ingredients.

Add the egg yolks, one at a time, and incorporate them, always stirring in the same direction. Add the olive oil, little by little, stirring constantly but very gently. Add the coriander, nutmeg, ginger, cayenne pepper, salt, and black pepper; mix them in very well.

Add the lemon juice, little by little, always stirring with the wooden spoon, and add the shrimp tails, mixing them in very gently.

Transfer the sauce to a sauceboat and serve.

Salsa di Capperi
(Caper Sauce) (SERVES 4)

A light caper sauce, made from a base of *salsa bianca*, that is, with broth. The caper sauce is placed over the fish dish after each is cooked separately. It is not to be confused with the technique of cooking the capers together with the fish as used in the dish *pesce ai capperi*. Used best with roasted fish, but also with poached.

    4 ounces capers in wine vinegar
    6 tablespoons (¾ stick) butter
    ¼ cup all-purpose flour
    1¼ cups meat broth
      Salt and freshly ground pepper to taste

Drain the capers and chop them coarsely. Set aside. Heat the meat broth to boiling in saucepan.

Meanwhile, melt the butter in a heavy saucepan over a low flame. When the butter is completely melted and very hot, add the flour and mix it in with a wooden spoon. Stir for 1 or 2 minutes, then pour all the hot meat broth into the pan at one time and stir for 1 or 2 minutes, to prevent lumps from forming.

Add the chopped capers; taste for salt and pepper. Let the sauce simmer for 10 to 15 minutes, then transfer it into a sauceboat and serve hot.

Salsa di Funghi
(Mushroom Sauce) (SERVES 6)

A light sauce of dried wild mushrooms, on a *salsa bianca* base, this is used for roasted meat and fish and for poached fish. It depends on the strong flavor of *porcini* mushrooms, imported from Italy.

    1 ounce dried *porcini* mushrooms
    1½ cups lukewarm water
    4 tablespoons (½ stick) butter
    ¼ cup all-purpose flour
      Salt and freshly ground pepper to taste

Soak the dried mushrooms in the lukewarm water for 20 minutes, then drain, but save the water. Place the mushrooms on a board and chop them coarsely. Set aside.

Let the water settle for 10 minutes, so that any sand present can drop to the bottom, then pour into a heavy enameled saucepan, being careful to leave any sand in the bowl. This water from the mushrooms will be used as the basis of the sauce. Heat until the water is close to the boiling point. Put the butter in another heavy saucepan and place it on a low flame. When the butter is melted and quite hot, add the flour and stir with a wooden spoon. When flour is all incorporated and begins to sizzle, pour all the hot mushroom water in at one time. Stir continuously for 3 to 4 minutes, to prevent lumps from forming.

Add the chopped mushrooms; taste for salt and pepper. Simmer for 12 to 15 minutes more, stirring every so often, then transfer to a sauceboat and serve hot.

SAUCES FOR PASTA, RICE, AND SOUPS

Sugo di Pomodoro Fresco
(Fresh Tomato Sauce)   (MAKES ABOUT 2 CUPS)

This simple sauce, which really deserves the adjective "classic," is perhaps the best recipe to demonstrate the basic point of view of Florentine cooking—that it is enough to combine absolutely necessary ingredients, of high quality and in the classic proportions, in order to produce the best cooking. It is antithetical to the Florentine point of view to "improve" a dish by adding one's favorite herbs, cooked butter or cream, for these additions destroy the classical proportions of the dish and obscure the fundamental combination of flavors, each of which must be tasted.

We also feel that this version of fresh tomato sauce brings out the intrinsic flavor of the tomato better than versions that add onion and/or sugar.

The basil is used not primarily for its own flavor, but because it is the best thing to bring out the flavor of the tomato itself. When fresh basil is available, it is not even cooked with the tomatoes. If basil preserved under salt must be substituted, the leaves are cooked with the tomatoes for only about 2 minutes and then removed.

This sauce is used with fresh and dried pasta, *topini di patate*, and with rice. It is also the base for the sauce of fresh mint used for *tortelli alla menta* (see page 168).

> 2 pounds fresh, very ripe plum tomatoes or 1 can (1 pound) imported Italian plum tomatoes
> Salt to taste
> 10 leaves fresh basil or under salt (see page 14)

If the tomatoes are fresh, cut them in half and place them in a high-sided saucepan; do not add anything else. Simmer slowly for about 1 hour. (If canned tomatoes are used, use the entire contents of the can, including the liquid, and cook for only about 20 minutes. After cooking, pass the tomatoes through a food mill, then place back in the pan and add salt to taste. If fresh basil is not available, place the preserved basil leaves in the pan. Simmer for 2 or more minutes, then remove the basil leaves, if present.

When fresh basil is available, tear the leaves in two or three pieces and place them on the bottom of the serving dish. Place freshly cooked pasta over them, then place the sauce over.

Note: To serve, add a little uncooked olive oil or butter, freshly ground pepper, and freshly grated Parmigiano cheese to pasta and sauce. (Notice that olive oil or butter are added uncooked. This typical Tuscan usage is consistent with modern ideas of healthy cooking.)

Pommarola
(Summer Tomato Sauce)   (SERVES 6)

This is the type of tomato sauce in which the *odori* (aromatic vegetables—the standard combination of carrots, celery, onions, garlic, parsley, and basil) are simmered together with the tomatoes rather than sautéed first. We feel that the classic *odori* should include garlic, and we do not recommend that sugar be added to fresh or canned tomatoes to sweeten them; the result is artificial.

Pommarola is used as the summer tomato sauce, and should really be made strictly with fresh tomatoes. If only canned tomatoes are available, it is better to make *sugo scappato* (or *di magro*), in which the *odori* are sautéed. Simmering the *odori* with canned tomatoes does not produce a very convincing result.

In some parts of Italy, people eat a small portion of pasta as much as once a day, so *pommarola* is usually made in large quantities, to last four or five days. The following recipe is only for one meal for six people.

2½ pounds fresh, very ripe plum tomatoes
1 medium-sized red onion
1 large carrot
1 celery rib
1 small clove garlic
4 or 5 sprigs Italian parsley
2 or 3 leaves fresh basil
Salt to taste

Cut the tomatoes in half. Cut the onion, carrot, and celery into small pieces; do not chop them.

Place all the ingredients in a stock pot; do not add oil or water. Simmer, covered, very slowly for 1½ to 2 hours, then pass everything through a food mill. (If the sauce is to be stored, do so at this point without adding anything else.)

Reheat the sauce (whether freshly made or stored), adding salt.

Note: Pommarola may be eaten with fresh or dried pasta, rice, or with *topini*. Only after the sauce is placed on these freshly cooked dishes should you add uncooked olive oil or butter and fresh pepper. On pasta or *topini* you also add freshly grated Parmigiano.

Sugo Scappato (or *di magro*)
(Winter Tomato Sauce)   (SERVES 6)

In the winter, when canned tomatoes generally form the basis of the tomato sauce, the sauce changes accordingly. The *odori* (aromatic vegetables) are chopped and sautéed. Wine and broth are added. It is really like a meat sauce without the meat, and so the name *scappato* means the meat has "escaped." (The alternate general term *di magro* also usually means without meat.)

This recipe is enough for 6 portions of dried pasta.

     2 carrots
     1 large red onion
     2 celery ribs
     1 clove garlic
     5 or 6 sprigs Italian parsley
     2 or 3 leaves basil, fresh or under salt (see page 14)
     5 tablespoons olive oil
     ¾ cup dry red wine
     1 cup hot meat or chicken broth
     1 pound fresh, ripe tomatoes, skin and seeds removed, or 1 can
          (1 pound) tomatoes
        Salt and freshly ground pepper to taste

Chop the carrots, onion, celery, garlic, parsley, and basil very fine, then transfer to a flameproof saucepan (preferably terra-cotta, but a heavy enameled one will do), along with the olive oil, salt and pepper. Heat over a low flame and sauté very gently until golden brown (about 12 minutes).

Add the wine and let it evaporate; then, stirring very well with a wooden spoon, pour in the hot broth and reduce on a low flame for about 15 minutes. Add the tomatoes and simmer very slowly for about 20 minutes until they are completely cooked and the sauce is homogenous.

Taste for salt and pepper. If more salt is needed, add an extra ½ cup of lukewarm water also, in order to integrate the additional salt, and reduce.

Sugo di Carne
(Meat Sauce)   (MAKES 2 TO 2 ½ CUPS)

This type of meat sauce for pasta is Tuscan, and is probably the type most commonly used throughout northern Italy. Many people mistakenly believe that any meat sauce means "Bolognese." There are three types of meat sauces used in the Bologna region, of which only one is *salsa bolognese*, the others being two types of *ragù*, one of which uses milk or cream and omits wine.*

The excellence of the Tuscan meat sauce comes from the famous Chianina beef, the red Chianti wine, and the *porcini* mushrooms of the area. Little more need be added to come up with a fine sauce, and the simplest possible one for the purpose.

* *Salsa bolognese* has garlic and a number of other ingredients that are different from Bolognese *ragù*.

1 ounce dried *porcini* mushrooms
1 carrot
1 celery rib
1 medium-sized red onion
6 or 7 sprigs Italian parsley
1 clove garlic
   Small piece of lemon peel
¼ cup olive oil
½ pound beef sirloin, in one piece
½ cup dry red wine
   Salt and freshly ground pepper to taste
1 can (1 pound) Italian plum tomatoes
1 tablespoon tomato paste
2 cups hot meat or chicken broth

Soak the mushrooms in lukewarm water to cover for 25 to 30 minutes.

Finely chop the carrot, celery, onion, parsley, garlic, and lemon peel, then place in a flameproof casserole (preferably terra-cotta) with the olive oil. Sauté very gently until golden brown (about 15 to 20 minutes).

With scissors, snip the meat into tiny pieces and add to the contents of the casserole. (The authentic meat sauce uses snipped pieces of meat rather than ground meat; this way the pieces retain their identity and flavor instead of amalgamating into a homogenous mixture.) Sauté the meat pieces for 12 to 15 minutes, then add the wine and cook until it evaporates (15 to 20 minutes).

Taste for salt and pepper, then add the tomatoes and tomato paste and let cook very slowly for 20 to 25 minutes.

Drain the soaked mushrooms, reserving the soaking liquid. Add the mushrooms to the sauce and simmer very slowly for at least 1½ hours, adding hot broth and the water in which mushrooms have been soaked as liquid is needed, until all the broth and mushroom water have been added. (The sauce should be of medium thickness, neither too liquid nor too dense.)

Sugo di "Cipolle"
(Sauce of Chicken Gizzards)   (SERVES 6)

A really fine sauce that has a flavor related to game. The concentration of chicken gizzards gives a taste you might not predict, one that is close to that of pheasant or other game birds.

Use with spaghetti and other dried pasta.

> 1 medium-sized red onion
> ½ celery rib
> 1 clove garlic
> 7 or 8 sprigs Italian parsley
> ¼ cup olive oil
>   Salt and freshly ground pepper
> 1 pound whole chicken gizzards, cleaned
> 1 cup dry red wine
> ¼ cup tomato paste
> 2 cups of hot chicken or meat broth

Finely chop, by hand, the onion, celery, garlic, and parsley, then place in a heatproof terra-cotta or enameled saucepan with olive oil. Add salt and pepper and sauté very gently, on a low flame, until golden brown (about 30 minutes). Add the chicken gizzards and sauté, still on a low flame, for at least 35 to 40 minutes.

Add wine and simmer until it evaporates, then add the tomato paste and stir very well. When the tomato paste is all incorporated, pour in ½ cup of the hot broth. Simmer for 1 hour longer, adding ½ cup more of broth, little by little as needed.

Remove the chicken gizzards and chop them extremely fine, either by hand or with food processor. Put back in the casserole and add the remaining cup of broth. Taste for salt and pepper and simmer very slowly until all the liquid is incorporated; the sauce should be quite thick and smooth.

Salsa di Tonno
(Tuna Sauce)   (SERVES 4)

A good winter sauce for dried pasta. Fresh tomatoes and tuna are not necessary; the result is excellent with canned ingredients. This is used all over Italy for all kinds of dried pasta. As with any sauce made with fish, do not add Parmigiano or other grated cheese.

> 1 small red onion
> ¼ cup olive oil
> 1 cup canned tomatoes

    1 can (3 ½ ounces) tuna in olive oil
    Salt and freshly ground black pepper

Chop the onion very fine, then place in a flameproof terra-cotta or enameled saucepan with the olive oil. Sauté very gently, on a low flame, until golden brown. Add the tomatoes and simmer until the liquid is evaporated.

Drain the tuna and transfer directly from can to pan, breaking the tuna up with a fork and mixing it in with the tomatoes.

Taste for salt and pepper.

After 8 to 10 minutes, remove the pan from flame; the tuna should be well incorporated.

Cibreo
(Sauce of Chicken Livers, Crests, and Wattles)
(MAKES 2 TO 2 ½ CUPS)

Cibreo, the sauce of chicken livers, crests, wattles, and the little yellow unborn eggs, was so beloved of that legendary *buona forchetta* ("a good fork," as the Italians call a good eater) Caterina de' Medici, that she literally almost ate herself to death on it. She ate so much *cibreo* one evening that she took violently ill and barely survived. If eaten in moderation, however, those results do not follow, and, especially if you can find the crests and eggs (get to know a chicken farmer), you may understand why Caterina went to such extremes.

    ¼ pound chicken crests, wattles, and unlaid eggs
    ½ red onion
    5 or 6 sprigs Italian parsley
    3 tablespoons butter
    1 tablespoon all-purpose flour
    ¾ pound fresh chicken livers (including some cut up veal kid-
          neys, optional)
    1 cup dry white wine
    ½ cup meat or chicken broth
    1 egg yolk
       Salt and freshly ground pepper to taste

Heat 2 cups of salted water in a saucepan. When the water reaches the boiling point, put in the crests and wattles (setting aside the unlaid eggs) and cook them for about 5 minutes. Drain the crests and wattles and cool them under running water.

Chop the onion and parsley finely.

Heat the butter in a saucepan over medium heat, and when it is hot, mix in the flour with wooden spoon and sauté for 1 minute. Then add chopped onion and parsley and sauté, stirring constantly for 3 or 4 minutes more. Add the whole chicken livers and the boiled crests and wattles, and then, after 3 or 4 minutes, the wine. Lower the flame and allow the wine to evaporate very slowly (about 5 or 6 minutes).

While the wine is evaporating, heat the broth in a second saucepan. When lukewarm (and no warmer), remove the broth from the flame and mix in the egg yolk.

When the wine has evaporated, taste for salt and pepper. Add the broth with the egg yolk and the unlaid eggs and stir very well. Let simmer for 2 to 3 minutes more, until the chicken livers, crests, and wattles are soft.

Remove the saucepan from the flame and serve very hot.

Note: The sauce is used both for fresh pasta (*tagliatelle con cibreo*, page 148) or for a main dish (*ciambella con cibreo*, page 361).

Balsamella con Parmigiano
(Béchamel with Parmigiano Cheese)

(MAKES 2 TO 2 ½ CUPS)

Balsamella mixed with Parmigiano cheese is used so often that it merits separate consideration. Indeed, the French give it a separate name, *sauce Mornay*. Needless to say, however, the sauce is of Italian origin.

This sauce is used over pasta dishes, some of which include a second sauce as well.

     2 to 2½ cups *balsamella* (see page 52)
     ¼ cup freshly grated Parmigiano cheese

When the *balsamella* is removed from the flame, still hot, add the Parmigiano and mix through very well with a wooden spoon. (The cheese should be incorporated only *after* the sauce has been removed from the flame.)

Salsa di Fegatini
(Chicken Liver Sauce)   (SERVES 6)

A sauce, based on chicken livers, white wine, and broth, that is superb with delicate fresh pasta. Butter is used with the olive oil, unusual in a Tuscan recipe. There is no tomato, and Parmigiano should not be added.

   1 medium-sized white onion
   3 tablespoons butter
   2 tablespoons olive oil
   8 chicken livers
     All-purpose flour for dredging
   ¾ cup dry white wine
   1 cup hot meat or chicken broth
     Salt and freshly ground pepper

Chop the onion very fine, then place in a heavy saucepan with the butter and olive oil and sauté very gently until golden brown.

Cut the chicken livers in quarters and flour them lightly, then add to the pan and sauté for 2 to 3 minutes. Add the wine and let the livers cook in it very slowly until the wine evaporates.

Taste for salt and pepper, then add the hot broth, mix very well, and simmer for 10 minutes, at which point the sauce should be smooth and homogenous.

Note: You can use this sauce for fresh pasta (*tagliatelle con fegatini*, see page 149) or as accompaniment to *riso in bianco* (buttered rice).

Pesto (Battuto alla Genovese)
(Basil Sauce)   (MAKES 4 TO 5 CUPS)

Pesto, an uncooked sauce, is one of the most typical products of Genoese cooking, and contributes much to the distinction of that fine *cucina.* It is used with pasta such as *trenette* or lasagne, with soups such as minestrone or *zuppa di pesce,* and with boiled potatoes. It is also known as *battuto alla genovese.* Genoese friends of mine like to point to a recipe in Virgil as the oldest known version of *pesto.* It is also related to the many types of *salse verdi* that one finds in old Renaissance cookbooks.

The name *pesto* of course refers to the pestle, as the grinding was originally done with that implement and a mortar. It is no exaggeration that every Genoese family has a mortar and pestle that is actually used. Centuries ago, all over Italy these implements were used to grind everything. The name "mortadella," which now refers to a Bolognese sausage, originally referred to any kind of forcemeat made with mortar and pestle. The Genoese are wonderfully conservative about food, so that medieval and Renaissance dishes that have disappeared elsewhere still hang on in Genoa.* Therefore the making of *pesto* in Genoa is a rite and must be done with mortar and pestle.

In other parts of Italy it is rare to find *pesto* still made with mortar and pestle. Though the Genoese would be scandalized, in Tuscany we make it with a *mezzaluna*, like other *battuti*. Much less laborious than doing it the Genoese way, it still results in a texture close to the original. It is also possible to make *pesto* in the blender or food processor, but this should be the third choice, as the texture is more liquid and the taste somewhat different. All three ways of making it are described.

Recipes for *pesto* vary widely in detail. I know that in Florence there are Tuscan touches to it. I have found that these go back to a period when many kinds of green sauces based on herbs were used in Tuscany, including one based on basil. Probably this merged with the famous Genoese one at some point. I think, however, that this Tuscan *pesto* should not be regarded merely as an inauthentic version, since it probably has its own claims to validity.

I have had some lively discussions with several Genoese friends in order to arrive at the "true" Genoese *pesto*:

1. Basil, garlic, olive oil, and grated cheese are basic to all the recipes.

2. Nuts exist in the older recipes; they were not a later addition. We should not be surprised, as nuts were commonly used in all green sauces of the Renaissance. Pignoli or walnuts or both may be used.

3. Cheese: The older Ligurian recipes used sheep's cheese, such as

---

* *Biancomangiare* is an example. It is a dish probably of Catalan rather than Provencal origin that was very important in medieval and Renaissance Italy. It was the main dish of the *bianco* or white category.

It was made with rice pulverized into flour, hens, almonds, and spices. It was not originally a sweet like the French *blancmange* that derives from it. It survived in close to its original form in Genoa until quite recently.

the local pecorino or pecorino Sardo. Local pecorino is difficult to find now in Liguria, so Sardo is used, mixed with Parmigiano, which is made from cow's milk. Other aged pecorino, such as Romano, is often substituted for Sardo, particularly outside of Liguria.

4. Many modern published recipes mix a little butter into the ingredients to be ground. Even many of the old Genoese families have adopted this.

5. The basil stays somewhat greener when crushed with mortar and pestle than with other methods. However, even in Genoa, a little parsley is sometimes added to keep the color greener.

As for Tuscan *pesto:*

1. Both walnuts *and* pignoli are used.

2. Since pecorino is still widely available in Tuscany, we grate local aged pecorino and mix it with Parmigiano.

3. *Pancetta* is used in place of butter.

4. Since *pesto* is made with a *mezzaluna* in Tuscany, something must be added to keep the green color. A little cooked spinach is used instead of parsley.

Whichever method you use, 1½ cups of olive oil will produce quite a thick pesto. It is best to start with a thick sauce. Additional liquid is added in the pasta recipes that use it, and, of course, in the soups.

To preserve *pesto*, it is not necessary to freeze it, nor even strictly necessary to refrigerate it. Omit the cheese and add enough olive oil to come about ½ inch above the *pesto*. This is the way *pesto* has been preserved through the winter for centuries, a method that retains more of the original taste than when frozen. Mix in the cheese before serving whatever amount of *pesto* you wish to use.

Making pesto with mortar and pestle

      12 walnuts, shelled
       2 tablespoon pignoli
       1 teaspoon coarse salt
       4 or 5 peppercorns
       3 cloves garlic
       4 tablespoons (½ stick) unsalted butter
       6 handfuls fresh basil leaves (about 3 cups)
       4 ounces Parmigiano cheese, freshly grated
       4 ounces Sardo, Romano, or additional Parmigiano cheese,
           freshly grated
    1½ cups of olive oil, approximately

Place the walnuts, pignoli, salt, peppercorns, and garlic in a stone mortar, along with the butter. Use a wooden pestle, not to crush, but rather to push the ingredients in a circular motion against the stone, which will grind them.

Add the basil leaves and grind until well integrated, then add the grated cheeses and grind the mixture a bit more. (Originally the cheese was cut into pieces and also ground in the mortar. I know of no one who still does this.)

Transfer the mixture to a bowl. Add the olive oil, little by little, mixing with a wooden spoon, as with a *maionese*, until the *pesto* is creamy and smooth.

Making pesto with mezzaluna

> 12 walnuts, shelled
> 2 tablespoons pignoli
> 4 ounces *pancetta* or salt pork
> 6 handfuls fresh basil leaves (about 3 cups)
> 1 heaping teaspoon chopped, cooked spinach
> 3 cloves garlic
> 4 ounces Parmigiano cheese, freshly grated
> 4 ounces Sardo, Romano, or additional Parmigiano cheese, freshly grated
> Salt and freshly ground black pepper
> 1½ cups of olive oil, approximately

Chop the walnuts, pignoli, and *pancetta* very fine with *mezzaluna*, then transfer to a bowl.

Chop the basil leaves, cooked spinach (squeezed until it is quite dry), and garlic very fine, then add to the bowl as well.

Add the grated cheeses and season with salt and pepper. Add the olive oil, little by little and stirring constantly, until you have a smooth sauce.

Making pesto with blender or food processor

Use the same ingredients as for *pesto* made with the *mezzaluna*. Place ½ cup of the olive oil, plus all the other ingredients, in the blender or food processor and grind very fine. Add the remaining olive oil and blend for a few seconds, until very smooth.

Agliata
(Garlic Sauce)   (SERVES 6)

A white sauce, uncooked, creamy, and only mildly spicy. The
cold sauce is placed on hot, cooked dried pasta or rice *in bianco,* that
is, with uncooked butter melted over it. Rather widely used in
northern Italy today, *agliata* appears in the first known Italian recipe
book, from Florence in the 1300s. Half the garlic was left raw, and the
other half cooked under hot wood ash. As in most white sauces of
that time, almonds provided the binding ingredient and the color. The
recent versions of the sauce, currently used in northern Italy, use all
raw garlic and *mollica,* the inside part of the bread, in place of almonds.

It will dress 1 pound of dried pasta or 2 cups of raw rice.

  3 slices Tuscan bread (see page 32) or white bread, if Tuscan
       bread is not available
1½ cups cold milk
  4 ounces shelled walnuts
  2 cloves garlic
     Salt and white pepper to taste

Remove the crust from the bread slices. Soak the bread in the cold
milk for 20 minutes in a crockery bowl.

Place the shelled walnuts and garlic in a stone mortar and grind very
fine with a wooden pestle, then transfer to the bowl containing the
bread and milk.

Stir continuously with wooden spoon; after 2 or 3 minutes, taste for
salt and pepper.

Stir for 10 minutes more in order to break up the bread and make a
homogenous sauce, then cover the bowl and place it in the refrigerator for 1 hour. Serve the sauce in a sauceboat.

Agliata may also be made by placing all ingredients together in a
blender.

Briciolata
(Bread Crumb Sauce)   (SERVES 6)

An excellent sauce for dried pasta, based on quality olive oil and good bread crumbs, *briciolata* derives from the word *briciole* for bread crumbs. Widely used all over Italy when homemade bread and bread crumbs were staples, it really depends on the high quality of its two principal ingredients. It uses no tomato or Parmigiano.

    1 cup olive oil
    3 tablespoons homemade bread crumbs (see page 45)
    Salt and freshly ground black pepper

Five minutes before your pasta has finished cooking, begin to make the *briciolata:*

Heat the olive oil in a saucepan over a low flame. When the oil is hot, add the bread crumbs and salt to taste. Sauté very gently until the bread crumbs are lightly golden brown, then remove the pan from the heat and sprinkle with pepper.

When the pasta is drained, pour the *briciolata* over it and mix thoroughly. Serve immediately. Absolutely do *not* add grated cheese.

Note: You can, if you wish, add 4 or 5 sprigs of Italian parsley, chopped.

Antipasti

Sedano, Finocchi, Carciofi in Pinzimonio
(Raw Celery, Fennel, and Artichoke *in Pinzimonio*)

Italians are very fond of raw vegetables dipped in a sauce as an antipasto. The Tuscan version of this is called *in pinzimonio*, which means that the vegetables are eaten held between two fingers, grasping the vegetable as in *pinze*, or tweezers. This metaphor is necessary for the Italians because, as the inventors of forks and eating implements, they do not readily accept the idea of eating anything with their hands, and they must turn it into a story.

The "sauce" for *pinzimonio* in Tuscany is just high-quality olive oil with lots of salt and pepper. The saltiness of dishes such as *pinzimonio* is the opposite extreme from the saltlessness of their bread and some other dishes. The range in salting in Tuscan food is very wide; there is not a single degree of saltiness that applies to all dishes. It is the two extreme ends, saltlessness and extreme saltiness, that takes some getting used to, but I believe one eventually comes to see the advantages of this nonuniformity. (Perhaps the closest approach to this is in Chinese cooking, in which "salt" dishes are in a special category of their own.)

Fresh celery and fennel are the best vegetables to use in America for this dish. Leave the small, fresh leaves of the celery on, as they are the best part for catching the sauce and are delicious eaten in this way. Slice the fennel into long, thin sticks, removing the leaves, of course. In Florence itself, the favorite vegetable for *pinzimonio* is the small, tender raw artichoke. If you are ever there in the winter, do try it.

For each serving

    ¼ cup olive oil, preferably virgin
    1 heaping teaspoon salt
    ½ teaspoon of freshly ground black pepper

Pinzimonio: Fresh raw vegetables (artichokes, fennel, celery) to be dipped in fine olive oil with salt and pepper.

Combine all the ingredients.

To serve, place the sliced vegetables on a serving dish. At each setting, place a small bowl with a portion of sauce as described above.

Each diner helps himself to vegetables, dips them, and eats.

Polenta Fritta
(Fried Polenta Appetizer)

Leftover polenta (page 367) without sauce, can be utilized as a delicious salty, crisp appetizer by deep-frying, then salting thin slices of it. It is particularly appropriate for the winter months.

Take polenta (a day old and still cold from refrigeration) and slice it into strips ½ inch thick and 2 inches long.

Heat a large quantity of olive oil, or a mixture of solid vegetable shortening and lard in a frying pan. When the oil is hot, add some polenta strips and deep-fry, turning them, until they are golden brown on all sides.

Prepare a serving dish by placing some paper towels on the bottom. As the polenta slices are cooked, transfer them to the dish. When all the slices are on the serving dish, sprinkle them with salt and remove the paper towels.

Serve immediately, very hot.

Insalata di Riso
(Rice Salad) (SERVES 8)

This cold rice appetizer, very often served at buffets, is especially good in the summer, when it is also useful as a first course. With good Arborio rice, a little crispness from the celery and tomato, and a piquant touch from capers, anchovies, tuna, and olives, it is a welcome opener to a meal.

> Coarse salt
> 1 pound raw rice, preferably Italian Arborio
>   Juice of 3 lemons
>   *Maionese* (see page 55)
> 5 whole anchovies in salt or 10 anchovy fillets in oil
> 1 8-ounce can tuna fish
> 4 ounces capers in wine vinegar
> 1 celery heart
> ¾ pound large Greek olives
>   Salt and freshly ground pepper to taste
> 3 eggs
> 3 firm, not overripe, fresh tomatoes

Put a large quantity of water in a stockpot, add coarse salt, and bring to the boiling point. Put in the rice, stir with a ladle, and cook until the rice is al dente (about 14 minutes). When rice is ready, drain it in a colander, then place in a bowl and add the lemon juice and salt to taste. Mix thoroughly and let cool until needed.

Prepare the *maionese;* refrigerate until needed. If whole anchovies preserved in salt are used, clean and bone them under cold running water. Cut the anchovies into small pieces and place them in a large bowl.

Drain the capers and add them to the large bowl containing the anchovies. Cut the celery heart into ½-inch pieces, then add to the bowl, along with the tuna and two-thirds of the olives. Add the *maionese* to the bowl with the other ingredients and mix very well.

Add the cooled rice to the bowl. Season with salt and pepper to taste, then mix thoroughly. Place the bowl, covered with a lid or aluminum foil, in the refrigerator until needed.

Place a saucepan containing 4 or 5 cups of cold, salted water on a flame. When the water reaches the boiling point, put in the eggs and let them cook until hard (about 11 minutes). Meanwhile, slice the tomatoes into ½-inch slices. When the eggs are ready, shell them and cut them in quarters.

Remove the bowl containing the rice mixture from the refrigerator and transfer the contents to a large serving dish. Arrange two rings of garnish around the rice, the first of tomato slices, the second of egg quarters. Finally, garnish with the remaining olives and serve, quite cold.

Riso Forte or *Pasticcio di Riso Amaro*
(Peppery Rice Pasticcio)   (SERVES 8)

This is a very special dish, in which the rice is mixed with three kinds of cheese: pecorino Romano, a sheep's cheese; Parmigiano, and pecorino Toscano, the Tuscan sheep's cheese. Since the third is not available in America, it is necessary to find a cheese that has a similar soft, unaged sheep's cheese flavor. *Ricotta salata*, a lightly salted dry ricotta, works very well. This ricotta is imported into the United States from southern Italy and is available at many cheese stores. If you can't find it, substitute more Parmigiano, though it is likely that cheese shops that carry really good Parmigiano could also obtain *ricotta salata*, since there are American distributors for it.

What may come as a shock at first is the quantity of fresh black pepper that is called for. The pepper is really the main flavoring of this rice *pasticcio*, and should be tasted not only for its "hot" quality but also for its flavor. After the initial jolt, it is a discovery to find that pepper is not only a condiment, but a taste in its own right.

    10 cups cold water
     1 tablespoon coarse salt
    10 ounces raw rice, preferably Italian Arborio
     4 ounces freshly grated Parmigiano
     2 ounces *ricotta salata* or additional Parmigiano
     2 ounces freshly grated Romano

4 teaspoons freshly ground black pepper
6 tablespoons bread crumbs, preferably homemade (see page 45)
  Freshly grated nutmeg to taste
¼ teaspoon ground cinnamon
6 eggs
2 cups milk

Put the water in a heatproof casserole, along with the salt, and bring to the boiling point. Add the rice, stir with a wooden spoon, and cook until the rice is soft (about 13 to 15 minutes).

Meanwhile, put the cheeses in a large bowl; preheat the oven to 375°.

When the rice is done, drain it in a colander and cool under cold running water. Add it to the bowl with the cheeses. Mix well with a wooden spoon, then add the pepper, 2 tablespoons of the bread crumbs, the nutmeg, and cinnamon. Add the eggs, one at a time, mixing thoroughly, then the cold milk.

Butter a loaf pan and coat with the remaining bread crumbs. Place the rice mixture in the pan and bake in the preheated oven for 40 or 45 minutes.

Remove from oven, allow to cool for 15 minutes, then unmold onto a serving dish. Serve immediately or cold, as an appetizer.

Foglie di Salvia Ripiene
(Sage "Sandwiches")   (SERVES 6)

These miniature deep-fried "sandwiches" of sage leaves between mozzarella squares make a very good appetizer to serve with *aperitivi*, before sitting down at the table. They are also useful for buffets.

1 cup all-purpose flour
  Salt
2 tablespoons olive oil
1 egg, separated
3 tablespoons dry white wine
½ cup cold water, approximately (for a medium-thick batter)
8 ounces mozzarella
30 small leaves sage, fresh or under salt (page 14)
1 pound solid vegetable shortening

Sift the flour, then combine in a bowl with a pinch of salt, the olive oil, egg yolk, white wine, and cold water. Mix well with a wooden spoon, then let stand in a cool place (not the refrigerator) for 2 hours.

Pat the mozzarella dry with a paper towel. Cut first into slices ½ inch thick, then into 1-inch squares. (If the cheese is still not very dry, absorb the excess liquid by patting the squares with more paper towels.) Using 2 sage leaves for each "sandwich," make miniature three-layer "sandwiches" by placing sage leaves between squares of mozzarella.

Heat the vegetable shortening in a large frying pan. While it is heating, beat the egg white and fold it into the batter.

When the fat is hot, dip the mozzarella "sandwiches" in the batter and deep-fry until golden brown all over. Remove from the fat, drain on paper towels, and immediately sprinkle with salt. Serve hot.

Mozzarella in Carrozza
(Mozzarella "in a Carriage")   (SERVES 6)

Mozzarella "in a carriage"—that is, wrapped in bread slices, dipped in egg, and deep-fried—is sprinkled with salt and served hot, as an appetizer. It is especially good served with an *aperitivo* of cold white wine.

   8 ounces mozzarella
  12 slices white bread
   4 eggs
     Salt
  ½ pound solid vegetable shortening

Cut the mozzarella into 6 slices, then cut each slice in half. Cut each slice of bread in half and place a piece of mozzarella between 2 bread slices.

Beat the eggs in a bowl with a pinch of salt.

Heat the shortening in a frying pan. While it is getting hot, prepare a serving dish by lining the bottom with paper towels.

When the fat is hot, dip each "sandwich" into beaten egg and deep-fry until golden brown on one side. Turn over to fry other side; the mozzarella will melt. Place the deep-fried "sandwiches" on the serving dish to drain.

In Italy mozzarella is unsalted, but in America it is sometimes salted. If the cheese is unsalted, when the "sandwiches" are on the serving dish, sprinkle them with salt. Serve hot.

Pasticcetti con Acciuga
(Anchovy Pastries) (SERVES 6)

Little deep-fried anchovy pastries. Crisp and salty, they make a perfect accompaniment to a cold *aperitivo* wine. They should be cooked at the last moment, as they must be served hot.

- 2 anchovies in salt or 4 anchovy fillets in oil
- 1¾ cups all-purpose flour
- 4 tablespoons (½ stick) butter
- 1 egg
- Salt
- ½ cup cold milk, approximately (for a smooth dough)
- 1 pound solid vegetable shortening

If using anchovies in salt, bone them under cold running water to remove excess salt. If using anchovy fillets in oil, dry them very carefully. Cut each anchovy into 8 pieces and set aside.

Place the flour in a mound on a pasta board. Make a well in the center.

Melt the butter and allow to cool for 10 minutes, then put in the well, along with the egg and a pinch of salt, and mix together thoroughly, not yet incorporating any flour. Add the milk and mix until all the ingredients are well incorporated into the flour.

Knead the dough for 20 minutes, until very smooth, then divide into halves. Spread out one half with your hands and arrange the anchovy pieces over the surface.

Spread out the other half of the dough until it is the same size as the first half, then place the second half evenly over the first. Press it down lightly, then roll with a rolling pin until the dough is ⅓ inch thick. Using cookie cutters of different shapes, cut out the dough.

Heat the shortening in a large frying pan. When it is hot, deep-fry *pasticcetti* on both sides until golden brown.

Remove them from the pan, drain on paper towels, and sprinkle with salt. Serve very hot.

Melanzane Marinate
(Marinated Eggplant)   (SERVES 6 TO 8)

Eggplant slices, fried, marinated in olive oil, wine vinegar, basil, garlic, salt and pepper, and then served cold. The dish may be served in the evening if prepared in the morning, but it is better if it marinates for at least a day. Best for an antipasto course at the table or for a buffet.

> 2 large or 4 medium-sized eggplants
> Coarse salt
> 1 cup fresh basil leaves
> 2 large cloves garlic
> Vegetable oil (such as safflower) for deep frying
> Salt and freshly ground pepper
> ½ cup very good quality wine vinegar

Slice the eggplants vertically into ½-inch slices; do not peel. Place the slices on a large plate, sprinkle liberally with coarse salt, and let stand for 1 hour. (The eggplant will shed some dark liquid.)

Chop the basil leaves and place in small bowl. Chop the garlic fine and add to the chopped basil. Mix very well with a wooden spoon.

Dry the eggplant slices with paper towels, and deep-fry them, in a large quantity of vegetable oil, until golden brown all over. After all the slices are fried, do not drain off the oil on absorbent paper as usual; you will layer the undrained slices in a serving dish.

Put down a layer of eggplant; cover with chopped basil and garlic, then sprinkle with salt and pepper. Put down another layer of eggplant; cover with more basil and garlic, then salt and pepper. Repeat until all the eggplant slices are in the serving dish.

Pour in the wine vinegar, let cool, and then place in refrigerator, covered with aluminum foil.

After 1 hour, gently turn the eggplant slices over. Return to the refrigerator, still covered, for at least 3 hours more. (This dish is even better when made a day in advance.)

Note: Since the eggplant is refrigerated after it is deep-fried, a solid vegetable shortening can't be used for the deep frying because it would resolidify in the cold temperature.

The marinated eggplant can be preserved through the entire winter by covering it with olive oil in a jar with a lid and keeping it in the refrigerator.

Crostini al Ginepro
(Canapés of Liver Paste and Juniper Berries)   (SERVES 6)

Crostini are the Italian canapés. However, hearty country bread is used, the slices, though thin, are not delicate, and the crusts are left on the bread. *Crostini* of liver paste cooked with juniper berries evoke the autumn hunting season.

- 10 chicken livers
- 2 cloves garlic, peeled but left whole
- 4 or 5 sage leaves
- ¼ cup olive oil
- 1 tablespoon butter
   Salt and freshly ground pepper to taste
- 7 juniper berries
- 2 cups chicken or meat broth
- 2 anchovies in salt or 4 anchovy fillets in oil
- 1 teaspoon capers in wine vinegar
- 24 small, thin slices day-old Tuscan bread (see page 32)

Chop the chicken livers coarsely, then place them in a saucepan with the garlic cloves, sage, olive oil, and butter. Sauté very lightly for 10 to 15 minutes, then add a pinch of salt, pepper, and the juniper berries. Add 1 cup of the broth and let cook until broth has completely evaporated.

Remove the pan from the stove. Drain out the liquid and save it. Place the solid contents of the pan on a board and chop fine, then return to the pan, along with the reserved liquid. Add the remaining cup of broth and cook again, very gently, until almost all the broth has evaporated.

If using anchovies in salt, fillet them under cold running water to remove excess salt. Chop the anchovies fine, along with the capers, then incorporate with a fork into the chicken livers. Taste for salt and pepper and remove the pan from the stove.

Spread some of this paste on each slice of bread, either toasted or plain, place them in a serving dish, and serve. *Crostini* on untoasted bread are eaten cold.

In Tuscany the bread is either toasted or used plain. However, bread slices fried in olive oil also work very well.

Crostini con Burro di Acciughe
(Crostini with Anchovy Butter)   (MAKES ABOUT 14)

Anchovy butter spreads on rustic slices of Tuscan bread—one of the simplest of appetizers, widely used with before-dinner drinks and at the beginning of a buffet.

    8 tablespoons (1 stick) salted butter
    8 anchovies in salt or 16 anchovy fillets in oil
    5 slices bread, preferably Tuscan (see page 32)
    1 to 2 ounces capers in wine vinegar

Place the butter in bowl and mash it gently with a wooden spoon for 15 minutes, until it has a soft, creamy texture.

If using anchovies in salt, bone and clean them under cold running water. Place the anchovy fillets in the bowl with the butter and mash them into a paste, then incorporate the paste into the butter. Continue to mix until the butter and anchovies are completely combined and homogenous. Cover the bowl with aluminum foil and refrigerate for 1 hour.

Cut the bread into slices; leave the crusts on. Cut each slice into halves or quarters for *crostini*. Spread the anchovy butter on the *crostini* and place on a serving dish. Garnish each *crostino* with one or two capers in the center and serve.

Panzanella
(Bread Salad)   (SERVES 6)

One of the most characteristic of all Florentine dishes, the earliest recipe for this was written down among the poems in the notebooks of the great painter Bronzino, pupil of Michelangelo himself, in the sixteenth century. Without doubt a summer dish, because it depends upon fresh summer vegetables.

Most important for making a good *panzanella* is to have a good, dark Tuscan bread, some days old, so that when it is soaked and the water squeezed out, it flakes into a texture that is very light and dry, almost a powder. (What must be avoided is sogginess, a danger lurking in light bread, or bread that is too fresh.)

This is probably one of the most difficult dishes to imagine if you have never experienced it, but follow the instructions carefully, take the trouble to make Tuscan dark bread, use good virgin olive oil, and you will have a real addition to your repertoire of refreshing dishes for summer eating.

(If the ingredients are not available, especially the Tuscan bread, do not attempt to make substitutions. All attention in the dish is focused on just these ingredients, and it cannot succeed without them.)

    1 large red onion
    8 to 10 large, fresh basil leaves
    2 large, ripe tomatoes
    1 pound Tuscan dark bread (see page 37), several days old
      Salt and freshly ground black pepper to taste
    ½ cup virgin olive oil
    1 tablespoon wine vinegar, approximately

Peel the outer skin from onion and wash very carefully. Wash the basil leaves and tomatoes as well.

Soak the bread in very cold water with the whole tomatoes, onion, and basil for 15 to 20 minutes, then squeeze the bread to remove all liquid and place in a plastic container.

Cut the onion in quarters and finely slice each quarter. Place the onion pieces over soaked bread. Tear each basil leaf into two or three pieces and arrange them over the onions, then dice the tomatoes into ½-inch squares and place these on top of the basil. Cover the plastic container and place in the refrigerator for at least 2 hours.

Remove the container from refrigerator and transfer the contents to a bowl. Season with salt, pepper, oil, and vinegar and mix thoroughly. Serve immediately.

Uova Ripiene
(Stuffed Eggs)   (SERVES 8 AS AN APPETIZER)

Removing the yolks of hard-cooked eggs, mashing them with flavorings, and refilling the whites with the mixture is a technique that again goes back at least as far as the fourteenth century. This is a version of somewhat more recent origin that is often used in present-day Italy. It is useful both as an appetizer and for buffets.

    4 eggs
    2 anchovies in salt or 4 anchovy fillets in oil
    1½ ounces capers in wine vinegar
    1 can (10 ounces) tuna in olive oil
    4 or 5 sprigs Italian parsley
      Salt and freshly ground pepper to taste
    1 tablespoon olive oil
      Maionese (made with 1 egg yolk, 1 cup oil, and 1 teaspoon
        lemon juice; for procedure see page 55)
    4 green olives stuffed with pimento

Hard-cook the eggs for 12 or 13 minutes. Let cool, then remove the shells and cut in half lengthwise. Remove the yolks, taking care not to break the whites. Place the whites on a sheet of aluminum foil and the yolks on a chopping board.

If using anchovies in salt, clean and fillet them under cold running water, then place, along with the capers, tuna, and parsley, on the chopping board with the yolks. Chop everything fine, then put in a bowl, taste for salt and pepper, and add the olive oil. Mix until thoroughly combined.

Fill each white half with enough of the yolk mixture to reconstruct the shape of a whole egg. Place the stuffed egg halves on a serving dish and cover with the *maionese*. Cut the green olives in half crossways, and place around the plate for garnish. Serve cold.

Peperoni Ripieni
(Stuffed Peppers)   (SERVES 4)

These baked peppers are stuffed with a rather elaborate filling in which the meat is flavored with a variety of elements, including *odori* (aromatic vegetables), the chopped pepper tops, wine, prosciutto, Parmigiano, and broth. Green peppers are used in this recipe even though the yellow, orange, and red ones that are found in Italy are also occasionally available in Italian markets (do not confuse the sweet red ones with fresh pimentos). I personally prefer the yellow or orange ones for flavor, but the green ones are also excellent and have the advantage of being easy to find.

This Tuscan version of stuffed peppers does not cover them with tomato sauce. The stuffing itself provides enough flavor. The baked peppers may be eaten cold as an appetizer, warm as a main dish, or as part of a buffet. When served as the main course, *peperoni ripieni* may be accompanied by *spaghetti alla fiaccheraia* (page 156) and *fagioli al forno* (page 403) with *ricotta fritta* (page 469) for a dessert.

    4 large green peppers
    1 small red onion
    1 clove garlic
    4 or 5 sprigs Italian parsley
    ½ medium-sized carrot
    3 tablespoons olive oil
    ½ pound ground meat
       Salt and freshly ground pepper to taste
    ½ cup dry red wine
    2 tablespoons canned tomatoes
    1 slice prosciutto, *pancetta*, or boiled ham (about 2 ounces)
    1 egg yolk
    2 tablespoons freshly grated Parmigiano cheese
    ½ cup bread crumbs, preferably homemade (see page 45)
    ½ cup meat or chicken broth

Soak the peppers in cold water for 10 minutes, then drain. Cut the tops off the peppers and remove the seeds from inside. Set the pepper bottoms aside and chop the top parts of the peppers fine, along with the onion, garlic, parsley, and carrot.

Place a saucepan containing 2 tablespoons of the olive oil on a medium flame. When the oil is hot, add the chopped ingredients and sauté for 5 to 8 minutes, until lightly golden brown. Add the ground meat, season with salt and pepper, and sauté for 10 more minutes. Add the wine and simmer until it is evaporated (about 6 to 8 minutes), then put in the tomatoes and cook until the sauce is thick (about 15 minutes), stirring continuously with a wooden spoon. Remove the saucepan from the stove and allow to cool (about 20 to 25 minutes).

Preheat the oven to 375°.

When the contents of the pan are cool, coarsely chop the prosciutto (or *pancetta* or boiled ham) and add to the pan. Mix very well with a wooden spoon, then add the egg yolk and Parmigiano, mixing thoroughly.

Fill the reserved peppers with the contents of the pan. Sprinkle the tops with the bread crumbs, then put the peppers in a rectangular Pyrex baking dish (13½ x 8¾ inches) and pour in the broth and remaining 1 tablespoon olive oil. Place the baking dish in the preheated oven for 40 minutes, until the peppers are soft.

Remove the baking dish from oven, allow to cool for 10 minutes, then transfer the peppers to a serving dish with a spatula. Serve hot or cold.

FRITTATE

There is no translation of *frittata* that conveys what it is. (See the photo opposite for a *frittata di porri*.) They are not omelets, which are really closer to egg *crespelle*, nor are they thin, pancakelike forms that are stuffed and rolled up. Rather, the pieces of vegetable or meat are sautéed or fried and incorporated into the eggs in the form of a low cake.

Frittate are used cold for appetizers and warm for main dishes of a light dinner. Like omelets, they are made with a large variety of different vegetables or meats cut into pieces and mixed into the egg.

Among the great favorites are *frittate* of leeks (*porri*), of fried green tomato slices, and with basil. The technique of cooking them once the eggs have been added is described in detail in each individual recipe.

Frittata di Porri
(Frittata of Leeks)   (S E R V E S 4)

   5 large leeks
  ¼ cup olive oil
     Salt and freshly ground pepper to taste
   6 eggs

Rinse the leeks well, then cut them into rings ½ inch thick. Place the pieces in a bowl of cold water and let them soak for 20 minutes, then drain and rinse carefully under cold running water.

Heat 3 tablespoons of the olive oil in a flameproof casserole. When it is warm, add the leeks, season with salt and pepper, and sauté for about 30 minutes, until soft. Transfer the leeks to a bowl and allow them to cool for 1 hour.

In a large bowl, beat eggs with a pinch of salt. Add the cooled leeks and mix thoroughly.

Place a large omelet pan on the flame with the remaining tablespoon of olive oil. When the oil is hot, add the leek-egg mixture. When eggs are well set and the *frittata* is well detached from the bottom of the pan, put a plate, face down, over the pan. Holding the plate firmly, reverse the pan and turn the *frittata* out.

Frittata di porri.

Return the pan to the flame. Carefully slide the *frittata* onto the pan to cook the other side. After 2 minutes, reverse the *frittata* onto a serving dish. It may be served either hot or cold.

Frittata di Pomodori Verdi
(Frittata of Green Tomatoes)   (SERVES 6)

>   4 large green tomatoes
>   1 cup plus 1 tablespoon olive oil
>   1 cup all-purpose flour, approximately
>   6 eggs
>   Salt and freshly ground pepper

Wash the tomatoes very well and cut them into ½-inch slices.

Heat the 1 cup oil in a frying pan. (Do not use more than 1 cup of oil, as the tomato slices should not be completely covered.) While the oil is heating, flour the tomato slices.

When the oil begins to sizzle, place only as many tomato slices in pan as will make a single layer. Sauté until golden brown on both sides, then transfer to a paper towel to drain; sprinkle with salt and pepper. Fry the remaining tomato slices the same way.

Beat the eggs very lightly with a pinch of salt and set aside.

Heat the 1 tablespoon of olive oil in an omelet pan. When it is hot, add the tomato slices to the pan. (The slices are reduced in size from having been sautéed, so they should all fit in one layer.) Pour the eggs over the tomato slices. When the eggs are well set and the *frittata* is well detached from the bottom of the pan, place a plate, face down, over the pan. Holding the plate firmly, reverse the pan and turn the *frittata* out.

Return the pan to the flame. Carefully slide the *frittata* into the pan to cook the other side. After 1 minute, reverse the *frittata* onto a serving dish. It may be served either hot or cold.

Frittata al Basilico
(Frittata with Basil)   (SERVES 6)

>   ½ cup fresh basil leaves
>   7 eggs

3 tablespoons grated Parmigiano cheese*
Salt and freshly ground pepper
1 ½ teaspoons olive oil

Wash the basil leaves and dry them with a paper towel. Tear each leaf into two or three pieces and place them in a dish.

In a large bowl, lightly beat the eggs with a pinch of salt and pepper.

Add the Parmigiano to bowl and mix thoroughly, then add the basil leaves and stir gently.

Heat the olive oil in an omelet pan. When the oil is hot, pour in the contents of the bowl. When the eggs are well set and the *frittata* is well detached from the bottom of the pan, place a plate, face down, over the pan. Holding the plate firmly, reverse the pan and turn the *frittata* out.

Return the pan to the flame. Carefully slide the *frittata* into the pan to cook the other side. After 1 minute, reverse the *frittata* onto a serving dish. It may be served either hot or cold.

Porrata
(Leek Pie)   (SERVES 12)

Strangely enough, the word "puree" seems to derive from the Italian word for leeks, *porri*. A soup made from *porri* was called a *"porrea."* At the annual festival held at San Lorenzo (of the famous Michelangelo sacristy), from the fourteenth century on they served a *passato*, or puree, of leeks, and it appears that anything pureed gradually came to be called a *"purea,"* which became "puree" in French and English.

Porrata is a large leek pie with a crust made of yeast dough. The leeks are sautéed in olive oil and butter and flavored with *pancetta*. This is even better cold than warm, and may be prepared in advance. A perfect antipasto to serve at a buffet or with before-dinner drinks, it is also suitable for a fancy occasion, and can serve a function similar to a quiche.

* In Italy this dish is made with Tuscan pecorino cheese which is unavailable in the United States.

5 bunches leeks (about 20 leeks)
3 tablespoons olive oil
1 tablespoon butter
  Salt and freshly ground pepper to taste
2 ounces (4 cakes) compressed fresh yeast or 4 packages active
    dry yeast
3 cups all-purpose flour
1 cup lukewarm or hot water, depending on the yeast
6 eggs
6 ounces *pancetta* or 3 ounces salt pork plus 3 ounces boiled ham

Rinse the leeks well, then slice them into rings. Place the pieces in a large bowl of cold water for 10 minutes. Rinse several times to remove all grains of sand.

Heat the olive oil and butter in a large flameproof casserole. When the butter is melted, add the leeks and sprinkle with salt and pepper. Cover the casserole and cook very slowly until the leeks are soft (30 to 40 minutes), stirring frequently with a wooden spoon. Remove the casserole from the heat and let the leeks stand until cold (about 1 hour). Meanwhile, make the crust.

Dissolve the yeast in the lukewarm or hot water.

Place the flour in a mound on a pasta board. Make a well in the flour, then pour in the dissolved yeast and add 2 eggs and salt. Mix with a wooden spoon, incorporating the flour from the inside rim of the well, little by little. When the dough is firm, start kneading. Knead until all but 2 tablespoons of flour is incorporated (about 20 minutes).

Sprinkle the dough with the remaining flour and cover it with a cotton dishtowel. Let stand in a warm place, away from drafts, until doubled in size (about 1½ hours).

Chop the *pancetta* coarsely and set aside in a dish until needed; place the remaining 4 eggs in the casserole with the leeks and mix well with a wooden spoon.

Oil a 10-inch springform; preheat the oven to 400°.

When the dough has risen, gently roll it, using a rolling pin, into a large sheet less than ½ inch thick. Fit the sheet of dough into the springform, letting the excess dough hang out over the edges.

Sprinkle the chopped *pancetta* over the dough, then, using a strainer-skimmer, fill the springform with the leeks. With a knife, cut off the dough around the edges of the springform. Turn the edges inward, over the leeks, to make a border. Sprinkle with abundant freshly ground pepper (the dish should be peppery), then place the spring-form in the preheated oven for 45 to 50 minutes.

Remove the *porrata* from the oven and allow it to cool for 15 minutes before opening the springform. Remove from the springform and transfer to a serving dish. To serve, cut it like a pie. (The *porrata* may also be eaten cold.)

Fettunta
(Tuscan Garlic Bread)   (S E R V E S 4)

In the regions of Italy that have olive oil, it is a great treat for snack or appetizer to have large slices of country bread toasted, rubbed with garlic, and covered with green oil, especially in the season of the year when the olives are newly pressed. The oil, still warm from the olive press, is poured over the bread, creating a flavor never to be forgotten. The Tuscan word for this is *fetta unta*, or "oily slice." In Rome and southern Italy, it is called *"bruschetta."* To compare the Roman and Tuscan ways of preparing it gives an insight into the way the Tuscans have of lightening their cooking. In Rome the bread is fried in the oil, while in Tuscany the bread is toasted, over charcoal or wood, if possible. Then the oil is heated, but not cooked, and poured over.

Fettunta can be successfully prepared in your kitchen with Tuscan bread (see page 32) and good olive oil. The bread may be toasted in the oven. If you are preparing something on the charcoal broiler, it is even better to toast the bread that way. Unlike the more usual garlic bread prepared to eat with the meal in America, *fettunta* is a dish in its own right and should be eaten as an appetizer or as a snack.

    4 large slices Tuscan bread (see page 32)
    2 cloves garlic, peeled and cut in half
    ½ cup olive oil
       Salt and freshly ground pepper

Place the bread slices on aluminum foil and place them in an oven preheated to 375°. Toast the bread for about 8 minutes on each side, then rub both sides of the bread with the cut garlic.

Warm the oil in a small saucepan on a very low flame for 5 minutes, then immediately pour onto the bread arranged on a serving dish. Sprinkle with salt and pepper and serve immediately.

Fagioli, Tonno e Cipolle
(Tuscan Beans, Tuna, and Fresh Onions)   (SERVES 4)

A very basic, rustic appetizer. Easier to make if you have some cooked beans left over, and always very satisfying. Quite popular in Italy.

> 2 cups dried cannellini beans
>   Coarse salt
> 2 medium-sized red onions
> 1 can (6 ounces) tuna
> 3 tablespoons olive oil
>   Freshly ground black pepper
>   Salt to taste

Soak the beans overnight in a bowl of cold water (about 6 cups).

The next day, drain the beans and place in a stockpot with about 10 cups cold water and coarse salt. Simmer very slowly for about 3 hours, until soft, then remove the stockpot from the heat and allow the beans to cool in the liquid for 1 hour. Drain the beans in a colander and transfer to a bowl. Cover with aluminum foil and refrigerate for about 1 hour.

Meanwhile, soak one of the onions in cold water for 30 minutes, then chop coarsely and place in a small bowl.

Drain the tuna and add to the small bowl containing the onion.

Break the tuna up with a fork and mix it with the onion. Add the olive oil and let stand in the refrigerator until needed.

When the beans have been refrigerated for 1 hour, remove both bowls from the refrigerator and add contents of the small one to the beans. Mix very well with a wooden spoon and transfer to a serving dish. Sprinkle generously with freshly ground black pepper, then taste for salt and garnish with the second red onion, left whole, placed in the center of the serving dish.

Note: This dish may be prepared several hours in advance; if so, keep the serving dish in the refrigerator, covered with aluminum foil.

Carote all' Agro
(Marinated Raw Shredded Carrots). See page 388.

Pomodori e Tonno
(Tomato Halves with Tuna, Capers, and Mayonnaise). See page 393.

Soups

THE great range of Italian soups is often unjustly overshadowed by the popularity of the pastas. In many parts of Italy, pasta is eaten perhaps less than many non-Italians suppose, not at the evening meal and not every day at lunch. Soups are most often eaten instead, soups ranging from light broth and consommé, both with a little pasta, through broth- and stock-based soups of many kinds—onion, leek, vegetable, and so forth.

There are stock-based purees of vegetables and, of course, the substantial hearty *minestre*, minestroni, and finally bean and pasta soups, the latter with almost no liquid at all. I include examples of the entire range of these.

Let me begin, however, with a discussion of broth and consommé, stock and *gelatina;* then I present four lighter soups, in which the broth or stock base still determines the basic thickness: the very special *ginestrata;* two onion soups, one old and one modern; and a leek soup covered with grated cheese.

BROTH AND CONSOMMÉ

IN ITALY, when one wants to make a really quality broth, one only uses beef. When one wants to economize, bones and scraps may be substituted, but we should not think that this is to be preferred. If the meat is of top quality, and if one begins with cold water and coarse salt and allows the stockpot only to simmer slowly, little or no impurity will come to the top of the pot. While Florentines are as well known as the Genoese for economy, this is one thing they feel is too important to compromise on.

The above rule applies to a soup broth or basic broth for consommé. For stock used in the preparation of other dishes, a less refined result is satisfactory, and bones and scraps may be substituted. On the other hand, chicken is never used for soup broth or consommé, though of course chicken stock is called for in making some dishes, and may often be substituted for beef stock.

The meat that is used in making broth must cook for 3 hours. If a cut that also requires so long a cooking time is used, such as brisket or short ribs, then the meat can also be eaten. If a meat is used that ordinarily requires a somewhat shorter cooking time, then it will be cooked out and useless. Often in Italy, where the meat is cut differently, it is necessary to discard the meat used for making broth.

The meat used for making broth into consommé is of necessity discarded.

See recipes for such dishes as *lesso rifatto con porri* (page 272), *polpettone con tonno* (page 319), or simply, boiled beef (page 268) for utilization of beef left over from making broth.

Many Italians prefer to clarify broths and aspics with whole eggs rather than whites alone. That is the older tradition there, and I personally still prefer it, but I have used egg whites in the instructions here.

Meat Broth   (MAKES ABOUT 2½ QUARTS)

    1¼ pounds beef
    15 cups of cold water (3¾ quarts)
    1 tablespoon coarse salt
    1 medium-sized carrot
    1 small red onion
    1 medium-sized celery rib
    4 or 5 sprigs Italian parsley
    1 small ripe tomato or 2 ripe cherry tomatoes

Place a stockpot containing the meat, cold water, and coarse salt on a low flame. When the water reaches the boiling point, add the carrot, onion, celery, Italian parsley, and tomato, all whole, and simmer very slowly for 3 hours, half covered. While simmering, spoon off any foam or impurities that come to the surface of the broth.

Remove the meat from stockpot. Strain the broth through a colander into a large nonmetal bowl.

Allow the broth to cool completely (about 1 hour), then place the bowl, covered with aluminum foil, in the refrigerator for at least 1 hour. Then remove all fat from the surface.

Clarified Broth   (MAKES ABOUT 2 QUARTS)

Lightly beat 2 egg whites in a small bowl with 2 tablespoons of broth.

Place the beaten whites in the bowl with cold broth and stir thoroughly with a whisk.

Transfer the contents of the bowl to a stockpot, turn the heat on to medium, and stir continuously until the broth reaches the boiling point, then let simmer, very slowly and without stirring, for about 10 minutes.

Meanwhile, wet a piece of cheesecloth with cold water and place it in the refrigerator for about 10 minutes.

Place the cheesecloth over a large bowl and pour the hot broth through it; the broth should be absolutely transparent.

Coloring Broth

It is possible to give different shades to broth, from very light brown to dark brown. This is done with 2 tablespoons of dry Marsala or from 1 to 2 teaspoons of caramelized sugar (melt the sugar in a spoon over a flame). The Marsala or sugar must be added to the broth when it reaches the boiling point while clarifying. Marsala flavors the broth a bit, while the caramelized sugar has almost no taste.

Consommé   (SERVES 6)

9 cups clarified broth (see above), made without the tomato
½ pound beef, without any fat
1 small carrot

1 very small red onion
1 small celery rib
3 or 4 sprigs Italian parsley
1 egg white

After the broth is clarified, put it back into a clean stockpot.
Chop the beef coarsely and place it in a small bowl. Add the egg
white to the bowl and mix it thoroughly into the meat, stirring for 5 or
6 minutes. Add the contents of the bowl to the stockpot and stir it into
the broth.

Add carrot, onion, celery and parsley, all whole, then place the
stockpot on a low flame and simmer for 1 hour, covered.

Wet a piece of cheesecloth with cold water and place it in the refrigerator for 10 minutes. Place the cheesecloth over a large bowl and
pass the broth through it. The consommé may be eaten warm or cold.

Note: Consommé is served in a cup rather than a bowl, probably because it is concentrated and a smaller portion of it is served than of
broth or soup.

Stock

Stock to be used in making other dishes is a by-product of boiled
meat and fish dishes (see page 239 and 266). Simply save the broth
that results from boiling the meats, strain it, let it cool, defat it, and
use it as stock.

Gelatina

Gelatina is the Italian form of what is called aspic in English
French, and German. The kind of meat used to make it depends on
the dish it accompanies. To make a *gelatina* to accompany a capon, a
second capon will be the base of the *gelatina*. The same would be true
of chicken, fish, pork, or beef. The recipe below is based on beef and
may accompany boiled beef, chicken, or capon.

10 cups cold water
 2 pounds beef for boiling
 1 medium-sized calf's foot   (*continued*)

1 pig's foot (optional)
1 chicken neck or one small piece of chicken
1 carrot
1 celery rib
1 small red onion
1½ teaspoons coarse salt
¼ pound lean boneless veal
3 egg whites
1 to 2 teaspoons sugar

Place the water, beef, calf's foot, optional pig's foot, chicken neck, carrot, celery, onion, and salt in a large stockpot. Set on a medium flame and let simmer very slowly, half covered, for about 4½ hours. By that time, the water should have reduced to less than half.

Remove the pot from the heat. Strain the broth through a piece of cheesecloth into a large bowl and let stand until cool (about 1 hour). When cool, cover the bowl with a lid or aluminum foil and place it in the refrigerator until completely cold (at least 4 hours).

Remove the bowl from refrigerator; all the fat will have risen to the top. Carefully remove it with a small spatula, wiping up the last bits with a paper towel.

Clarifying Gelatina

Using a wire whisk, beat egg whites with 2 tablespoons of the broth. Coarsely chop the veal, then add along with the beaten egg whites to the bowl with the cold broth. Mix thoroughly, then transfer the contents of the bowl to an absolutely clean stockpot. Place it on a very low flame and stir continuously with the whisk until the broth reaches the boiling point. (In this way the beaten egg whites will become completely absorbed in the broth.)

At the moment the broth reaches boiling point, half-cover pot with lid and lower flame to minimum. Let simmer for 10 to 12 minutes. In this time eggs rise to the top with all the impurities absorbed and the broth should at a critical moment become completely transparent.

Coloring Gelatina

You can give *gelatina* the shade you like, depending on the quantity of caramelized sugar you add.

Put sugar in a metal spoon and place spoon directly on flame until sugar liquifies and turns brown.

Pour it in simmering broth drop by drop and stop when it reaches the shade you wish.

Straining and Clarifying Gelatina

Wet cheesecloth with cold water and place it in refrigerator for five minutes.

Place cheesecloth on colander and rest colander on large bowl.

Gently pour broth into colander with cheesecloth. Broth passing through should be absolutely clear and transparent.

Wet the mold you have chosen with cold water.

Transfer broth to mold and let stand until cool.

Place mold in refrigerator until firm.

Unmolding Gelatina

Hold serving dish upside down tightly over mold and reverse them together.

Wet towel with hot water and squeeze it.

Place hot towel over reversed mold. Repeat procedure with hot towel until *gelatina* detaches. Lift off mold.

You can serve *gelatina* in the shape of the mold or cut it into 1 inch squares.

Taglierini in Brodo
(Pasta in Broth)   (S E R V E S 6)

Finely cut fresh pasta in broth. A light and versatile first dish, suitable for all occasions.

> 2 cups all-purpose flour, preferably unbleached
> 2 eggs
>   Pinch of salt
> 2 teaspoons olive or other vegetable oil
> 4½ cups meat broth (see page 105), approximately
>   Coarse salt
> 6 tablespoons freshly grated Parmigiano cheese

Make the *taglierini*, using the flour, eggs, salt, and oil. For procedure, see pages 133–137, and to cut into *taglierini*, see page 138. Let the *taglierini* stand on a pasta board, covered with a cotton dishtowel, until needed.

Heat a large quantity of salted water in a stockpot. Meanwhile, in a second stockpot, heat the broth.

When the water in the first stockpot reaches the boiling point, add the *taglierini*, stir with a wooden spoon, and let them cook for 15 seconds, then strain quickly and transfer to the second stockpot, with the heated broth.

Serve immediately, sprinkling each serving with a tablespoon of freshly grated Parmigiano.

Palline Ripiene in Brodo
(Little Mushroom-filled Puffs in Broth)   (S E R V E S   6)

Little balls of cream-puff pastry, filled with dried wild mushrooms, in a fine broth. Appropriate to the most formal and elegant occasions.

For the palline (pasta soffiata)

    ¾ cup cold water
        Pinch of salt
    6 tablespoons (¾ stick) butter
    ¾ cup flour
    2 eggs
        Pinch of freshly grated nutmeg

       Salsa di funghi (see page 68)

    5 cups meat broth (see page 105), approximately
    6 tablespoons freshly grated Parmigiano cheese

Make the *pasta soffiata* with the ingredients listed above. For procedure see page 440, adding the pinch of nutmeg when the eggs are incorporated.

Butter a cookie sheet; preheat the oven to 375°.

Place the *pasta soffiata* in a syringe or pastry bag and form small balls (about ½ inch in diameter) with it on the cookie sheet, then bake in the preheated oven for about 20 minutes. Do not open the oven for 15 minutes after you put the cookie sheet in.

Remove the cookie sheet from oven and let *palline* rest until cool (about 30 minutes).

Prepare *salsa di funghi* as described on page 68, but make sure the mushrooms are chopped very fine. Let the sauce rest until cool (about 30 minutes), then place in a syringe and fill the *palline*. Place 5 or 6 *palline* in each individual soup bowl.

Heat the broth. When it is warm, pour one ladleful of broth (about ¾ cup) in each soup bowl with the *palline*, then sprinkle with Parmigiano and serve immediately.

Topini di Patate con Petto di Pollo in Brodo
(Topini of Potato and Chicken Breast in Broth) (s e r v e s 8)

A marvelous variant of *topini* of potatoes (see page 232) is one made with chopped chicken breast added to the potatoes. The recipe is slightly more complicated, requiring egg yolks and Parmigiano to be added as well, but the procedure is the same. They are eaten in broth, rather than with sauce.

      1¼ pounds boiling potatoes
        1 whole chicken breast
        2 egg yolks
        ½ cup freshly grated Parmigiano cheese
      4 or 5 sprigs Italian parsley
      2½ cups all-purpose flour
           Salt, freshly ground pepper, and freshly grated nutmeg to
           taste
        6 cups chicken or meat broth

Steam (do not boil) potatoes until cooked but firm. Set aside until needed.

Heat 3 cups of salted water in a saucepan. When it reaches the boiling point, add the chicken breast and let cook until soft (about 20 minutes).

Meanwhile, place the egg yolks in a small bowl. Add ¼ cup of the grated Parmigiano and mix very well with a wooden spoon. Chop the parsley fine and add to the bowl with the egg yolks and Parmigiano.

When the chicken breast is done, transfer it from saucepan to chopping board and remove both skin and bone. Chop the meat fine and add it to the bowl with the other ingredients.

Spread the flour on a pasta board. Peel the potatoes and pass them through a potato ricer onto the flour. Sprinkle the potatoes with salt, a little pepper, and a pinch of nutmeg, then add the contents of the small bowl to potatoes. Start incorporating flour, little by little, into the potato mixture until the dough is homogenous and firm. Knead gently for 5 or 6 minutes.

Cut the dough into several pieces and roll each piece into a long thin roll about ½ inch in diameter. Cut each roll into 1-inch pieces.

Use the dull inside of a convex hand cheese grater. Hold a 1-inch piece at the top of the grater with the middle fingers of one hand. Lightly draw the piece around in a motion that makes the cursive letter "c." The resultant shape should be the quasi-shell the Florentines think resembles "little mice," and which they prefer to the more usual gnocchi.

Heat the broth in a stockpot; heat a large quantity of salted water in a second stockpot.

When the water is boiling, raise the flame and quickly drop all the *topini*, one by one, into the stockpot. Lightly stir the water with a wooden spoon, to keep the *topini* from sticking. After a few seconds, the *topini* will come to the surface of the water; let them cook for 1 minute more. With a strainer-skimmer, remove the *topini* from the stockpot to individual soup bowls. Quickly pour some hot broth over the *topini* in each bowl, sprinkle with some of the remaining Parmigiano, and serve immediately.

Ginestrata
(Renaissance Cinnamon Broth)   (SERVES 6)

Ginestrata starts with a rich "eating" broth (not a stock). Making it requires more technique than the usual soup. The cold, defatted broth is mixed with the egg yolks and other ingredients and strained through cheesecloth. Then it is placed on a low flame and stirred without stopping. It must be taken from the flame just before it reaches the boiling point.

The texture should be a homogenous, creamy one, a suspension, in which the egg particles should not be separately visible. Be sure to use very fresh eggs and a rich eating broth, completely defatted, which must not be allowed to boil. When the *ginestrata* does not succeed, it curdles in part, and the egg particles are separately visible. When it succeeds, which it should always do with care, it is a dream;

an unforgettable flavor in which individual ingredients lose their identity in a perfect whole.

Ginestrata is a classic Renaissance broth, and appears in sixteenth-century cookbooks. The name refers to the yellow color of broom flowers, *ginestre*. Dishes the color of *ginestre* formed one of the color groups so dear to Renaissance Florentines. It is unusual for a dish of this color not to contain saffron, but the desired color is achieved in other ways, with egg yolks and Marsala.

At that time there were many sweet fortified wines that were used, but since the eighteenth century Marsala has gradually replaced most of them.

5 egg yolks
2 teaspoons ground cinnamon
¾ cup dry Marsala
1 quart cold chicken or meat broth (not stock), completely defatted
6 tablespoons butter
3 teaspoons granulated sugar
Freshly grated nutmeg

Place the egg yolks in a large bowl and add the cinnamon and Marsala. Mix very well with a wooden spoon, then add the cold broth and mix thoroughly. Pass the ingredients of the bowl through a piece of cheesecloth into a large flameproof casserole and add the salt and butter.

Warm 6 terra-cotta soup bowls in the oven.

Place the casserole on a low flame and stir continuously until the moment before the broth reaches the boiling point; do not allow it to boil. Remove immediately from the flame and ladle into the individual heated soup bowls. Sprinkle each bowl with ½ teaspoon sugar and a "smell" (less than a pinch) of freshly grated nutmeg. Serve immediately.

Carabaccia
(Renaissance Onion Soup) (SERVES 8)

Carabaccia has the Renaissance flavorings of ground almonds and a little sugar and cinnamon, but the lemon juice and olive oil make the taste a little sweet and sour. The soup does not require the careful technique of *ginestrata*, and the base can be an ordinary stock, left over from a *bollito*. It also dates from a sixteenth-century cookbook.

    8 large red onions
    ¼ cup olive oil
    3 quarts chicken or meat broth, defatted
       Juice of 3 lemons
    8 ounces blanched almonds
       Salt and freshly ground pepper
    5 teaspoons ground cinnamon
    4 teaspoons granulated sugar

Put a large quantity of water in a stockpot, add salt, and bring to a boil.

Peel the onions; leave them whole. Cook the onions in boiling water for 5 minutes, then drain and dry them and chop them coarsely.

Heat the olive oil in a large saucepan. When it is hot, add the chopped onions and sauté them very gently for 5 to 8 minutes. Heat the broth in a stockpot, then pour it into the saucepan with the onions. Simmer until the onions are soft (about 1 hour).

Warm the lemon juice in a small saucepan, then add the blanched almonds and simmer very slowly for 4 or 5 minutes.

Remove the onions from the broth by straining it into a bowl. Pass the onions through food mill, then return, along with the broth, to the saucepan. Taste for salt and pepper, add 1 teaspoon of the cinnamon, and place the saucepan back on the heat. At the moment the broth reaches the boiling point, add the almonds in the lemon juice and let everything simmer very gently for 2 or 3 minutes more. Meanwhile, heat 8 terra-cotta soup bowls in the oven.

Remove the saucepan from the heat and ladle the *carabaccia* into the individual heated bowls. Sprinkle ½ teaspoon each sugar and cinnamon on each portion and serve very hot.

Cipollata
(Modern Tuscan Onion Soup)   (S E R V E S 4)

Lighter than French onion soup because the onions are parboiled rather than sautéed in butter. *Pancetta*, olive oil, and Parmigiano provide the Italian flavor, while the specifically Tuscan touch is the slices of good bread placed at the bottom of the bowl. Though post-Renaissance, the recipe is still an old one.

4 large white onions
2 ounces *pancetta* or 1 ounce salt pork plus 1 ounce boiled ham, if *pancetta* is not available
¼ cup olive oil
5 cups hot chicken or meat broth
4 slices Tuscan bread (see page 32)
  Salt and freshly ground black pepper
¼ cup freshly grated Parmigiano cheese, approximately

Peel the onions; leave them whole. Cook them in a large quantity of boiling, salted water for 10 minutes, then drain them, place under cold running water to cool, and chop coarsely. Transfer to a bowl.

Chop the *pancetta* coarsely and sauté very lightly in the olive oil in a flameproof casserole, preferably terra-cotta. Add the chopped onions and sauté until they are golden brown, then add the hot broth. Cover the casserole and simmer for 35 minutes.

Toast the bread slices on both sides. Place one in each of 4 heated terra-cotta soup bowls.

Taste the soup for salt and pepper, then pour into the bowls. Sprinkle with Parmigiano and freshly ground black pepper, then cover the bowls with lids or aluminum foil and allow to rest for 5 minutes before serving. (If you used aluminum foil to cover the bowls, remove it before serving.)

Zuppa di Porri
(Leek Soup)   (SERVES 4)

The leeks are sautéed in butter, and then simmered in a stock. The soup is poured over toasted Tuscan bread in a terra-cotta bowl, the grated Groviera is sprinkled generously over and allowed to melt just from the heat of the hot soup. Not a thick soup, but a rich one.

There are two variants: in one ½ cup of rice is cooked in the simmering broth and the bread is omitted; in the second, a separately poached chicken breast is cut into long, thin strips and used instead of either bread or rice. (The similarity of this leek soup and French onion soup is worth noting. There is no evidence, however, that either derived from the other.)

> 5 medium-sized leeks
> 4 tablespoons (½ stick) butter
> 2 tablespoons all-purpose flour
> 4 cups hot meat or chicken broth
>   Salt and freshly ground pepper
> 4 slices Tuscan bread (see page 32)
> ½ cup freshly grated Swiss cheese

Rinse the leeks well, then cut leeks into ½-inch slices. Wash the pieces very well in cold water.

Heat the butter in a large flameproof casserole, preferably terra-cotta. When the butter is completely melted, add the leeks and sauté until golden brown (15 to 20 minutes). Sprinkle the flour over the leeks and mix it in well with a wooden spoon, then pour in the hot broth and stir thoroughly for 1 minute. Taste for salt and pepper and simmer, covered, for 25 minutes.

Toast the bread slices on each side and place one in each heated terra-cotta soup bowl. Sprinkle 1 tablespoon of grated cheese over each bread slice, then pour over the soup, and sprinkle with the remaining cheese and freshly ground black pepper. Cover the individual bowls with their lids, if they have them, or with aluminum foil. Let rest for 10 minutes, then serve. (If you used aluminum foil to cover the bowls, remove before serving.)

PASSATI

THIS CATEGORY of Italian soups deserves to be better known. Pureed vegetables are added to a stock, then Parmigiano is sprinkled over and sometimes good homemade croutons float on top. Though they are sometimes also known as *creme*, comparable to our "cream of," no cream is used. It is the creaminess of the soup itself that suggests that name. *Passato* means "passed through."

The favorite types are those made from mixed vegetables, from spinach, and from Tuscan beans; the recipes for all three follow. The first two are useful for a light repast in the evening.

Passato di Verdura
(Pureed Vegetable Soup)   (SERVES 4)

Pureed mixed vegetables in a meat- or chicken-stock base, with some homemade croutons and good Parmigiano floating on top, is a very satisfying beginning to a light meal.

Of the vegetables specified, if Savoy cabbage, Swiss chard, or string-beans are out of season, increase the quantities of all the other vegetables to compensate; there should be about 1¼ pounds of vegetables in all.

The vegetables are simmered first without any water or broth; they create their own liquid. Then they are passed through a food mill and added to the broth.

> 2 leaves Savoy cabbage
> 1 small potato
> 1 small red onion
> 1 carrot
> 5 or 6 sprigs Italian parsley
> 2 celery ribs
> 5 or 6 large leaves Swiss chard
> 2 or 3 ounces fresh spinach
> 1 fresh ripe tomato or ½ cup canned Italian plum tomatoes
> 1 handful stringbeans
> 5 tablespoons olive oil
>   Salt to taste
> 5 cups warm chicken or meat broth, defatted
>   Pinch of freshly ground black pepper
> ¼ cup freshly grated Parmigiano cheese
> 4 heaping tablespoons deep-fried *crostini* (see page 46) or 4 tablespoons of rice, preferably Italian Arborio (optional)

Trim and clean, then cut or slice all the vegetables (except the canned tomatoes, if used) into medium-sized pieces, then place in a bowl of cold water and let soak for 20 minutes. Then, without drying them, transfer all the vegetables (including the fresh tomato, if used) from bowl to stockpot. (If canned tomatoes are used, add them to the stockpot.)

Add the olive oil and salt to the stockpot and place on a medium flame. Cover and let simmer very slowly, without lifting the lid and without adding any water or broth, for about 25 minutes. Remove the stockpot from the heat and pass all the vegetables through a food mill into a large bowl.

Heat the broth in a saucepan.

Place the pureed vegetables back in the stockpot and add the warm broth. Place on a medium flame and let simmer slowly, uncovered, for about 25 minutes, stirring every so often. Taste for salt and add black pepper.

After 25 minutes, the *passato di verdura* is ready to be served. If you prefer to eat it with *crostini*, prepare them while the soup is simmering. Then place them in individual soup bowls, and when the *passato* is ready, pour it over the *crostini*, sprinkle with Parmigiano, and serve immediately.

If you prefer to eat *passato di verdura* with rice, cook the rice in salted water in a small saucepan for about 15 minutes and add to the stockpot when *passato* is ready, after it has cooked for 25 minutes. Serve in individual soup bowls, sprinkled with grated Parmigiano.

Passato di Spinaci
(Creamed Spinach Soup)   (SERVES 4)

The spinach is cooked in water with some *odori* (aromatic vegetables) and then strained. This is to remove the bitterness from the spinach before it is added to the stock.

    1½ pounds fresh spinach
         Coarse salt
    ½   carrot
    1   small red onion
    ½   celery rib
    3   cups chicken or meat broth, preferably homemade (see page
         105)
    ¼   cup freshly grated Parmigiano cheese

Remove the large stems from the spinach, then wash the leaves several times in cold water, in order to remove all sand.

Put 4 cups of cold water in a flameproof casserole, along with some coarse salt. When the water reaches the boiling point, add the spinach, carrot, onion, and celery and boil for 6 or 7 minutes. Meanwhile, heat the broth in a large saucepan. Drain the spinach, carrot, onion, and celery and add them to the saucepan with broth. Simmer for about 20 minutes, covered, then remove the saucepan from the heat and pass the contents through a food mill into a second saucepan.

Place the second saucepan, with the *passato*, on the flame. Taste for salt and pepper and simmer very slowly for 10 minutes more. Remove the saucepan from stove and serve the soup immediately. Sprinkle each serving with a tablespoon of grated Parmigiano.

Note: Homemade croutons (see *crostini*, page 46) may be added to the soup when served.

Passato di Fagioli
(Tuscan Pureed Bean Soup)   (SERVES 4)

    1½ cups dried cannellini beans
     2 ounces *pancetta* or salt pork
     1 clove garlic, whole and unpeeled
        Salt
    ¼   cup olive oil
     1 large slice Tuscan bread, white (see page 32) or dark (see page 37)
     1 tablespoon rosemary leaves
     4 ounces good-quality imported dried pasta (small shells)
        Freshly ground pepper to taste

Soak the beans overnight in cold water. The next day, drain and rinse the beans and put them in a stockpot with 7 cups of cold water.* Add the *pancetta*, unpeeled garlic, and 1 tablespoon of salt. Place the

* Cannellini beans are picked in June and are eaten fresh at that time. For the rest of the year, the beans become increasingly dry and require longer cooking time. The dried beans of September are still almost fresh; those which remain until May are much drier. Those packed in plastic remain softer than those left in open barrels. Since most American cooks will be using imported beans, it is necessary to check the cooking time. It could be as long as 2½ hours for old beans. When soaking older beans, add 1 tablespoon of flour to the water to tenderize them.

pot on the flame and simmer until the beans are very soft (1 to 2 hours).

Drain beans, saving the cooking water, and pass them through a food mill. Put back into stockpot, along with the water. Return the pot to the flame and simmer until the texture of the soup resembles a smooth light cream.

Heat the olive oil in a frying pan. Cut the bread slice in quarters and fry lightly. Remove the bread from the oil and add the rosemary leaves to the pan. Let them sauté for 3 or 4 minutes, then pour the oil containing the rosemary into the bean soup. Taste for salt and pepper; there should be a lot of both.

Cook the dried pasta in the soup until al dente (10 to 15 minutes), then remove the soup from the heat and let rest for 10 to 15 minutes.

Place one piece of bread in each of 4 soup bowls and pour the *passato* over. Serve hot.

Note: This soup is equally good served cold the following day, especially in summer. If you are making the soup to be served cold, add the bread pieces to the stockpot at the time you are putting in the dried pasta.

MINESTRONI AND MINESTRE

Every part of Italy has its own particular minestrone, with vegetables, beans, and pasta or rice. In Tuscany, slices of Tuscan bread are usually substituted for pasta.

Following are the recipes for a number of different types: *minestrone di riso*, eaten hot or cooled; *minestrone alla contadina*, the usual Tuscan "country" minestrone; and the *ribollita* that is made from it the next day.

There are two special *minestre* from the mountainous Garfagnana region: *incavolata*, featuring kale and cannellini, lightly thickened with a little yellow corn meal, and the *minestra povera* of potatoes.

Finally, we have the *pasta e fagioli* (pasta and beans) category. Again, every part of Italy has its own version. Included here are two Tuscan versions, one with cannellini beans and the other with chickpeas, or *ceci*.

Minestrone di Riso
(Tuscan Minestrone with Rice)   (S E R V E S 8)

One of the few Tuscan soups not using bread, obviously because rice is used. Unlike most minestroni, it begins with chicken and meat stock. Even the rice is cooked separately in stock before it is added to the minestrone.

Minestrone di riso may be eaten hot, but it is more often eaten cooled (*semifreddo*), not chilled or refrigerated, in the summer. It is one of the staples of the *trattoria* menu in the summertime.

To get the authentic flavor, be careful to use wrinkled Savoy cabbage rather than the more common type and to get a piece of the rind of the prosciutto from your Italian market. Otherwise, it can be made with no great difficulty and with sure result.

1 ½	cups dried cannellini beans
8	ounces fresh or frozen spinach
1	small bunch Swiss chard
½	small head Savoy cabbage
7 or 8	sprigs Italian parsley
2	cloves garlic
2	ounces prosciutto
1	small piece prosciutto rind
3	tablespoons olive oil
2	celery ribs
1	carrot
1	medium-sized red onion
1	medium-sized potato
1	handful stringbeans
1	small zucchini
1	tablespoon tomato paste
2	quarts chicken or meat broth, approximately
	Salt and freshly ground pepper to taste
¾	cup raw rice, preferably Italian Arborio
½	cup freshly grated Parmigiano cheese

Soak the cannellini beans in cold water overnight. The next day, drain the beans and partially cook them in salted water for 30 to 60 minutes.

Wash the spinach, Swiss chard, and cabbage, then cut into strips.

Cook in another saucepan for 15 minutes, with salt and only the water left on the leaves after washing. Drain the cooked vegetables, squeeze them dry, and set aside.

Coarsely chop the parsley, garlic, prosciutto, and prosciutto rind. Place in a stockpot with the olive oil and sauté very gently for 15 minutes, until golden brown. Meanwhile, cut celery, carrot, onion, potato, stringbeans, and zucchini into ½-inch pieces. Add to the stockpot and sauté for 5 minutes more.

Transfer the partially cooked beans, and their water, to the stockpot, then add the spinach, Swiss chard, and cabbage. Add the tomato paste and enough broth (about 6 cups) to cover the vegetables by about 4 inches. Simmer very slowly until all the ingredients are cooked (about 40 minutes).

While the vegetables are cooking, partially cook the rice (for 10 minutes) in the remaining broth with water. Drain the rice, add it to the stockpot, and cook until the rice is completely cooked (8 to 10 minutes more). Taste for salt and pepper and serve immediately, hot (sprinkling about a tablespoon of Parmigiano over each serving), or serve cool the next day.

Minestrone alla Contadina
(Tuscan Minestrone, Country Style)   (S E R V E S 6 T O 8)

The standard Tuscan "country" minestrone, including among its vegetables Savoy cabbage, kale, and a few cannellini beans, served over slices of Tuscan bread with Parmigiano floating on top. It is flavored with the full battery of *odori* (aromatic vegetables) and with olive oil. If you have homemade croutons, you may substitute them for the bread slices.

Minestrone alla contadina is also served the following day as *ribollita* (see page 124).

> 8 ounces dried cannellini beans
> 1 slice prosciutto (about 3 ounces) or 1 ounce salt pork plus 2 ounces boiled ham
> 1 large red onion
> 1 celery rib
> 2 large cloves garlic
> 1 carrot

    7 or 8 sprigs Italian parsley
    6 tablespoons olive oil
    ½ small head Savoy cabbage
  1½ bunches kale
    1 potato
    1 cup canned tomatoes
    1 small bunch Swiss chard
  12 large, thick slices Tuscan bread (see page 32), several days
        old, or 9 to 12 tablespoons homemade *crostini* (see page
        46)
      Salt and freshly ground pepper
    6 to 8 tablespoons freshly grated Parmigiano cheese

Soak the dried beans overnight in cold water. The next day, drain the beans and cook them in a large flameproof casserole with 2 quarts of salted water and the prosciutto or salt pork and ham. As the beans absorb water, keep adding enough to maintain 2 quarts of liquid (*broda*) at the end of the cooking time. When the beans are tender (about 1 hour),* remove from the flame and let stand until needed.

Coarsely chop the onion, celery, garlic, carrot, and parsley and sauté them in a stockpot, with the olive oil, for 12 to 15 minutes. Meanwhile, finely slice the Savoy cabbage; remove the stems from the kale and cut into small pieces; peel the potato and cut it into small squares.

When the *odori* are light brown, add the cabbage, kale, and potato to the stockpot, along with the tomatoes. Cover and simmer for 15 minutes, then add the Swiss chard, stems removed and cut up.

Remove the prosciutto (or salt pork and ham) from the bean casserole. Pass two-thirds of the beans through a food mill into the stockpot. Simmer together for about ½ hour more, until Savoy cabbage and kale are almost cooked.

Drain the remaining beans, reserving the broth, and return them to the original casserole. Add the bean broth to the stockpot, little by little, whenever more liquid is needed, until all is used.

When the cabbage and kale are ready, add the remaining beans, whole. Taste for salt and pepper, then let cook for 5 minutes more.

If using bread, make a layer of bread slices on the bottom of a tureen and pour over two full ladles of soup. Make other layers of bread, each time pouring the soup over, until all the bread is used.

* See footnote, p. 119.

Pour the remaining soup on top, cover the tureen, and let stand for 20 minutes before serving, with a tablespoon of grated Parmigiano sprinkled over each portion.

If using croutons instead of bread slices, place 1½ tablespoons of croutons in each individual soup bowl. Allow the soup to stand for 20 minutes after cooking, then pour over the croutons. Sprinkle with Parmigiano and serve.

Ribollita
("Reboiled" Tuscan Minestrone)   (SERVES 6)

Minestrone alla contadina is usually made in a large quantity so there will be enough left over to make *ribollita* the next day. *Ribollita* means, literally, "reboiled."

Most Florentines prefer the *ribollita* to the minestrone itself, so it is a very popular, standard winter dish. One of the standard items on all *trattoria* menus in Florence, it resembles *pappa*, the "bread soup" (see *pappa al pomodoro*, page 230), more than a *minestra*. Try it.

Overnight, the minestrone will thicken even further. Heat it, and allow it to boil for about 1 minute. With a wooden spoon, mix well, breaking up the bread slices until the texture is almost homogenous. Ladle into individual bowls, preferably of terra-cotta with handles, and pour 2 teaspoons of good olive oil over each serving.

Incavolata
(Kale and Bean Soup)   (SERVES 6 TO 8)

A *minestra* of kale and beans, flavored with sage and *pancetta*. At a certain point, a little yellow corn meal (*farina gialla*) is added, creating a unique texture, only slightly thick. *Incavolata* is a specialty of the mountain villages north of Lucca, called the Garfagnana. That area of Tuscany has its own, very special *cucina*.

Special care must be taken when the corn meal is added; this must be done very slowly, while stirring, so it does not lump together.

    1 pound dried cannellini beans
    3 or 4 leaves sage
    4 ounces *pancetta* or salt pork

1 clove garlic, peeled but left whole
Coarse salt
1 pound kale
1 tablespoon tomato paste
½ cup corn meal
Salt and freshly ground pepper to taste

Soak the beans overnight in a large bowl of cold water. The next day, drain the beans and put in a stockpot, preferably terra-cotta, along with the 12 cups cold water, the sage, the whole clove of garlic, and *pancetta* or salt pork, cut into pieces. Season with coarse salt, cover, and simmer very slowly until the beans are tender (at least 1 hour, depending on the freshness of the beans).*

Meanwhile, remove the stems completely from the kale and cut up the leaves coarsely. Soak in a large bowl of cold water for 1 hour.

Drain the cooked beans in a colander, letting the bean water pour off into another large bowl. Pour the bean water back into the stock-pot. Pass half of the beans through a food mill back into the stockpot; leave the remaining beans in the colander.

Return the stockpot to the heat and add the kale and tomato paste. Simmer until the kale is very soft (about 1 hour), then pour in the yellow corn meal, little by little, stirring continuously with a wooden spoon. Simmer very slowly for 30 minutes.

Just 5 minutes before removing the pot from the flame, add remaining whole beans from the colander and mix thoroughly. Taste for salt and pepper, then remove from the flame and serve immediately.

Minestra "Povera" di Patate
(Simple Potato Soup)   (SERVES 4)

A potato soup, also from the Garfagnana. In Tuscany, the word "*povera*," meaning "poor," is sometimes used, in a form of reverse snobbism, to mean "genuine" or "good" when referring to food. The implication is that nothing sophisticated and unnatural is used. Most times *taglierini* are added (see note below), but there is also an alternate version that adds thin strips of chicken breast. This second version would be less starchy and probably more to American tastes. It is, however, a completely authentic alternative.

* See footnote, p. 119.

    1 ½   pounds of boiling potatoes
    12   cups cold water
    1   celery rib
    1   large red onion
    1   clove garlic
    1   carrot
    5   or 6 sprigs Italian parsley
    2   ounces of *pancetta* or salt pork
    ¼   cup olive oil
    2   small tomatoes, fresh or canned
    Salt

For poaching the chicken breast

    1   carrot
    1   very small red onion
    ½   celery rib
    3   or 4 sprigs Italian parsley
    Coarse salt
    1   whole chicken breast, boned

    ¼   cup freshly grated Parmigiano cheese
    Freshly ground black pepper

Peel and wash the potatoes, then place them in a stockpot, preferably terra-cotta, with the cold water. Coarsely chop the celery, onion, garlic, carrot, parsley, and *pancetta*. Add to the stockpot, along with the olive oil, tomatoes (skinned and seeded, if fresh), and salt. Place the stockpot on the heat and simmer, covered, for 3 ½ hours.

While the soup is simmering, place the poaching *odori* (carrot, onion, celery, and parsley) in a saucepan with water to cover and coarse salt. When the water boils, poach the chicken breast for 16 to 18 minutes. Transfer to a board, remove the skin, and cut the meat into long thin strips.

When the soup is ready, place a few strips of chicken breast on bottom of each individual terra-cotta soup bowl. Pour the soup over, and sprinkle each serving with 1 tablespoon of Parmigiano. Grind some fresh black pepper into each bowl, then cover each bowl with its lid, if it has one, or aluminum foil and let stand for 5 minutes before serving. (If you use aluminum foil to cover the bowl, remove it before serving.)

Note: This soup is most frequently served with fresh *taglierini* in place of the strips of chicken breast. (Rice may also be substituted.) We prefer the version with chicken breast because it is lighter. If you wish to use *taglierini* instead of chicken breast, make them according to the recipe on page 133, using 1 egg, 1 cup all-purpose flour, a pinch of salt, and 1 teaspoon olive oil.

Pasta e Fagioli
(Pasta and Bean Soup)   (S E R V E S 6)

The famous "hearty" pasta and beans.

Flavored with prosciutto rind (*cotenna*), garlic, and pepper, it is served with Parmigiano. A high-quality imported dry pasta should be used, one that is also fairly substantial in shape, such as the medium-sized *chiocciole* (snails or shells), which are known by some other names as well.

      2 cups dried white cannellini beans
      1 small slice prosciutto rind (unsmoked) or salt pork
      1 small potato
      1 medium-sized red onion
      2 cloves garlic
    ¼ cup olive oil
    10 cups water
      1 cup canned tomatoes
         Salt and freshly ground black pepper
      8 ounces good-quality imported dried pasta (medium-sized
         shells or large elbow macaroni)
      6 heaping teaspoons freshly grated Parmigiano cheese

Soak the beans overnight in cold water.

The next day, cook the prosciutto rind in boiling water for 2 minutes, then rinse well under cold running water and cut into small pieces; peel the potato and cut into small dice.

Chop the onion and garlic coarsely and place them in a stockpot, preferably terra-cotta, along with the olive oil. Sauté very gently until golden, then add the drained beans, the potato pieces, cold water, tomatoes, and pieces of prosciutto rind. Cover and simmer very slowly for at least 2 hours. Taste for salt and pepper, then add the pasta to the pot and cook until al dente. Allow to cool for 10 minutes, then serve, sprinkling Parmigiano and freshly ground black pepper over each individual serving.

Pasta e Ceci
(Pasta and Chick-Peas)   (SERVES 6)

Chick-peas, *ceci*, are widely used in Tuscany and all over Italy. There is a well-known *torta* or "pie" of *ceci*, and we have seen that they were used in Renaissance cooking, antedating cannellini. Their fine flavor is well complemented by olive oil, rosemary, garlic, and pepper. Use the smaller type of pasta, such as *avemaria*. Grated cheese is not used with this dish; instead, some good uncooked olive oil is spooned over each bowl when the *pasta e ceci* is served.

        8 ounces dried chick-peas
        8 cups cold water
        6 tablespoons olive oil
        1 clove garlic, peeled but left whole
        ½ cup canned tomatoes
        1 teaspoon rosemary leaves
           Salt and freshly ground pepper to taste
        6 ounces good-quality imported dried short pasta (such as *ave-maria*)

Soak the chick-peas overnight in a large bowl of cold water.

The next day, put 8 cups of cold water in a flameproof casserole, preferably terra-cotta, along with the olive oil, the whole clove of garlic, tomatoes, and rosemary leaves. Set it on the heat, and when the water is warm, add the chick-peas. Season with salt, cover, and simmer very slowly until the chick-peas are soft (about 3 hours).

Remove half the chick-peas from the casserole and pass through a food mill back into the casserole. Taste for salt and pepper, then add the dried pasta and cook until al dente (about 10 minutes for pasta of this size).

Remove the casserole from flame and serve; the soup should be quite thick and smooth. Put 1 teaspoon of the remaining olive oil, uncooked, on each serving; do *not* add any grated Parmigiano.

Zuppa Lombarda
(Bean Soup for the Lombards)   (SERVES 4)

Soup *for* the Lombards, not Lombard soup. When the Milanese Lombards, fighting for the German emperor, succeeded in their siege of Florence in 1525, they were famished when they broke into the city. The besieged Florentines had very little food left, but they put together this dish with some beans, days-old bread, olive oil, and some broth. If you think it doesn't sound appetizing, try it and you'll know why it is still eaten very often, without the benefit of a siege. It is a useful dish to make with leftover *fagioli* (see page 400). But as often as not, the beans are made on purpose just to be able to make this dish.

It was in this siege that the Germans set fire to the Renaissance façade of the famous Cathedral of Florence. For some centuries it stayed without a façade, until a reconstruction was made in the nineteenth century.

> 6 large thick slices Tuscan bread (see page 32), at least 3 days old
> 2 cups beans and all the liquid from the flask from *fagioli al fiasco* (see page 400)
> 4 cups meat broth, approximately
> 4 teaspoons olive oil
> Abundant fresh black pepper, coarsely ground

Cut the bread slices into thirds and place in a tureen.

Heat the beans, with their liquid, in a saucepan; in another saucepan, heat the broth. When hot, pour the beans and liquid over the bread. Add enough broth so the liquid covers the beans and bread by ½ inch. (The amount of broth will vary depending on the amount of bean broth already present.) Cover tureen and let stand for about 20 minutes.

Mix the beans and bread together with a ladle, then ladle out into terra-cotta soup bowls. Sprinkle 1 teaspoon of olive oil and abundant coarsely ground black pepper over each serving.

Pasta

THE widespread myth that Marco Polo introduced pasta from China into Italy is not true. There still exists the manuscript of a will, drawn up in Genoa two years before the return of Marco Polo, which leaves the heirs a chestful of dried pasta.

In any case, most historians of gastronomy trace the origins of pasta to ancient Roman times. Sicily's woods had been cut down in order to make it the granary of the Roman Empire, a one-crop area for wheat. The Romans of Sicily made the excess wheat into pasta, which was preserved by drying it in the sun.

Though stuffed pasta dishes appear in Renaissance cookbooks, the standardization of the large-scale use of any pasta for the first course did not occur until rather recently, well into the nineteenth century in northern Italy, perhaps a little earlier in the south. The order of courses fixed in the sixteenth century in Florence continued, as we have mentioned before, into the nineteenth century in Italy and France, the first course after antipasti consisting of a variety of boiled dishes. By the beginning of the nineteenth century this had narrowed down to a *minestra* course. With the passage of the nineteenth century, pasta gradually moved north and began to alternate with *minestra* as the first course. Friends of mine in the Veneto tell me that pasta was not eaten there as recently as the generation of their grandparents.

Unstuffed pasta did not come into its own until Corrado, the great cook of the Neopolitan Bourbon court, made it respectable in court circles in the second half of the eighteenth century. As a matter of fact, the three-pronged fork was invented to make it possible to eat spaghetti in a polite way, not with the hands, as was done on the street by the common folk. The triumphant progress northward began in the early nineteenth century, when a machine was invented to produce dried pasta in quantity. (The adoption of dried pasta as the chief first course for many families was a product of the Industrial Revolution.)

Stuffed fresh pasta has been used at least since the fourteenth century, when Florentine cookbooks discuss *tortelli*. It was probably taken to Bologna from Florence. Fresh pasta is not always made with eggs, as exemplified by the pasta that is made in modern Genoa.

We begin with a discussion of fresh pasta—how to make it, how to cut it for various dishes—and then we present recipes for dishes made with it.

Following is a discussion of some popular types of dried pasta, some advice about buying it, and some recipes using it.

Finally, we have a section on stuffed fresh pasta—how to make the various kinds, along with a variety of stuffings and recipes for dishes made with it. ·

FRESH PASTA

THIS IS the basic "yellow" egg pasta. It is cut into *taglierini*, *tagliatelle* (fettucine), *pappardelle*, *farfalle*, homemade spaghetti, and *penne* to be eaten with sauce. It is cut into *taglierini* (again) and *quadrucci* to be eaten with broth. And finally, it is used to make the stuffed pasta: *tortelli* (ravioli), *tortellini*, and *cappelletti* (smaller tortellini for broth) and *cannelloni*. The squares made for *cannelloni* are also used to make the layered lasagne.

> 1 cup all-purpose flour, preferably unbleached
> 1 "extra-large" egg
> 1 teaspoon olive or other vegetable oil
> Pinch of salt

The proportion of ingredients to each other is given, rather than a fixed amount per serving, because the amounts vary depending on which dish the pasta is being made for. Definite amounts are given in ingredients for each recipe.

Flour: Unbleached all-purpose flour in America is not significantly different from Italian flour used for making pasta. (Semolina is almost never used in Italy to make fresh pasta.) Indeed, since much of the wheat used in Italy is imported, some of it is probably American. The difference in method of grinding becomes significant only for dark flour used in making bread (see page 38). Unbleached flour is preferable, but bleached is also usable. All-purpose flour is generally partially sifted and states this on the package. Use it as it comes, without additional sifting.

Eggs: If you use "large" instead of "extra-large" eggs, you will need an extra egg for every 5 or 6. If the eggs are still smaller, add an extra one for every 3 or 4. Flour absorbs less egg in damp weather, so you may have to add a little more egg under such conditions.

Oil: If you do not use olive oil, be sure that the vegetable oil you do use is one such as safflower or peanut oil, which does not have a strong taste.

Tuscan fresh pasta varies from that of the Bologna region. Oil and salt are used in Tuscany, and the pasta is generally rolled finer. A little oil makes the pasta more flexible so it can be rolled a little finer, and is lighter when cooked. This pasta when stuffed can be sealed without being dampened, or if left to dry a little, may be sealed by being dampened very slightly with a finger dipped in water.

I repeat that the amount of pasta necessary for each serving varies, especially according to whether it is used with sauce or with broth, or again whether it is to be filled. The proportion of the ingredients remains the same. See each individual recipe for specific amounts.

Making fresh pasta is an area in which I take a slightly heretical position. I believe that pasta made with a pasta machine is at least as good as that rolled out with a wooden rolling pin. Perhaps this is because I have the Tuscan preference for pasta that is fine and soft. (The Bolognese *sfoglia* of 1 millimeter is too thick for my taste.) Taking the pasta machine's roller to the last notch, it can be made even finer. The little oil in the Tuscan pasta makes that fineness possible, without holes.

Hand-rolled pasta is necessary, however, for dishes that require a large single sheet, wider than is possible with the machine, such as the *rotolo di pasta ripieno* on page 198, where the hand rolling process is described. Even by hand, however, I still prefer it finer than the thickness that is usual in Bologna or in the south of Italy.

Pasta board: A pasta board 18 x 26 inches provides a good wooden surface to work on.

Rolling pin: The long, thin Italian rolling pin is difficult to find here, but I see no reason why the American rolling pin, which is shorter and rotates, cannot be used equally well. The rotary action actually makes it easier to use.

Pasta machine: When you invest in a pasta machine, be careful of the trademark. They are not equally good, and some of the brands that are most often imported are inferior. Among the brands I find satisfactory is the Imperia. Use of the different parts of the machine is explained below.

MAKING FRESH PASTA

Place the flour in a mound on a pasta board. Make a well in the center and put in the egg, olive oil, and salt (see photo 1). With a fork, first mix together the yolk, white, oil, and salt, then begin to incorporate the flour from the inner rim of the well, always incorporating fresh flour from the lower part, pushing it under the dough to keep the dough detached (see photo 2).

Making fresh pasta: 1. Breaking the eggs into the well in the flour.

2. Incorporating the flour into the egg mixture.

When half of the flour has been absorbed, start kneading, always using the palms of your hands, not the fingers (see photo 3). Continue absorbing the flour until almost all of it has been incorporated. The small fraction of flour that remains unabsorbed should be passed through a sifter to remove bits of dough and kept to coat dough during the succeeding steps. Now you are ready to use the pasta machine.

The machine has two main parts, one for rolling, the other for cutting. The first part of the machine consists of two rollers, the distance between which can be adjusted by a little wheel on the side. On the opposite side fits a detachable handle, to turn the rollers. The second part, for cutting, is sometimes detachable. It consists of two rows of teeth, one to cut into narrow strips (*taglierini*), the other wide (the width of *tagliatelle*).

Attach the machine to your table by tightening the clamp at the bottom. (See photo 4 for the position of the body in relation to the pasta machine.) Set the wheel for the rollers at the widest setting.

If the dough has been made with more than one egg, cut it into the same number of pieces as eggs. Repeat the following steps with each piece of dough.

Turning the handle, pass the dough through the rollers. Fold the dough into thirds and press down (see photo 5). Sprinkle with flour

3. Kneading with the palms of the hands.

4. Pasta hanging over the whole left hand. Notice the position of the body in relation to the pasta machine.

and repeat the rolling and folding eight to ten times, until the dough is very smooth. (These steps take the place of hand kneading.)

Move the wheel to the next notch (see photo 6), which places the rollers a little closer together. Pass dough through rollers once; do not fold. Move the wheel to each successive notch, each time passing the dough through the rollers once. After passing each time, sprinkle the dough with a little flour. Each successive notch produces a thinner layer of pasta. Stop when the layer reaches the thickness desired; I always go to the last notch.

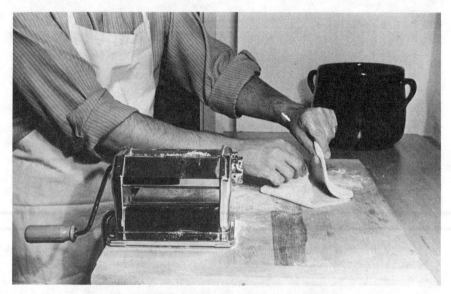

5. Folding the dough into thirds.

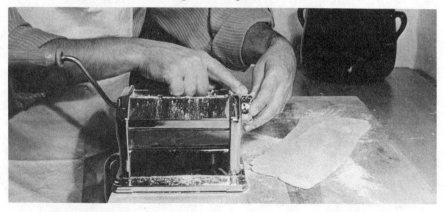

6. Moving the wheel to the next notch on the pasta machine.

Caution: Beginning with the step in which you first pass the pasta through the rollers without folding, do not hold it with your fingers, but let it hang over your whole left hand (see photo 4).

When the long sheet of pasta has finished passing through the rollers, take the end gently in your fingers and carefully pull the layer out to its full length, free of folds (see photos 7 and 8). Sprinkle a cot-

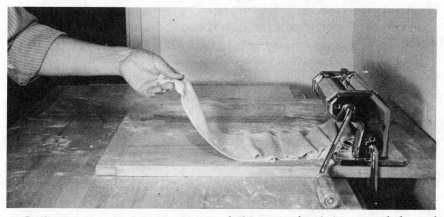

7. Pulling the layer of pasta out to its full length after it has passed through the rollers.

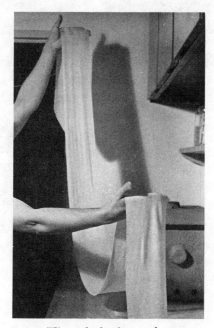

8. The whole sheet of pasta.

ton dishtowel with flour and lay the sheet of pasta upon it to dry for 10 minutes before cutting. If the kitchen is hot or drafty, cover the pasta with another dishtowel.

CUTTING FRESH PASTA (*Types made by machine*)

Tagliatelle: For *tagliatelle*, simply pass the sheet of pasta through the the wide teeth of the cutting section (see photo 1).

Taglierini: For *taglierini*, pass the sheets of pasta through the narrow teeth of the cutting section (see photo 2).

Spaghetti: For homemade spaghetti, when you are passing the pasta through the rollers to thin them, stop when you arrive at two notches from the last and leave the sheets of pasta this thick. When the pasta has dried a bit, pass it through the narrow teeth. The shape of the cut pasta will be almost round (see photo 3). (Generally, the dried pasta form of spaghetti is used; the freshly made ones are an infrequent treat.)

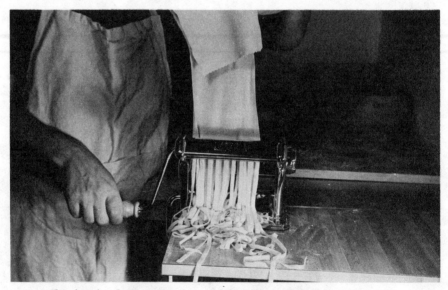

Cutting fresh pasta (types made by machine): 1. *Tagliatelle.*

2. *Taglierini.*

3. Spaghetti.

CUTTING FRESH PASTA (Types made by hand)

Pappardelle: See the recipe for *pappardelle sulla lepre* (page 151) and photo 1.

Farfalle (or *fiocchi*): With a pastry wheel, cut your sheet of pasta in half lengthwise, and every 2 inches widthwise, making rectangles (see photo 2).

Take each rectangle in the center, lengthwise, between two fingers, and press the two sides toward each other, making the pasta piece take the shape of a bow (photos 3 and 4). This shape of fresh pasta may be substituted for *tagliatelle* in any of the recipes given and used with any kind of tomato sauce.

Penne: Using the same rectangles as for *farfalle* (see above), roll the pasta around the end of a wooden spoon (see photo 5). Press down the outside edge of the pasta to seal the side; the form should be a tube. Pull the spoon end off and let dry. (For sealing, see photo 6.)

Do not substitute these for dry *penne*, but rather for other fresh pasta.

Cannelloni: See the recipe for *cannelloni con carne* (page 178).

Lasagne: See the recipe for *lasagne* (page 191).

Tortellini: See the recipe for *tortellini* (page 165).

Mezzelune: See the recipe for "half-moon" *tortelli* (page 164).

Tortelli: See the recipe for *tortelli* (page 162).

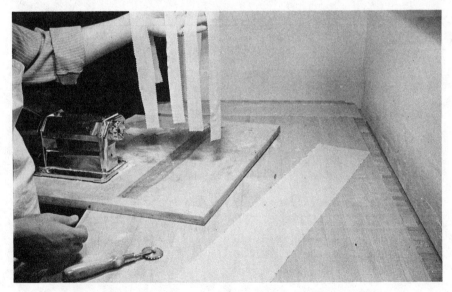

Cutting fresh pasta (types made by hand): 1. *Pappardelle.*

2. Cutting the dough for *farfalle*, or *fiocchi*, into squares.

3. Shaping the *farfalle*, or *fiocchi*.

4. Pressing the centers of the *farfalle*, or *fiocchi*, together.

5. Rolling a pasta square around the handle of a wooden spoon to make *penne*.

6. Sealing the outside edge of the *penne* tube.

Pasta Verde
(Green Pasta)   (S E R V E S   3)

> 5 to 6 ounces fresh spinach, weighed before stems are removed
> 2 "extra-large" eggs
> 3 ½ cups all-purpose flour, preferably unbleached
> 2 teaspoons olive or other vegetable oil
>   Pinch of salt

Remove the stems completely from the spinach, leaving only the leaves.

Place a large saucepan containing a large quantity of salted water on the heat. Meanwhile wash the spinach leaves thoroughly.

When the water has reached the boiling point, add the spinach leaves and cook for 10 to 12 minutes. Drain the spinach, cool under cold running water, and squeeze very dry. Chop the spinach extremely fine and measure 1 heaping tablespoon of it. (If there is a little left over, discard it.) At this point, using the remaining ingredients, follow the directions on pages 133–138, noting that this recipe uses 1 ¾ cups of flour for each egg instead of 1 cup, and placing the chopped spinach in the well along with the other ingredients. Follow the remaining directions exactly, but allow the pasta to dry for 15 or 16 minutes instead of 10.

Green pasta may be used for *tagliatelle* and *taglierini*. To cut pasta into those shapes, see pages 138–139.

To cut green pasta for lasagne or cannelloni, see *cannelloni con carne* (page 178).

Green pasta and red pasta: spinach for green, beets for red.

Pasta Rossa
(Red Pasta)   (SERVES 3)

        1 medium-sized red beet
    3 ½ cups all-purpose flour, preferably unbleached
        2 "extra-large" eggs
        2 teaspoons olive or other vegetable oil
            Pinch of salt

Discard the stem of the beet and wash the beet very well.

Place a saucepan containing a large quantity of cold salted water on the heat. When the water has reached the boiling point, add the beet and cook for 1 to 1 ½ hours, until soft. Peel off the beet's outer layer under cold running water, then chop the beet extremely fine. Measure 1 heaping tablespoon of finely chopped beet. (If there is a little left over, discard it.)

At this point, using the remaining ingredients, follow the directions on pages 133–138, noting that this recipe uses 1 ¾ cups of flour to each egg instead of 1 cup. Place the chopped beet in the well along with the other ingredients. Follow the remaining directions exactly, but allow the pasta to dry for 15 to 16 minutes instead of 10.

Red pasta may be used for *taglierini, tagliatelle,* or even cannelloni. To cut pasta into these shapes, see pages 138–139 and 178.

Taglierini al Pomodoro Fresco
(Taglierini with Fresh Tomato Sauce)   (S E R V E S   4)

The thinly cut, delicate *taglierini* go best with the lightest sauce, one made from ripe, fresh tomatoes, cooked very lightly and then adorned only with fresh basil leaves to bring out the quality of the tomatoes.

With good imported Italian canned plum tomatoes, and basil preserved in salt, a very creditable version can also be made in the winter. The fresh *taglierini* need be cooked for only 15 seconds. Green *taglierini* (see page 143) are also used to good advantage in this dish.

For the pasta

> 2 cups all-purpose flour, preferably unbleached
> 2 "extra-large" eggs
> 2 teaspoons olive or other vegetable oil
>   Pinch of salt
>
>   *Sugo di pomodoro fresco* (see page 69)
>   Coarse salt
> 4 tablespoons (½ stick) butter or ¼ cup olive oil
> ¼ cup freshly grated Parmigiano cheese
>   Freshly ground black pepper
> 3 or 4 leaves fresh basil (see note below)

Make the *taglierini,* using the quantities listed above, according to directions on pages 133–138. To cut into *taglierini,* see page 138. Let the *taglierini* stand on a pasta board, covered with a cotton dishtowel, until needed.

Make the sauce as directed on page 69. Let it stand in the casserole, covered, until needed.

Put a large quantity of cold water in a stockpot, add coarse salt, and set on the heat.

Prepare a serving dish with butter or olive oil. Cut the butter into pats and spread them over the bottom of the dish, or spread olive oil over instead. Then spread on about 6 tablespoons of tomato sauce. Heat the remaining sauce in its casserole.

When the water reaches the boiling point, put in the *taglierini*, stir with a wooden spoon, and allow them to boil for 15 seconds *only*. Immediately drain the *taglierini* in a colander and arrange them on the serving dish, over the tomato sauce.

Pour the remaining tomato sauce over the *taglierini* and sprinkle with Parmigiano and black pepper. Tear the basil leaves into 3 or 4 pieces and sprinkle them over sauce. Serve immediately.

Note: If fresh basil is not available, omit basil garnish at the end. Do not substitute basil under salt or dried basil leaves.

Tagliatelle al Sugo di Carne
(Fresh Tagliatelle with Meat Sauce)   (S E R V E S 6)

Tagliatelle, somewhat wider than *taglierini* but no thicker, go best with a richer sauce, a meat sauce. Indeed, this is the cut of fresh pasta that is generally used with meat sauce. (On San Lorenzo day, sometimes the wider *pappardelle* are used with meat sauce if the hare sauce is not available.)

This is one of the most widely used pasta dishes in Italy and abroad. Cooking time for fresh *tagliatelle* is about 30 seconds. Green *tagliatelle* (see page 143) may also be used.

> *Sugo di carne* (see page 72)

For the pasta
> 3 cups all-purpose flour, preferably unbleached
> 3 "extra-large" eggs
> 1 tablespoon olive or other vegetable oil
>   Pinch of salt
>
>   Coarse salt
> 6 tablespoons freshly grated Parmigiano cheese

Make the sauce as directed on page 72. Let it stand in the casserole, covered, until needed.

Make fresh *tagliatelle*, using the quantities listed above, according to the directions on page 133. To cut into *tagliatelle*, see page 138. Let the *tagliatelle* stand on a pasta board, covered with a cotton dishtowel, until needed.

Put a large quantity of cold water in a stockpot, add coarse salt, and set on the heat. Meanwhile, prepare a serving dish by spreading 4 or 5 tablespoons of sauce over the bottom; heat the remaining sauce in its casserole.

When the water reaches the boiling point, put in the *tagliatelle*, stir with a wooden spoon, and let them cook for only about 30 seconds. Immediately drain the *tagliatelle* in colander and arrange in the serving dish.

Pour the remaining sauce over the *tagliatelle*. Toss very well, sprinkle with the Parmigiano, and serve immediately.

Tagliatelle alla Panna
(Fresh Tagliatelle in Cream Sauce) (SERVES 6)

The simple, classic butter-and-cream sauce used for fresh pasta is called by several different names, *alla panna* or cream sauce in Bologna and Florence, *doppio burro* being the correct term for it in Rome. The sauce is probably of northern rather than Roman origin, and calling it "Alfredo" is giving too much credit to a restaurateur in Rome who clearly did not invent it. The fresh pasta, called in standard Italian *tagliatelle*, are known in Roman dialect as *fettuccine*.

In Italy, there are two kinds of heavy cream, that used for whipping and an almost solid cream used for cooking. For this dish you would use whipping cream, which fortunately corresponds to the heavy cream we find in America.

For the pasta

> 3 cups all-purpose flour, preferably unbleached
> 3 "extra-large" eggs
> 1 tablespoon olive or other vegetable oil
> Pinch of salt

> 12 tablespoons (1 ½ sticks) unsalted butter
> ½ pint heavy cream
> 8 ounces freshly grated Parmigiano cheese
> Freshly ground white pepper
> Freshly grated nutmeg

Make fresh *tagliatelle*, using the quantities listed above, as directed on page 133. To cut into *tagliatelle*, see page 138. Let the *tagliatelle* stand on a pasta board, covered with a cotton dishtowel, until needed. Place a stockpot containing a large quantity of salted water on the heat. After about 10 minutes, when the water is giving off steam but is not yet boiling, place a frying pan containing the butter over the stockpot to melt the butter. Keep the butter warm, but do not allow it to boil.

When the water is boiling vigorously, add the fresh pasta. The pasta will rise to the surface, cooked, almost immediately. Quickly drain it in a colander.

Place the frying pan containing the butter on a very low flame and add the cooked pasta. Toss gently with two forks.

Add the heavy cream, unheated, and the Parmigiano, and keep tossing gently until the sauce is homogenously creamy (about 2 minutes). Sprinkle with white pepper and nutmeg and serve.

Tagliatelle con Cibreo
(Fresh Tagliatelle with Cibreo Sauce) (SERVES 6)

Tagliatelle also go well with the special *cibreo* sauce, the sauce with the almost gamelike flavor, made from chicken livers and crests and little unlaid eggs if they are available. Like *sugo di carne*, this sauce requires the slightly wider pasta. It can also be made with green *tagliatelle* (see page 143).

> *Cibreo* (see page 75)

For the pasta

- 3 cups all-purpose flour, preferably unbleached
- 3 "extra-large" eggs
- 1 tablespoon olive or other vegetable oil
   Pinch of salt
   Coarse salt

Make the sauce according to the directions on page 75. (If you cannot get the crests and unlaid eggs, use 1 whole pound of chicken livers.) Let the sauce stand covered, until needed.

Make fresh *tagliatelle* using the flour, eggs, oil, and salt, according to the direction on page 133. To cut into *tagliatelle*, see page 138. Let the *tagliatelle* stand on a pasta board, covered with a cotton dishtowel.

Put a large quantity of cold water in a stockpot, add coarse salt, and set on the heat. While the water is heating, prepare a serving dish by spreading 4 or 5 tablespoons of sauce over the bottom; heat the remaining sauce in its casserole.

When the water reaches the boiling point, put in the *tagliatelle*, stir with a wooden spoon, and let them cook for only about 30 seconds. Immediately drain the *tagliatelle* in a colander and arrange in the serving dish.

Pour the remaining sauce over the *tagliatelle*. Toss very well, and serve immediately.

Tagliatelle al Sugo di Fegatini
(Fresh Tagliatelle with Chicken Liver Sauce)   (S E R V E S 6)

This sauce differs from the straight chicken liver version of *cibreo* in that it is made with a thickened broth base and less wine. The texture of this sauce again calls for the *tagliatelle* cut; it can also be made with green *tagliatelle* (see page 143).

> *Salsa di fegatini* (see page 77)

For the pasta

 3 cups all-purpose flour, preferably unbleached
 3 "extra-large" eggs
 1 tablespoon olive or other vegetable oil
  Pinch of salt
  Coarse salt

Make the sauce according to the directions on page 77. Let it stand in its pan until needed.

Make fresh *tagliatelle*, using the quantities listed above, according to the directions on page 133. To cut into *tagliatelle*, see page 138. Let the *tagliatelle* stand on a pasta board, covered with a cotton dishtowel.

Put a large quantity of cold water in a stockpot, add coarse salt, and set on the heat. While the water is heating, prepare a serving dish by spreading 4 or 5 tablespoons of sauce over the bottom; heat the remaining sauce in its pan.

When the water reaches the boiling point, put in the *tagliatelle*, stir with a wooden spoon and let them cook for only about 30 seconds. Immediately drain the *tagliatelle* in a colander and arrange in the serving dish.

Pour the remaining sauce over the *tagliatelle*. Toss very well and serve immediately.

Sformato di Tagliatelle Verdi
(Green Pasta "Soufflé")   (SERVES 4)

This is a soufflé-like dish made with green *tagliatelle*. The green pasta is cooked a little less than usual, for about 20 seconds. Then it is mixed with *balsamella*, Parmigiano, and egg yolk. Stiffly beaten egg whites are folded in, and the soufflé dish is placed in the oven. After it is baked, it is unmolded in the manner of Italian *sformati*.

An elaborate treatment, suitable for a stylish dinner.

For the green pasta

    1 "extra-large" egg
1 ¾ cups all-purpose flour, preferably unbleached
    1 teaspoon olive or other vegetable oil
    4 ounces fresh spinach, weighed with part of the stems removed (enough to make 1 scant tablespoon chopped, boiled spinach)
    1 tablespoon vegetable oil
       Pinch of salt

For the balsamella

    6 tablespoons butter
  ½ cup all-purpose flour
    2 cups milk
       Pinch of salt

For the soufflé

    3 eggs, separated, plus 1 egg white
    2 tablespoons freshly grated Parmigiano cheese
    4 ounces boiled ham
       Salt, freshly ground white pepper, and freshly grated nutmeg to taste

Using the ingredients in the proportions listed above, make the green pasta according to the directions on page 143.

Cut the green pasta into *tagliatelle* (see page 138). Set aside, covered with a cotton dishtowel, until needed.

Using the ingredients in the proportions listed above, make the *balsamella* according to the direction on page 52. Cover the saucepan and let the *balsamella* cool for 20 minutes.

Place a stockpot containing a large quantity of salted water on the heat. While the water is heating, put about 10 cups of cold water and 1 tablespoon of oil into a large bowl.

When the water reaches the boiling point, put in the *tagliatelle* and cook for about 20 seconds. Drain them, then put into the bowl of cold water for about 1 minute.

Wet a cotton dishtowel with cold water and spread it out on a pasta board. Lifting the *tagliatelle* very gently, place them on the damp towel.

Preheat the oven to 400°.

Beat the egg yolks in a large bowl with a wooden spoon. Add the cooled *balsamella* and grated Parmigiano. Mix very well, then add the ham, coarsely chopped, and seasonings and mix very gently. Let rest for 15 minutes. Meanwhile, beat the egg whites until stiff.

Add the *tagliatelle* to the bowl containing the ham mixture, then fold in the egg whites. Toss very gently, taking care not to break up the *tagliatelle*. Pour carefully into a soufflé dish well greased with butter and a little olive oil and bake in the preheated oven for 40 minutes. Serve immediately.

Pappardelle sulla Lepre
(Pappardelle with Hare Sauce)   (S E R V E S   6)

One of the great Tuscan dishes, a still wider pasta with a sauce made from wild hare. This famous dish is of course characteristic of the hunting season in Italy. Hare may be found in many markets, Italian, German, and so on, in the United States, and in those specializing in game. If you hunt yourself, so much the better. Be careful when buying hare that it be a "wild rabbit" with dark meat rather than just a large rabbit, as there seems to be some confusion in America about the term "hare." (If the animal is very large, with light meat, it is not what you are looking for to make this dish.)

The sauce of hare is not given separately, as it is used only for this dish, wedded (without the possibility of divorce) with the *pappardelle*. *Pappardelle* are always made with "yellow" pasta.

For the pasta

    4 cups all-purpose flour, preferably unbleached
    4 "extra-large" eggs
    4 teaspoons olive or other vegetable oil
      Pinch of salt

For the sauce

    1 hare, liver reserved
  ½ cup wine vinegar
    1 medium-sized red onion
    1 carrot
    1 celery rib
    7 or 8 sprigs Italian parsley
    4 ounces *pancetta* or 2 ounces boiled ham plus 2 ounces salt
      pork
  ¼ cup olive oil
    4 tablespoons (½ stick) butter
      Salt and freshly ground pepper to taste
  ½ cup red wine
    2 tablespoons tomato paste
 2½ cups chicken or meat broth, approximately
      Pinch of freshly grated nutmeg
      Freshly grated Parmigiano cheese

Make the pasta, using the ingredients in the quantities listed, according to the directions on page 133. When the sheet of pasta has dried for 10 to 15 minutes, cut it with jagged pastry cutter into strips ¾ inch wide and about 12 inches long. Place the *pappardelle* on a floured board, cover with a cotton dishtowel, and let stand until needed.

Cut the hare into large pieces. Wash the pieces and place them in a large bowl with 3 cups cold water and ½ cup strong wine vinegar. Let soak for 1 hour; this will remove the strong "gamey" flavor.

Finely chop the *odori* (onion, carrot, celery, and parsley); coarsely chop the *pancetta* (or ham and salt pork).

Heat the olive oil and butter in a large casserole. When they are hot, add the chopped ingredients and sauté until golden brown (about 20 minutes), stirring continuously with a wooden spoon.

Wash the hare pieces under cold running water and add them to the casserole. Sprinkle with salt and pepper, then sauté, turning, until the pieces are golden brown on all sides (about 20 minutes). Add the wine and let evaporate very slowly (from 15 to 20 minutes). Meanwhile heat the broth in a saucepan.

When the wine has evaporated, add the tomato paste and 1 cup of the hot broth. Let cook very slowly, adding hot broth as needed, for about 1 hour. Coarsely chop the reserved hare liver and add it to the casserole. Sauté for about 10 minutes more, then remove the hare from the casserole. (The hare meat is not needed in this sauce and may be eaten separately at another meal.)

Taste for salt and pepper and add a pinch of nutmeg. Reduce the sauce very slowly, for about 10 minutes, until it is quite thick, then remove the casserole from the heat and let the sauce rest until needed.

Put a large quantity of salted water in a stockpot and heat until it reaches boiling point. Meanwhile, spread 4 or 5 tablespoons of the sauce over the bottom of a large serving dish; heat the remaining sauce in its casserole.

When the water reaches the boiling point, put in the *pappardelle*. If the pasta is very fresh, it will rise to the surface almost immediately. Let the pasta cook only 30 seconds from that point; quickly remove it from the water. (If the pasta has been made several hours in advance, and is somewhat dried, cooking time will be from 1 to 1½ minutes after the pasta rises to the surface.

Drain the *pappardelle* in a colander, then transfer to the serving dish. Pour the remaining sauce on top, sprinkle with the Parmigiano, and serve immediately.

Trenette al Pesto
(Trenette with Basil Sauce)   (SERVES 4)

The pasta classically associated with *pesto* is called *trenette*. Since the spread of dried pasta in the last century and a half, packaged dried *trenette* are gradually replacing the fresh pasta even in Genoa itself. Indeed, fresh *trenette* have become sufficiently rare so that some current cookbooks confuse them with *tagliatelle* or *fettuccine*. *Trenette* have a different shape from *tagliatelle*, having curled edges, but the significant difference is that *trenette* are made without eggs.

Most genuinely Genoese pasta, such as *trofie* and the specifically Ligurian ravioli, is eggless. Genoese cookbooks of the nineteenth and twentieth centuries began to include the egg pastas from other places, and that has added to the confusion that exists even in cookbooks published in Italy.

The following is the way some Genoese friends of mine of the older generation make fresh *trenette*. The pasta without egg is more elastic when cooked.

For the pasta

> 2½ cups all-purpose flour, preferably unbleached
> 1 cup cold water
> 2 teaspoons olive or other vegetable oil
> Pinch of salt
>
> *Pesto* (see page 77)
> 1 large potato
> Coarse salt

Prepare the pasta, using the quantities listed above, according to the directions on page 133. The technique of making this kind of pasta, without eggs, is just the same as for that with eggs. Place the cold water, olive oil, and salt in the well in the flour but omit eggs. Then continue with the same procedure and technique.

When the sheet of pasta has dried for 10 to 15 minutes, cut it with a jagged pastry cutter into strips ½ inch wide and about 12 inches long. Place the *trenette* on a floured board and cover with a cotton dishtowel. Let stand until needed.

Prepare the *pesto*. (Since quantities and ingredients depend on whether you wish to make it with mortar and pestle, *mezzaluna*, or blender, see the recipes for all three, pages 77–81.)

When the *pesto* is done, place a large stockpot containing salted cold water on the heat. While the water is heating, peel the potato, then cut it into paper-thin slices; put them into stockpot. Place a large serving dish and the bowl of *pesto* sauce close by. When the pasta is cooked, you must work quickly.

When the water reaches the boiling point, let it boil for 2 minutes before adding the pasta. Put in the *trenette*, stir with a wooden spoon, and let them boil for 30 seconds. Meanwhile, take 2 tablespoons of boiling water from the stockpot and put them into a bowl with the *pesto* sauce. Mix thoroughly.

Quickly drain the *trenette* and place in the serving dish. Put the *pesto* on top, toss gently, and serve immediately.

Note: If dried *trenette* (widely available both in Italy and America) are used, the only difference will be in the cooking time of the pasta. Dried *trenette* require about 12 minutes to cook.

DRIED PASTA

THERE ARE scores of varieties of dried pasta. Italians feel that a particular shape and thickness lends itself best to certain sauces or treatments. And, conversely, each sauce has a particular dried pasta, or perhaps two, especially suited to it.

Dried pasta made in the south of Italy is still in a class by itself. For this reason I would recommend not merely imported pasta, but pasta made in Naples or Abruzzo. It is lighter and more finely made than versions made outside of Italy, and fortunately it is widely available, especially in Italian markets in America.

Of the multitude of dried pasta dishes, I am going to suggest a limited number that I feel have culinary distinction, though they are often simple enough. Spaghetti (from *spaghi*, meaning "little strings") remains the prototype and the most popular kind of dried pasta. I include five treatments that are best for this type of pasta and two more recipes, one for *chiocciole* (snails or shells) and another for *penne* (short tubular pasta). Most of these are Tuscan treatments, but several come from other parts of Italy. My principal criterion has been that they retain a relative lightness consistent with the approach in the rest of the book.

Al dente cooking time for dried pasta is given as 12 minutes. With some brands, it may be as little as 8 minutes. Check package instructions.

Spaghetti alla Carbonara
(Spaghetti with Egg-Pancetta Sauce)   (SERVES 4)

This Roman dish is sometimes called "spaghetti with bacon and eggs" on tourist menus. *Pancetta*, of course, is not bacon, because it is not smoked; do not substitute bacon. To make it well and with as much lightness as possible, cook the *pancetta* slowly to remove the fat. This recipe contains just enough *pancetta* fat and eggs to have all the sauce well incorporated. There is nothing worse in *carbonara* than to have excess fat and unincorporated egg sitting on the bottom. This version should give a spicy, but not greasy *carbonara*, one that is as light as the dish can be.

4 ounces *pancetta* or salt pork
2 large cloves garlic
3 tablespoons olive oil
½ teaspoon hot pepper flakes
  Salt
2 eggs
⅓ cup freshly grated Parmigiano cheese
1 pound spaghetti
  Freshly ground black pepper

Put a large quantity of salted water in a stockpot. Set on the heat.

While the water is heating, cut *pancetta* into small pieces and chop the garlic very fine. Put the *pancetta* and garlic in a saucepan with the olive oil, salt, and hot pepper flakes. (Salt should be added depending on the saltiness of the *pancetta; alla carbonara* should be rather salty.) Place the saucepan on very low heat for 12 to 15 minutes. The *pancetta* should brown very, very slowly, so that all the fat is rendered out.

In the meantime, beat the eggs and combine with the grated Parmigiano.

When the water reaches the boiling point, add the pasta and cook until it is al dente (about 12 minutes). Drain the spaghetti well, then place it in a serving bowl. Quickly spoon the hot contents of saucepan over it. Toss; then, just as quickly, add the eggs and Parmigiano. Grind black pepper plentifully over the dish, as it should be very peppery, then toss very well and serve hot.

Spaghetti alla Fiaccheraia
(Spaghetti, Coachmen's Style)   (SERVES 4)

A very spicy red-peppery dish that is Tuscan, but also close to similar dishes in other parts of Italy—a dish that should give lie to the idea that red-peppery dishes exist only in the south of Italy. The name means "in the style of coachmen," who are supposed to be the prototypical tough, rough-hewn city types in Italy.

2 ounces *pancetta* or 1 ounce of boiled ham plus 1 ounce of salt
    pork
5 tablespoons olive oil

1 small red onion
1 cup canned tomatoes
1 tablespoon tomato paste
  Salt and freshly ground black pepper to taste
½ teaspoon hot pepper flakes
1 pound spaghetti
¼ cup freshly grated Parmigiano or Romano cheese

Chop the *pancetta* (or boiled ham and salt pork) coarsely.

Heat the olive oil in a saucepan. When it is hot, add the *pancetta* and sauté until golden brown (about 15 minutes). Meanwhile, chop the onion coarsely.

Remove the *pancetta* from the saucepan with a slotted spoon and set it aside. Add the onion to the oil in the saucepan and sauté gently until soft and golden brown (about 15 minutes). Add the tomatoes and tomato paste, then taste for salt and pepper and add the hot pepper flakes. Reduce the sauce very slowly for about 20 minutes.

While the sauce is reducing, place a stockpot containing a large quantity of salted water on the heat. When the water boils, add the spaghetti and cook until al dente (about 12 minutes, depending on the brand).

When the sauce is reduced and the spaghetti almost cooked, place the *pancetta* back in the sauce and simmer it for 1 minute more. Remove the pan from the flame.

Drain the spaghetti in a colander and place it in a serving bowl. Pour the sauce on top and sprinkle with the Parmigiano. Toss very well and serve hot.

Note: No extra cheese should be added at the table.

Spaghetti al Sugo di "Cipolle"
(Spaghetti with Chicken Gizzard Sauce)   (SERVES 4)

A really unusual and delicious dish. The long-cooked sauce of chopped chicken gizzards has a rich flavor reminiscent of game. Spaghetti is the pasta that goes best with it.

  Sugo di "cipolle" (see page 73)
  Coarse salt
1 pound spaghetti
¼ cup grated Parmigiano

Make the sauce according to the directions on page 73. Let it stand in the casserole, covered, until needed.

Put a large quantity of cold water in a stockpot, add coarse salt, then set on the heat. While the water is heating, prepare a large serving dish by spreading 4 or 5 tablespoons of the sauce over the bottom; heat the remaining sauce in its casserole.

When the water reaches the boiling point, put in the spaghetti, stir with a wooden spoon, and cook on a medium flame until al dente (about 12 minutes). When the pasta is cooked, drain it in a colander and place it in the serving dish.

Pour the remaining hot sauce over the spaghetti and toss very well. Sprinkle with Parmigiano and serve immediately.

Spaghetti con Briciolata
(Spaghetti with Bread Crumb Sauce)   (SERVES 4)

Spaghetti with *briciolata*, the sauce made with homemade bread crumbs, was one of the most popular first courses throughout Italy when everyone still made his own bread crumbs. It is worth going to that trouble if only to be able to retain this dish in your repertoire. (Commercial bread crumbs just aren't good enough to carry the entire burden of the dish.)

> Coarse salt
> 6 or 7 sprigs Italian parsley
> 1 pound spaghetti
> *Briciolata* (see page 82)
> Freshly ground black pepper

Heat a large quantity of salted water in a stockpot. Meanwhile, chop the parsley coarsely and let stand until needed.

When the water reaches the boiling point, put in the spaghetti, stir with a wooden spoon, and let cook until al dente (about 12 minutes).

Meanwhile, prepare the *briciolata* as directed on page 82.

When the spaghetti is ready, quickly drain it in a colander and place it in a serving dish. Pour on the hot sauce, then sprinkle with the chopped parsley and freshly ground black pepper. Toss thoroughly and serve immediately; do not add grated cheese.

Spaghetti all' Acciugata
(Spaghetti with Anchovy Sauce)   (SERVES 4)

Spaghetti is the best pasta for anchovy sauce and this dish is perhaps the most useful of all for last-minute cooking if you need a quick first dish.

> Coarse salt
> *Acciugata* (see page 64)
> 1 pound spaghetti
> Freshly ground black pepper

Put a large quantity of water in a stockpot, add coarse salt, and set on the heat. While the water is heating, prepare the *acciugata* according to the directions on page 64. Let stand until needed.

When the water reaches the boiling point, put the spaghetti in the pot, stir thoroughly with a wooden spoon, and let it cook until al dente (about 12 minutes). Immediately drain the spaghetti in a colander and place it in a serving dish.

Pour the *acciugata* over and toss thoroughly. Sprinkle with freshly ground pepper and serve immediately; do not add any grated cheese.

Pasta alla Puttanesca
(Pasta with a Sauce of Uncooked Tomatoes and Herbs)
(SERVES 4)

The most perfect of all summer pasta dishes, for freshness and for lightness. Everything in the sauce—tomatoes, basil, and olive oil—is uncooked. The fresh, summery ingredients must be made very cold (even left for a few minutes in the freezer), and then quickly tossed with the steaming pasta, just out of the boiling water. The contact of the very hot with the very cold releases an unforgettable flavor; this dish should be a real discovery for many people. A substantial pasta, shaped to catch some of the sauce, is called for. (I won't translate the name, nor even speculate as to why those ladies should prefer their pasta this way.)

    1 pound very ripe tomatoes or 12 ounces canned tomatoes
    4 medium-sized cloves garlic
  25 large leaves fresh basil, approximately
  ½ cup olive oil
    Salt
    Generous amount of freshly ground black pepper
    1 pound dried pasta, such as *chiocciole* (shells or snails) or *penne*

Wash the tomatoes, then cut them into small pieces and put in a bowl.

Chop the garlic coarsely and add to bowl, then tear the basil leaves into thirds and add to the bowl, along with the oil, salt, and pepper. Mix all the ingredients together, then cover the bowl with aluminum foil and place it in the refrigerator for at least 2 hours before serving time.

About 30 minutes before serving time, put a large amount of salted water in a stockpot and set it on the heat. When the water boils, cook the pasta until al dente (about 12 minutes). Drain quickly and place it in a serving bowl.

While the pasta is still extremely hot, pour the refrigerated sauce over it. (It is the reaction of very hot to very cold that releases the unique flavor of this dish.) Toss very well and serve at once; absolutely do *not* add grated cheese.

Chiocciole con Salsa di Tonno
(Shells with Tuna Sauce)   (SERVES 4)

Another treatment useful for those evenings when you would like a first dish, but have almost no time to make it. The flavorsome *salsa di tonno* (tuna sauce) requires a heavier pasta that will, again, "catch" some of the sauce. *Chiocciole* are perfect.

    Salsa di tonno (see page 74)
    Coarse salt
  1 pound *chiocciole* (shells or snails)

Make the sauce according to the directions on page 74. While the sauce is cooking, put a large quantity of water in a stockpot, add coarse salt; and set on the heat.

When sauce is almost ready and the water in stockpot has reached the boiling point, put the *chiocciole* in the boiling water. Stir with a wooden spoon, and allow them to cook until al dente (about 12 minutes). Drain the pasta in a colander and place in a serving bowl.

Pour over the sauce; toss thoroughly, and serve very hot; do not add any grated cheese.

STUFFED FRESH PASTA

TORTELLI, the earliest known stuffed pasta, appear along with lasagne in the earliest Florentine cookbooks and were always made with egg pasta. The Bolognese would probably be shocked to know, as they certainly do not know any longer, that their beloved egg pasta and *tortellini* came to Bologna from Florence. The earliest Bolognese cookbook is a copy of an earlier Florentine one that contains these types of pasta.

Tortelli are similar to what are known in other places as "ravioli." They may be cut in a circular shape with a special *tortelli* or ravioli cutter, or even a cookie cutter. They may also be made in a rectangular form, cut with a pastry wheel. It is typical that the edges of the circles or rectangles be jagged. (It is difficult to understand why many books state that this type of stuffed pasta is of more recent Genoese origin. If you wish to be amused, read *Larousse Gastronomique*'s account of the source of "ravioli," in which the origin is left ambiguously hovering between Genoese and French.)

Tortellini means, of course, "little *tortelli*." In Florence the term refers to something close to "half-moon" *tortelli*, but curved around a finger and joined at the end. They are made with circles of pasta about 1½ inches in diameter. The smaller versions are called *cappelletti* in Florence, and are eaten in broth.

The names *tortellini*, *cappelletti*, and even *tortelloni* differ slightly in meaning depending on the region in which they are used, but they all derive from the ancient Florentine stuffed pasta called *tortelli*. The packages of dried *tortellini* that one sometimes sees in stores are most appropriate for broth, and resemble *cappelletti*.

First, we present the directions for making *tortelli*, and "half-moon" *tortelli*, and *tortellini*. Then recipes for *tortelli* with a fresh mint sauce; for half-moon *tortelli* stuffed with spinach and ricotta and covered with butter and cheese; for *tortelli* with a gorgonzola stuffing and a light tomato sauce. There is a special recipe that features a rabbit sauce from the mountainous Mugello and, finally, one for the sweet *tortelli* of pumpkin from Modena. Two recipes for *tortellini* conclude the section, demonstrating the versatility of one filling for two very different sauces.

Half-moon *tortelli*, filled with a *tortellini* chicken-breast stuffing, are also used in the dish *cannelloni alla sorpresa* on page 187, and *tortellini* are also used in the dish *timballo di tortellini* on page 212.

MAKING TORTELLI

Follow the recipe for fresh pasta on pages 133–138, through the drying of the pasta sheet before cutting. Then lay out the long sheet of pasta, and starting an inch from the top and side edges, begin a lengthwise row of dots of filling, each one 2 inches from its neighbor. Each dot should be made with 1 teaspoon of filling. Continue the row until it reaches close to halfway down the length of the pasta sheet. If sheet is narrow, make only 1 such row. If it is wide enough, make a second row, 1 inch in from the other side. (See photo 1.)

Tortelli: 1. Placing dots of filling on the pasta sheet.

With a wet finger, draw 3 vertical lines (2 if only 1 row of dots), half the length of the pasta, one down each side and one through the center; then draw lines across, between the dots of filling (see photo 2). In this way, when cut, the edges of each *tortello* will be moist enough to seal well.

Carefully pick up bottom end of pasta sheet and fold it over the top half (see photo 3). Quickly press down around the dots of filling. Using a 2-inch round scalloped pastry cutter, cut out circles, pressing well to be sure all edges are detached. As you lift out each *tortello*, press the edges all around between two fingers, to make sure they are completely sealed.

2. Moistening the pasta so it will seal well.

3. Folding the pasta sheet over the filling.

Let rest until needed on a floured wooden surface or floured cotton dishtowel. If the *tortelli* are to stand more than 30 minutes before cooking, cover them with a cotton towel so they do not become too dry.

Note: *Tortelli* may also be made square (photo 4). Cut into squares using a pastry wheel instead of a round cutter.

4. Cutting out the *tortelli*.

MAKING "HALF-MOON" TORTELLI

Follow the recipe for fresh pasta on pages 133–138, through the drying of the pasta sheet before cutting. Then lay out the long sheet of pasta on a wooden surface. With a pastry wheel or knife, cut the sheet in half lengthwise

Starting 1½ inches from top, begin a lengthwise row of dots of filling, in the center of each half-sheet. Each dot should be made with 1 teaspoon of filling. Continue the row down entire length of the half-sheet.

With a wet finger, moisten entire length of one edge of each half-sheet. Then make lines of moisture across, between the dots of filling. In this way, when cut, each half-moon will be moist enough to seal well.

Carefully pick up one of the sides with both hands and fold the half-sheet lengthwise in half. Quickly press down around the dots of filling. Repeat with the other half-sheet.

Cut out half-moons, that is semicircles, by placing only half of a round 2-inch jagged pastry cutter over the area containing the filling. As you lift out each half-moon, press the edges on the semicircular side between two fingers, to be sure they are completely sealed.

Let rest until needed on a floured wooden surface or floured cotton dishtowel. If the half-moon *tortelli* are to stand more than 30 minutes before cooking, cover them with a cotton towel so they do not become too dry.

MAKING TORTELLINI

To make *tortellini*, make fresh pasta according to the directions on pages 133–138, but do not wait for the pasta to dry. As each piece of dough is rolled out, begin to make *tortellini* with it immediately.

Cut the sheet of pasta into circles with a 1½-inch round cookie cutter (see photo 1). Place a scant ½ teaspoon of filling in the center of each circle (see photo 2). Moisten the edges (photo 3), then double over one side of the pasta circle, but not all the way to the other side; leave a little border arc of the pasta undoubled (it should show from the bottom side). Seal the moistened edges (see photo 4).

Tortellini: 1. Cutting the sheet of pasta into circles with a cookie cutter.

2. Placing the filling on the pasta circles.

3. Moistening the edges of the pasta circles so they will seal well.

4. Doubling the pasta over and sealing it.

Wrap the half-moon around your index finger, the top of the finger reaching only to the top of the filled section (see photo 5). With your thumbs, connect the two edges of the half-moon. The overlap of pasta above your index finger should be curled outward.

5. Curving the *tortellini* around the finger.

Tortelli alla Menta
(Tortelli with Fresh Mint)   (SERVES 8)

How can one adequately describe the summery freshness of this dish, in which the fresh mint plays the role usually assigned to fresh basil in bringing out the full flavor of fresh tomato? The mint leaves are chopped up and placed in the stuffing itself, while basil leaves are placed in the fresh sauce.

For the sauce

     2 pounds tomatoes, fresh or canned
        Salt and freshly ground pepper to taste
     8 tablespoons (1 stick) butter
    10 to 12 large basil leaves

For the filling

    15 ounces of ricotta
     4 egg yolks
     1 cup freshly grated Parmigiano cheese
    1½ tablespoons finely chopped fresh mint leaves
    1½ tablespoons coarsely chopped mint leaves
        Salt, freshly ground pepper, and freshly grated nutmeg to
        taste

For the pasta

     4 cups all-purpose flour, preferably unbleached
     4 "extra-large" eggs
     4 teaspoons olive or other vegetable oil
        Pinch of salt
     ¼ cup freshly grated Parmigiano cheese

Prepare the sauce first. Cut the tomatoes into pieces, if fresh, and put them in a saucepan with salt. Place the pan on a medium flame and simmer for 20 to 30 minutes, then pass the tomatoes through a food mill into a bowl. Return the tomato sauce to saucepan and place it again on a low flame. Simmer for 5 more minutes, then taste for salt and pepper. Meanwhile, cut the butter into pats and place them on a serving dish. Set both sauce and serving dish aside while you prepare the filling.

Place the ricotta in a bowl and add the egg yolks, grated Parmigiano, and mint. Mix very well with a wooden spoon, then season with salt, pepper, and nutmeg, and set aside.

Make the pasta, using the ingredients in the proportions listed above, according to the directions on page 133. Form the *tortelli* as directed on page 162, using the filling you have just prepared.

Bring a large quantity of salted water to a boil in a stockpot. Meanwhile, heat the sauce, then pour half of it over the butter in the serving dish. Tear 6 or 7 of the basil leaves in quarters and add them.

When the water is boiling, add the *tortelli* quickly but gently, being careful not to break them. If the *tortelli* have been made as much as an hour or two before, they will cook and rise to surface of water in 1 minute. If they are already dried, cooking time will be longer (about 3 to 4 minutes). Remove the *tortelli* with a strainer-skimmer and place them on the serving dish. Pour the rest of the sauce over them. Tear the remaining basil leaves and add them, sprinkle with the Parmigiano, and serve.

Tortelli della Vigilia
("Half-moon" Tortelli Stuffed with Spinach and Ricotta)

(SERVES 8)

Perhaps the best-known stuffing for *tortelli,* that of ricotta, spinach, Parmigiano, eggs, and flavorings. Originally the stuffing for the eve of a holiday when meat was not eaten, it has surpassed the original meat stuffings in popularity. Serve the *tortelli* with a light butter and cheese sauce.

For the filling

    3 pounds fresh spinach or 4 packages frozen
  15 ounces ricotta
    2 eggs plus 2 egg yolks
    1 cup freshly grated Parmigiano cheese
      Salt, freshly ground pepper, and freshly grated nutmeg

For the pasta

    4 "extra-large" eggs
    4 cups all-purpose flour, preferably unbleached
    4 teaspoons olive or other vegetable oil
      Pinch of salt

For the sauce

    12 tablespoons (1½ sticks) butter
   1½ cups freshly grated Parmigiano cheese
       Freshly ground black pepper and freshly grated nutmeg

Rinse the spinach very well and cut off the larger stems, then cook in a large quantity of boiling, salted water for about 15 minutes. If frozen spinach is used, cook according to package directions. Drain the spinach, cool it under cold running water, and squeeze very dry.

Chop the spinach very fine, then place it in a bowl, along with ricotta, eggs, egg yolks, Parmigiano, salt, pepper, and nutmeg. Blend with a wooden spoon until the mixture is thoroughly combined, then cover with aluminum foil and let stand in the refrigerator until needed.

Make the pasta, using the ingredients in the proportions listed above, according to the directions on page 133, then form the "half-moon" *tortelli* as described on page 164, using the filling you have just made.

Begin preparing the sauce by melting 8 tablespoons (1 stick) of the butter in a saucepan; let it stand, covered, until needed.

Bring a large quantity of salted water to a boil in a stockpot. Meanwhile, prepare a serving dish by pouring in half the melted butter. When the water is boiling, add the *tortelli* quickly but gently, being careful not to break them. If the *tortelli* have been made as much as an hour or two before, they will cook and rise to surface of water in 1 minute. If they are already dried, cooking time will be longer (about 3 to 4 minutes). Remove the *tortelli* with a strainer-skimmer and place them on the prepared serving dish.

Pour the rest of the melted butter over the *tortelli*, arrange the remaining 4 tablespoons of butter, in pats, on top, then sprinkle with the Parmigiano, freshly ground black pepper, freshly grated nutmeg, and serve.

Tortelli al Gorgonzola
(Tortelli with Gorgonzola Stuffing)   (SERVES 8)

Gorgonzola dolce, the sweet gorgonzola cheese is mixed with ricotta, Parmigiano, egg yolks, and nutmeg to produce a rich and unusual stuffing for *tortelli*. It is covered with a very light tomato sauce and some melted, but not cooked, butter. Useful for those occasions when you crave something "rich."

For the sauce

  2 pounds tomatoes, fresh or canned
  8 tablespoons (1 stick) butter
  6 tablespoons freshly grated Parmigiano cheese
     Salt and freshly ground pepper to taste

For the stuffing

  7 ounces ricotta
  8 ounces gorgonzola, preferably *dolce*
  4 egg yolks
  3 tablespoons freshly grated Parmigiano cheese
     Salt, freshly ground black pepper, and freshly grated nutmeg
        to taste

For the pasta

  4 "extra-large" eggs
  4 cups all-purpose flour, preferably unbleached
  4 teaspoons olive or other vegetable oil
     Pinch of salt

Make the sauce first.

Place the fresh or canned tomatoes in a flameproof casserole and simmer very slowly for 25 to 30 minutes. Season with salt and pepper, then pass through a food mill back into the casserole. Simmer for 5 minutes longer. Remove the casserole from the stove and add 4 tablespoons of the butter, then cover and let rest until needed.

Make the filling by combining the ricotta and the gorgonzola in a bowl. Mix with a wooden spoon until thoroughly combined, then add the egg yolks and Parmigiano. Season with salt, pepper, and nutmeg and mix thoroughly with the wooden spoon.

Make the pasta, using the ingredients in the proportions listed above, according to the directions on page 133 Form into *tortelli* as directed on page 162, using the filling you have just made.

Bring a large quantity of salted water to a boil in a large stockpot. Meanwhile, reheat the sauce, then pour half of it into a serving dish.

When the water is boiling, add the *tortelli* quickly but gently, being careful not to break them. If the *tortelli* have been made as much as an hour or two before, they will cook and rise to surface of water in 1 minute. If they are already dried, cooking time will be longer (about

3 to 4 minutes). Remove the *tortelli* with a strainer-skimmer and place them on the prepared serving dish.

Pour the remaining sauce over, dot with remaining butter, sprinkle with the Parmigiano, and serve.

Tortelli al Coniglio
(Tortelli in Rabbit Sauce)   (S E R V E S   8)

A rather elaborate country dish, from the mountainous Mugello, the area where Giotto and Fra Angelico were born.

The sauce is made by cooking out the essence of the rabbit with *odori* (aromatic vegetables), red wine, *pancetta*, butter, and olive oil, broth, and a little tomato. The liver is chopped up and added; the rabbit is discarded or saved for a family snack. The *tortelli* are lightly stuffed with a potato, egg, and cheese filling flavored with a little of the sauce and butter. But the lion's share of the sauce is put over the *tortelli* after they are cooked.

This is a dish very little known even in Florence itself, and once when I made it for a public occasion there, it became the subject of an article in one of the Florentine newspapers. (My co-citizens are not used to coming in contact with a new dish that they actually like.)

For the sauce

    1 small rabbit, liver reserved
    4 ounces *pancetta* or salt pork
    4 tablespoons (½ stick) butter
    3 tablespoons olive oil
    1 medium-sized red onion
    1 large or 2 small carrots
    1 medium-sized celery rib
    4 or 5 sprigs Italian parsley
    1 clove garlic
    1 cup dry red wine
      Salt and freshly ground pepper to taste
    3 ounces tomato paste
    2 cups meat broth

For the filling

    2 large boiling potatoes
    8 tablespoons (1 stick) butter
    ½ cup of the sauce (see above)
    2 egg yolks
    ¼ cup freshly grated Parmigiano
    Salt, freshly ground pepper, and freshly grated nutmeg to taste

For the pasta

    4 "extra-large" eggs
    4 cups all-purpose flour, preferably unbleached
    4 teaspoons olive or other vegetable oil
    Pinch of salt

    4 tablespoons (½ stick) butter
    4 or 5 tablespoons freshly grated Parmigiano cheese

Prepare the sauce first.

Be sure the cavity of rabbit is well cleaned. Wash the rabbit very well and place it in a metal casserole. Cover the casserole and place on a medium flame for 10 minutes; do not add anything, as the rabbit will shed liquid. Remove the casserole from flame and throw away the liquid the rabbit has shed (it would give the dish too gamey a taste), then wash rabbit in cold water again and set it aside.

Chop the *pancetta* (or salt pork) coarsely, then place it in a flame-proof casserole with the butter and olive oil and sauté very gently for 10 to 12 minutes. Add the rabbit and sauté until golden brown all over (about 15 minutes).

Meanwhile, finely chop the onion, carrots, celery, parsley, and garlic. Add these chopped *odori* to the casserole and sauté very slowly until golden brown. Add the red wine and let it evaporate (about 15 minutes), then season with salt and pepper. Add the tomato paste and 1 cup of the meat broth, cover, and let simmer very slowly for 15 to 20 minutes until the broth is reduced and the tomato paste is completely incorporated. Taste for salt and pepper, add 1 more cup of broth, and simmer again until almost all the broth is evaporated (about 20 minutes).

Remove rabbit and set aside for another purpose (it is no longer needed for this dish), then chop the rabbit liver very fine and add it to the casserole. Cook for 5 minutes more, continually stirring with a wooden spoon, then remove the casserole from the heat, cover, and let rest until needed.

Make the filling. Boil the potatoes, in their skins, in salted water (about 25 to 35 minutes, depending on the potatoes), then peel and pass them through a potato ricer into a small flameproof casserole. Add the butter and ½ cup of the rabbit sauce to riced potatoes and place the casserole on a medium flame for about 15 minutes, stirring constantly with a wooden spoon. Remove the casserole from the heat and transfer the contents to bowl to cool for about 20 minutes.

When cool, add the egg yolks, grated Parmigiano, salt, pepper, and nutmeg and mix very well with a wooden spoon.

Make the pasta using the ingredients in the proportions listed above, according to the directions on page 133. Form into *tortelli* as directed on page 162, using the filling you have just made.

Bring a large quantity of salted water to a boil in a stockpot. Meanwhile, reheat the sauce and pour half of it into a serving dish with 4 tablespoons of butter.

When the water is boiling, add the *tortelli* quickly but gently, being careful not to break them. If the *tortelli* have been made as much as an hour or two before, they will cook and rise to surface of water in 1 minute. If they are already dried, cooking time will be longer (about 3 to 4 minutes). Remove the *tortelli* with a strainer-skimmer and place them on the prepared serving dish.

Pour over the remaining sauce, sprinkle with Parmigiano, and serve.

Tortelli di Zucca alla Modenese
(Pumpkin Tortelli, Modena Style)   (S E R V E S 8)

Festive, sweet *tortelli*, eaten as a first dish. Made with fresh baked pumpkin, the bitter almond taste of *amaretti*, egg, bread crumbs, and Parmigiano, its mixture of sweet and "salt" reveals it as a survivor of the Renaissance. It is really a good idea for a Thanksgiving Italian dinner, because the fresh pumpkins are appropriate and available. Do not make it if fresh pumpkins cannot be found; they are the closest to the Italian *zucche* used for the dish.

For the stuffing

   1 very small pumpkin (for a yield of 1 cup of pulp after baking
      and straining)

   1 ounce of *amaretti* (imported Italian cookies)
  ¼ cup bread crumbs, preferably homemade (see page 45)
   1 egg
   5 heaping tablespoons freshly grated Parmigiano cheese
       Salt to taste
       Pinch of freshly grated nutmeg

For the pasta

   4 "extra-large" eggs
   4 cups all-purpose flour
   4 teaspoons olive or other vegetable oil
       Pinch of salt

For the sauce

   6 tablespoons butter
   5 or 6 heaping tablespoons freshly grated Parmigiano cheese

For the stuffing, bake the pumpkin on an aluminum cookie sheet in an oven preheated to 400° for about 1 hour, then remove from the oven and lower the heat to 375°. With fork and knife, peel the pumpkin, divide in quarters, and remove the seeds and filaments. Place the pulp in a bowl and mash it with a fork, then strain it into another bowl.

Crush the *amaretti* very fine and pass them through a sifter. Toast the bread crumbs in the 375° oven on a sheet of aluminum foil, until golden brown (about 15 minutes).

Place the *amaretti* and toasted bread crumbs in the bowl containing the pumpkin; mix very well with a wooden spoon, then add the egg, freshly grated Parmigiano, salt, and nutmeg. Mix very well, without stopping, for about 10 minutes, then place the bowl in the refrigerator until the pasta is ready.

Make fresh *tortelli*, using the ingredients in the quantities listed, according to the directions on page 133. Form the *tortelli* as directed on page 162, using the filling you have just made.

Melt the butter for the sauce in a saucepan. Set aside until needed. Bring a large quantity of salted water to a boil in a stockpot. Meanwhile, prepare a serving dish by coating the bottom with 2 tablespoons of the melted butter. When water reaches the boiling point, add the *tortelli* quickly but gently, being careful not to break them. If the *tortelli* have been made as much as an hour or two before, they will cook and rise to the surface of the water in 1 minute. If they are already dried, cooking time will be longer (about 3 or 4 minutes). Remove the *tortelli* from the boiling water with a strainer-skimmer and arrange them in a layer in the prepared serving dish. Sprinkle with 2 more tablespoons of the butter and half the Parmigiano, then make a second layer of *tortelli* and cover with the remaining melted butter and Parmigiano. Serve hot.

Tortellini alla Panna
(Tortellini in Butter and Cream Sauce)   (S E R V E S   6)

Tortellini tossed in the same butter and cream sauce as in *tagliatelle alla panna*. The sauce must be made in the pan with the cooked *tortellini;* it does not exist in its own right.

The dish is very popular in Bologna. It requires homemade *tortellini,* very tender, and should not be made with the prepackaged kind.

For the stuffing

    2 ounces prosciutto, in 1 or 2 slices
    2 ounces mortadella of Bologna, in 1 large slice
  ¼ pound chicken breast
  ¼ pound pork
    1 whole bay leaf
    1 teaspoon butter
    1 tablespoon olive oil
       Salt, freshly ground black pepper, and freshly grated nutmeg
    2 eggs
    1 cup freshly grated Parmigiano cheese

For the pasta

    3 "extra-large" eggs
    3 cups all-purpose flour, preferably unbleached
    1 tablespoon olive oil
       Pinch of salt

For the sauce

  12 tablespoons (1½ sticks) unsalted butter
  ½ pint heavy cream
    8 ounces Parmigiano cheese, freshly grated
       Freshly ground white pepper to taste
       Freshly grated nutmeg to taste

To make the stuffing, cut the prosciutto and mortadella into small squares.

Heat the butter and oil in a saucepan and add the meat squares, along with the chicken breast, pork, bay leaf, salt, pepper, and nutmeg. Sauté very lightly for 10 minutes, remove the mixture from the pan, discarding the bay leaf, and chop very fine. Mix in the eggs and Parmigiano, then stir well until entire mixture is thoroughly combined.

Make the pasta, using the ingredients in the quantities listed, according to the directions on page 133. Form the *tortellini* as directed on page 165, using the stuffing you have just made.

To cook the *tortellini*, put a large quantity of salted water in a stockpot and set on the heat. When the water reaches the boiling point, add the *tortellini*, a few at a time, until all are in the pot. Freshly made *tortellini* will be cooked in 2 or 3 minutes, those made several hours before require a few minutes more. (Test them, as cooking time can also vary with the weather.)

When they are cooked, quickly remove the *tortellini* with a strainer-skimmer.

Place a large frying pan containing the 12 tablespoons of butter on a very low flame and add the *tortellini*. Toss gently with a large metal spoon. Add the heavy cream, unheated, and the grated Parmigiano. Keep mixing gently until the sauce is homogenously creamy (about 2 minutes). Sprinkle with white pepper and nutmeg and serve immediately.

Tortellini al Sugo di Carne
(Tortellini in Meat Sauce) (SERVES 6)

These little stuffed pasta are very versatile; they also go very well with the *sugo di carne* used with *tagliatelle*. Throughout Italy this is the sauce which is most often used with them.

Make the *sugo di carne* as described on page 72. After the *sugo* has cooked for 1 hour and has another hour to cook, make the *tortellini*, preparing the pasta, filling it, and then cooking the *tortellini*, all as described in the recipe for *tortellini alla panna*, using the same stuffing but omitting the sauce.

When the *tortellini* are cooked, quickly remove them from the boiling water with a strainer-skimmer.

Arrange the *tortellini* in a serving bowl and pour the *sugo di carne* over them. Serve hot, sprinkling each serving with a tablespoon of grated Parmigiano.

Note: The *sugo di carne* may be prepared as much as a day in advance.

LARGE STUFFED PASTA DISHES

Cannelloni con Carne
(Cannelloni with Meat)   (MAKES 8 TO 10)

Cannelloni are stuffed, rolled-up squares of pasta. They may be made from yellow or green pasta and stuffed with a variety of fillings. Sometimes they are also made with *crespelle* instead of pasta squares; this is not in imitation of French crêpes, but rather a survival of Italian *crespelle* from earlier centuries. The recipes given here are for the more usual type made with pasta.

After the long strips of pasta have been cut into squares, the squares are precooked for some seconds. A few tablespoons of the stuffing to be used are placed at one end, and the square is rolled up in the form of a tube.

It has become the custom in America to serve *cannelloni* as a main dish. This is never done in Italy. *Cannelloni* are always a first dish, even if they are stuffed with meat, and are eaten in a quantity appropriate to that course. Two *cannelloni* is an adequate portion, and for light eaters one often suffices.

This basic recipe, for meat *cannelloni*, contains the procedure for how to prepare them in detail. Following are *cannelloni* for the eve of a holiday, containing spinach and ricotta, *cannelloni* filled with ricotta and cheese, green *cannelloni* stuffed with ricotta and cheese, and the very special *cannelloni alla sorpresa*, the apotheosis of *cannelloni*, which are filled with *tortelli alla panna*.

Cannelloni are always baked, covered with "strips" of *balsamella* so the top does not become dry.

For the stuffing

       1 ounce dried *porcini* mushrooms
       1 small carrot

  1 medium-sized red onion
  ½ celery rib
  6 or 7 sprigs Italian parsley
  1 clove garlic
  5 tablespoons olive oil
  ¼ pound pork
  ¼ pound ground beef
  ½ chicken breast
  ½ cup dry red wine
  1 tablespoon tomato paste
  2 cups hot meat or chicken broth
  ¼ pound prosciutto
    Salt and freshly ground pepper to taste
  ¼ cup freshly grated Parmigiano cheese
    Freshly grated nutmeg to taste

For the pasta

  2 cups all-purpose flour, preferably unbleached
  2 "extra-large" eggs
  2 teaspoons olive or other vegetable oil
    Pinch of salt
  2 tablespoons olive oil

For the balsamella

  3 tablespoons butter
  ¼ cup all-purpose flour
  1½ cups milk
    Salt and freshly grated nutmeg to taste

Prepare the stuffing first.

Soak the mushrooms in lukewarm water for 15 to 20 minutes.

Meanwhile, chop the carrot, onion, celery, parsley, and garlic very fine. Place in a saucepan, preferably terra-cotta, along with the olive oil and sauté very gently until golden brown.

Add the pork, beef, and chicken breast and sauté for 15 to 20 minutes more, then add the wine and cook until evaporated (about 15 minutes). Add the tomato paste and 1 cup of the hot broth and reduce for 15 minutes.

Transfer the pork and chicken breast to a board and chop them very fine. Place them back in the pan, adding the second cup of broth, the soaked, drained mushrooms, salt, and pepper. Reduce for about 15

minutes, until the sauce is quite thick, then chop the prosciutto very
fine and add it to the sauce.

Remove the pan from flame. Add the grated Parmigiano and nutmeg and mix very well, then let the sauce cool before stuffing the pasta.

Make fresh pasta, using the ingredients in the quantities listed, according to the directions on page 133. Then, with a jagged-edged
wheel, cut the pasta sheets across to make squares (see photo 1).

Cannelloni con carne: 1. Cutting the pasta into squares.

Bring a large amount of salted water to a boil. Meanwhile, fill a large
bowl with cold water and 2 tablespoons of olive oil; dampen 2 cotton
dishtowels with cold water.

When the water is boiling, one by one, put squares of pasta into the
pot for several seconds, until they rise to the top of the water. Transfer
each to the bowl of cold water with a slotted spoon to cool, then place
on the dampened towels and allow to rest for 20 minutes (see photos
2–4).

Meanwhile, make the *balsamella*, using the ingredients in the quantities listed, following the directions on page 52. Cover the pan and
let stand until needed.

When you are ready to put the *cannelloni* together, preheat the
oven to 375°, then transfer a pasta square to a board. Spread 3 table-

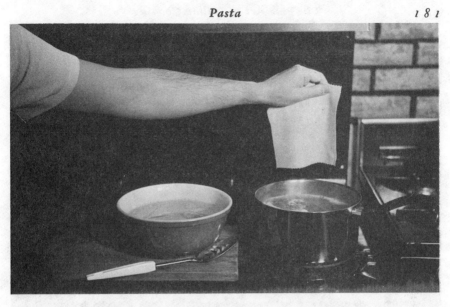

2. Putting the squares of pasta in boiling water.

3. Transferring the half-cooked pasta square to the bowl of cold water.

spoons of the stuffing along one of the jagged edges, then roll, starting at the edge containing the stuffing and ending with the other jagged edge on top (see photos 5–7). Repeat until all the *cannelloni* are rolled.

Place the *cannelloni* in one or two well-buttered rectangular Pyrex

4. Placing the pasta squares on the dampened cotton dishtowel.

5. Placing the filling on a pasta square.

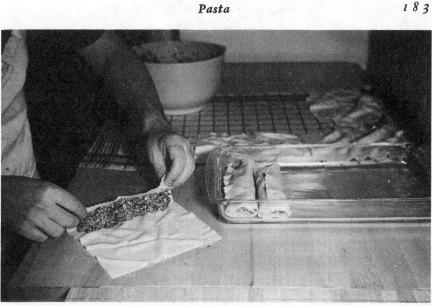

6. Preparing to roll up the stuffing in the pasta.

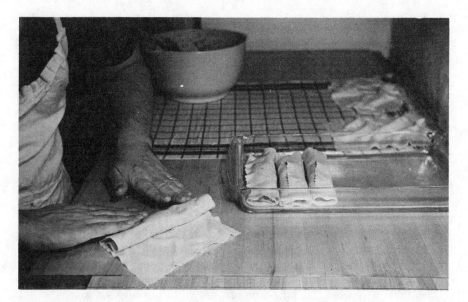

7. Rolling the *cannelloni* . Notice that the rolled *cannelloni* in the baking dish have the jagged end of the pasta on top.

baking dishes 13 ½ x 8 ¾ inches. A maximum of 8 will fit in one dish of this size, so be guided by the number of *cannelloni* you have.

Pour a "strip" of *balsamella* along the length of each of the *cannelloni* and another strip between each two, then bake in the preheated oven for 20 minutes. Allow to cool for 10 minutes before serving, then serve with a large spatula.

Cannelloni della Vigilia
(Cannelloni Stuffed with Spinach and Ricotta)

(MAKES 8 TO 10)

The stuffing for these *cannelloni* is made of spinach, ricotta, eggs, Parmigiano and seasonings.

For the filling

    3 pounds fresh spinach or 4 packages (10 ounces each) frozen
   15 ounces ricotta
    2 eggs plus 2 egg yolks
    1 cup freshly grated Parmigiano cheese
      Salt, freshly ground pepper, and freshly grated nutmeg to taste

For the balsamella

    3 tablespoons butter
   ¼ cup all-purpose flour
  1 ½ cups milk
      Salt to taste

For the pasta

    2 "extra-large" eggs
    2 cups all-purpose flour, preferably unbleached
    2 teaspoons olive or other vegetable oil
      Pinch of salt

Make the filling first.

If using fresh spinach, rinse it very well and cut off the larger stems. Put a large quantity of salted water in a stockpot and set it on the heat. When the water boils, add the spinach and cook for about 15 minutes. For frozen spinach, cook according to directions on the package.

Drain the spinach, cool it under cold running water, and squeeze very dry.

Chop the spinach very fine, then place it in a bowl with the ricotta, eggs, egg yolks, Parmigiano, salt, pepper, and nutmeg. Mix together with a wooden spoon until well combined, then cover with aluminum foil and let stand in the refrigerator until needed.

From this point on, proceed exactly as directed in the recipe for *cannelloni con carne* on page 178. The procedures for making the pasta and *balsamella* and assembling the dish are identical.

Cannelloni con Ricotta

(Cannelloni Stuffed with Ricotta)   (M A K E S   8   T O   1 0)

Here the ricotta–eggs–Parmigiano stuffing is flavored with Italian parsley.

For the filling

        12 or 14 sprigs Italian parsley
        15 ounces ricotta
         1 cup freshly grated Parmigiano cheese
         2 eggs plus 2 egg yolks
            Salt, freshly ground pepper, and freshly grated nutmeg to
            taste

For the balsamella

         3 tablespoons butter
        ¼ cup all-purpose flour
        1½ cups of milk
            Salt

For the pasta

         2 cups all-purpose flour, preferably unbleached
         2 "extra-large" eggs
         2 teaspoons olive or other vegetable oil
            Pinch of salt

First, prepare the filling.

Remove the stems from the parsley and chop the leaves fine. Place in a bowl with the ricotta, Parmigiano, eggs, egg yolks, salt, pepper, and nutmeg. Mix together with a wooden spoon until all the ingredients are well combined. Cover the bowl with aluminum foil and let stand in the refrigerator until needed.

From this point on, proceed exactly as directed in the recipe for *cannelloni con carne* on page 178; the procedures for making the pasta and *balsamella* and assembling the dish are exactly the same.

Cannelloni Verdi di Ricotta
(Green Cannelloni with Ricotta Filling)

(MAKES 10 TO 12)

The stuffing for the *cannelloni* is standard, made of ricotta, eggs, Parmigiano, and seasonings, but the pasta is green.

For the stuffing

  8 ounces ricotta
  1 cup freshly grated Parmigiano cheese
  2 whole eggs plus 2 egg yolks
15 sprigs Italian parsley, approximately
     Salt, freshly ground pepper, and freshly grated nutmeg to taste

For the balsamella

  3 tablespoons butter
 ¼ cup all-purpose flour
1½ cups milk
     Salt to taste

For the pasta

3½ cups all-purpose flour, preferably unbleached
  2 "extra-large" eggs
  5 to 6 ounces fresh spinach, weighed before stems are removed
  2 teaspoons olive or other vegetable oil
     Pinch of salt

Make the stuffing first.

Remove the stems from the parsley and chop the leaves coarsely. Place in a large bowl with the ricotta, Parmigiano, eggs, and egg yolks. Mix well with a wooden spoon, then season with salt, pepper and nutmeg and mix thoroughly. Cover the bowl with aluminum foil and place it in the refrigerator until needed.

From this point on, proceed as directed in the recipe for *cannelloni con carne* on page 178, but making the green pasta according to the directions on page 143.

Cannelloni alla Sorpresa
(Green Cannelloni Stuffed with Tortelli alla Panna)

(MAKES 1 6)

The apotheosis of *cannelloni*, a very fancy treatment in which green pasta is used for the outside roll, while inside, under a lining consisting of a thin slice of *prosciutto cotto*, is a stuffing of "half-moon" *tortelli*, made of yellow pasta and stuffed in turn with chicken breast, prosciutto, and seasonings, then tossed in *alla panna* sauce, some of which is spooned inside the cannelloni along with the *tortelli*. A noteworthy dish, worth the trouble of making the two kinds of pasta and the *tortelli*. It makes a strong impression at an important dinner.

Pasta for the green cannelloni

> 5 to 6 ounces fresh spinach, weighed before stems are removed
> 3 ½ cups all-purpose flour, preferably unbleached
> 2 "extra-large" eggs
> 2 teaspoons olive or other vegetable oil
> Pinch of salt

For the tortelli filling

> 3 tablespoons olive oil
> 2 tablespoons butter
> 1 whole chicken breast
> 1 bay leaf
> Salt and freshly ground pepper to taste
> ¼ cup freshly grated Parmigiano cheese
> 2 eggs yolks
> Freshly grated nutmeg to taste

Pasta for the "half-moon" tortelli

> 3 cups all-purpose flour, preferably unbleached
> 3 "extra-large" eggs
> 1 tablespoon olive or other vegetable oil
> Pinch of salt

For the balsamella

> 3 tablespoons butter
> ¼ cup all-purpose flour
> 1½ cups milk
> Pinch of salt

For the alla panna sauce

> 8 tablespoons butter
> ½ pint heavy cream
> 5 tablespoons freshly grated Parmigiano cheese
> Freshly ground white pepper and freshly grated nutmeg to taste

Plus

> 16 thin slices boiled ham

Make the green pasta, using the ingredients in the quantities listed, according to the directions on page 143. Prepare the pasta for *cannelloni*, cutting it and precooking it, as directed on page 180. Let stand on the damp cotton dishtowel until needed. Prepare the "half-moon" *tortelli*, making the filling first.

Heat the oil and butter in a saucepan. When the butter is melted, add the whole chicken breast, along with the bay leaf. Season with salt and freshly ground black pepper and sauté lightly for about 20 minutes, turning several times.

Remove the saucepan from the flame, discarding the bay leaf but saving the sautéing fat, and transfer chicken breast to a chopping board. Remove the bones and chop the meat fine.

Place the chopped meat in a small bowl, along with the Parmigiano, egg yolks, and reserved sautéing fat. Taste for salt and pepper, add a pinch of freshly grated nutmeg, and mix thoroughly with a wooden spoon. Cover the bowl with aluminum foil and let stand until needed.

Make the pasta for the "half-moon" *tortelli*, as directed on pages 133–138, using the ingredients in the quantities listed, then form the *tortelli* as directed on page 164, using the filling you have just made.

When you have finished making the *tortelli*, put a large quantity of salted water in a stockpot and set it on the heat. While the water is heating, melt 8 tablespoons of butter in a large frying pan to prepare for making *tortelli alla panna*.

When the water in the stockpot reaches the boiling point, put all the *tortelli*, one by one, into the pot. Stir with a wooden spoon and let cook about 35 seconds, in the meantime turning on a low flame under the pan containing the melted butter. When the *tortelli* are ready, quickly transfer them with a strainer-skimmer from pot to the warm butter in the frying pan. Pour the heavy cream over the *tortelli*, and then sprinkle them with the Parmigiano, a little white pepper, and nutmeg to taste.

With a slotted spoon, very gently mix the heavy cream, Parmigiano, and *tortelli* together. Allow the *tortelli* to simmer for 30 seconds, gently stirring without stopping, then remove the pan from the flame and let the *tortelli* cool for 1 hour.

Meanwhile make the *balsamella*, using the ingredients in the quantities listed, according to the directions on page 52, then cover the saucepan and let the *balsamella* cool for 1 hour.

Preheat the oven to 375°.

To assemble the dish, place a whole slice of boiled ham on each square of green pasta. Arrange 5 or 6 *tortelli*, with a little of the sauce, along one jagged edge of each pasta square and roll up. Place the rolled cannelloni in two well-buttered rectangular Pyrex baking dishes (13½ x 8¾ inches), then pour a "strip" of *balsamella* along the length of each pasta roll. Place the baking dishes in the preheated oven for 20 minutes. Allow to cool for 10 minutes, then serve with a wide spatula.

Note: You can prepare this dish as much as 1 day in advance. Put the dish together up to and including pouring on the *balsamella*. Wrap the baking dishes in aluminum foil and place in refrigerator until needed.

Forty-five minutes before serving, remove the aluminum foil and place in an oven preheated to 375° for 30 minutes. Allow to stand for about 10 minutes and serve.

Lasagne al Forno
(Baked Lasagne, Northern Italian Style)

(SERVES 8 TO 10)

Lasagne are layers of pasta, made from the same squares of pasta as *cannelloni*, with layers of sauce or stuffing placed between the layers of pasta. The dish is then baked in the oven.

The northern Italian lasagne are made with light fresh pasta, yellow, green or both. The classical dish is an alternation of three sauce/stuffings: meat sauce, *balsamella*, and a mixture of coarsely grated mozzarella and grated Parmigiano. It is quite different from lasagne made with dried lasagne noodles and heavier sauces, and is usually a revelation of lightness to Americans.

The recipe as given here includes the three sauces and suggests the alternation of yellow and green pasta. (When made completely with green pasta it is called *alla ferrarese*, in the style of Ferrara.) The alternation of the two colors adds a further touch of distinction to the presentation, and of course to the taste.

The meat sauce uses the same ingredients as the filling for *cannelloni con carne* on page 178, but in different proportions.

For the meat sauce

    1 ounce dried *porcini* mushrooms
    1 large carrot
    1 large red onion
    1 celery rib
    6 to 8 sprigs Italian parsley
    1 clove garlic
    5 tablespoons olive oil
    ¼ pound ground pork
    ½ pound ground beef
    ½ chicken breast
    ½ cup dry red wine
    1 tablespoon tomato paste
    2 cups hot meat or chicken broth
    ¼ pound prosciutto or boiled ham
    Salt, freshly ground pepper, and freshly grated nutmeg to taste

For the balsamella

    6 tablespoons butter
    ½ cup all-purpose flour
    3 cups milk
    Salt and freshly grated nutmeg to taste

For the cheese stuffing

    8 ounces mozzarella
    1½ cups grated Parmigiano cheese

For the pasta

>   4 "extra-large" eggs
>   4 cups all-purpose flour, preferably unbleached
>   4 teaspoons olive or other vegetable oil
>   Pinch of salt

Make the meat sauce using the ingredients in the quantities listed, according to the directions given in *cannelloni con carne* on page 178, omitting the Parmigiano. Otherwise, follow the procedure exactly. When the meat sauce is cooked, cover the saucepan and be sure you allow it to cool for 1 to 1½ hours before using.

Make the *balsamella*, using the ingredients in the quantities listed, according to the directions on page 52. When finished, cover the saucepan and let rest until needed.

Make the cheese stuffing by coarsely grating the mozzarella into a bowl. Add the grated Parmigiano and mix together with a wooden spoon, then cover and place in the refrigerator until needed.

Make fresh pasta, using the ingredients in the quantities listed, according to the directions on page 133, then cut and precook it as for *cannelloni* (see page 180). Make the green pasta according to the directions on page 143. (If you prefer, use green pasta only, which would make the dish *lasagne alla ferrarese*.) An especially beautiful dish is made by alternating layers of yellow pasta with green pasta.

Preheat the oven to 375°.

To put the dish together, heavily butter a rectangular Pyrex baking dish (13½ x 8¾ inches). Spread 1 tablespoon of the meat sauce over bottom of dish (see photo 1); then fit in enough squares of precooked pasta to cover the bottom of the baking dish and to allow about 1 inch to hang out over the edges all around the dish; sprinkle with some of the cheese stuffing (see photos 2 and 3).

Add another layer of pasta, this time covering only the inside of the dish. Cover with *balsamella* (see photo 4). Keep alternating the three fillings (meat sauce, *balsamella*, and cheese), covering each layer of filling with a layer of pasta (see photos 5 and 6). The last layer should be either cheese or *balsamella*, covered with 3 squares of pasta.

Take the pasta ends hanging over the edges of the baking dish and fold them in, over the top layer of pasta (see photo 7); then place the dish in the preheated oven for about 25 minutes; top layer should be lightly golden brown and crisp. Remove the dish from the oven and allow to cool for 15 minutes before serving.

When ready to serve, cut the lasagne, in the baking dish, in half lengthwise, then cut each half into 4 or 5 servings. Transfer the servings to individual plates with a spatula.

Note: This dish may be prepared a day in advance. If so, after the dish is assembled but not baked, wrap in aluminum foil and place in the refrigerator. When needed, unwrap and place in a preheated 375° oven for 35 to 40 minutes.

Lasagne al forno: 1. Putting some of the sauce in the prepared baking dish.

2. Covering the bottom of the baking dish with squares of pasta.

3. Putting down a layer of cheese "stuffing."

4. Making a layer of *balsamella*.

5. Making a layer of meat sauce.

6. Adding a layer of pasta squares.

7. Ready for the oven.

Lasagne all' Anitra all' Aretina
(Lasagne with Duck, in the Style of Arezzo)

(SERVES 8 TO 10)

Lasagne with duck as made in the Tuscan town of Arezzo, home of
the frescoes by the great Piero della Francesca and an old Etruscan
town with its own tradition of cooking. Only an authentic version of
Peking duck matches the haughtiness with which the duck meat itself
is treated after it is used to make the dish. Here the essence is extracted
from the duck by cooking it for a long time in the sauce. And it is
only the sauce, and a little of the duck fat and its liver, which are then
used for the dish. As far as the Aretini are concerned, the duck itself
may be tossed out. (But if you have some close family or friends,
who won't tell on you, you can keep it for a snack, because as you can
imagine it is still quite good.)

The pasta squares prepared for the lasagne must be all yellow pasta.
The duck sauce is alternated with each layer of pasta until you reach
the last one. Then a substantial layer of *balsamella* is placed over the
last layer of pasta, and is then itself covered with a thin coating of
homemade bread crumbs. This is a rare dish, in all senses, and one you
will remember.

For the sauce

       1 duck (about 4 pounds), liver reserved
         Salt and freshly ground pepper to taste
       1 tablespoon butter
    ¼ cup olive oil
       1 large red onion
       2 large carrots
       1 large or 2 small cloves garlic
       5 or 6 sprigs Italian parsley
       4 medium-sized celery ribs
    ¼ pound boiled ham
       2 ounces prosciutto, *pancetta*, or salt pork
         Salt, freshly ground pepper, and freshly grated nutmeg
       4 large, ripe fresh or canned tomatoes (about 12 ounces)
       1 cup meat or chicken broth, approximately

For the pasta

       4 cups all-purpose flour, preferably unbleached
       4 "extra-large" eggs
       4 teaspoons olive oil
         Pinch of salt

For the balsamella

       3 tablespoons butter
    ¼ cup all-purpose flour
    1½ cups milk

For the filling and topping

       8 ounces Parmigiano cheese, freshly grated
    ⅓ cup bread crumbs, homemade, if possible, from Tuscan
         bread (see pages 45 and 32)

Start with the sauce.

Clean the duck very well, setting the liver aside, then sprinkle inside and out with salt and pepper. Put 1 tablespoon of butter inside the duck, then place it in a large oval aluminum or steel casserole, along with the olive oil. Put the casserole on a medium flame and sauté the duck until it is lightly golden brown on all sides (about 30 to 35 minutes). Meanwhile, chop the onion, carrots, garlic, parsley, celery, boiled ham, and prosciutto (or *pancetta* or salt pork), all very fine.

When duck is browned, add the chopped ingredients to the casserole and sauté gently for 25 to 30 minutes more, turning the duck over two or three times. Add salt, pepper, and nutmeg and mix thoroughly.

Pass the fresh or canned tomatoes through a food mill and add them to the casserole. Simmer slowly, covered, for 1 hour, adding a little broth if the sauce becomes too thick, then remove the duck from the sauce. (The cooked duck may be eaten separately, but it is no longer necessary for this dish.) Chop the reserved duck liver very fine and add it to the sauce. Taste for salt and pepper and let simmer for 5 or 6 minutes more.

Transfer the sauce to a bowl and allow it to cool for at least 1 hour. Remove half of the grease from the top.

Make fresh pasta, using the ingredients in the proportions listed, according to the directions on page 133, then cut and precook it as for *cannelloni* (see page 180).

Make the *balsamella*, using the ingredients in the quantities listed, according to the directions on page 52, then let cool, covered.

Preheat the oven to 400°.

Butter a rectangular Pyrex baking dish (13½ x 8¾ inches) generously, since in this type of lasagne no sauce is placed on the bottom, then fit in enough precooked pasta squares to cover the bottom and allow about ½ inch to hang out over the edges all the way around. Cover the layer of pasta generously with the duck sauce, then sprinkle abundant grated Parmigiano over the sauce.

Make another layer of pasta (with no overlap) and repeat the procedure with sauce and Parmigiano. Keep making layers (this amount of pasta should make about 6 or 7), putting sauce and Parmigiano over each layer except the last. Cover the last layer with the *balsamella* and cover the *balsamella* with the bread crumbs. Fold the pasta edges over the ends of the bread crumb layer.

Bake in the preheated oven for 20 to 25 minutes, then allow to cool for 15 minutes before serving.

Note: This dish may be prepared a day in advance. If so, after the dish is assembled but not baked, wrap it in aluminum foil and place in the refrigerator. When needed, unwrap and place in a preheated 400° oven for 35 to 40 minutes.

Rotolo di Pasta Ripieno
(Stuffed Pasta Roll)   (SERVES 8)

For the filling

   3 pounds fresh spinach or 4 packages (10 ounces each) frozen
 15 ounces ricotta
   2 whole eggs plus 2 egg yolks
1½ cups freshly grated Parmigiano cheese
     Salt, freshly ground pepper, and freshly grated nutmeg to taste

For the balsamella

  2 tablespoons butter
  8 teaspoons all-purpose flour
  1 cup milk

For the pasta

  2 cups of all-purpose flour, preferably unbleached
  2 "extra-large" eggs
  2 teaspoons olive or other vegetable oil
    Pinch of salt
  2 tablespoons olive oil

If using fresh spinach, remove the large stems and rinse the leaves very carefully. Put a large quantity of salted water in a stockpot and set on the heat. When the water reaches boiling point, put in the spinach and cook for about 15 minutes, then drain in a colander, cool under cold running water and squeeze very dry. For frozen spinach, follow package directions.

Chop the spinach fine, then put it in a large bowl, along with the ricotta, eggs, and egg yolks. Mix very well with a wooden spoon, then, when well combined, add 1 cup of the Parmigiano and salt, pepper, and nutmeg to taste. Stir until the mixture is homogeneous, then cover with aluminum foil and put in the refrigerator until needed.

Prepare the *balsamella*, using the ingredients in the quantities listed, according to the directions on page 52, then cover the saucepan and let stand until needed.

Make fresh pasta, using the ingredients in the proportions listed, according to the directions on page 133, then knead it and roll it out by hand as directed below.

After the flour has been absorbed, knead the dough for about 10 minutes more. (This parallels the early steps of passing it through the machine.)

After making sure that your pasta board and American-style ball-bearing rolling pin are absolutely dry and smooth, dust the board with the sifted remaining flour.

Note: The pasta for the *rotolo* should be a bit thicker than that rolled by machine. That paper-thin pasta is less than 1/32 of an inch. But the large single *rotolo* sheet must be a bit thicker in order to handle it as a single whole sheet that must be precooked and then stuffed and placed in the oven, all in one piece.

Gently roll out the ball of dough to a uniform thickness between 1/16 and 1/32 of an inch, in the following stages:

Holding the rolling pin firmly in both hands, quickly roll back and forth over the ball of dough until it is flat (see photo 1). At this point it will be longer than it is wide. Turn the dough 45 degrees and roll it until the width is about equal to the length.

Making pasta by hand: 1. The first stage in rolling out the pasta.

Sprinkle with flour and turn the pasta over (see photo 2). Repeat the rolling as described above. Sprinkle with flour and turn over again.

Repeat the procedure about 4 times on both sides. At that point, the sheet should be almost as thin as needed. (After the second rolling out,

2. Turning over the sheet of pasta.

it becomes more difficult to lift the sheet for turning. To make it easier, lightly wrap the sheet of pasta around the rolling pin. Then, hold the end of the sheet and reverse the direction of the rolling pin. The sheet of pasta should unroll on the reverse side; see photos 3 and 4).

3. Wrapping the sheet of pasta around a rolling pin.

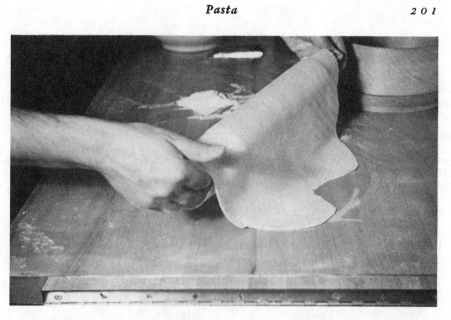

4. Unrolling the sheet of pasta on the other side.

In the final stage, pay careful attention to rolling the edges to the same thickness as the rest of the sheet. (With the American rolling pin it is not necessary to use any special procedure for the edges, such as rolling them around the pin.) Before stopping, be sure the sheet of pasta is of uniform thickness all over (see photo 5).

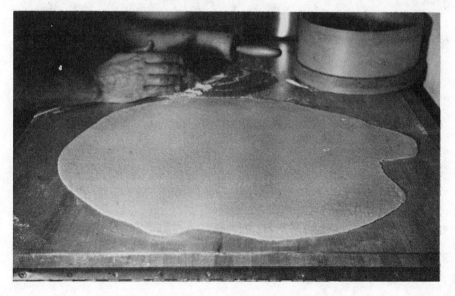

5. The completely rolled-out sheet of pasta.

Let the sheet of pasta dry on the board for 10 to 12 minutes, depending on the weather. Meanwhile, put a large quantity of salted water in a large spaghetti stockpot with insert. Set on the heat.

Prepare a very large bowl (or substitute a second stockpot) with about 20 cups of cold water and 2 tablespoons of oil.

When the water in the spaghetti pot reaches the boiling point, carefully place the entire sheet of pasta in insert of the pot, holding the ends with both hands and being sure not to fold it (see photo 6). Let the sheet of pasta cook for 30 seconds, than remove the insert with the sheet of pasta inside and quickly place it in the bowl of cold water and oil and let cool for 10 to 15 minutes (see photos 7 and 8).

Wet a cotton dishtowel with cold water and spread it out on a board. Remove the sheet of pasta from the cold water and spread it out flat on the towel. Let it dry for 15 to 20 minutes, then, with a jagged pastry wheel, trim edge of one side in a straight line. Cut the opposite side similarly to make a sheet uniformly 13 inches wide. (The other two sides need not be cut, and can be as long as the pasta board.)

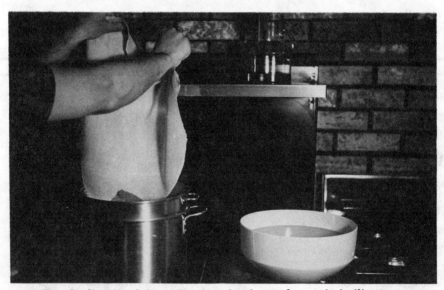

6. *Rotolo di pasta ripieno:* Putting the sheet of pasta in boiling water.

7. Removing the insert from the pot with the sheet of pasta inside.

8. Placing the insert containing the layer of pasta in the bowl of cold water and oil.

Transfer the filling from the bowl onto the sheet of pasta. Using a long spatula, spread out the filling to cover the sheet, leaving a ½-inch edge of pasta all around (see photo 9). Sprinkle the remaining ½ cup of grated Parmigiano over.

Preheat the oven to 375°.

To roll up *rotolo*, take one of the untrimmed sides in both hands and fold it over about 1 inch of the filling. Then pick up the edge of the towel in both hands. As you keep lifting the edge of the towel a little higher, the pasta sheet will continue to roll over until it is rolled up like a jelly roll (see photo 10); the other untrimmed end should now be on top.

Place the *rotolo* in a well-buttered rectangular Pyrex baking dish (13½ x 8¾ inches). Cover the top with a thin layer of the *balsamella* (see photo 11). Place in the preheated oven for about 25 minutes, until the top part is lightly golden brown. Remove from oven and allow to cool 10 to 15 minutes before serving.

To serve, slice through, like a jelly roll, so that all of the layering shows through.

Note: This dish may be prepared, up to and including the rolling and covering with *balsamella*, in advance. If you don't wish to cook the *rotolo* immediately, wrap the dish in aluminum foil and place it in the refrigerator. When you wish to serve it, unwrap it and bake it at 375° for 35 to 40 minutes.

9. The filling spread over the pasta sheet.

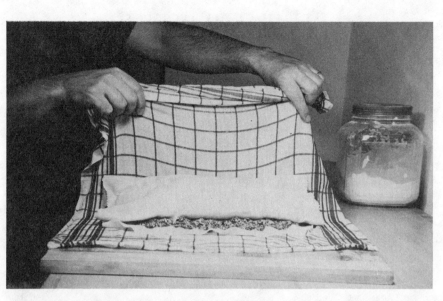

10. Roll up the *rotolo* by picking up the edge of the towel in both hands.

11. Ready for the oven.

TIMBALLO DISHES
(Pastry Drums)

THE *timballo,* or pastry drum, is used for elegant presentation of various dishes, consisting of chicken, meat, pasta, or dessert. The French who also use it, call it *timbale.* The type of pastry used depends on whether it holds a "salty" or "sweet" dish (two opposing categories that are used in Italian cooking, "salty" meaning anything not sweet). Both types of pastry may be eaten, but an elaborate pretense is made that they are for presentation only. Sooner or later, however, someone wants to taste the pastry and everyone joins in.

There are simpler dishes that are called by this name that have crisp bread crumb crusts, but they are not real *timballi,* being rather more like *pasticci.*

For sweet *timballi,* see pages 449–450.

Timballo di Piccioni
(Squab with Macaroni in a Pastry Drum)   (SERVES 6)

This "salty" *timballo* dish includes the recipe for the nonsweet timballo pastry and directions for making the drum.

For the pastry drum

  12 tablespoons (1½ sticks) butter
  6 cups all-purpose flour
  2 egg yolks
  1 cup cold water
  3 tablespoons olive oil
    Pinch of salt
  1 egg (for the glaze)
  2 pounds of any dried beans, the cheaper the better

For the balsamella

  3 tablespoons of butter
  ¼ cup all-purpose flour
  1½ cups of milk
    Salt to taste

For the squab-macaroni sauce

 2 squab
 2 small celery ribs
 1 small red onion
 2 small carrots
 3 tablespoons olive oil
 ½ cup dry red wine
 1 cup chicken or meat broth
  Salt, freshly ground pepper, and freshly grated nutmeg to taste
 ¾ pound dried elbow macaroni
 4 ounces boiled ham

For the topping

 6 tablespoons (¾ stick) butter (in small pats)
 2 tablespoons freshly grated Parmigiano cheese
  Freshly grated nutmeg to taste

Make the pastry drum first.

Melt the butter in a small saucepan and let cool for about 30 minutes.

Make a mound of the flour on a pasta board. Make a well in the flour and in it put the melted butter, egg yolks, water, olive oil, and salt. Mix the ingredients in the well together, then incorporate the flour from the inside rim of the well until only 3 or 4 tablespoons of flour remain. Knead for only about 1 minute, just enough to make the dough into a ball, then place the dough in a floured cotton dishtowel and let rest in a cool place for 4 hours. Do not refrigerate.

Preheat the oven to 375°.

Unwrap the dough and knead it for 1 minute on a board. Sprinkle board with remaining flour, then, using a rolling pin, roll it out to a thickness of less than ¼ inch.

Make the "lid" of the *timballo* by placing the removable bottom of a 10-inch springform on the sheet of dough and cutting around it with a pastry wheel (see photo 1).

Butter an aluminum pastry sheet and place the *timballo* "lid" on it. Using a fork, make several punctures, arranged in any design you please, in the lid so the dough will not rise while baking; with a 2-inch cookie cutter, cut out a circle of pastry and place it in the center of the *timballo* lid to make a little handle (see photo 2).

Making a *timballo:* 1. Cutting out the pastry lid.

2. Puncturing the lid with a fork, so it will stay flat while baking.

Beat the egg in small bowl. With a pastry brush, paint the top of the *timballo* lid with the egg, then place the baking sheet in the pre-heated oven for 30 to 35 minutes, until the lid is golden brown. Remove from the oven and let stand until the rest of the *timballo* is ready. While the lid is baking, cut out a circular bottom for the *timballo*. Place the removable springform bottom on the pastry sheet again, but this time cut the circle about ½ inch larger than the springform bottom itself.

Put the springform together and butter it generously. Carefully fit the bottom layer of the *timballo* into the springform; the ½-inch overlap of pastry should be curled up along the sides of the springform (see photo 3).

3. Fitting the bottom of the pastry drum into the springform.

To make sides for the *timballo*, cut long strips of dough about 1 inch wider than the height of the springform (about 3½ inches). Fit the strips inside the springform, along the sides; they should fit *inside* the overlapping pastry from the *timballo* bottom (see photo 4). (Try to use strips as long as possible so there will be relatively few separate pieces; also, when connecting the separate pieces, be sure to allow a ½-inch overlap at the point of connection.) With a knife, cut around the top of the springform to remove overlapping pastry. (Do not cut it too close; there must be enough pastry to cling

4. Forming the sides.

to the top so the sides do not fall. On the other hand, the pastry should not be pressed to the form or it could stick when baked.) Fit a sheet of aluminum foil loosely inside the *timballo*, then put all the dried beans in the form to keep the shape of the *timballo* while baking (see photo 5).

Place the springform in the preheated oven for 50 to 60 minutes, then remove and lift out the aluminum foil containing the beans (saving the beans to use again for the same purpose). Do not remove the *timballo* from the springform; set it aside to cool.

Make the *balsamella*, using the ingredients in the quantities listed, according to the directions on page 52. Cover the saucepan and let rest until needed.

To make the sauce with the squab and macaroni, wash the squab well, discarding the livers, and set aside.

Coarsely chop the celery, onion, and carrot, then heat the olive oil in a large flameproof casserole and sauté the chopped ingredients for 15 minutes, stirring with a wooden spoon, until golden brown. Add the squab and sauté very slowly for 15 to 20 minutes, turning them over two or three times. Add the wine, season with salt and pepper, and let the wine evaporate very slowly (about 10 minutes).

5. Filling the pastry drum with beans so the bottom will stay flat in baking.

Heat the broth in a saucepan. When the wine has evaporated, add the broth and simmer for about 25 minutes more.

Remove the casserole from the flame. Transfer the squab to a board, remove all the meat from the bones, and coarsely chop it. Coarsely chop the boiled ham as well, and set both meats aside.

Put a large quantity of salted water in a stockpot and set on the heat. When the water reaches the boiling point, put in the macaroni and let them cook for 11 or 12 minutes only. Meanwhile, put the casserole back on a low flame.

Drain the macaroni in a colander, then transfer it to the casserole. Mix thoroughly with a wooden spoon. Add the squab meat, chopped ham, and *balsamella*. Stir while the sauce simmers.

Meanwhile, preheat the oven to 400°.

Remove the casserole from the flame. Fill the *timballo*, still in the springform, with the contents of the casserole, top with the pats of butter, and sprinkle with Parmigiano and freshly grated nutmeg. Cover the *timballo* with its own lid and place in the preheated oven for 15 or 16 minutes, then remove from the oven and allow to cool for 5 minutes before opening the springform.

Transfer the *timballo* to a serving dish and put its lid in place for presentation. Serve immediately, lifting the lid, using serving spoons to dish out each portion.

Timballo di Tortellini
(Tortellini in a Pastry Drum) (SERVES 6)

In this dish, *tortellini alla panna* (see page 176) are served in a pastry drum, made and baked as described on page 206.

Make the *timballo* first, then, when it is out of the oven and cooling, make the *tortellini*. The *timballo* may even be made as much as a day in advance and kept, but while the *tortellini* can be made up several hours in advance (to be cooked a few minutes longer if they dry out a bit), they must be cooked and combined with the *alla panna* sauce only immediately before they are poured into the pastry drum and served.

Rice First Courses

---◆---

RISOTTI

RISOTTO is an entire category of first courses, based on a particular way of cooking rice, a way that as far as I know is unique to northern Italy. This area, and the Po Valley in particular, produces a wide-grained rice that has a pearly white spot on it. It is especially suitable for *risotti*, because when cooked in that manner it remains al dente, firm and chewy. In making *risotto* it is worth the trouble to find the Po Valley rice, the Arborio type, which is generally found in Italian markets in America as well as in "gourmet" shops, where you should ask for Italian Arborio rice.

The rice is not precooked in water at all, and no water as such is used in making the dish, so that nothing of the flavor of the rice is lost. The raw rice is sautéed first in hot butter and seasonings until it is very hot. Then hot broth is added, little by little, while stirring, and the hot rice quickly absorbs the broth. More broth is added only after that previously put in has been absorbed. It is important to stir without stopping so that the rice does not stick or burn. Only enough hot broth is used to get the rice to that point of al dente firmness and chewiness. Then the *risotto* is done.

There are many kinds of *risotti*. We include nine, the first being the simplest and most common treatment, *in bianco*—with the rice sautéed in butter and olive oil and a little onion, with Parmigiano added—the last being the marvelous *risotto di mare*, made with the broth of the *cacciucco* fish soup on page 257. The section ends with a rustic *timballo* of *risotto*, hearty enough for a second course.

Risotto in Bianco
(Risotto)   (S E R V E S 3)

>   1 small white onion
>   2 tablespoons olive oil
>   5 tablespoons butter
>   1 cup raw rice, preferably Italian Arborio
>   2 cups meat or chicken broth
>   ¼ cup freshly grated Parmigiano cheese
>   Salt and freshly ground pepper to taste

Chop the onion fine.

Put the olive oil and 4 tablespoons of the butter in a large casserole. Set on a medium flame, and when the butter is melted, add the chopped onion and sauté until lightly golden brown (3 to 5 minutes). Meanwhile, heat the broth to boiling in a saucepan.

Place the rice in the casserole with the onion and sauté for a minute, stirring constantly with a wooden spoon. Pour in ½ cup of the boiling broth and keep stirring very gently until the rice has incorporated all the broth (3 or 4 minutes). Season with salt and pepper. Then continue to add hot broth, little by little, stirring continuously until all the broth is absorbed and rice is cooked (about 16 minutes). The rice should be al dente, not overcooked, and no liquid should be left unabsorbed.

Remove the casserole from flame and add the remaining tablespoon of butter and all the grated Parmigiano. Mix thoroughly with a wooden spoon, then transfer the *risotto* into a tureen and serve.

Risotto in Bianco con Agliata
(Risotto with Garlic Sauce)   (S E R V E S 3)

This *risotto* is prepared using the same ingredients and procedure as for *risotto in bianco* (see above). However, omit the Parmigiano and pour some *agliata* sauce, the ancient white garlic sauce (see page 81), over each portion at serving time.

Risotto con Funghi
(Risotto with Dried Mushrooms)   (S E R V E S 6)

Imported dried *porcini* mushrooms (Folci brand, if available) are prepared by soaking them, then, when the risotto is prepared, red wine is added before the broth. The soaked mushrooms are added after the first cup of broth. Like all dishes depending on the flavor of the dried *porcini*, this is a memorable one.

> 2 ounces dried *porcini* mushrooms
> 1 medium-sized red onion
> 1 clove garlic
> 6 or 7 sprigs Italian parsley
> 6 tablespoons (¾ stick) butter
> 1 tablespoon olive oil
> ⅓ cup red wine
> 4 cups chicken or meat broth
> 2 cups raw rice, preferably Italian Arborio
> ¼ cup freshly grated Parmigiano cheese
> Salt and freshly ground pepper

Soak the dried mushrooms in a small bowl of lukewarm water for 20 minutes. Meanwhile, chop the onion, garlic, and parsley fine.

Put 4 tablespoons of the butter and the oil in a flameproof casserole and set on medium heat. When the butter is melted, add the chopped ingredients and sauté very gently until golden brown (about 12 to 14 minutes), then add the wine and let evaporate slowly (3 or 4 minutes). Meanwhile, heat the broth to boiling in a saucepan.

Place the rice in the casserole and sauté for 2 or 3 minutes, stirring constantly with a wooden spoon. Add 1 cup of boiling broth and keep stirring. Season with salt and pepper.

When the first cup of broth is completely incorporated (about 2 or 3 minutes), add the soaked, drained mushrooms and, still stirring constantly, add hot broth as needed until the rice is completely cooked (about 16 to 18 minutes). All the broth should be completely absorbed.

Remove the casserole from the flame. Add the remaining butter and Parmigiano and mix thoroughly, then transfer the *risotto* to a tureen and serve immediately.

Risotto con Carciofi
(Risotto with Artichokes)   (s e r v e s   3)

The artichoke pieces are soaked in lemon, then sautéed together with garlic, prosciutto, and *pancetta*. After the *risotto* has been made, the artichoke and its seasoning are mixed in and Parmigiano is added.

      1 large artichoke
      1 lemon
      1 clove garlic
      3 or 4 sprigs Italian parsley
      2 ounces prosciutto
      1 ounce *pancetta* or salt pork
      1 small red onion
      3 tablespoons olive oil
      4 tablespoons (½ stick) butter
      1 cup raw rice, preferably Italian Arborio
      2 cups meat or chicken broth
         Salt and freshly ground pepper to taste
         Freshly grated Parmigiano cheese

Place whole artichoke in cold water with a lemon half, for 20 minutes. Meanwhile, coarsely chop the garlic, parsley, prosciutto, and *pancetta* (or salt pork) on a board; chop the onion separately and set it aside.

After the artichoke has soaked, remove the outer leaves and inside "choke" (see page 394). Cut the remainder in small pieces, using both body and stem, and place, along with the chopped ingredients, in a saucepan with the olive oil. Sauté very gently for 10 to 12 minutes, then taste for salt and pepper and simmer for 10 minutes more, until the artichoke pieces are soft. Remove the saucepan from the stove, cover, and let stand until needed.

Heat 2 tablespoons of the butter in a flameproof casserole. When the butter is completely melted, add the chopped onion and sauté slowly, stirring with a wooden spoon, until the onion is golden brown (about 12 minutes). Meanwhile, in another saucepan, heat the broth to boiling.

When the onion is golden brown, add the rice and stir for 1 minute. Pour in 1 cup of boiling broth, and keep stirring. Continue mixing and adding hot broth as needed until the rice is completely cooked (about 18 minutes). All the broth should be completely absorbed.

Remove the saucepan from the stove, add the artichoke pieces and remaining butter, and mix very well. Transfer the *risotto* to a serving dish, sprinkle with the Parmigiano, and serve immediately.

Risotto alla Toscana
(Risotto with Meat Sauce)   (S E R V E S 3)

A meat sauce is prepared with chopped beef, coarsely chopped chicken livers, red wine, a little tomato, and *odori* (aromatic vegetables). After the rice is sautéed, a little sauce is stirred in before the broth is added. After the *risotto* is cooked, the rest of the sauce is served with it, to be added to the individual servings.

For the sauce

- ½ small red onion
- 1 small celery rib
- 1 small clove garlic
- 1 carrot
- 5 or 6 sprigs Italian parsley
- 2 tablespoons butter
- ¼ cup olive oil
- ½ pound ground beef
- ½ cup dry red wine
- 1 cup canned tomatoes
- 2 or 3 chicken livers
- Salt and freshly ground pepper to taste

For the risotto

- ½ small red onion
- 4 tablespoons (½ stick) butter
- 2 tablespoons olive oil
- 1 cup raw rice, preferably Italian Arborio
- 2 cups chicken or meat broth
- ¼ cup fresh grated Parmigiano cheese

Make the sauce first.
Finely chop the onion, celery, garlic, carrot, and parsley.
Heat the butter and oil in a saucepan, and when the butter is melted

and the oil hot, put in the chopped *odori* and sauté until lightly golden brown (about 15 minutes), stirring constantly with a wooden spoon. Add the ground meat and sauté for 10 minutes more, then season with salt and pepper.

Add the wine and let evaporate slowly (about 9 or 10 minutes), then pass the tomatoes through a food mill into the saucepan and simmer for 25 minutes more.

Coarsely chop the chicken livers and place in the saucepan. Cook for 5 minutes, then remove the saucepan from the flame and let rest while you start the *risotto*.

Chop the onion coarsely.

Put the butter and oil in a flameproof casserole and set on medium heat.

When the butter is melted, add the chopped onion and sauté very gently until golden brown (about 12 minutes). Meanwhile, heat the broth to boiling in a saucepan.

Add the rice to the casserole and sauté for 4 minutes, stirring constantly, then add ¼ cup of sauce to the casserole and stir for 2 minutes more. Add 1 cup of boiling broth, stirring with a wooden spoon. Keep stirring and adding broth as needed; in about 18 minutes all the broth should be absorbed and the rice properly cooked al dente.

Remove the casserole from the stove and transfer the *risotto* to a serving dish. Place the remaining sauce all around the rice in a ring, then sprinkle with the Parmigiano and serve immediately.

Risotto con Salsicce
(Risotto with Sausage)   (SERVES 3)

    1 sweet sausage (about 6 ounces)
    1 medium-sized red onion
    6 tablespoons (¾ stick) butter
    2 tablespoons olive oil
    1 cup raw rice, preferably Italian Arborio
    2 cups meat or chicken broth
    ¼ cup freshly grated Parmigiano cheese
       Salt and freshly ground pepper to taste

Remove the skin from the sausage and cut it into small pieces; coarsely chop the onion.

Heat 4 tablespoons butter and olive oil in a flameproof casserole, then add the sausage pieces and chopped onion and sauté very gently until golden brown, stirring every so often. Meanwhile, heat the broth to boiling in a saucepan.

When the contents of the casserole are golden brown, add the rice and stir constantly for 4 or 5 minutes. Add 1 cup of boiling broth, still stirring constantly. Keep stirring for about 17 minutes, adding broth as needed; by then the rice should be al dente and all the broth absorbed. Taste for salt and pepper.

Remove the casserole from the heat, add the remaining butter and grated Parmigiano, and mix thoroughly. Serve immediately.

Risotto con Gamberetti in Bianco
(Risotto with Shrimp)   (S E R V E S 3)

The shrimps are sautéed in a saucepan with the olive oil and white wine. Then the *risotto* is prepared and 5 minutes before it is finished cooking, the shrimp are added to the rice. Fish broth may be used instead of meat or chicken broth in this dish, but it is not essential.

         1 large clove garlic
        10 sprigs Italian parsley
        ½ pound small shrimp
         5 tablespoons olive oil
            Salt and freshly ground black pepper to taste
        ½ cup dry white wine
        ½ small white onion
         3 tablespoons butter
         1 cup raw rice, preferably Italian Arborio
      1 ½ cups of fish, meat, or chicken broth, approximately

Chop the garlic fine, and chop the parsley coarsely; shell the shrimp and place them in a bowl of salted water.

Heat 3 tablespoons of the olive oil in a saucepan, and when it is warm, add the garlic and parsley and sauté very lightly for about 4 minutes. Add the shrimp, season with salt and pepper, and stir thoroughly with a wooden spoon. Sauté for 2 or 3 minutes longer.

Pour the wine into the saucepan and let it evaporate very slowly (about 12 minutes), then remove the saucepan from the heat and transfer the shrimp to a small bowl, leaving the liquid in the saucepan. Add about 1½ cups of broth to the saucepan; there should now be about 2 cups of liquid. Set aside while you start the *risotto*.

Chop the onion fine.

Heat an additional 2 tablespoons of butter and the remaining olive oil in a flameproof casserole. When the butter is melted, add the chopped onion and sauté very gently until golden brown (about 12 minutes). Meanwhile, heat the liquid in the saucepan.

When onion is golden brown, add the rice and stir constantly for about 4 minutes with a wooden spoon. Add ½ cup of boiling broth to the casserole and keep stirring very gently until the rice has incorporated all the broth (3 or 4 minutes). Taste for salt and pepper, then continue to add broth, little by little, stirring continuously, until all the broth is absorbed and the rice is al dente (about 16 minutes).

Just 5 minutes before the rice is completely cooked, add the shrimp to the casserole. Remove the casserole from the flame, add the remaining butter, and mix thoroughly. Transfer the *risotto* to a serving dish and serve immediately.

Risotto alla Marinara
(Risotto with Fish Broth)   (SERVES 3)

Fish broth is essential to this dish. The procedure is basically the same as for *in bianco* (see page 214), but after the onions are sautéed, a little tomato paste is mixed in before the raw rice is added. This is a good first course for a fish dinner.

    2 cups broth left over from poaching a fish
    1 small white onion
    2 tablespoons olive oil
    2 tablespoons butter
    2 tablespoons tomato paste
    1 cup raw rice, preferably Italian Arborio
      Salt and freshly ground pepper to taste

Strain the poaching broth; chop the onion fine.

Heat the oil and 1 tablespoon of the butter in a flameproof casserole. When the butter is melted, add the chopped onion and sauté gently until lightly golden brown. Meanwhile, heat the broth to boiling in a saucepan.

Add the tomato paste to the casserole and stir thoroughly until it is completely incorporated. Add the rice and sauté for a minute, stirring constantly with wooden spoon, then pour in ½ cup of the boiling broth and keep stirring very gently until the rice has absorbed all the broth (about 3 minutes). Taste for salt and pepper, then continue to add hot broth, little by little, stirring continuously until all the broth is absorbed and the rice is al dente (about 16 minutes).

Remove the casserole from the flame, add the remaining butter, and mix thoroughly. Transfer the *risotto* to a serving dish and serve immediately.

Risotto di Mare
(Risotto with Cacciucco Broth)   (SERVES 3)

It is difficult to decide which is more delicious, the *cacciucco* itself or the *risotto* made with its broth. It is good to save some little morsels of fish and shellfish from the *cacciucco* along with the broth, to mix in at the last moment in order to make an even more interesting texture.

    1 small red onion
    2 tablespoons olive oil
    2 tablespoons butter
    2 cups broth left over from *cacciucco* (see page 257)
    1 cup raw rice, preferably Italian Arborio
      Salt and freshly ground pepper to taste

Chop the onion fine. Heat the olive oil and 1 tablespoon of the butter in a flameproof casserole. When the butter is melted, add the chopped onion and sauté gently until lightly golden brown. Meanwhile, heat the broth to boiling in a saucepan.

Add the rice to the casserole with the onion and sauté for 1 minute, stirring continuously with a wooden spoon. Pour in ½ cup of the boiling broth and keep stirring very gently until the rice has incorporated all the broth (3 or 4 minutes). Taste for salt and pepper (generally no salt or pepper are necessary because the broth left over from *cacciucco* is very spicy), then continue to add hot broth, little by little, stirring continuously until all the broth is absorbed and the rice is al dente (about 16 minutes).

Remove the casserole from flame, add the remaining butter, and mix thoroughly with a wooden spoon. Transfer the *risotto* to a serving dish. Place any pieces of fish left over from *cacciucco* over the *risotto* and serve immediately.

Timballo di Riso (Bomba con Salsicce)
(Rice Timballo Stuffed with Sausages)   (S E R V E S   6)

Molded to the shape of a drum, this rustic dish from the Apennine Mountains is called a *timballo*, though the outside of the drum is not of pastry. It is, rather, shaped in the mold from half-cooked rice. The stuffing is of sausage pieces, dried wild mushrooms, and seasoning. The whole is then covered with homemade bread crumbs, and when baked acquires a crisp outer crust. A gastronomic treat that is also useful as a hearty second dish, it is served hot.

For the crust

    3 cups raw rice, preferably Italian Arborio
       Coarse salt
    3 whole eggs
   .3 tablespoons freshly grated Parmigiano cheese
       Salt and freshly ground pepper to taste
       Pinch of freshly grated nutmeg
   ½ cup bread crumbs, preferably homemade (see page 45)

For the filling

    2 ounces dried *porcini* mushrooms
    1 medium-sized red onion
    2 tablespoons olive oil
    1 teaspoon butter
    6 sweet sausages
    6 medium-size ripe fresh or canned tomatoes
    1 cup meat or chicken broth
       Salt and freshly ground pepper to taste

Prepare the crust first.

Put the rice in a saucepan with a large quantity of cold water and a pinch of coarse salt. Set the saucepan on medium heat and stir the rice with a wooden spoon until the water reaches the boiling point. When the rice is half cooked (about 10 to 12 minutes), remove the saucepan from the heat and drain the rice. Run cold water over it to cool it completely, then drain again and put it in a bowl. Add the eggs, Parmigiano, salt, pepper, and nutmeg and stir well until completely combined. Set aside while you prepare the filling.

Soak the dried mushrooms in lukewarm water for 20 minutes. Meanwhile, chop the onion coarsely. Heat the olive oil and the butter in a saucepan. When they are hot, add the chopped onion and sauté gently for 10 to 12 minutes.

Remove the skin from the sausages and cut them into 5 or 6 pieces each. When the onion is golden brown, add the sausage pieces and sauté for 10 to 15 minutes, then add the tomatoes and simmer very slowly for 15 minutes more. Add the broth, taste for salt and pepper, and let cook slowly, until the broth has completely evaporated and the mixture is thick and homogeneous (about 30 minutes).

Add the soaked mushrooms and 3 or 4 tablespoons of the water in which the mushrooms soaked. Let cook until the water has evaporated, then remove the saucepan from the flame and transfer the filling mixture to another bowl to cool (about 30 minutes).

When cool, transfer 2 or 3 tablespoons of liquid from the filling mixture to the bowl with the rice.

When you are ready to assemble the *timballo*, preheat the oven to 400°; butter well the bottom and sides of a 10-inch round Pyrex casserole and sprinkle it with some of the bread crumbs.

Stir the rice very well once more and cover the bottom and sides of the prepared mold with three-quarters of it. Pour the filling mixture sauce into the center, then make a layer on top with the rest of the rice. Sprinkle the remaining bread crumbs over, then place the casserole in the preheated oven and bake for 25 to 30 minutes.

Remove from the oven and let cool for 15 minutes, then unmold on a serving dish. The rice should form a uniform outer crust, in one piece, to resemble a *timballo*. Serve hot, slicing it like a cake.

Miscellaneous First Courses

Gnocchi di Farina Gialla
(Corn Meal Gnocchi)   (SERVES 6 TO 8)

The corn meal is prepared as though you were going to make polenta. It is then put in individual terra-cotta bowls in layers, alternating with layers of *sugo di carne* (meat sauce), with Parmigiano sprinkled on each layer of sauce. The polenta is not cut into discs nor into layers, but is ladled into the bowls while still hot. The dish is allowed to rest after all the layers are made, to permit the ingredients to amalgamate into a single delicious whole.

> *Sugo di carne* (page 72)

For the gnocchi

- ¾ pound corn meal
- 8 cups cold water
- 2 teaspoons salt

- 1 cup freshly grated Parmigiano cheese

Make the sauce, then set aside, covered, until needed. Prepare the gnocchi, with the quantities listed above, according to the directions on page 367, up to and including the cooking and stirring for 35 minutes. (More water is added to the corn meal in this recipe than in that for polenta as the cooked *farina gialla* should be less thick for gnocchi than for polenta.) Keep it on a low flame while you prepare 6 or 8 small terra-cotta bowls with handles.

Put a tablespoon of meat sauce in each individual bowl, then make a layer of gnocchi, using about ¼ cup, or half a ladleful, in each bowl. Sprinkle with some more sauce and some of the grated Parmigiano.

Make another layer of gnocchi and again add sauce and Parmigiano. Continue this alternation of layers until you have used everything up. The top layer should be meat sauce and Parmigiano. Cover each terra-cotta bowl with its lid, if it has one, or aluminum foil and let rest for about 15 minutes. Then serve. (If you used aluminum foil to cover the bowls, remove before serving.)

Pomodori Ripieni
(Stuffed Tomatoes)   (SERVES 6)

The tomatoes are stuffed and baked with a very light touch. The stuffing is basically tomato itself, with chopped garlic and basil, and just a little rice. The tomatoes are covered with their own "lids" and baked in a dish containing tomato-flavored liquid, olive oil, and more basil. Served warm or cold, they make a good opener or addition to a buffet, and they have a refreshing taste in which everything contributes to bring out the flavor of the tomato itself.

    6 large, ripe tomatoes and 1 small, very ripe tomato
   10 or 11 large leaves basil
    1 large clove garlic
    6 heaping tablespoons raw rice, preferably Italian Arborio
    5 tablespoons olive oil
    1 cup water
    2 tablespoons tomato paste
       Salt and freshly ground pepper to taste

Soak all the tomatoes in cold water for 10 minutes, then drain and slice off the tops of the 6 large tomatoes. Put the tops aside to be used later. Using a melon-ball cutter, empty the seeds and juice of the tomatoes into a large bowl without breaking up the inside pulp. Put the tomatoes into a rectangular Pyrex baking dish (13½ x 8¾ inches); strain the juice into another bowl and save seeds in a strainer.

Pass the small tomato through a food mill into the bowl containing the juice of other tomatoes. Chop the garlic and 6 of the basil leaves fine and add them to the bowl, then put in the rice and season with salt and pepper.

Fill each tomato two-thirds full with the stuffing mixture. Sprinkle ½ teaspoon of the olive oil on top of the stuffing in each tomato, then cover each with its top.

Preheat the oven to 375°.

Pass the 1 cup of water through the seeds left in strainer into a bowl. Then mix in the tomato paste, remaining 2 tablespoons olive oil, salt, pepper, and the remaining 4 or 5 basil leaves. Pour into the baking dish with tomatoes. If the liquid does not reach one-third the height of the tomatoes, add enough water to do so.

Bake in the preheated oven for about 40 minutes, then remove the dish from the oven and transfer the tomatoes very carefully to a serving dish. Allow to cool 10 to 15 minutes before serving; you may also serve the tomatoes cold.

Gnocchi di Pesce
(Fish Gnocchi)   (SERVES 6)

A recipe of Jarro, the famous Florentine gastronome of the turn of the century. This was the period when Florence had emerged from its life as the charming capital of the Grand Duchy of Tuscany to become briefly the capital, and then the artistic and intellectual center of the kingdom of Italy. The cafés of the Piazza Vittorio Emanuele* were ablaze with the great literary and artistic groups of their day. The international social set, including many of the reigning monarchs, spent the winter season in Rome and summered in their villas in the hills outside of Florence, Henry James's American social set joining in. Bernard Berenson in his villa entertained everyone from Bertrand Russell to the King of Sweden and, in his last days, Harry Truman. This was the period when Jarro was one of the arbiters of Florentine gastronomy.

The chopped raw fish, all light in flavor, are held together with egg yolks and cheese and flavored with other ingredients. They are baked, much in the manner of *gnocchi di semolino*. A delicious and unusual first dish to begin a fish dinner.

* Now Piazza della Repubblica.

For the fish mixture

> 2 pounds of raw fish, a combination of 2 or more light-flavored fleshy fish (pike, striped bass, mullet, red snapper, whiting)
> 2 whole eggs, separated, plus 2 egg yolks
> 1 cup milk
> ½ cup all-purpose flour
> 2 tablespoons butter
>   Salt and freshly ground pepper to taste
> 4 tablespoons freshly grated Parmigiano cheese
>   Freshly grated nutmeg to taste
>
> 1 tablespoon olive oil
> 2 tablespoons butter
> 3 tablespoons Parmigiano cheese

Remove bones, skin, and heads from all the fish, so that only filleted meat remains. Chop the fish very fine, until homogenous and soft. Put into a large bowl.

Beat the egg whites in a bowl, preferably copper, until stiff. Add the egg yolks to the fish, and when they are thoroughly incorporated, fold in the beaten egg whites.

Put the fish mixture into a saucepan on a low flame and begin stirring gently with a wooden spoon. When the fish mixture begins to bubble, add the milk and then the flour, little by little. When the flour is all incorporated and the mixture is smooth, add 4 tablespoons of the butter, salt, and pepper. Keep stirring for 10 to 12 minutes more, to allow the flour to cook.

Remove from the heat and add 4 tablespoons of the Parmigiano and the nutmeg. Season with additional salt and pepper.

Preheat the oven to 375°.

Using 1 tablespoon of oil, oil a marble, formica, or aluminum foil surface. Place the contents of the pan upon the oiled surface. With a wet spatula, spread out uniformly to a thickness of ½ inch. Let rest until cool, then cut into round shapes with a cookie cutter.

With the remaining butter, butter a rectangular Pyrex baking dish (13½ x 8¾ inches). Place the rounds in it, in a single layer, then place in the preheated oven for 15 to 17 minutes.

Remove from the oven, sprinkle with the remaining 3 tablespoons Parmigiano, and serve hot.

Ravioli Nudi di Pesce
(Naked Fish Ravioli)	(SERVES 6)

The chopped fish is held together like *ravioli nudi* (see below), with egg yolks and cheese, but also with a little flour. They are poached like their namesake. Another good fish first course.

    1 egg yolk
    2 heaping tablespoons all-purpose flour
    6 tablespoons freshly grated Parmigiano cheese
    2 tablespoons butter

Prepare and cook the fish mixture as described on page 226, up to and including the addition of the Parmigiano, salt, and pepper.

Place the contents of the saucepan in a bowl and let rest until cool. Then add the egg yolk, 2 tablespoons more of Parmigiano, and 2 heaping tablespoons of flour. Mix very well until all these ingredients are incorporated, then make little balls 1 inch in diameter and coat them very gently with additional flour.

Meanwhile, put a stockpot containing abundant salted water on the heat; melt the butter in another saucepan and pour over the bottom of a serving dish.

When the water boils, drop in the little fish balls, one at a time. In about 30 seconds they will rise to the surface of the water; let them cook for 1 minute more and then, with a slotted spoon, remove them from the water and place in the buttered serving dish. Sprinkle the remaining 4 tablespoons Parmigiano over them and serve hot.

Ravioli Nudi
(Naked Ravioli or Ravioli alla Fiorentina)	(SERVES 8)

Ravioli nudi, one of the prides of the city on the Arno, are never called "spinach gnocchi" there—for that is another dish made in other places. The recipe is a simple, classic one, with enough egg yolks and cheese to bind together the chopped spinach and ricotta mixture. If properly done, it should not be necessary to add flour to hold the mixture together; this makes the "ravioli" too tough. Though the standards for making this dish are very high in its native city, or perhaps because of it, you will never find the dish on the menu of a restaurant. Perhaps because of the confusion with the above-mentioned gnocchi, one sees some very strange recipes for this dish in cookbooks.

The *nudi* part of the name refers to the fact that the filling is not covered with pasta.

    3   pounds fresh spinach or 4 packages frozen
   15   ounces ricotta
    5   egg yolks
    3   cups freshly grated Parmigiano cheese
        Salt and freshly ground pepper to taste
   ½   teaspoon freshly grated nutmeg
    2   cups all-purpose flour
    8   tablespoons (1 stick) butter

Using fresh spinach, rinse it very well and cut off the large stems. Place a stockpot containing a large quantity of salted water on the heat. When the water boils, add the spinach and cook for about 15 minutes, then drain and cool under cold running water. Squeeze very dry. For frozen spinach, follow package directions for cooking.

Chop the spinach very fine, then place in a bowl, along with the ricotta, egg yolks, 2 cups of the Parmigiano, salt, pepper, and nutmeg. Mix together with a wooden spoon until thoroughly combined. Refill the stockpot with a large quantity of salted water and set on the heat.

While the water is heating, place a sheet of aluminum foil on the table and spread the flour over. Take 1 tablespoon of the mixture from the bowl and roll it on the floured foil surface into a little ball. Be sure the ball is uniformly compact, with no empty spaces inside; the outside should be uniformly floured.

When the water is boiling, drop this first ball in, to test it. It should retain its shape and rise to the top, cooked, after a minute or two. (If it falls apart, you have allowed too much liquid to remain in the spinach. To save the dish, you can add 2 tablespoons of flour to the mixture. However, this is a compromise and should not be done regularly; even that little flour will make the taste inauthentic.) After testing, as described above, continue to make ravioli, rolling them in flour, until all the contents of the bowl have been used up.

Melt the butter and pour into a serving dish; place the serving dish close to the stockpot.

Drop the ravioli into the boiling water, 5 or 6 at a time, and as they rise to the surface, remove them with a strainer-skimmer, transferring them directly onto the serving dish. They should be placed in one layer, not one on top of another.

When all the ravioli are on the serving dish, sprinkle with the remaining Parmigiano and serve immediately.

Pappa al Pomodoro
(Bread Soup)   (SERVES 4)

Perhaps another descendant of the ancient Roman *puls*, but made with bread instead of polenta. Though similar dishes exist in other parts of Italy, it is the Florentine version that is the most famous and that is considered one of the most characteristic dishes of that town, for simple home dinners or in *trattorie*. As with *panzanella* (see page 92), it is most important that the bread not be soggy. It should be sufficiently old, several days at least, rather hard, and if possible dark rather than light. The quantities of liquid given are just enough to produce the right texture. The broth, tomatoes, olive oil, basil, and garlic provide the marvelous flavor.

Another dish that makes it even more worthwhile to take the trouble to make the Tuscan bread.

> 3 large cloves garlic
> ½ cup olive oil
>   Pinch of dried hot pepper flakes
> 1 pound very ripe tomatoes, fresh or canned
> 1 pound Tuscan bread, white (see page 32) or dark (see page 37), several days old
> 3 cups hot chicken or meat broth
>   Salt and freshly ground black pepper
> 4 to 5 leaves basil, fresh or under salt (see page 14)

Chop the garlic coarsely, then place in a stockpot, preferably terracotta, along with ¼ cup of the olive oil and the pepper flakes. Sauté very gently for 10 to 12 minutes.

Cut the tomatoes into 3 or 4 pieces, remove the seeds, and add them to the pot. Simmer for 15 minutes.

Cut the bread into small pieces and add to the pot, along with the broth, salt, black pepper, and whole basil leaves. Stir very well and simmer for 15 minutes longer, then remove from the heat, cover, and let rest for 1 to 2 hours.

When ready to serve, stir very well and place in individual soup bowls. At the table, sprinkle 1 tablespoon of the remaining olive oil on each serving, and grind some fresh black pepper into each bowl.

Note: Though considered a soup, the consistency of *pappa* is not liquid at all. It may be eaten lukewarm or cold, or reheated and hot the following day. Do not add any grated cheese.

Gnocchi di Semolino
(Semolina Gnocchi)   (S E R V E S 4)

Gnocchi of semolina or *alla romana*. First the milk is boiled and some butter and flavorings added. The semolina flour must be added slowly and carefully in a steady stream so that lumps do not form, and it must be stirred without stopping while cooking for the same reason.

When the semolina is cooked and cooled, the egg yolks and Parmigiano are added. The mixture is spread out, cut into discs and arranged in one or more layers for baking. (Occasionally, with the same proportions, the cooled mixture becomes too soft and does not hold its shape. If this happens, reduce the amount of butter a little the next time.)

5 cups milk
8 tablespoons butter
  Salt, freshly ground pepper, and freshly grated nutmeg to taste
1¼ cups semolina flour
4 egg yolks
1¾ cups freshly grated Parmigiano cheese, lightly packed

Reserve 2 tablespoons of milk; pour the rest into a flameproof casserole. Heat the milk. The moment before it boils, add 4 tablespoons of the butter and a pinch each of salt, pepper, and nutmeg. Then add the semolina, pouring in a continuous slow stream, at the same time mixing steadily with a wooden spoon. As soon as all the semolina is in the casserole, quickly raise the flame so the contents will reach the boiling point almost immediately. (The longer it takes to reach the boiling point, the more possibility there is for lumps to form.) Lower the flame and allow the mixture to boil slowly for 15 to 20 minutes, stirring continuously, until smooth and homogenous. Remove from the heat and let cool for 10 minutes.

Dilute the egg yolks with the 2 tablespoons cold milk, mixing with a wooden spoon. Add this to the semolina mixture, then add half the Parmigiano. Continue to stir, being careful to keep the mixture from sticking to the bottom and sides of the pan.

Oil a marble or formica surface or aluminum foil. Pour the semolina mixture over this surface, and spread it out with a cold spatula to make a sheet about ⅓ inch thick. Let the sheet rest for 1½ hours.

Meanwhile, melt the remaining butter in a saucepan; preheat the oven to 400°.

Cut the semolina mixture into discs with a 2-inch round cookie cutter. Make a layer of semolina discs in a buttered rectangular Pyrex baking dish (13½ x 8¾ inches). Cover this layer with some of the melted butter and some of the remaining grated Parmigiano. Make additional layers of semolina discs, covering each layer with butter and Parmigiano until you get to the final semolina layer. Leave this layer without butter or cheese. (A top layer of cheese would brown and become bitter in taste.)

Place the baking dish in the preheated oven. When the top is golden brown (25 to 30 minutes), remove from the oven. Sprinkle with Parmigiano and serve hot.

Topini di Patate
(Potato Gnocchi)   (SERVES 6)

Topini di patate are the Florentine counterpart of gnocchi, but are made into the shape of "little mice." The potatoes must be steamed, not boiled, both to retain all their flavor and to absorb as little moisture as possible. They are passed through a ricer and mixed with flour to make a dough. The knack of pulling the dough pieces across a curved grater to acquire the proper shape is acquired with just a little practice in making the right hand movement.

Topini are versatile, and may be served with a variety of sauces—fresh tomato, butter and cheese, *pesto*.

    1 pound boiling potatoes
1¾ cup all-purpose flour

Salt
2 tablespoons butter

Steam (do not boil) the potatoes until cooked but firm, then peel.

Spread the flour on a pasta board. Pass the potatoes through a potato ricer onto the flour. Sprinkle with a pinch of salt, then start incorporating the flour, little by little, into the potatoes until the dough is homogeneous and firm. Knead gently for 5 or 6 minutes.

Cut the dough into several pieces and roll each piece into a long thin roll about ½ inch in diameter. Cut each roll into 1-inch pieces.

Use the dull inside of a convex hand cheese grater. Hold a 1-inch piece of dough at the top of the grater with the middle fingers of one hand. Lightly draw the piece around in a motion that makes the cursive letter "c" (see photo). The resultant shape should be the quasi-shells which the Florentines think resemble "little mice," and which they prefer to more usual gnocchi. Continue until all the dough is shaped.

Place a stockpot containing a large quantity of salted water on the heat. While the water is heating, melt the butter in a small saucepan and pour it onto a serving dish. Place the serving dish next to the stockpot.

Topini di patate: Shaping the *topini.*

When the water is boiling, raise the flame and quickly drop all the *topini*, one by one, into the stockpot.

Lightly stir the water with a wooden spoon, to keep the *topini* from sticking. After a few seconds, the *topini* will come to the surface of the water; let them cook for 1 minute more. With a strainer-skimmer, remove the *topini* to the serving dish. Serve hot, with the sauce of your choice.

Torta Pasqualina
(Easter Torta)   (SERVES 12)

One of the specialties of the fine Genoese cooking. The *torta pasqualina* reveals in its very name that it is primarily a dish for the Easter holiday. The pastry is the Genoese pastry without eggs or yeast, and with a minimum of oil; it is almost a severe flour and water dough. It must be rolled very, very thin, and about ten layers of it are used, five on the bottom and five on top. The manifold thin layers separated by air are a little related to strudel, but this pastry is even more difficult to handle because it has very little shortening in it; the layers do not quite become paper thin. There are two layers of stuffing, one of sautéed artichokes with dried wild mushrooms and another with ricotta and Parmigiano, with whole eggs broken into it.

One of the great specialties of northern Italian cooking, at one time no Easter feast would have been conceivable without its *torta pasqualina*. If you are fond of artichokes, mushrooms, and fine pastry, this makes a spectacular antipasto for an elegant dinner. It is served cold.

Though in Italy, a large one is often eaten over a period of several days, in the course of which the pastry loses its crispness, I believe Americans would prefer to eat it fresh, while the pastry is still crisp. It may be followed by a lamb dish and fruit dessert.

For the dough
>   5 cups all-purpose flour
>   2 cups very cold water
>   1 tablespoon olive oil
>   Pinch of salt

For the artichoke stuffing
>   2 ounces dried *porcini* mushrooms
>   5 medium-sized artichokes

　　　Juice of 2 lemons
　2　medium-sized onions
　2　cloves garlic
10　sprigs Italian parsley, approximately
¼　cup olive oil
　2　tablespoons butter
　　　Salt and freshly ground pepper to taste
½　cup meat or chicken broth, approximately

For the ricotta stuffing

15　ounces ricotta
　3　eggs
¼　cup freshly grated Parmigiano cheese
　1　tablespoon all-purpose flour
　　　Salt, freshly ground pepper, and freshly grated nutmeg to taste
½　cup olive oil, approximately
　7　or 8 pats butter
　4　eggs

Make the dough first.

Arrange the flour in a mound on a pasta board and make a well in the center. Put the cold water, olive oil and salt in the well. Little by little, mix the flour from the inside rim of the well into the liquid; absorb as much flour as possible. When a solid dough is formed, start kneading, always using a folding motion. Knead the dough for about 25 minutes.

Dampen a cotton dishtowel with cold water. Place the dough in the damp towel and let rest for 2 hours in a cool place (do not refrigerate) while you make the stuffings.

For the artichoke stuffing, soak the mushrooms in a small bowl of lukewarm water for 20 minutes.

Meanwhile, clean the artichokes (see page 394) and cut them into ½-inch pieces. Put the artichoke pieces into a bowl of cold water with the lemon juice and let stand until needed.

Coarsely chop the onions, garlic, and parsley.

Heat the olive oil and butter in a large flameproof casserole, terracotta if possible, and when the melted butter is hot, add the chopped ingredients and sauté very gently for about 15 minutes, until lightly golden brown. Add the artichoke pieces, mix thoroughly, and sauté for 15 minutes more.

Drain and squeeze the mushrooms dry, then add to the casserole. Season with salt and pepper and let cook very slowly until artichokes are done (about 25 minutes), adding broth as needed (about ½ cup).

Remove the casserole from the heat and transfer its contents to a large bowl. Let cool completely (about 1 hour) while you make the ricotta stuffing.

Drain the ricotta in cheesecloth to remove excess liquid, then place in a large bowl and add the eggs, Parmigiano, and flour. Mix all the ingredients together with a wooden spoon, then add salt, freshly ground pepper, and nutmeg to taste and mix thoroughly. Cover the bowl with aluminum foil and place it in the refrigerator until needed.

When you are ready to assemble the dish, preheat the oven to 375°. Cut the dough into 10 equal pieces. With a rolling pin, roll each piece of dough into a circular sheet, as thin as you can get it.

Oil a 10-inch springform and line it with a first layer of dough, letting an overlap of pastry hang over the sides. Oil the top side of the pastry sheet in the springform and place a second sheet on top of it; oil the second sheet. Repeat this procedure until there are 5 sheets of pastry in all.

On top of the fifth layer, arrange the cold artichoke stuffing, then put 3 or 4 pats of butter on top. Make a layer of the ricotta stuffing on top of the layer of artichokes. In this ricotta layer, make 4 small depressions, each the width of an egg; in each one break a raw egg. Place a pat of butter on top of each egg and sprinkle with salt and pepper.

Over the ricotta layer, place a sixth sheet of pastry, still letting the sides overlap. Oil the sixth sheet of pastry and add the remaining sheets, oiling each except for the last one. (With these top 5 sheets it is important to leave some air between the layers.) Gently press all the layers together at the edge of the springform and cut off all the overlapping parts with a knife.

Place the springform in the preheated oven and bake for about 40 minutes, then remove from the oven and let cool for about 4 or 5 hours. Do not cover the springform; otherwise, the crust will become soggy.

When cool, open the springform, place the *torta pasqualina* on a serving dish, and serve, slicing it like a cake.

Fish

THE Arno river is one of the central facts of Tuscany. Florence, Pisa, and a host of smaller towns are situated on it. At one time the river was not only navigable by large vessels but also the river and its tributaries were teeming with fish. Sturgeon was not a rarity. In 1558 two gigantic sturgeon fished from the Arno fed the entire company at one of the gigantic Medici royal weddings. The old cookbooks have recipes for carp, salmon, turbot, as well as sturgeon. The tributaries such as the Bisenzio, a few miles from Florence, were famous throughout Europe for the quality of their fresh pike, tench, and so on. These recipes which have remained on after the fish themselves have gone from the local waters are useful in areas where many of these species are still to be found, among them the United States. In recent times the specialties of the Arno are tiny fish and baby eels which the Arno folk love to deep-fry.

Standing also at the foot of the Apennine mountains, Florence nowadays depends on the mountain streams for marvelous and abundant fresh trout, which are prepared in a wide variety of ways. Eels and lampreys, snails, and frogs have also given rise to a large repertoire of dishes.

The long seacoast of Tuscany gives access to the varieties of fish on Italy's western Mediterranean coast. (It is often said that the Adriatic has the best fish but the Mediterranean side the best ways of cooking it.) Since the sea receded several centuries ago and Pisa is now inland, the most famous sea dishes are those of Livorno (Leghorn), Viareggio, and Massa. The fish soup of Livorno is a direct descendant of the ancient Greek ones, and shares the highly spiced quality of Livornese cooking.

Among the varieties of sea fish used in Tuscan cooking that are available in America are the following: *spigola*, sea bass and its relative, striped bass; *triglia*, the larger ones like red mullet; *cernia*, spotted grouper; *pesce spada*, swordfish; *tonno*, fresh tuna; *cefalo* or *muggine*, striped or grey mullet; *nasello* or *merluzzo*, hake or its less tasty relative whiting. Fresh sardines are sometimes available in America, and in some dishes the more common smelts may be substituted. Though only dried salted cod, *baccalà*, is available in Italy, fresh cod is available in America and makes a more subtle and not inauthentic version of some, though not all, of the Italian cod dishes. Salted herring is used more in Italy than most Americans suspect. Bluefish, though related to *ombrina*, is too strong in taste to substitute for it, as delicious porgy is really too strong to approximate its relative, *dentice*, though one sees these substitutions suggested often enough in American Italian cookbooks. Though the American sole is related to the flounder family of flatfish (*Pleuronectidae*) rather than that of the Mediterranean and Dover sole (*Solidae*), if the dish is not a subtle and very exposed one, small, thin American sole can sometimes be substituted with success.

Squid and ink-squid or cuttlefish are also much used. The smaller shrimp are generally preferred to the larger ones for most dishes, except for grilling on the spit. Italian clams are much smaller than American ones and are eaten steamed in the shell with flavorings or used with pasta. Mussels are used in fish soups and cooked *alla marinara*. Oyster, crab, and turtle recipes exist in old cookbooks, though these species are rarely used in Italy now. (Turtles may always have been imported for eating, even in the sixteenth century.) Lobsters are characteristic of the islands off Tuscany, Giglio, and Elba.

The sampling of fish dishes which follows is just an introduction to this large area of Tuscan cooking.

BUYING AND HANDLING FISH

THERE are some basic things you should know about buying and handling fish, most important of all is how to recognize whether a fish is fresh:

1. The smell of ocean fish must be extremely light; there should be no smell at all for fresh-water fish.
2. The eyes must be very bright and not sunken.

3. The skin must be smooth and still pulled tight.
4. The gills must be rose or red in color.
5. The body of the fish must be firm and not soft.

When using slices cut from a very large fish (such as cod, haddock, etc.), note that the fish is generally tougher than a small whole fish and should be soaked in cold milk for an hour, then dried with paper towels, before using.

Finally, always handle fish with wet hands. To remove any smell from your hands it will be enough to moisten them with some lemon juice and then wash them as you ordinarily do.

Pesce Bollito
(Poached Fish)

One of the most common ways of cooking fish is by poaching. Many kinds of fish can be prepared this way, and the fish-poaching broth we give below can be generally used (see page 241 for an exception). Observe the directions below in order to obtain the best taste result with each kind of fish.

First of all, the best pot for poaching fish is a long, heavy tin-lined copper fish poacher, which in Italy is called a *"pesciaiola."* If you don't have a fish poacher, copper or tin, make a cheesecloth sling on which the fish may rest immersed in the broth in a large saucepan.

Before poaching, ocean fish must be washed in salted cold water, while fresh-water fish must be washed in cold water containing some lemon juice (*acqua acidulata*, as it is called in Italy). The fish can then be poached in the following broth (the amount of water is for 2 pounds of fish).

Poached fish should be preceded by a light soup or pasta, accompanied by boiled vegetables, and followed by almost any dessert.

    1 carrot
    1 medium-sized red onion
    1 celery rib
    1 clove garlic
    5 or 6 sprigs Italian parsley
    1 large bay leaf
    ½ teaspoon dried thyme
    ½ cup dry white wine   (*continued*)

1 tablespoon coarse salt
2 quarts water
2 pounds fish, ocean or freshwater

Place all the ingredients in your fish poacher, then cover and place on a medium flame. Let the broth simmer very slowly for about 30 minutes, then strain through a wire strainer into a large bowl. Return the broth to the poacher.

Then follow either of these procedures; the first is for ocean fish.

Allow the broth to become cold. Place the ocean fish in the cold broth, then cover the poacher and heat until the broth reaches the boiling point. Simmer very slowly until cooked. (Time depends on individual fish and its size; see the list below for times for various fish.) Remove the poacher from the flame and let stand without opening the pot for 5 or 6 minutes.

For freshwater fish, place the fish in very hot broth (not yet boiling), then cover the poacher and simmer very slowly until the fish is cooked. Remove the poacher from the flame and let stand without opening for about 10 minutes.

Note: The broth left over after poaching fish may be used for *risotto di mare* (see page 221).

Cooking times: Sea bass, 2 lbs., or striped bass, 2-lb. piece, 20–25 min. Swordfish, 2-lb. piece, 20–30 min. Fresh cod or haddock, 2-lb. piece, 20–30 min. Hake or whiting, 2 lbs., 15–20 min. Sole filet, medium-sized, about 12 min. Dried, salted cod, soaked overnight, boiled 20–30 min. Trout, see page 241.

A SUGGESTED DINNER

WINE
Bolla Soave

Gnocchi di pesce (see page 226)

Trota bollita con maionese (see below)

Spinaci saltati (see page 421)

Torta di ricotta (see page 448)

Trota Bollita con Maionese
(Boiled Trout with Mayonnaise) (SERVES 4)

Freshwater trout, poached in a good broth and served with home-made *maionese*, is one of the great treats, though it is among the simplest of things to prepare. Trout is widely available, and this dish may be served in either the most informal or highly formal circumstances.

Trout is a very delicate fish, and for this reason the broth in which it is cooked differs from ordinary fish poaching broth in that the garlic and onion are omitted.

> *Maionese* (see page 55)
> 1 lemon, cut in wedges
> 6 or 7 sprigs Italian parsley
> Broth for poaching fish (see page 239), but omitting the garlic and onion
> 4 trout (about 2 pounds)

Make the *maionese* according to the directions on page 55, then set aside until needed.

Prepare the broth for poaching fish as directed on page 239, then poach the trout in it for about 15 minutes.

When the trout are done, let them stand, covered, for about 10 minutes, then lift them out of the fish poacher and carefully cut off the heads and tails. Open each trout lengthwise and gently lift out the central bone, leaving each filleted half-fish in one piece. Place the trout fillets on a serving dish and surround with the lemon wedges and parsley sprigs. Serve, accompanied by the *maionese* in a sauceboat.

Note: This dish can be served either warm or cold.

———◆———

A SUGGESTED DINNER

WINE
Ruffino Orvieto (*secco*)

Risotto con gamberetti in bianco (see page 219)

Trota al piatto (see below)

Pomodori al forno (see page 424)

Meringhe alla panna (see page 468)

———◆———

Trota al Piatto
(Trout Cooked on a Plate)   (SERVES 4)

A special way to cook filleted trout. The fillets are put on oven-proof plates with a little wine, lemon juice, and olive oil, then the plate is placed over a steaming stockpot. While simple to prepare, the presentation of this fish generally provides a touch of drama, and the result is delicious.

    4 brook trout (about 2 pounds)
    4 or 5 sprigs Italian parsley
       Juice of ½ lemon
    ¼ cup dry white wine
    2 teaspoons olive oil
       Salt and freshly ground white pepper

Wet your hands, then cut off the heads and tails of the trout with a knife. Open stomachs to clean out the viscera. With a boning knife, extend each stomach opening down to the tail end, to open the fish completely, then insert the point of the knife alongside the backbone, at the head end. Move the knife downward to the tail end. Repeat the procedure on the other side of the bone, then lift the bone out.

Coarsely chop the parsley and set it aside.

Put the lemon juice in a small bowl, along with the wine, olive oil, and salt and white pepper to taste. Stir very well with a wooden spoon.

Oil 4 ovenproof plates and on them place the trout fillets, with their skins on (see photo 1). Pour the liquid in the bowl over the trout and sprinkle the chopped parsley on top, then wrap the plates completely in aluminum foil.

Put a large quantity of water in 4 saucepans and set them on the heat. When the water reaches the boiling point, lower the flame to a simmer and place the plates on top of the saucepans (see photo 2). Let the fish steam for 16 to 18 minutes.

Remove the plates from the saucepans, carefully unwrap the foil, and serve immediately.

Trota al piatto: 1. Trout fillets on the plate.

2. Plate of trout fillets steaming over a boiling stockpot.

————◆————

A SUGGESTED DINNER

WINE
Antinori Est! Est!! Est!!!

Risotto all marinara (see page 220)

Pesce arrosto (see below)

Cardi dorati (see page 408)

Budino di ricotta (see page 491)

————◆————

Pesce Arrosto
(Roasted Fish)   (S E R V E S   4)

A roasted fish retains its full flavor if it is left whole, with the head and tail still on, since cutting these off would create openings through which a large part of the flavor vanishes. (If the head and tail bother you, cut them off only before serving.)

The touch of garlic here blends ideally with the fish, at least as well as with meat. Be careful not to overcook. Test with a fork; the bones may still be slightly pinkish when the fish is ready to be removed from the oven.

> 1 large whole fish such as striped bass, spotted grouper, or gray
>   mullet (about 4 pounds)
> 3 cloves garlic
> 1 tablespoon rosemary leaves
>   Salt and freshly ground pepper to taste
> 5 tablespoons olive oil
>   Juice of 1 lemon
>   Lemon wedges

Clean the fish very well, removing the scales but not the head, and cutting off only the lower half of the tail. Make 2 or 3 short slits in the skin of the fish.

Cut the garlic cloves into quarters, then put some inside each slit and inside the fish's cavity, along with the rosemary, salt, and pepper.

Preheat the oven to 375°.

Place 4 tablespoons of the olive oil in a roasting pan. Place the fish on the oil, sprinkle on the remaining olive oil and a little salt, and place in the preheated oven for about 30 minutes. (It is very difficult to give the exact time for roasting fish, because not only do different kinds of fish take different lengths of time to cook, but even among fish of the same kind there are big differences, according to the size of fish, how big the bones are, the freshness of the fish, in which period of the year the fish has been caught and where.) The best judge for doneness of fish is a fork. When the fork goes down very easily and the meat makes no resistance, the fish is ready.

Remove the fish from the oven, sprinkle with the juice of a lemon, and serve in the same roasting pan, garnished with lemon wedges.

———◆———

A SUGGESTED DINNER

WINE
Ruffino Lugana

Risotto con agliata (see page 214)

Pesce al cartoccio (see below)

Fagiolini in fricassea (see page 404)

Frittura mista di frutta (see page 497)

———◆———

Pesce al Cartoccio
(Fish Cooked in a Paper Bag)   (S E R V E S 4)

Another way of roasting fish, this time wrapped up to hold in the flavor and to keep the fish moist. Years back, the fish used to be cooked in an oiled brown paper bag, but aluminum foil produces just as good a result and has taken the place of the oiled paper. Garlic, rosemary, and lemon are the flavorings. This method is very widely used in Italy.

> 1 sea bass or striped bass (about 3 ½ pounds)
> Salt and freshly ground pepper to taste
> 1 tablespoon rosemary leaves
> 2 cloves garlic
> Lemon wedges

Make sure that the cavity of the fish is very well cleaned, then wash the fish in salted water and wipe it off with paper towels.

Preheat the oven to 375°.

Place a large sheet of aluminum foil on a board and sprinkle it with a little salt, pepper, and some of the rosemary leaves. Place the fish on the aluminum foil.

Cut the cloves of garlic into small pieces. Into the cavity of the fish put half of the remaining rosemary leaves, half of the garlic pieces, salt, and pepper. Sprinkle the outside of the fish with the remaining rosemary leaves, garlic, and more salt and pepper.

Wrap fish completely in the aluminum foil and place it in a baking pan, then place in the preheated oven for 17 minutes. Gently turn the fish over and bake for 17 minutes more, then remove the pan from oven and let the fish cool for 10 minutes.

Unwrap the fish onto a serving dish and serve hot, garnished with lemon wedges.

SQUID

THE squid in the photos are much larger than those recommended for eating, but it is easier to see how they are prepared. For most dishes, the smaller the squid the better, and more tender. For *calamari ripieni* (see page 252) the squid should be larger, since they are to be stuffed, but not extremely large.

To clean the squid, pull the tentacles away from the casing, or stomach, until the entire head is outside. Detach the head from the stomach by pulling. Cut off the head below the eyes and discard, leaving the tentacles attached to the lower part (see photo 1).

Turn the lower part upside down. The tentacles will now hang over the sides, and the inside of the lower head will be pulled open to reveal a black spot, which is the mouth. Pull it out (see photo 2).

Cleaning squid: 1. Cutting the head below the eyes, leaving the tentacles attached to the lower part of the head.

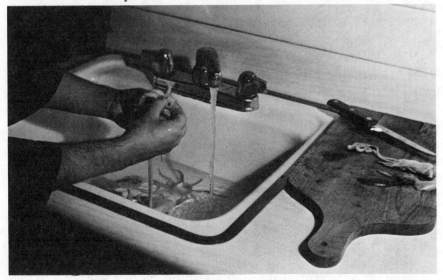

2. Pulling out the mouth.

Remove the membranes remaining inside the stomach by squeezing the stomach from the bottom. Discard the membranes, then pull out the transparent "bone" from inside the stomach (see photo 3) and wash out the inside of the stomach very carefully.

Under cold running water, pull the thin layer of dark outer skin from the stomach and tentacles so the white under layer is exposed (see photo 4). (Leaving on the outer skin is the most common mistake of

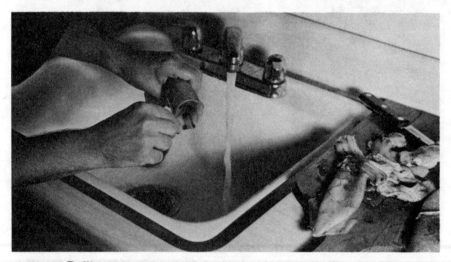

3. Pulling out the transparent bone from inside the stomach.

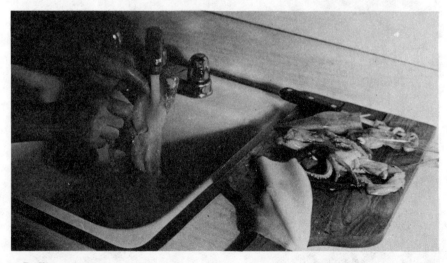

4. Pulling the thin layer of dark outer skin off the stomach, under cold running water.

those inexperienced with squid; no amount of cooking can remove its toughness.)

The "fins" attached along the sides of the bottom half of the stomach are of the same quality as the stomach. Cut them off, being careful not to open the stomach, and save them.

At this point the squid is ready to be used for a variety of dishes. Unless you are going to stuff the whole stomach, cut it into rings (see photo 5). If the tentacles are larger than an inch or so, cut them into 1-inch sections.

5. A stuffed squid and how to cut squid into rings.

A SUGGESTED DINNER

WINE
Lungarotti Torre di Giano

Pomodori ripieni (page 225)

Fritto di calamari e gamberi (see below)

Zucchini fritti (see page 426)

Biscotti di Prato (see page 462)

Fritto di Calamari e Gamberi
(Deep-Fried Squid and Shrimp)   (S E R V E S   4)

The lightness and crispness of fried shrimp and squid in Tuscany is widely admired. It is important not to use a thick batter. The Tuscan method is to shake the shellfish in a bag of flour, so that only what clings to the fish remains. Then, after being lightly dipped in egg, it is cooked in very hot, light shortening and placed on paper towels to absorb any excess grease. As in any kind of deep-frying, if the shortening is light and hot enough, very little fat is absorbed by the fish, as you will see when you place them on towels and see how little excess grease comes off. All fish in Tuscany is fried according to this method or the *alla pescatora* method described on pages 274–5.

    1 pound squid
    ½ pound medium-sized shrimp
       Salt to taste
    3 eggs
    2 cups all-purpose flour
    1 pound solid vegetable shortening
       Lemon wedges

Clean the squid well according to the directions on page 246, then cut the stomachs into rings and the tentacles into 2 or 3 pieces; shell the shrimp. Soak the squid and shrimp in a bowl of cold water, with a pinch of salt, for 10 to 15 minutes, then drain on paper towels to absorb excess water.

Put the flour into a plastic bag, then drop in the slightly damp fish pieces and shake very well. The pieces should be fully, but lightly, covered with flour.

Beat the eggs in a second bowl with a pinch of salt and set aside while you heat the vegetable shortening in a deep-fat fryer. While it is getting hot, cover a serving dish with a layer of paper towels.

When the shortening is very hot, dip each piece of floured squid or shrimp into the beaten eggs and fry until golden brown. Transfer onto the serving dish lined with paper towel, so grease is absorbed.

When all the fish is cooked, remove the paper towels from the bottom of the serving dish, sprinkle with salt, and garnish with lemon wedges. Serve hot.

A SUGGESTED DINNER

WINE
Melini Lacrima d'Arno

Gnocchi di semolino (see page 231)

Calamari in zimino (see below)

Pomodori in insalata (see page 391)

Fresh fruit

Calamari in Zimino
(Squid with Spinach)   (SERVES 4)

When Americans overcome their resistance to squid, they are generally very happy with their discovery; it is, after all, one of the very best gifts of the sea. For most dishes, the smaller squid are best because they are more tender. Squid rings and pieces, cooked together with spinach in white wine and slightly spiced with red pepper flakes, is one of the classic Florentine recipes. All Italian fish markets in America carry fresh squid.

2 pounds of squid
3 pounds fresh spinach or 4 packages (10 ounces each) frozen
1 small onion
1 carrot
5 tablespoons olive oil
  Salt and freshly ground pepper to taste
  Pinch of hot red pepper flakes
½ cup dry white wine
1 tablespoon tomato paste
5 or 6 sprigs Italian parsley
  Juice of 1 lemon

Clean the squid according to the directions on page 246, then cut the stomachs into rings and the tentacles into small pieces. Leave squid pieces to soak in a bowl of salted water until needed.

Put a large quantity of salted water into a stockpot and bring it to a boil. Cook the spinach in the water for 15 minutes, then squeeze as dry as possible and chop it coarsely. Set aside.

Chop the onion and carrot coarsely, then transfer to a flameproof casserole, along with the olive oil, salt, pepper, and red pepper flakes. Lightly brown them, add the squid and sauté for 15 or 16 minutes.

Add the white wine and continue to sauté until the wine is evaporated, then add the spinach and tomato paste and cook very slowly for 20 minutes more.

Chop the parsley coarsely, then add it to the casserole and cook for 1 minute more. Remove from the flame, add the lemon juice, and serve hot.

Note: Swiss chard (*bietola*) may be used instead of or in combination with the spinach.

A SUGGESTED DINNER

WINE
Castello di Poppiano Bianco

Frittata di porri (see page 97)

Calamari ripieni (see below)

Finocchi in sugo finto (see page 414)

Pesche ripiene (see page 492)

Calamari Ripieni
(Stuffed Squid)   (S E R V E S   4)

Stuffed squid requires larger squid, as the so-called stomach sections must be large enough to stuff. When cooked, these look like attractive white sausages, and they are stuffed with the squids' tentacles, chopped, mixed with *mollica* (the inside part of bread), white wine, and seasoning. We strongly urge you to try this, especially if you share the implicit American resistance to squid.

> 8 large squid
> 2 large cloves garlic
> 12 to 15 sprigs Italian parsley
> 2 slices white bread
> ½ cup olive oil
> 1½ cups dry white wine
> Salt and freshly ground pepper

Clean the squid very well, without cutting the stomachs, according to the directions on page 246, then remove the tentacles from the bottom part of the heads and soak them, along with the stomachs, in cold salted water for 10 to 15 minutes. Be sure that nothing remains in the bottom of the stomachs.

Chop the tentacles fine, together with the garlic and parsley; remove the crusts from the bread slices.

Heat ¼ cup of the oil in a saucepan, and when it is warm, add the chopped ingredients and the bread slices. Sauté on a medium flame, mixing very well until the bread is completely incorporated with the other ingredients (about 12 to 15 minutes). Season with salt and pepper, then remove the saucepan from the flame and allow to cool for 20 minutes.

Preheat the oven to 375°.

Stuff the squid stomachs with the contents of the saucepan, but not too full or they will split. Fasten the open end of each with a toothpick, then place in a rectangular Pyrex baking dish (13½ x 8¾ inches).

Combine the wine and remaining ¼ cup of olive oil and pour over the *calamari*. Sprinkle with salt and pepper, then place in the preheated oven and cook for 25 to 35 minutes or until tender; the squid should be tender when pricked with a fork.

Remove the dish from the oven, transfer the squid to a serving dish, and serve hot.

———◆———

A SUGGESTED DINNER

WINE
Antinori Castello della Sala Orvieto Classico (*secco*)

Risotto alla toscana (see page 217)

Baccalà alla fiorentina (see below)

Boiled potatoes

Fresh fruit

———◆———

Baccalà alla Fiorentina
(Dried Salted Cod, Florentine Style)   (S E R V E S 4)

Baccalà is dried salted cod. It can be found in most Italian markets, as well as in other ethnic markets such as Greek, Spanish, and Chinese. (In Italy, dried cod is also found unsalted and called *stoccafisso*.)

The dried fish must be soaked before cooking. In Italy, the classic way to do this is to leave it in a bowl under slowly running water overnight, for 9 or 10 hours. Many trying to sleep, however, would consider this "the Italian torture treatment," so most will prefer the below-mentioned compromise; it is, however, important to change the water quite often.

Every part of Italy has its own way of cooking *baccalà*. In Florence, in common with some other parts of Italy, it is done with olive oil, garlic, and tomatoes. But it is crisped in the oil before the tomatoes are added, in moderation, and because it is not cooked too long, it does not become heavy.

In America we have fresh cod, which they do not in Italy. However, the dried salted cod has its own special flavor.

    1 pound dried salted cod fillet
    ½ cup all-purpose flour
    3 cloves garlic
      Scant ½ cup olive oil

  1 cup fresh or canned tomatoes
     Salt and freshly ground pepper to taste
  7 or 8 sprigs Italian parsley

Cut the dried cod into large pieces (about 4 x 3 inches) and let soak in cold water for 24 hours, changing the water quite often. Dry on paper towels

Spread the flour on a sheet of aluminum foil and flour the pieces well; coarsely chop the garlic. Heat the olive oil in a large frying pan. When it is hot, add the *baccalà* to the pan, along with the garlic, and fry lightly on both sides until golden brown (about 12 minutes). Pass the tomatoes through a food mill into the pan and let simmer for 15 minutes on a low flame. Taste before adding salt (the saltiness of the fish is variable) and add fresh pepper to taste. Simmer for 4 to 5 minutes more.

Transfer the *baccalà* pieces from pan to serving dish, coarsely chop the parsley and sprinkle it over. Pour over the hot sauce from the pan and serve.

A SUGGESTED DINNER

WINE
Tristo di Montesecco

Risotto con carciofi (see page 216)

Sogliola alla livornese (see below)

Boiled potatoes

Fragole al vino rosso (see page 496)

Sogliola alla Livornese
(Sole, Livorno Style)   (SERVES 4)

Mediterranean sole is a species we do not find here. It is very delicate and thinner than ours, which is related to the flounder family. For this reason, I don't recommend it for light sautéing or frying. But if you can find small whole sole, this spicy treatment of *sogliola alla livornese* will not suffer with the domestic species. Leave the sole whole; do not have them filleted, just cleaned.

A very Mediterranean treatment of a small whole fish, in the style of the seaport of Livorno (Leghorn).

    4 small whole sole
    6 or 7 sprigs Italian parsley
    2 cloves garlic
    ½ celery rib
    6 tablespoons olive oil
    ½ cup canned tomatoes
      Salt and freshly ground pepper to taste

Be sure that sole are cleaned well, then wash them in salted water; finely chop the parsley, garlic, and celery.

Heat 3 tablespoons of the olive oil in a frying pan on a medium flame. When the the oil is hot, add the chopped ingredients to the pan and sauté them very gently for 10 minutes. Pass the tomatoes through a food mill into the frying pan. Taste for salt and pepper and let cook for 10 minutes more, then remove all the solid ingredients from the pan with a strainer-skimmer and set aside.

Add the remaining 3 tablespoons of olive oil to the pan, and when it is hot, place all 4 whole sole in the pan. Sprinkle salt and freshly ground black pepper over the fish and sauté for 1 minute.

Sprinkle the sole with the solid ingredients previously set aside, then cover the pan and very gently cook for about 16 minutes, turning the fish once after about 8 minutes.

Serve very hot.

———◆———

A SUGGESTED DINNER

WINE
Umani Ronchi-Verdicchio Classico dei Castelli di Jesi

Sformato di carciofi (see page 426)

Cacciucco (see below)
Bruciate ubriache (see page 477)

———◆———

Cacciucco
(Tuscan Fish Soup, Livorno Style)   (SERVES 6)

One of the favorite dishes of the ancient Greeks was a rich fish soup, and all of the cities the Greeks settled along the Mediterranean—such as Marseille and Naples—retain this great old tradition. Each Italian seacoast town has its *zuppa di pesce*, and the one characteristic of the Tuscan seacoast is *cacciucco*. It uses a variety of fish and shellfish, which are served over toasted Tuscan bread slices covered with some of the rich broth as sauce. However, the bulk of the broth is retained for making another dish the next day, *risotto di mare* (see page 221). A great treat that yields two unforgettable meals, *cacciucco* is a main course, and should be preceded by something quite light.

The Mediterranean fish used in Italy such as *palombo*, small *triglie*, or *cicale* (a type of shellfish that has no meat but is added for flavor), are not all found here. For *palombo*, a full-fleshed fish may be substituted, such as cod, haddock, or striped bass. Smelts may be substituted for *triglie*, and crabs, preferably soft-shelled, for the sweet flavor of the *cicale*. Seafood used in Italy and found here are *calamari* (squid) and shrimp (used raw, in their shells), and while clams and mussels are also used, some people may prefer to avoid them. The *cacciucco* can be made perfectly well without them. To be avoided are fatty fish and any with a flavor so strong as to overwhelm the others.

> 6 pounds assorted fish and shellfish (see above), plus 2 or 3 additional large fish heads
> 1 large red onion
> 18 or 19 sprigs Italian parsley
> 6 cloves garlic
> 7 tablespoons olive oil
> 2 cups canned tomatoes
> 2 tablespoons tomato paste
> Salt and freshly ground black pepper to taste
> 1 teaspoon hot red pepper flakes
> ¼ cup wine vinegar

(*continued*)

8 cups meat broth

6 large slices Tuscan bread, preferably dark (see page 37)

Clean all the fish, detaching heads and tails, and cut into pieces about 1½ inch square (cutting full-fleshed fish across the width to leave the bones in, rather than filleting); reserve heads. Clean squid well (see page 246) and cut the stomachs into rings and the tentacles into small pieces. Leave shrimp in their shells.

Place all the seafood in a large bowl containing 2 quarts of cold water and 1 tablespoon of salt, and let stand until needed.

Coarsely chop the onion, 8 or 9 sprigs of the parsley, and 2 cloves of the garlic, then place them in a large stockpot, along with the olive oil, and sauté until lightly golden brown (about 15 minutes).

Add the tomatoes and tomato paste to the stockpot, season with salt, pepper, and red pepper, and simmer for 15 minutes longer. Add the wine vinegar and all the reserved fish heads and bones and cook for 15 minutes more.

In a saucepan, heat the broth to the boiling point, then add to the stockpot and simmer, with the lid on, for 2 hours.

Strain the contents of the pot, forcing the solids through the strainer, into another bowl, then transfer the contents of the bowl back to the stockpot and return the latter to the heat. Taste for salt and pepper, remembering that it should be spicy.

Pour the soaked fish pieces into a colander, letting the water run off, then wash them under cold running water and add them to the stockpot in the following stages:

First put in squid, which take about 30 minutes; then, 20 minutes later add the full-fleshed fish. A few minutes after that, add shrimp, crabs, and smelts, which all take 10 to 12 minutes.

Meanwhile, chop the remaining 10 sprigs of parsley and set aside; cut the remaining garlic cloves into halves; preheat the oven to 375°.

Toast the bread slices in the preheated oven for about 10 minutes on each side, then remove from the oven and immediately rub them on both sides with the cut garlic. Place 1 slice of bread in each individual soup plate.

When all the fish is cooked, remove the stockpot from the flame and let rest for 10 minutes, then, with a large ladle, select a sampling of each fish for each serving. Pour about ½ cup of broth over the fish and bread in each plate. Sprinkle with a little chopped parsley, and serve hot.

Note: There will be abundant broth remaining, which is sometimes eaten separately the next day but is most often used to make *risotto di mare.*

———◆———

A SUGGESTED DINNER

WINE
Melini Lacrima d'Arno

Tagliatelle alla panna (see page 147)

Pastello di pesce (see below)

Spinaci alla fiorentina (see page 422)

Timballo di pere (see page 449)

———◆———

Pastello di Pesce
(Boned Whole Fish, Baked in a Crust)   (SERVES 6)

An elaborate, impressive dish, it is appropriate for a special occasion. The recipe comes from a Florentine cookbook of the 1300s. Much Florentine food of that period was extremely complicated and used many different spices; the classic Florentine food, using a few excellent ingredients in just the right proportions, was developed in the course of the centuries of the Renaissance. Dishes such as this *pastello* were indirectly responsible for the discovery of America, as these were the famous spices of the Indies that Columbus sought, after the Venetians and other shippers were cut off from the East by the Turks.

Fish should be used which has only one, central bone, and whose flesh is not too soft. In America, striped bass is ideal and of the same family as the Italian *spigola.* In Italy *spigola* or *orata* is best.

  2 cups all-purpose flour
  ⅔ cup cold water
  3 tablespoons olive oil
   Salt
  1 large fish (about 4 or 5 pounds before boning), such as striped
   bass
  ½ teaspoon freshly ground black pepper
  ¼ teaspoon cayenne pepper
  ½ teaspoon ground ginger
  ½ teaspoon ground cloves
  1 level teaspoon ground cumin
  ½ teaspoon freshly grated nutmeg
   Pinch of ground saffron
  1 level teaspoon ground cardamom
  4 or 5 black peppercorns
   Pinch of ground cinnamon
  5 or 6 sprigs Italian parsley
  2 ounces *pancetta* or salt pork
  ¼ cup rose water

First make the crust. Place the flour in a mound on a pasta board and make a well in it. Pour in the water, 1 tablespoon of the olive oil, and a pinch of salt. Using a fork and mixing outward from the center, completely absorb the flour into the liquid. Keep mixing until very smooth (about 15 minutes), then knead for at least 15 minutes. Wrap the dough in a dampened cotton dishtowel and put it in a cool place for 2 hours; do not refrigerate.

Meanwhile, prepare the fish. Wash it very carefully, then, after wetting your hands with cold water, completely remove the scales from the outside.

Now bone the fish. Open the stomach completely, using a boning knife, then cut out the backbone in one piece, without cutting the back, and cut the connection to the head on one end and to the tail on the other. Cut off the bottom half of the tail; the upper part of the tail should be left so the bottom end of the fish remains completely closed (see photos 1–4).

Open the fish flat, with the inside facing up, and sprinkle 1 level tablespoon salt and all the spices uniformly over the entire cavity. Arrange the parsley sprigs down the length of the fish, in the center, then

Boning a fish: 1. Opening the stomach of the fish completely before boning.

2. Removing the backbone in one piece.

3. Cutting the connection of the backbone to the head.

4. Opening the fish out flat.

cut up the *pancetta* (or salt pork) coarsely and arrange it uniformly all over the cavity. Close the fish.

Preheat the oven to 350°.

With a rolling pin, roll out the dough into a large, paper-thin sheet. Place the fish on the sheet of dough and wrap it completely, but only once.

Lay out a large sheet of aluminum foil and puncture it all over with about 20 little holes. Place a grill on a jelly-roll pan and put the punctured aluminum foil on the grill; oil the aluminum foil with the remaining 2 tablespoons of oil.

Place the fish on the aluminum foil. (In this way, if there is excess fat, it can drip off without softening the crispness of the bottom crust.) Make two little holes on the top side of the dough enclosing the fish, one near the head, the other near the tail (these will be necessary at a later stage to pour in the rose water), then place the pan in the preheated oven for 20 minutes.

Remove the pan from the oven and pour the rose water in through the two holes in the crust. Replace the pan in the oven and raise the oven temperature to 375° for about 15 minutes more. (Be careful not to overcook the fish, but be sure the crust is a light golden brown.)

Remove the pan from the oven and let cool for 5 minutes, then transfer the fish to a serving dish. Starting from the tail end, cut the fish across into at least 6 pieces and serve.

———◆———

A SUGGESTED DINNER

WINE
Serristori Bianco

Ravioli nudi di pesce (see page 228)

Pesce ripieno in gelatina (see below)

Bietole saltate (see page 423)

Ciambella di frutta (see page 487)

———◆———

Pesce Ripieno in Gelatina
(Stuffed Whole Fish in Aspic)   (SERVES 6)

Stuffed whole fish in aspic is a dish for an important dinner. The fish is boned before it is stuffed with a shrimp and mushroom filling. When it is served it can be cut right through, each slice containing fish and stuffing and still encased in aspic.

We prefer beef aspic, as that made from fish, in our experience, produces too "fishy" a result for most people. The beef aspic blends quite well with the stuffed fish.

This dish may be served at the most formal of dinners and is also useful for a fancy buffet. Since it is cold, it goes particularly well in warm weather, but need not be restricted to that time.

Gelatina

        20 cups cold water
         4 pounds beef for boiling
         1 large calf's foot
         2 carrots
         2 celery ribs
         1 large onion
         1 tablespoon coarse salt
         8 ounces lean boneless veal
         5 egg whites
         2 or 3 teaspoons sugar

Stuffing

         4 or 5 sprigs Italian parsley
         2 cloves garlic
        ½ pound shrimp
        ½ pound fresh mushrooms
         3 tablespoons olive oil
            Salt and freshly ground pepper to taste
         2 heaping tablespoons bread crumbs

         1 large striped bass (about 3½ pounds)
         2 teaspoons rosemary leaves, approximately

Make the aspic with quantities listed above, according to the directions on page 107, but do not place it in the refrigerator to solidify.

Chop the parsley and garlic coarsely; shell the shrimp and wash them with salted water; clean the mushrooms, removing the stem ends, then wash and dry them with paper towels.

Heat the olive oil in a saucepan. When it is warm, add the parsley and garlic and sauté gently for 4 or 5 minutes, then add the shrimp, taste for salt and pepper, and cook for 2 or 3 minutes longer. Cut the mushrooms into quarters and add them to the saucepan. Mix thoroughly with a wooden spoon and let them cook for about 10 minutes. Add the bread crumbs, mix thoroughly, and cook for 5 minutes more.

Remove the saucepan from the flame. Transfer the contents of the pan to a bowl and let rest until completely cold (about 1 hour).

Preheat the oven to 375°.

Clean and bone the fish, leaving on the head and tail, as described on page 260. Sprinkle the cavity of the fish with salt and pepper, then stuff it with the contents of the bowl, being careful not to overstuff the fish. Sew the fish up.

Oil a sheet of aluminum foil and place the whole fish on it. Sprinkle the outside part with salt, pepper, and rosemary leaves, then with 2 or 3 drops of olive oil. Place the aluminum foil containing the fish in a baking dish and put it in the preheated oven for about 40 minutes.

Remove the dish from the oven and allow the fish to cool completely (about 1 hour), then place the fish in the refrigerator for 2 hours more.

Meanwhile prepare a mold, the same size as the fish, by lightly oiling it all over. Put ¾ cup of the aspic, cool but still liquid, in the mold and place in the refrigerator until the aspic is completely solid (about 3 hours).

When the aspic is solid, remove the fish from the refrigerator and carefully remove the thread. With a paper towel, gently remove the rosemary leaves from the top of the fish.

Lay the fish in the mold, on the solid aspic, and pour over the remaining, still-liquid aspic. Place the mold in the refrigerator until the second layer of aspic is solid (about 5 hours).

When the aspic is solid, remove the mold from the refrigerator and reverse it onto a serving dish. Loosen the aspic by placing hot towels on the outside of the mold (the aspic should unmold with ease) and serve.

The Boiled Course

W<small>E</small> have seen in the discussion of a sixteenth-century Florentine dinner that the boiled course was a part of every large meal. Generally five different boiled and poached dishes were included in it. Here are some more examples of the Renaissance boiled course. A boiled course of March 18, 1546 included Malta eels with little green cabbages (probably Brussels sprouts), squid in a thick soup, ground pignoli soup, and filleted herrings with a walnut-garlic sauce. This more elaborate boiled course was for a feast day in August 1546: stuffed stomach of baby veal (like the modern *cima alla genovese*), boiled tripe, boiled kid Florentine style, boiled salted beef, boiled sausages and salamis with *ginestrata* soup (see recipe page 112) and *viscole* sour cherry sauce. We can see that this really approaches quite closely the modern *gran bollito misto* for feast days such as Christmas. The stuffed veal nowadays would be a main dish by itself. But boiled veal, kid, and beef could be contained in an elaborate *bollito*. The sausages and salamis have continued into the present as the boiled *cotechini* and *zamponi* still included in the modern *bollito*.

What happened to the boiled course as an everyday feature? Mainly, it evolved into the *minestra* or soup course. Also, boiled meats became occasional main dishes when the distinction "boiled course," then "fried course," or "roasted course" gave way to the modern *primo piatto* and *secondo piatto* in the nineteenth century.

Fortunately, some of the good boiled dishes survive—and many more that have become rare deserve to be revived. Following are the most basic boiled dishes of the modern-day repertory, as well as the combination *bollito misto*, used on feast days.

Boiled meats, fowl, and fish are always accompanied by boiled vegetables, never fried or roasted or prepared in any other way.

A SUGGESTED DINNER

WINE
Chianti Classico Catignano

Spaghetti alla fiaccheraia (see page 156)

Boiled chicken or *Boiled beef* (see below)
with *Salsa verde* (see page 57)

Bietole all'agro (see page 423)

Fragole al vino rosso (see page 496)

Boiled Fowl

Fowl that are often eaten in boiled dishes are chicken, hen (*gallina*) capon, and turkey. A hen is used exclusively for boiling because it is usually about two years old and must be cooked a long time. A boiled hen can be a marvelous dish, preferred by many to chicken for its richer taste. As we mentioned elsewhere, turkey was originally used to replace the very expensive and prestigious peacock in elaborate dishes, and is eaten boiled as well as roasted.

In the *gran bollito misto* (see page 271), there is always at least one fowl included and sometimes more than one. Boiled chicken is also used to make *pollo forte* (see page 302).

Great care must be taken in boiling a chicken not to overcook it. It is also pointless to boil a small, young chicken that can be better used for frying or broiling.

BOILING TIMES
Chicken: 45 minutes
Hen: 4 to 5 hours
Capon: 1½ hours
Turkey: 2 hours, approximately

     Enough cold water to well cover the fowl
     Coarse salt
1 large carrot
1 medium-sized red onion
1 celery rib
4 or 5 sprigs Italian parsley
1 chicken, hen, capon, or turkey

Put a goodly amount of cold water in a stockpot, add coarse salt and bring to a boil. Add the carrot, onion, celery, and parsley and return to a boil.

When the water has reached the boiling point, add the fowl and let it boil very slowly, with the stockpot uncovered, until done according to the chart above. (The fowl must be well covered with water. Keep a saucepan of boiling water on a low flame next to the stockpot to add if the stockpot water reduces to too low a level. For boiled hen it may be necessary to add water several times because of its long cooking time.)

Note: Boiled fowl are always served with one or more sauces on the side. See the recipes for sauces on pages 57–64.

Boiled Beef

The perfect meat for boiling is beef. Italian *manzo* is usually a little younger than our beef, and different cuts of it are used boiled, depending on the relative festiveness and importance of the dinner. In America I generally use the cut called "brisket" and boil it for about 2½ hours. It is a meat that requires this long cooking time, and it is excellent for boiling, since it remains moist and retains its fine taste when boiled enough to become soft. Take care not to overcook it, however; if too soft, it becomes difficult to cut.

Boiled beef is almost always included in the *gran bollito misto* (see page 271).

For ingredients and procedure, see the recipe for boiled fowl on page 267.

Note: Boiled beef is always served with one or more sauces on the side; see pages 57–64.

Boiled Veal Tongue

This may be eaten as a separate dish or as part of the *bollito misto* (see page 271).

Veal tongue should be boiled for about 1½ hours; for ingredients and procedure, see recipe for boiled fowl. After boiling, the outer skin must be pulled off whole before the tongue is sliced and served.

Note: See pages 57–64 for sauces to accompany the tongue.

Boiled Cotechino and Zampone

Cotechino and *zampone* are large pork sausages in the shape of salami. Though they are cured, they are always eaten boiled. Both can be eaten as a separate dish, usually accompanied by puree of potatoes, or as part of the *gran bollito misto* (see page 271). *Cotechino* resembles an ordinary sausage, but *zampone* has a special shape as it is a stuffed pig's foot. The *zamponi* made in the town of Modena are celebrated in Italy, and when I am there for Christmas I make a trip to Modena to obtain one for Christmas dinner. Imported Italian *cotechini* and *zamponi* are sometimes difficult to obtain in America, but domestic ones are obtainable in many Italian specialty markets.

Cotechini and *zamponi* must be soaked for several hours and cooked for a long time, *cotechini* for 2 to 3 hours and *zamponi* for 4 to 5 hours. Usually cooked in a long fish poacher (*pesciaiola*), they can be cooked together, but never in the same pot with other boiled meats because they give off a lot of grease. Unless they are served to a large group, generally these sausages are not completely consumed at one meal, so the water in which they are cooked is saved to be used for reheating them. They are always eaten hot.

1 *cotechino* or *zampone* sausage
Water to cover
Coarse salt

Place the *cotechino* or *zampone* in a large bowl of cold water and soak for 2 or 3 hours. After soaking, make several punctures in the sausage with a large needle, then wrap completely in a cotton dishtowel and tie both ends with thread.

Place the sausage in a large pot of cold water and bring to a boil on a medium flame. Meanwhile, put enough water to cover the sausage in a large fish poacher, add coarse salt, and set on the heat till it boils.

When the water containing the sausage reaches the boiling point, remove the pot from the flame, transfer the sausage to a board, and unwrap the towel. Place the *cotechino* in the boiling water in the fish poacher, then lower the flame and simmer until cooked. Cooking time varies even among *cotechini* or *zamponi* of the same brand, because cooking time is related to the freshness of the sausage and how coarsely chopped the meat inside is. The time for *zamponi* varies from 4 to 5 hours; for *cotechini*, 2 to 3.

Transfer the *cotechino* or *zampone* to a cutting board and cut into slices about ½ inch thick. (Cut only those slices you will need, as the rest will retain its flavor better if left in a large piece, resting in its own broth.) Arrange the discs of meat in a ring on a serving dish, and inside place a puree of potatoes or another accompanying vegetable (see note below).

Note: I feel it would be presumptuous to tell Americans how to make puree of potatoes, since their own is among the best. These dishes may also be accompanied by *fagioli al fiasco* (see page 400), *fagioli all'uccelletto* (see page 402), or *rape saltate in padella* (see page 420).

———◆———

A SUGGESTED DINNER

WINE
Chianti Classico Viticcio

Palline ripiene in brodo (see page 110)

Gran bollito misto (see below)
with *Salsa verde* (see page 57), *Salsa verde del Chianti* (see page 58),
and *Maionese* (see page 55)

Puree of potatoes

Ritortelli pieni alla fiorentina (see page 465)

———◆———

Gran Bollito Misto
("Grand" Mixed, Boiled Dinner)

The tradition of the elaborate boiled course, with many dishes, is principally represented today by the *gran bollito misto*. It is to Christmas what turkey is to American Thanksgiving. It can, of course, be served on other festive occasions, and in some *ristoranti* it is available on ordinary days.

The components may vary slightly, but generally there is boiled beef, one or two kinds of boiled fowl, *cotechino* and *zampone*, veal tongue, *guancia* (the cheek part of the calf's head), calf's foot, and even occasionally calf's tail. These last two might be too gelatinous for most American tastes, but if you should decide to use one or both, they must be cooked apart from the other meats—*zampa*, or foot, for 2½ to 3 hours and tail for about 2 hours. The latter has meat like oxtail. Cooking time for *guancia* is 2 to 2½ hours.

Hen, beef, turkey, capon, tongue, and chicken may all be cooked together and added in the order mentioned. Following the directions on page 267, start with the hen; after 2½ hours, add the beef, after ½ hour more add the turkey; after another ½ hour, capon and tongue; after 45 minutes more, the chicken. When the chicken is added, try the hen with a fork. If it is soft, remove it and put it back in when everything is finished. If it is not yet soft enough, leave it in to cook for the additional time.

Zampone should be placed to cook in the fish poacher at the same time as the hen in the other pot. Add *cotechino* 2 hours later. (See page 269 for directions on how to cook the sausages.)

In a third pot, boil *zampa*, starting about when you add the *cotechino*. Half an hour later, add *guancia;* another half hour later, add tail.

At the last moment before serving, combine all the boiled meats in a very large pot, preferably of copper, with some hot broth. To serve each individual, remove each meat one by one to a cutting board; cut off a slice and place the large piece back in the broth. Each person should get a slice of each meat. This is the most elegant way of serving the dish, painstaking though it may be.

If you don't have a large enough pot for everything, slice the different meats and arrange the different types in rings or rows on one or more serving dishes. Place puree of potatoes or another vegetable in the center and serve with a variety of the sauces found in pages 57–64.

Note: For Christmas, the first dish is usually *tortellini* (see page 165) in broth, which precedes the *bollito* very well.

———◆———

A SUGGESTED DINNER

WINE
Chianti Classico Castello di Cerreto

Melanzane marinate (see page 90)

Lesso rifatto con porri (see below)

Castagnaccio (see page 479)

———◆———

Lesso Rifatto con Porri
(Leftover Boiled Beef with Leeks)　　　　　(S E R V E S 4)

One of the best ways to convert leftover boiled meat into an exciting new dish. The meat is cooked a second time, covered with a layer of leeks. By covering the casserole, only the liquid given off by the leeks is used, so the boiled meat loses none of its own flavor but rather gains that of the leeks.

> 10　large leeks
> ¼　cup olive oil
> 1½　pounds of boiled beef, approximately
> 　　Salt and freshly ground pepper to taste

Wash the leeks well, then cut them into rings and soak them for 2 hours in a bowl of cold water.

Pour the olive oil into a large casserole, preferably terra-cotta, then add half the leeks. Place the whole piece of cold boiled meat over the leeks and cover it with the remaining leeks. Sprinkle with salt and freshly ground pepper, cover, and place the casserole on a medium flame. Simmer very gently, stirring every so often with a wooden spoon, for about 1½ hours. The leeks should give off enough liquid so it will not be necessary to add any. If extra liquid is necessary, add up to ½ cup of hot water. After 1½ hours, the leeks should be very soft. When you stir, be sure to leave boiled meat between two layers of leeks.

Taste for salt and pepper and simmer for 3 or 4 minutes more without the lid, then remove the casserole from the stove and let rest for 5 minutes.

Remove the boiled meat from the casserole and slice it on board. Arrange slices of meat on a serving dish and make a ring of leeks around them. Sprinkle with a little pepper and serve.

A fourteenth-century Venetian copy of a Florentine cookbook showing a recipe for *torta di latte*, a type of quiche. This manuscript also contains the recipe for *quinquinelle*, the original quenelles.

The Fried Course

⋖◆⋗

"Even a bedroom slipper tastes good if it is deep-fried."

This saying conveys how much the Florentines love deep-fried meats and vegetables, and over the centuries they have developed a wide variety of techniques for deep frying.*

Though in recent decades some Americans have attempted to minimize the consumption of fried foods because of their heaviness, it should be noted that this heaviness comes about only when the frying is poorly done. Indeed, roasted meats, which are often cooked for a very long time, are usually heavier. If the deep frying is properly done, the shortening is not absorbed into the food itself, but merely serves to make the outside crisp. The shortening—which in most cases should be a light vegetable shortening—must be allowed to become very hot, so it is not absorbed into the meat or vegetable but affects only the outside. Detailed instructions are given in each recipe.

There are five main methods of deep frying used in Florence, and all of them result in a very light dish. Even batter-dipped meat and vegetables have only a thin, light coating. (The kind of batter frying in which the batter is half an inch thick with a minute amount of meat inside, all very soggy, is unknown in Florentine cooking.)

The following are the procedures for coating different kinds of meats and vegetables; remember that fried meats are always accompanied by vegetables that are fried, not boiled, baked, pureed, or prepared in any other way:

1. Lightly floured by shaking the pieces in a bag with some flour. For fish and seafood, this method is sometimes referred to as *fritto alla*

---

* Again, the French owe all techniques of frying to Caterina de Medici's cooks, as frying was unknown in France before their arrival. Even *tempura* was introduced to Japan from the West, by the Portuguese, who probably got the technique from the Florentines.

pescatora because it is the method used by fishermen. A whole fish or fillet, not in pieces, is rolled in flour and the excess flour is shaken off.

2. Coating with bread crumbs only.
3. Flouring as described in method 1 above and then dipping lightly in salted beaten egg.
4. Marinated in lightly beaten egg with salt and coated lightly with bread crumbs.
5. Dipped in batter.

A SUGGESTED DINNER

WINE
Villa di Capezzana-Carmignano

Rotolo di pasta ripieno (see page 198)

Pollo fritto (see below)

Zucchini fritti
and *Fiori di zucca fritti* (see page 425)

Crespelle di farina dolce (see page 481)

Pollo Fritto
(Chicken Deep-Fried in Batter)   (SERVES 4)

Boned chicken pieces, dipped into a batter made with white wine and olive oil and flavored with nutmeg, are luscious, light, and crisp when deep-fried. Easy to make for a family dinner, when accompanied by zucchini or zucchini flowers dipped in the same batter and fried, a dish delicious enough to serve to the most discerning guests. On a family evening, if you really have little time, you can use the chicken unboned, and it will still work well. The batter must, however, be prepared 2 hours in advance and allowed to stand in a cool place, though not the refrigerator.

For the pastella (batter)

  1 ¾ cups all-purpose flour
  ½ teaspoon salt
  3 tablespoons olive oil
  2 eggs, separated
    Pinch of freshly grated nutmeg
  ⅓ cup dry white wine
  1 cup cold water

For the chicken

  1 small chicken, about 3 pounds
  2 pounds solid vegetable shortening
    Salt to taste
    Lemon wedges

Sift the flour into a large bowl. One at a time, add the salt, olive oil, egg yolks, nutmeg, wine, and water. After each ingredient is added, mix it well with the flour before adding the next. When all are added, stir until the batter is smooth.

Let stand in a cool place for 2 hours; do not refrigerate. Set the egg whites aside for incorporation later.

Meanwhile, cut the chicken into about 24 small pieces, then remove the bone from each piece of chicken. (This is not absolutely necessary, but the dish is better when the pieces are boned. Boning the individual small pieces requires no special technique and need not be time consuming.) Remove the skin, however, whether boned or not.

Heat the vegetable shortening in a deep-fat fryer until very hot. Just before the fat reaches the point where it is ready for frying, whip the reserved egg whites in a bowl until they are stiff. Fold the whites into the batter and mix very gently and very little.

Submerge each piece of chicken completely in the batter and drop it into the hot fat. Let cook for 7 or 8 minutes. (With the bone, it will take a few minutes longer.)

Cover a large serving dish with a layer of paper towels. As each piece of chicken is cooked, remove with strainer-skimmer and place on the paper towels.

When all the pieces are on the dish, remove the towels. Sprinkle with salt. Serve hot, garnished with lemon wedges.

A SUGGESTED DINNER

WINE
Chianti Classico Melini Riserva

Lasagne all'anitra (see page 195)

Cervello fritto (see below)

Sformato di verdura (see page 426)

Tortelli dolci (see page 458)

Cervello Fritto
(Fried Calf's Brains) (s e r v e s 4)

The calf's brains are soaked for an hour in cold water, the membranes are removed, and then are soaked for 15 minutes in lemon juice. They are cut into small pieces, lightly floured, dipped in egg and deep fried. This is a good dish to introduce you to brains if they are not already part of your repertory. Mixed together with fried artichoke pieces (see page 398), they make a very special dish called *fritto misto alla fiorentina* (see page 280).

1 whole calf's brain
  Salt
  Juice of ½ lemon
2 whole eggs
1 cup all-purpose flour, approximately
1 pound solid vegetable shortening
  Lemon wedges

Soak the brains in a bowl of cold water for an hour. Meanwhile, bring about 1 quart of water, with a little salt, to a boil in a saucepan.

Drain the brains, put them back in the bowl, then cover with the boiling water. Leave the brains in the hot water for 5 minutes, then put them under cold running water, holding them with one hand while you remove the membranes with the other.

Return the brains to the bowl. Add the lemon juice to 1 cup of cold water and pour it over the brains. Let soak for 15 minutes, then dry very well with paper towels and cut into pieces about 1 inch square.

Beat eggs in a bowl and add a pinch of salt; lightly flour the pieces of brain.

Heat the shortening in a deep-fat fryer. When it is very hot, dip the pieces of brain, one at a time, in the egg and drop into the hot shortening, turning them over when golden brown on one side.

Cover the bottom of a serving dish with a layer of paper towels. When pieces are brown on both sides, transfer them with slotted spoon onto the serving dish; the paper towels will absorb excess grease. When all the pieces are in the serving dish, remove the paper towels.

Sprinkle with salt, garnish with lemon wedges, and serve hot.

———◆———

A SUGGESTED DINNER

WINE
Chianti Classico Palazzo al Bosco

Incavolata (see page 124)

Polpette alla fiorentina (see below)

Broccoli strascicati (see page 406)

Pesche ripiene con mandorle (see page 493)

———◆———

Polpette alla Fiorentina
(Deep-Fried Chicken or Meat Croquettes)   (SERVES 6)

Though these croquettes are sometimes made with leftover chicken breast or boiled beef, more often the chicken is poached or the meat boiled especially to make this dish, which shows that it is important enough to the Florentines for them to start from scratch.

When the croquette filling is rolled in homemade bread crumbs and deep-fried in a light shortening, the result is a marvelously light, crisp *polpetta.*

2 large potatoes
4 slices white bread, crusts removed
1 cup cold milk
¾ pound boiled chicken breast or beef (see pages 267 and 268)
6 or 7 sprigs Italian parsley
1 clove garlic
2 eggs
¼ cup freshly grated Parmigiano cheese
  Salt and freshly ground pepper
1 cup bread crumbs, preferably homemade (see page 45), approximately
2 pounds solid vegetable shortening
  Lemon wedges

Boil potatoes in a saucepan of salted water for 25 to 30 minutes, until soft, then peel them and pass through a potato ricer into a large bowl.

Put the bread in a small bowl with the cold milk and soak for 10 to 12 minutes. Meanwhile, finely chop the boiled chicken (or beef), parsley, and garlic.

Transfer the chopped ingredients to the bowl with potatoes, then add the eggs and Parmigiano and mix very well with a wooden spoon. Squeeze the milk out of the bread and add to the bowl, then taste for salt and pepper and mix throughly.

Spread the bread crumbs out on a sheet of aluminum foil. Take a heaping tablespoon of the croquette mixture, form into a sausage shape, and roll in the bread crumbs. Repeat until all the mixture is used.

Prepare a serving dish by lining it with paper towels.

Heat the shortening in a frying pan, and when it is very hot, put in the *polpette* and fry until golden brown on both sides. As they are cooked, place them to drain on the prepared serving dish.

When all the *polpette* are on the dish, remove the paper towels, sprinkle with salt, and garnish with lemon wedges. Serve hot.

———◆———

A SUGGESTED DINNER

WINE
Chianti Classico Castell'in Villa

Risotto con funghi (see page 215)
Fritto misto alla fiorentina (see below)
Insalata verde (see page 387)
Pesche al vino (see page 496)

———◆———

Fritto Misto alla Fiorentina
(Mixed Fry, Florentine Style)

The fried-dish counterpart to the *bollito misto* is called *fritto misto*. It is again a holdover from the days when the boiled course and the fried course were the *primi e secondi*.

The most usual mixture, if only two dishes are included, is that of fried calf's brain (see page 277) and fried artichokes (see page 398), a combination that appears on most restaurant menus as *fritto alla fiorentina*. However, the *misto* can be a more elaborate combination. For a really grand *misto*, you may include, for meats, fried chicken (see page 275), croquettes (see page 278), and the brains; for vegetables, zucchini (see page 426), zucchini flowers (see page 425), cauliflower (see page 410), potatoes, or any combination thereof.

To serve *fritto misto*, divide the serving dish into as many wedges (like slices of a pie) as there are different dishes. Separate each wedge from the next by a row of lemon wedges. As much as possible, alternate wedges of meats with those of vegetables.

————◆————

A SUGGESTED DINNER

WINE
Chianti Classico Montagliari

Tortelli alla menta (see page 168)

Braciole fritte (see below)

Fiori di zucca fritti (see page 425)
or *Insalata mista* (see page 387)

Schiacciata unta di Berlingaccio (see page 472)

————◆————

Braciole Fritte
(Deep-Fried Veal or Beef Cutlets)   (S E R V E S 4)

This dish is the Florentine counterpart of *cotolette alla milanese*. Cookbooks from the turn of the century mention that a *milanese* has a bone when it is cut from the loin, and is boneless when it is cut from the upper leg. (These are called respectively *costola* and *noce*.) At that time the *milanese* was cooked in enough butter so that it was really deep-fried. Nowadays, most *milanese* are made with the bone and use less butter, so they are almost sautéed rather than deep-fried.

This recipe is for a dish that the Florentines sometimes call a *milanese*, but I believe that, though they were once the same, both it and the *milanese* have changed in the past century. I call it *braciola* because it is made from meat, either veal or young beef, without the bone, pounded thin and tender with the *batticarne* (meat pounder). In Milan the dish is often swimming in butter; some recommend that the butter in which it has been cooked be poured over the dish when served. This obviously would not appeal to the Florentines with their horror of fat and heaviness. So, in Florence, the deep frying of the old days remains, but done with the lighter *olio di semi*. The butter flavor is replaced by lemon juice and a little salt, which are added when the dish is served. It is also the practice there to marinate the meat in the beaten egg, rather than just dipping it.

4 boneless veal cutlets (about ¾ pound) or thin slices of a tender beef, such as sirloin

2 eggs
Salt

¾ cup very fine unflavored bread crumbs, preferably homemade (see page 45), approximately

½ pound solid vegetable shortening, approximately
Lemon wedges

If any fat has been left on the meat cutlets, remove it with a knife.

Wet two sheets of wax paper and place the cutlets between them. Pound the cutlets with a meat pounder until they are about ⅛ inch thick.

In a large bowl, beat the eggs with a pinch of salt. Place the cutlets, one by one, in the bowl with the beaten egg, making sure all are well coated with egg. Let the cutlets marinate for 1 hour.

Place a sheet of aluminum foil on a board and spread the bread crumbs over it. Remove one cutlet at a time from the bowl and bread it on both sides; with your fingers, gently press each cutlet all over to make sure the other side is absorbing bread crumbs.

Prepare a serving dish by lining it with paper towels.

Heat the vegetable shortening in a frying pan. When it is hot, place the cutlets, one by one, in the pan and cook them for about 1 minute on each side, until very lightly golden brown. (In Italy we say that the *braciole* must be "blonde" and that breaded lamb cutlets must be "brunette.")

Transfer the cutlets from the pan to the prepared serving dish with a strainer-skimmer. When all cutlets are on the dish, remove the paper towels. Garnish with lemon wedges, sprinkle with a little salt, and serve immediately.

Note: You can also eat the cutlets cold, or plain with anchovy sauce (see page 64). If so, use butter to fry the cutlets. While butter is heavier than the vegetable shortening, it will give a better taste to the cold dish.

A SUGGESTED DINNER

WINE
Dr. Antoniolo Gattinara

Tagliatelle al cibreo (see page 148)

Cotolette d'agnello (see below)

Carciofi fritti (see page 398)

Insalata verde (see page 387)

Pere al vino (see page 495)

Cotolette d'Agnello
(Lamb Chop, Florentine Style)   (SERVES 4)

Lamb is eaten in Italy only very young, in the spring. In order to make these deep-fried lamb chops, you have to convince your butcher to cut them very thin, usually requiring that he cut a single chop into two slices. Insist, because they must be very thin for this dish.

    8 small rib lamb chops, cut very thin
    2 eggs
       Salt
    ¾ cup very fine unflavored bread crumbs, preferably homemade
          (see page 45), approximately
    ¼ pound solid vegetable shortening, approximately
    ½ cup olive oil
       Lemon wedges

Remove all the fat from the chops.

Beat the eggs in large bowl with a pinch of salt. Place the lamb chops, one by one, in the bowl with the beaten eggs, making sure all are well coated with egg. Let them marinate for 1 hour.

Place a sheet of aluminum foil on a board and spread the bread crumbs over it. Remove the chops one at a time from the bowl and bread them on both sides. With your fingers, gently press each chop all over to make sure the bread crumbs are adhering to the other side.

Prepare a serving dish by lining it with paper towels.

Heat the vegetable shortening and olive oil in a frying pan. When they are hot, place the chops, one by one, in the pan and cook for 2 or 3 minutes on each side, then raise the flame to make the bread crumbs a darker brown (what Italians call "frying a brunette," rather than a "blonde," color).

With a strainer-skimmer, transfer the chops from the pan to the prepared serving dish. When all the chops are on the dish, remove the paper towels. Garnish with lemon wedges, sprinkle with salt, and serve immediately.

Eggs

E GGS make a very light but very satisfying main course. The first egg dish we present, the classically simple *uova al pomodoro* (eggs poached in tomatoes), is useful for the simplest of occasions or when a very light main dish is in order. Following is *eggs Florentine* the way the Florentines make it, and last comes *asparagi alla fiorentina* a succulent dish of tender, thin young asparagus, sautéed with butter and topped with eggs fried a very special way.

It goes without saying that any of the *frittate* on pages 96–99, when freshly made and warm, may also be served as main courses.

A SUGGESTED DINNER

WINE
Chianti Spicchio

Risotto con salsicce (see page 218)

Uova al pomodoro (see below)

Patate saltate alla salvia (see page 416)

Fresh fruit

Uova al Pomodoro
(Eggs Poached in Tomatoes)   (SERVES 6)

A dish that can be marvelous—if the ingredients are good. Poaching in tomatoes rather than water preserves the full flavor of the eggs. Especially good in the summer when tomatoes and basil are fresh, this dish also works well with preserved tomatoes and basil in the winter.

        2 pounds very ripe fresh or canned plum tomatoes
        1 clove garlic
        ¼ cup olive oil
           Salt and freshly ground pepper
        5 or 6 leaves fresh basil or basil under salt (see page 14)
       12 fresh eggs

If fresh tomatoes are used, first cut them into pieces (canned tomatoes may be left whole); cut the garlic into small pieces.

Heat the oil in a large saucepan, preferably terra-cotta. When it is hot, sauté the garlic lightly until light golden. Add the tomatoes and cook on a low flame for about 15 minutes. Check to be sure they are very soft and of a saucelike consistency, and if necessary cook a little longer; do not add any water or broth. Add salt and pepper to taste.

If the basil is fresh, tear the leaves in half or in thirds. If preserved, keep the leaves whole, as they must be removed before the dish is served. Add basil to the saucepan.

Very carefully, break the eggs into the tomato sauce. Sprinkle salt and pepper over the eggs and let them poach for about 8 minutes. (Remove the preserved basil at this point.)

Bring the eggs to the table, in the pan, and serve hot.

————————◆————————

A SUGGESTED DINNER

WINE
Chianti Classico Il Caggio

Spaghetti con briciolata (see page 158)

Uova alla fiorentina (see below)

Frittelle di riso (see page 485)

———◆———

Uova alla Fiorentina
(Eggs Florentine, the Florentine Way) (SERVES 4)

The dish that is widely disseminated under the name "eggs Florentine" consists of spinach sautéed in butter, egg placed over it, everything covered with *balsamella* and Parmigiano or *groviera* (Mornay sauce in France), and then baked.

Though even modern Florentine cookbooks use this recipe and call it "eggs Florentine," I believe that this is a completely French dish. The French tend to call anything with spinach and Mornay sauce "Florentine," and there probably is some basis in the history of food for doing so.

However, I have never come across the sautéing of spinach in butter in the Florence of either the past or present. And while Mornay sauce is quite probably of Florentine origin, and is used on spinach to make *spinaci alla fiorentina* (see page 422), it is not used on eggs. The baking also probably comes from *spinaci alla fiorentina*.

The following is a dish that is widely used in Florence and is possibly the authentic eggs Florentine.

        2 packages (10 ounces each) fresh spinach
        3 tablespoons olive oil
        1 clove garlic
          Salt, freshly ground pepper
          Freshly grated nutmeg to taste
        4 eggs

Using the spinach, olive oil, garlic, and salt and pepper make *spinaci saltati* as directed on page 421, preferably using a terra-cotta saucepan.

Make 4 small wells in the spinach and place a raw egg in each. Salt and pepper each egg, then cover the pan and cook on a very low flame for about 12 to 15 minutes; the eggs will steam inside the pan.

Sprinkle very lightly with nutmeg, then bring to the table in the pan and serve.

———————◆———————

A SUGGESTED DINNER

WINE
Chianti Classico Montepaldi

Tagliatelle al sugo di carne (see page 146)

Asparagi alla fiorentina (see below)

Lamponi alla panna (see page 497)

———————◆———————

Asparagi alla Fiorentina
(Asparagus, Florentine Style) (SERVES 4)

Because they have a short one-month season, in the spring, asparagus are much prized in Italy and are treated as a main dish. In contrast to American tastes, it is the thin asparagus that are preferred, for their delicacy and taste as well as tenderness. In America, we are lucky to have asparagus for much more of the year, and our large, thick asparagus are often very good and tender. But do try the thin ones, for taste. (They are also usually a great bargain in America, because nobody wants them.)

After the asparagus are boiled or steamed, they are sautéed in butter and sprinkled with Parmigiano. Then the master touch is applied: *uova in padella* (fried eggs) are arranged over them. The Italian expression, *"Non è buono a cuocere nemmeno un uovo"* (he is not even able to cook an egg) gives an incorrect impression, because to cook an egg well is really an art—and the eggs as prepared here are truly artistic. They can stand on their own, without the asparagus, very well indeed, and make an excellent main course in themselves.

     4 eggs
     3 pounds thin asparagus
       Coarse salt
    12 tablespoons (1½ sticks) butter
       Salt and freshly ground black pepper
     ½ cup freshly grated Parmigiano cheese

Remove eggs from the refrigerator at least 1 hour before you intend to use them; they must be at room temperature for this dish.

Wash the asparagus well, then clean the white part of each one by scraping it with a knife. Arrange all asparagus in a bunch, with tips even. Tie the bunch together, toward the bottom, with thread. Then, with a knife, even off the ends.

Place the bunch of asparagus, standing with tips up, in a tall stockpot. Add enough cold water to cover the white parts, at the lower end of the asparagus, and coarse salt, then cover the pot and place it on the heat. Bring the water to a boil, reduce the heat, and simmer for 20 minutes, without removing the lid.

Remove the pot from the heat and transfer the asparagus to a chopping board. Untie the bunch and cut off the hard white ends.

Heat the butter in a large frying pan. When it is melted, add the asparagus and sauté for 6 or 7 minutes, turning gently with a wooden spoon several times. Sprinkle the grated Parmigiano, salt, and freshly ground black pepper over the asparagus, then cook, still turning gently, for 1 minute more.

Leaving the sautéing butter in the pan, transfer the asparagus from the frying pan to a large serving dish and arrange in a ring, with all the tips facing the center of the dish. Keep the serving dish in a warm place, near the stove if possible.

Heat the butter left over from cooking the asparagus on a low flame. Break one of the eggs, and carefully pour the white into the pan with the asparagus butter, saving the yolk in its half-shell. Repeat with the remaining eggs, keeping each white separate from the others in the pan.

When all the egg whites are arranged in the frying pan, sprinkle with salt, then place a yolk on top of each white, taking care not to break the yolk. Sprinkle each yolk with pepper, then cover the frying pan and let simmer very slowly for about 4 minutes.

Remove the pan from the flame, arrange the eggs over the asparagus on the serving dish, and serve immediately, sprinkled with a little freshly ground black pepper.

Poultry and Game

A SUGGESTED DINNER

WINE
Chianti Classico Fattoria Casenuove

Lasagne al forno (see page 189)

Pollastrino alla griglia (see below)

Insalata mista (see page 387)

Torta di mele (see page 475)

Pollastrino alla Griglia
(Grilled Squab Chicken)   (SERVES 1)

Here, the celebrated, two-month-old Arno Valley chickens are
flattened and cooked simply on the iron *gratella*, the range-top grill.
A good butcher can obtain young squab fryers or fresh Cornish hens
for you, and they work very well for this dish. Each person is served
a whole tender, tiny chicken.

The *gratella* (see photo 1) is a wonderful way of cooking. It is
ridged so that the fat pours down and the chicken doesn't cook in it.
If the grill is well seasoned, you will need no shortening; just salt the
grill.

Pollastrino alla griglia: 1. The *gratella* (range top grill) and the flattened chicken.

    1 squab fryer chicken (1 to 1½ pounds) or fresh Cornish hen
    2 teaspoons salt
       Freshly ground black pepper
       Lemon wedges

Cut the chicken (or Cornish hen) lengthwise through the breast and open it. With your hands, flatten it out.

Heat a well-seasoned iron *gratella* on a low flame for about 5 minutes, then sprinkle the grill with 2 teaspoons of salt. When the grill is very hot and the salt turns brown, place the flattened chicken on it and top with a weight such as an iron skillet wrapped in aluminum foil (see photo 2). Cook for about 10 minutes, then turn the chicken over, put the weight back on, and cook for 10 minutes more. (If the chicken is really very young, at this point it should be completely cooked and of a dark, golden color. Try with a fork to see if it is really cooked; if not, cook it for several more minutes, until completely done.)

Transfer the grilled chicken to serving dish, sprinkle with a little freshly ground black pepper and serve, garnished with lemon wedges.

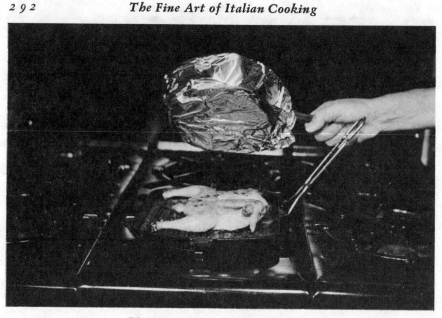

2. Placing the weight on the chicken.

A SUGGESTED DINNER

WINE
Conte Spalletti Orvieto Classico (*secco*)

Sformato di tagliatelle verdi (see page 150)

Petti di pollo alla fiorentina (see below)

Schiacciata con zibibbo (see page 473)

Petti di Pollo alla Fiorentina
(Chicken Breasts, Florentine Style)   (S E R V E S 6)

Chicken breasts and the tender insides of artichokes, cut into pieces
and sautéed together in white wine and sprinkled with lemon juice.
This is a dish that gives lie to the idea that artichokes and wine do

not go together. In this dish, only the tenderest part of the artichoke is used so it can be cooked in a very short time, conveying a little of the idea of the taste of the raw tender artichokes the Florentines love to eat *in pinzimonio* (see page 83).

This is a dish that can be prepared in a short time.

> 3 large artichokes
> 2 lemons
> ½ cup olive oil
>   Salt and freshly ground pepper to taste
> 3 whole chicken breasts
> 1 cup all-purpose flour, approximately
> ½ cup dry white wine

Clean the artichokes according to the directions on page 394 and cut them into small pieces. Put artichoke pieces in a large bowl of cold water with one of the lemons, cut into halves, and leave to stand for 30 minutes.

Remove artichokes and dry them with paper towels.

Heat ¼ cup of the olive oil in a large casserole. When the oil is hot, add the artichoke pieces and sauté, on a medium flame, for about 25 minutes, stirring every few minutes with a wooden spoon. Season with salt and pepper, then, with a strainer-skimmer, remove the artichokes from the casserole and transfer them to a second casserole. Cover with a lid and let stand until needed.

Remove the skin and bone from chicken breasts and cut them into 1 inch-square pieces. Lightly flour the chicken pieces.

Heat the remaining ¼ cup of olive oil in the first casserole and put in the chicken pieces. Sauté very gently until soft (about 20 minutes), then season with salt. When the meat is ready, transfer from the first casserole to the second, containing the artichokes.

Heat the wine in the first casserole and let it reduce very slowly (about 15 minutes), then pour it over the artichoke and chicken mixture; squeeze the juice of the remaining lemon over and mix throughly.

Transfer the contents of the casserole to a serving dish and serve immediately.

A SUGGESTED DINNER

WINE
Chianti Classico Carpineto

Carabaccia (see page 113)

Pollo alle olive (see below)

Insalata mista (see page 387) or *Insalata composta* (see page 388)

Dolce di polenta (see page 476)

Pollo alle Olive
(Chicken with Black Olives)   (SERVES 4)

Unboned chicken pieces cooked with olives and flavored with thyme and bay leaf. Though thyme grows wild in many gardens in Florence, it is not used as much nowadays as in olden times. There are, however, several traditional dishes that use it. Here its flavor blends well with the Mediterranean olive flavor.

Another dish which is not difficult or time consuming to prepare.

>   1 chicken (3 to 4 pounds)
>   8 tablespoons (1 stick) butter
>   1 tablespoon olive oil
>   Salt and freshly ground pepper
> 1½ cups chicken or meat broth
>   2 tablespoons all-purpose flour
>   1 bay leaf
>   1 teaspoon dried thyme
>   ½ pound black olives
>   5 or 6 sprigs Italian parsley

Cut the chicken into 16 pieces.

Heat the butter and olive oil in a large flameproof casserole. When they are hot, put in the chicken pieces and sauté gently, turning them, until they are golden brown all over (about 15 minutes). Season with salt and pepper.

Heat the broth to the boiling point in a saucepan.

Meanwhile, sprinkle the chicken with the flour and stir it thoroughly with a wooden spoon for 1 minute. Immediately pour in the hot broth, stirring thoroughly to prevent lumps from forming, then add the bay leaf and the thyme to the casserole and simmer slowly for 20 minutes, stirring every so often. Remove the bay leaf from the casserole and add the olives. Taste for salt and pepper and simmer for about 10 minutes more.

Remove the casserole from the heat and transfer its contents to a serving dish. Sprinkle over the parsley, coarsely chopped, and serve hot.

◆

A SUGGESTED DINNER

WINE
Borgogno Grignolino

Risotto con funghi (see page 215)
Fricassea di pollo (see below)
Sformato di fagiolini (see page 426)
Torta di mele (see page 475)

◆

Fricassea di Pollo
(Florentine Chicken Fricassee)   (S E R V E S 4)

Le Cuisinier of La Varenne, which appeared in France about 1650 is full of fricassees. However, the Florentine and Ferrarese cookbooks of more than a century earlier also contain them. In fact La Varenne's book, which many consider an important step in the history of the development of haute cuisine, really does not differ all that much from the Italian cookbooks of the previous century. The book was translated in Bologna about 1690, and because the French and the Bolognese share a predilection for rich, creamy food, it may have played a role in the development of Bolognese cooking.

This is the good old recipe for basic chicken fricasee as it has been made in Florence for centuries.

1½ ounces dried *porcini* mushrooms
1 chicken (about 3 pounds)
1 onion
1 celery rib
5 or 6 sprigs Italian parsley
1 carrot
1 clove garlic
½ teaspoon rosemary leaves
1 tablespoon butter
2 tablespoons olive oil
1½ tablespoons all-purpose flour
2½ cups chicken or meat broth, approximately
3 eggs
1 lemon
   Salt and freshly ground pepper to taste

Soak mushrooms in lukewarm water for 20 minutes; cut the chicken in 8 pieces; place the *odori* (onion, celery, parsley, carrot, garlic, and rosemary) on a piece of cheesecloth, tie into a bag, and set aside.

Heat the butter and olive oil in a flameproof casserole. When they are very hot, add the chicken pieces and sauté lightly on a medium flame for 10 to 12 minutes. When the chicken pieces are golden brown, remove them from the casserole to a serving dish.

Leaving the casserole on the flame, add the flour to the remaining oil and cook, stirring very well, until golden brown (about 3 to 4 minutes). Meanwhile, heat the broth to boiling in a saucepan, then pour 1½ cups of it into the casserole and mix very well, to prevent lumps from forming.

Put the chicken pieces back into the casserole and add the cheesecloth bag containing the *odori*. Cover and simmer very slowly for 20 minutes, then remove the cheesecloth bag and taste for salt and pepper. Add the soaked mushrooms and more hot broth if needed, cover, and simmer for 10 to 12 minutes more.

When the cooking time is almost up, beat the eggs in a bowl. Remove the casserole from the heat and quickly add the beaten eggs, stirring continuously with a wooden spoon. When the eggs are well amalgamated, squeeze in the juice from the lemon and mix thoroughly.

Transfer the contents of the casserole to a serving dish and serve hot.

———◆———

A SUGGESTED DINNER

WINE
Chianti Classico Fattoria Calcinaia

Risotto in bianco (see page 214)

Pollo alla cacciatora (see below)

Insalata composta (see page 388)

Bombe (see page 443)

———◆———

Pollo alla Cacciatora
(Chicken, Hunter Style)   (S E R V E S   4)

All over Italy, "hunter style," *alla cacciatora*, is applied to dishes made with fowl, perhaps originally with game birds. It is supposed to connote the basic but excellent style of preparation used by the hunters themselves. Naturally, the name covers a multitude of dishes, usually made with chicken rather than a game bird.

This is a Tuscan way of making it, using very little tomato but depending more on red wine and olive oil and full of herbs such as sage, rosemary, and bay leaf. The chicken is almost *spezzato*, that is, cut into small pieces, each around a piece of bone.

It is worthwhile to try this version, especially if you know the heavier tomato sauce ones. It is not difficult to prepare.

    1   chicken (3 to 3½ pounds)
    1   tablespoon rosemary leaves
    7   or 8 leaves sage, fresh or under salt (see page 14)
    2   cloves garlic   *(continued)*

¼ cup olive oil
Salt and freshly ground pepper to taste
Pinch of hot red pepper flakes
½ cup dry red wine
1 bay leaf
2 tablespoons tomato paste
1½ cups hot water

Cut the chicken into 16 pieces; coarsely chop the rosemary, sage, and garlic.

Heat the olive oil in a large casserole, preferably terra-cotta, and when it is hot, add the chopped ingredients and sauté gently until lightly golden brown (10 to 12 minutes). Add the chicken pieces and sauté them on a moderately high flame until golden brown on both sides (about 15 minutes), then add salt, pepper, and hot pepper flakes.

Lower the flame and pour in the wine. Let it evaporate very slowly (about 10 minutes), then add the bay leaf, tomato paste, and ½ cup of the hot water. Cover and let simmer very slowly for 20 minutes, adding more hot water if needed.

At this point, the chicken should be cooked, and there should be a small quantity of thick sauce. Remove the bay leaf and transfer the chicken pieces and sauce to a serving dish. Serve hot.

Note: This dish is even better when reheated.

———◆———

A SUGGESTED DINNER

WINE
Chianti Classico Castelli del Grevepesa

Cipollata (see page 114)

Pollo in porchetta (see below)

Fagioli all'uccelletto (see page 402)

Fresh fruit

———◆———

Pollo in Porchetta
(Chicken Made in the Manner of Suckling Pig)   (S E R V E S   4)

The famous *porchetta*, or suckling pig, is cooked filled with a large quantity of herbs, spices, and *pancetta*. This treatment is also very good with both chicken and duck. After the bird is stuffed, it is closed up tightly by sewing, and put in the oven. Suckling pig is indeed evoked, and one can make this dish more often than the *porchetta*, which after all requires a very special occasion.

For the stuffing

      4 ounces *pancetta* or 2 ounces boiled ham plus
             2 ounces salt pork
     14 large leaves sage, fresh or under salt (see page 14)
     10 juniper berries
      1 large bay leaf
      1 tablespoon rosemary leaves
      6 or 7 whole black peppercorns
         Salt and freshly ground black pepper

For the chicken

      1 broiler chicken (about 3 ½ pounds), left whole
     ¼ cup olive oil

Prepare the stuffing by coarsely chopping the *pancetta*, 10 of the sage leaves, the juniper berries, bay leaf, and rosemary leaves; then mix in the peppercorns, 2 level teaspoons of salt, and ½ teaspoon pepper.

Preheat the oven to 400°.

Wash the chicken inside and out; leave in all the chicken fat. Fill the cavity of the chicken with the stuffing mixture and sew up both ends, placing the 4 remaining sage leaves in the neck end before sewing it up, then tie the chicken up as you would a roast.

Abundantly salt and pepper the outside of the chicken and place in a roasting pan along with the olive oil. Cook in the preheated oven for about 65 minutes.

Transfer the chicken to a serving dish and serve hot.

———◆———

A SUGGESTED DINNER

WINE
Chianti Classico Castello di Gabbiano Riserva

Gnocchi di pesce (see page 226)

Pollo affinocchiato (see below)

Sformato di finocchi (see page 426)

Crostata di frutta (see page 444)

———◆———

Pollo Affinocchiato
(Fenneled Chicken)   (SERVES 4)

Chicken prepared with fennel and almonds is the oldest known Italian chicken recipe, going back at least to the fourteenth century, and for some centuries it was the favorite way of preparing chicken. When you try it, you'll understand why. The taste is a little unusual at first, but then you realize that it is one of the combinations that was meant to be. That it has disappeared in recent times can probably be explained by the movement away from using almonds as one of the bases of Mediterranean cooking. A dish that is worth reviving, that can be eaten often, with an unusual flavor, this is not extremely difficult to prepare, but makes a fine impression at an important dinner.

  1 chicken (about 3 to 3½ pounds)
  4 ounces *pancetta* or 2 ounces boiled ham plus 2 ounces salt pork
  1 medium-sized red onion
 ¼ cup of olive oil
  2 cups chicken or meat broth
  4 ounces blanched almonds
  2 tablespoons all-purpose flour
  1 heaping tablespoon fennel seeds
    Salt and freshly ground pepper to taste

Cut the chicken into 8 pieces, then wash very carefully and dry with paper towels. Chop the *pancetta* and onion coarsely.

Heat the olive oil in a flameproof casserole, then add the *pancetta* and onion and sauté on a medium flame until golden brown. Add the chicken pieces and let them sauté until light brown on both sides (about 15 minutes).

While the chicken is sautéing, heat the broth in a saucepan. When the broth is hot, lower the flame and put in the blanched almonds. Let the broth and almonds remain on a low flame until needed.

When the chicken pieces are light brown, sprinkle them with the flour. Wait a few seconds, then pour in the hot broth and almonds. Taste for salt and pepper, then add the fennel seeds and let everything simmer together for 25 to 30 minutes, until completely cooked, stirring every few minutes.

Remove the casserole from the flame, transfer the chicken and sauce to a serving dish, and serve hot. This dish is even better the next day, reheated, or served cold for a family dinner.

Note: Sometimes American chickens give off a great deal of fat. If there is more than a thin layer at the top, remove excess before transferring chicken and sauce to serving dish.

A SUGGESTED DINNER

WINE
Ruffino Rosatello

Panzanella (see page 92)

Pollo forte (see below)

Insalata composta (see page 388)

Pesche al vino (see page 496)

———◆———

A SUGGESTED BUFFET

WINES
Bianco "Le Fonti"
Lungarotti Torgiano
Marchese Antinori Nature (*brut*)

Insalata di riso (see page 85)

Pollo forte (see below)

Porrata (see page 99)

Melanzane marinate (see page 90)

Pesche ripiene con mandorle (see page 493)
with *Crema zabaione* (see page 435)

———◆———

Pollo Forte
(Spicy Chicken Appetizer)   (S E R V E S   8)

Boiled chicken pieces, flavorsome and not overcooked, in a delicious, piquant sauce made with olive oil, broth, wine vinegar, garlic, and ground red peppers preserved in wine vinegar. Served cold, it is an extremely useful and versatile dish. Used mainly as an antipasto to whet the appetite, it serves also as a refreshing main dish for the hot weather.

- 1 boiled chicken (about 4 pounds), with its broth (see page 267)
- 2 tablespoons capers in wine vinegar
- 4 anchovies in salt or 8 anchovy fillets in oil
- 2 cloves garlic
- ½ cup olive oil
- 1 ½ tablespoons all-purpose flour
- 2 red peppers in wine vinegar, whole or in pieces, or pimento (soaked in wine vinegar for 30 minutes)

Salt and freshly ground pepper to taste
3 tablespoon wine vinegar

Prepare the boiled chicken according to the directions on page 267. Remove from the broth and let cool. Strain the broth and let cool for 1 hour.

Meanwhile, remove the skin from the chicken and lift the meat off the bones. Cut the meat into strips and place on a serving dish. Sprinkle the capers over. Set aside.

When the broth is cool, defat it thoroughly. Set aside.

Prepare the sauce. Clean and fillet the anchovies under cold, running water if the anchovies in salt are used. Set the fillets aside until needed.

Heat 1½ cups of defatted broth to the boiling point in a saucepan. Meanwhile, chop the garlic coarsely.

Heat the oil in a flameproof casserole on medium heat. When it is hot, add the anchovies, mashing them with a wooden spoon into a paste. Add the flour and stir until the flour is golden brown. Continuing to stir, add the boiling broth, all at once, and stir for 2 or 3 minutes more. Add one of the peppers, unchopped, and the chopped garlic. Let simmer for about 10 minutes, then remove from the heat and put in a blender. Blend until homogeneous.

Return the blended mixture to the casserole. Taste for salt and pepper and place on a low flame. Simmer for about 15 minutes more, then remove the casserole from the flame. Add the wine vinegar, mix well, and pour immediately over the chicken.

Cut the remaining pepper into thin strips and use to garnish the serving dish.

Let cool for 30 minutes, then wrap the serving dish in aluminum foil and place in the refrigerator for at least 4 hours.

———◆———

A SUGGESTED DINNER

WINE
Calissano Barolo Riserva Speciale

Taglierini al pomodoro fresco (see page 145)

Pollo in pane (see below)

Lattaiolo (see page 436)

———◆———

Pollo in Pane
(Whole Chicken Baked in Bread) (SERVES 4)

The whole chicken baked inside a bread and the boned whole stuffed chicken (see page 307) are the most elaborate chicken dishes in the Tuscan repertory, and probably in all Italian cooking. They are both dishes with an elaborate presentation that is appropriate to the most festive and formal occasions.

This dish, the less complicated of the two, is presented as a very large, freshly baked Tuscan bread. Then it is sliced open and inside is a whole, unboned chicken, which is stuffed in turn with coarsely cut *odori* (aromatic vegetables), chicken livers, red wine, and prosciutto. The stuffing is not in the form of a forcemeat, but is in recognizable small pieces. The bread absorbs some of the juice of the chicken and stuffing on the inside, and is delicious when chunks of it are served with the meat and stuffing.

 1 chicken (3½ to 4 pounds)
 1 medium-sized red onion
 1 large celery rib
 1 clove garlic
 2 carrots
 3 ounces prosciutto or boiled ham
 5 tablespoons olive oil
  Salt, freshly ground pepper, and freshly grated nutmeg
 ½ cup red wine
 ¼ pound chicken livers
  Tuscan bread (see page 32)

Prepare the stuffing and the chicken first.

Wash the chicken, inside and out, then dry with paper towels; cut the onion, celery, garlic, carrots, and prosciutto (or boiled ham) into large pieces.

Heat the olive oil in a large frying pan, then add the cut-up ingredients and sauté gently for about 10 minutes.

Place the whole chicken in the frying pan. Season with salt, pepper, and nutmeg and sauté, turning on all sides, until golden brown all over (about 15 minutes). Add the red wine and let evaporate very slowly (about 15 minutes) continuing to turn the chicken on all sides.

Meanwhile, cut the chicken livers into quarters. Add them to the pan and cook for 2 or 3 minutes more, then remove the frying pan from the flame and let stand until cool (about 1 hour).

Prepare the "sponge" and then the dough for Tuscan bread according to the directions on page 32, up to the point that kneading of dough is completed.

Flour a pasta board. Spread the dough out very gently, with a rolling pin or with your hands, to a thickness of about 1 inch. Sprinkle the surface of the dough with salt and pepper.

Stuff the chicken with the ingredients in pan and then place the chicken on the dough (see photo 1). Sprinkle the top of the chicken with any ingredients left over in the pan, then fold the dough completely around the chicken so that from the outside it appears to be an oval-shaped bread (see photo 2).

Pollo in pane: 1. Placing the chicken on the dough.

2. Folding the dough around the chicken.

Lightly flour a large jelly-roll pan and carefully place the dough-covered chicken on it. Cover with a cotton towel and let stand in a warm place, away from drafts, until the dough has risen and almost doubled in size (about 1 hour).

Preheat the oven to 400°.

Place the pan in the preheated oven and bake for 60 to 70 minutes, depending on the size of the chicken, then remove the pan from the oven and transfer the whole bread with chicken inside onto a large serving dish (see photo 3).

To serve, cut off the top part of the bread; the chicken will appear, sitting in the middle of the loaf of bread with some vegetables surrounding it. Each serving should have a piece of chicken, some vegetable filling, and a piece of the bread crust.

3. The final result.

———◆———

A SUGGESTED DINNER

WINE
Chianti Classico Villa Cafaggio

Ravioli nudi (see page 228)
Pollo disossato ripieno (see below)
Fagioli al fiasco (see page 400)
Torta di riso uso Garfagnana (see page 486)

———◆———

Pollo Disossato Ripieno
(Boned Whole Stuffed Chicken)

(SERVES FROM 8 TO 12)

One of the great old Tuscan dishes, this requires much preparation, the time and skill to bone the chicken while leaving it whole, the elaborate stuffing, the cooking, weighting, and cooling. It is appropriate for the most elegant occasions, though it is eaten cold. The elaborate forcemeat with which it is stuffed contains four kinds of meat, red wine, Parmigiano, and boiled ham, in addition to *odori* (aromatic vegetables) and herbs. It is a much more complex dish than a *galantina*, with which it is occasionally confused.

It is well worth the trouble, however, for it is one of the most delicious dishes imaginable, and makes an extraordinary presentation. It also has the advantage that it must be prepared in advance, so it can be done at your leisure. Don't be afraid to try it. The instructions for boning the chicken, making the stuffing, etc., are given in complete detail. Just follow them carefully, and with a little practice you'll have a dish that will give you reason to be proud of yourself.

   3 eggs
   1 small red onion
   2 celery ribs
   6 or 7 sprigs Italian parsley
   2 cloves garlic
   1 carrot
   5 tablespoons olive oil
   1 bay leaf
   1 pork chop (for a yield of ¼ pound meat)
  ½ pound ground beef
   1 whole chicken breast
  ¾ cup dry red wine
      Salt and freshly ground pepper
   1 tablespoon tomato paste
  ½ cup canned tomatoes
 1½ cups chicken or meat broth
   1 package unflavored gelatin
  ¼ pound boiled ham
   1 cup freshly grated Parmigiano cheese
      Pinch of freshly grated nutmeg
   1 whole chicken (about 4 pounds)
 1½ teaspoons rosemary leaves

In a small saucepan, hard-boil one of the eggs in salted water (10 to 12 minutes). Set aside until needed.

Finely chop the *odori* (onion, celery, parsley, garlic, and carrot).

Heat the olive oil in a large flameproof casserole. When it is hot, add the chopped *odori* and sauté lightly until golden brown (about 15 minutes), then add the bay leaf, pork chop, ground beef, and chicken breast. Sauté, stirring every so often with a wooden spoon, for 15 minutes more.

Add the wine and let it evaporate slowly (15 to 20 minutes), then taste for salt and pepper. Add the tomato paste and tomatoes and simmer for 4 or 5 minutes more.

Remove the casserole from the flame, discard the bay leaf, and transfer the pork chop and chicken breast to a board. Remove the bones and chop the meat very fine.

Replace the casserole on the heat and add the chopped meat. Simmer for 5 or 6 minutes.

Meanwhile, heat the broth in a saucepan, then add it to the casserole and simmer very slowly for 10 minutes. Sprinkle the unflavored gelatin over the ingredients in the casserole and mix very well with a wooden spoon. Let simmer very slowly until all the broth has evaporated and the sauce has become thick (35 to 45 minutes).

Remove the casserole from the stove, and with a strainer-skimmer transfer the sauce to a large bowl. Let stand until cold (about 2 hours); do not refrigerate.

When the contents of the bowl are cold, chop the boiled ham coarsely and add it to the bowl, along with the remaining 2 eggs, grated Parmigiano, and nutmeg to taste. Mix very well with a wooden spoon and let stand until needed.

Shell the hard-boiled egg and let stand until needed.

Begin boning the chicken by cutting the two tendons at the end of each of the two legs (see photo 1). Free the bone on the inside by hand (there is nothing to cut here) and push out a little bit (see photo 2). Free the thigh bone by cutting the tendon between leg and thigh. Push the thigh bone from one end and pull from the other (see photo 3).

Starting from cavity end, with a knife, little by little scrape the meat, without breaking it, off the inside of the central carcass (see photo 4). Remove large central bone in one piece (see photo 5).

Cut off the two outer sections of each wing. Remove the bone of the inner section in the same way you did the legs (see photo 6).

Tuck the legs and wings inside and sew up the neck opening (see photo 7).

Pollo disossato ripieno: 1. Cutting the tendon at the end of the leg.

2. Freeing the leg bone on the inside.

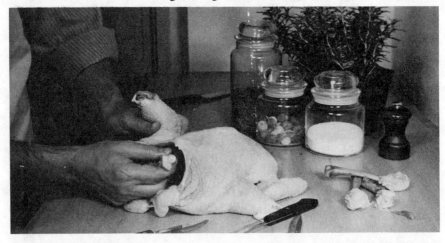

3. Pushing the thigh bone from one end and pulling from the other.

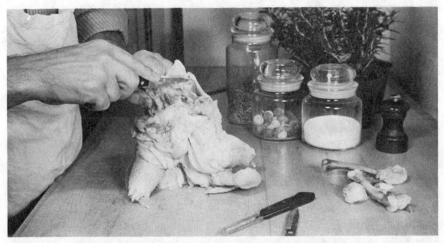

4. Scraping the meat from the rib cage.

5. Removing the carcass.

6. Cutting off the two outer sections of the wing.

7. The boned chicken, with wings and legs tucked inside and the neck cavity sewn up.

Preheat the oven to 350°.

Stuff the chicken from the remaining opening, at the bottom end. When you are halfway through, add the hard-boiled egg, then continue with the remaining stuffing; sew up the opening (see photos 8–10). Sprinkle freely with salt, pepper, and rosemary.

Wrap the chicken well in a large sheet of aluminum foil (see photo 11), then place the foil-wrapped chicken in a rectangular Pyrex baking dish (13½ x 8¾) (see photo 12) and bake in the preheated oven for 2 hours, turning the chicken over once, after 1 hour.

Remove the dish from the oven and allow the chicken to cool for 2 hours, first putting a weight (such as 2 Pyrex dishes or a brick) on top to flatten it (see photo 13). Then, still with the weight on top, place in the refrigerator until completely cold (about 4 hours).

When cold, unwrap the chicken and transfer to a board. Slice across the width, then place the slices on a serving dish, garnish with parsley and serve.

Note: It is better to prepare this dish one day in advance.

8. Stuffing the chicken.

9. Inserting the hard-boiled egg when the chicken is half stuffed.

10. Sewing up the remaining opening.

11. Wrapping the stuffed chicken in aluminum foil.

12. The foil-wrapped chicken in its baking dish.

13. The stuffed chicken cooling under a weight.

14. The final result, shown along with a large Tuscan bread (page 32).

A SUGGESTED DINNER

WINE
Negri Sassella

Spaghetti al sugo di "cipolle" (see page 157)

Petto di tacchino arrocchiato (see below)

Sformato di carote (see page 426)

Ciambella di frutta (see page 487)

A SUGGESTED DINNER
FOR THANKSGIVING DAY

WINES
Melini-Vernaccia di S. Gimignano
Chianti S. Fabiano
Cinzano Riserva Speciale (*brut*)

Polpettone di tacchino al tonno (see page 319)

Tortelli di zucca alla modenese (see page 174)

Petto di tacchino arrocchiato (see below)

Patate saltate alla salvia (see page 416)

Tartufi di castagne (see page 480)

Petto di Tacchino Arrocchiato
(Rolled Stuffed Turkey Breast)   (SERVES 6)

Turkey started to be used in Italy very soon after the discovery of America. In line with the general confusion about where Columbus and the Florentines, Amerigo Vespucci and Giovanni Verrazzano, had landed, it was at first called "rooster of India" (*gallo d'India*). (Even the name "turkey" reveals a mistaken geography.) Turkeys were probably adopted so quickly because of their resemblance to the peacock, which was a very expensive bird with enormous prestige.

Italians do not generally roast the turkey whole, but rather separate the breast and the remainder and give them different treatments. This is useful, because the dark meat usually takes much time to become tender, time in which the breast can dry out. In this treatment, the breast is "butterflied," covered with boiled ham and *pancetta* and then rolled, and tied. It is wrapped in foil and baked, and when it is served it is cut into slices like a jelly roll.

1 whole or half turkey breast (about 3 pounds), boned
6 ounces *pancetta* or 3 ounces salt pork plus 3 ounces boiled ham
3 ounces boiled ham
3 medium-sized cloves garlic
1 tablespoon plus 2 teaspoons rosemary leaves
2 leaves sage (optional), fresh or under salt
4 or 5 black peppercorns
Salt and freshly ground pepper

Preheat the oven to 400°.

Remove the skin from the turkey breast. Place the breast on a board and "butterfly" it, that is, slice it lengthwise through the breast from one side almost to the other, leaving the halves attached only at one side. Open it out into one long thin slice.

Cut the *pancetta* (or salt pork and ham) and boiled ham into strips and arrange the strips all over breast. Sprinkle the breast with the 1 tablespoon rosemary leaves, salt, pepper, sage, and peppercorns.

Roll up the turkey breast like a *braciola* (or jelly roll) and tie with thread; place it on aluminum foil (see photos 1–2). Sprinkle the out-

Petto di tacchino arrocchiato: 1. Rolling up the turkey breast.

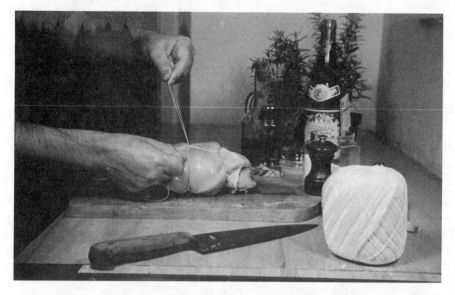

2. Tying the rolled-up turkey breast.

side of the roll with the 2 teaspoons rosemary leaves, salt and pepper (see photo 3), then wrap the rolled breast in the aluminum foil and place it in a baking dish. Bake in the preheated oven for from 45 to 55 minutes, then remove from the oven and let cool for 20 minutes.

3. Sprinkling the rolled turkey breast with rosemary, salt, and pepper prior to wrapping it in foil.

Unwrap the aluminum foil and slice the rolled turkey breast like a loaf. Arrange the slices on a serving dish and serve.

Note: This dish is even better when cold. In this case, slice it just a few minutes before serving.

———◆———

A SUGGESTED DINNER

WINE
Castello di Poppiano Bianco

Minestrone di riso (see page 121)

Polpettone di tacchino al tonno (see below)

Fagiolini in fricassea (see page 404)

Castagnaccio (see page 479)

———◆———

Polpettone di Tacchino al Tonno
(Poached Turkey Loaf with Tuna Flavor)

(SERVES 8 TO 10)

In this treatment boiled dark meat turkey is combined with tuna, ham, and seasonings, then shaped into a loaf, wrapped in cheesecloth, and boiled again. When unwrapped and cold, it emerges almost as a kind of pâté, quite far from its humble origins, and may be eaten as a cold main dish or as an excellent cold antipasto, worthy of a quite festive dinner. It is served cut into slices, with a light sauce of olive oil and lemon.

2 slices white bread, crusts removed
1 cup cold milk
5 or 6 sprigs Italian parsley
1 large clove garlic
2 ounces boiled ham
1 can (7 ounces) tuna in olive oil
1 pound boiled dark meat turkey

(continued)

    2 eggs
    4 ounces freshly grated Parmigiano cheese
       Salt and freshly ground black pepper

   ¼ cup wine vinegar
    1 large carrot
    1 celery rib

   ¾ cup olive oil
       Juice of 1 lemon

Soak the bread slices in the cold milk for 20 minutes.

Meanwhile, finely chop the parsley, garlic, and ham and transfer to a large bowl.

Drain the tuna to remove the oil, then place on a board with the turkey meat and chop very fine. Transfer the turkey and tuna mixture to the large bowl and mix very well its contents. Add the eggs, Parmigiano, and salt and pepper and incorporate them well with the other ingredients, then squeeze the liquid from the bread slices, add them to the bowl, and mix very well.

On a board, roll the mixture into a large sausage about 3½ inches thick. Spread out a piece of cheesecloth and place the turkey "sausage" on it (see photo 1). Wrap the cheesecloth around several times, and tie with thread as you would tie meat (see photos 2–3).

Polpettone di tacchino al tonno: 1. Placing the turkey "sausage" on cheesecloth.

2. Tying the *polpettone*.

3. The tied *polpettone*, before being placed in the pot.

Half fill a stockpot with cold water. Add the wine vinegar, carrot, celery, and salt. Put the *polpettone* in the pot (the water should completely cover it), cover, and place on a medium flame. Simmer for 1 hour after the water comes to a boil.

When the *polpettone* has finished cooking, press it by placing it in a Pyrex baking dish with a similar dish, full of water, on top of it. Let the *polpettone* cool this way, then transfer it to the refrigerator with the weight still on it. It should remain in this condition for at least 5 or 6 hours, or better still, overnight.

Unwrap the *polpettone* and cut it into about 20 slices (see photo 4). Place them on a serving dish and let stand while you prepare the following sauce:

Put the olive oil in a crockery bowl and add the lemon juice little by little, stirring with a wooden spoon. Add salt and freshly ground black pepper, then transfer to a sauceboat and serve with the *polpettone*.

4. The finished *polpettone*, sliced and ready to serve.

A SUGGESTED DINNER

WINE
Luigi Bigi Orvieto (*abboccato*)

Ginestrata (see page 112)

Anitra all'arancio (see below)

Spinaci saltati (see page 421)

Pesche ripiene (see page 492)

Anitra all' Arancio
(Duck in Orange Sauce)   (SERVES 6)

It is difficult for most people to believe that this almost prototypical French dish is really Florentine. One of the dishes that was transported to France through the good offices of Caterina de Medici, it appears in the earliest fourteenth-century Florentine cookbooks as *paparo o oca o anitra al melarancio* (gander or goose or duck in orange). The original is really closer to the modern French treatment, with its sweetness and glaze, than to the modern Florentine treatment, which has developed the dish away from its original sweetness. Originally, apparently, gander was the preferred bird and duck an acceptable substitute. We all know what happened subsequently.

You will notice that this present-day Italian recipe differs from the classical French ones a little. Try it, and don't be be too sure that you won't prefer this one once you know it well.

   1 duck (about 5 pounds)
   8 tablespoons (1 stick) butter
      Salt and freshly ground pepper to taste
   1 tablespoon olive oil
1 ½ cups dry white wine
   2 oranges with thick skins
   1 pound raw rice, preferably Italian Arborio   (*continued*)

5 sweet, juicy California oranges
⅛ teaspoon ground saffron
6 or 7 black peppercorns

Preheat the oven to 375°.

Clean the duck; remove the liver and set aside for another purpose. Into the cavity of the duck put 4 tablespoons of the butter, salt, and pepper.

Heat the olive oil and the remaining butter in a large casserole. When the butter is melted, put in the duck and sprinkle the outside with salt and pepper. Sauté on a low flame until the duck is golden brown all over (about 30 minutes), then add the wine and let it evaporate very slowly.

When the wine has evaporated, transfer the duck from the casserole to a large roasting pan with the grill removed. Place the pan in the preheated oven for 1½ hours, then remove from the oven. Lift the duck out of the roasting pan and pour the fat into the casserole. Replace the grill in the roasting pan, then put the duck back in, on the grill. Return the pan to the oven, still at 375°, for 30 minutes more.

Cut each of the two oranges into quarters and carefully remove the peel, in one piece, from each quarter. Cut the orange peel into very thin strips, cutting away most of the white underside of the peel. Reserve the peeled sections for another use.

Place a saucepan containing 3 cups of water and a pinch of salt on the heat. When the water reaches the boiling point, add the orange strips and blanch them for 5 minutes, then remove from the saucepan and cool under cold running water.

Add 1 cup of cold water to the casserole containing all the duck fat and simmer for 20 minutes.

Meanwhile, heat a large quantity of salted water in a stockpot. When the water reaches the boiling point, add the rice, saffron, and peppercorns and cook, stirring very frequently with a wooden spoon, until the rice is al dente (about 15 minutes).

While the rice is cooking, discard all but about 1 cup of fat from the casserole. When the duck has baked for 2 hours total, transfer it to the casserole and cook on a low flame for 5 minutes; turn it twice. Taste for salt and pepper, then transfer the duck to a large serving dish.

Squeeze 3 of the California oranges and add the juice and the orange strips to the fat left in the casserole. Place the casserole back on the flame and heat the sauce to the boiling point, then immediately pour it over the duck.

Drain the rice in a colander and arrange it in a ring around the duck. Cut the remaining two oranges into thin slices and place them as garnish around the outside of the rice ring, and serve.

———◆———

A SUGGESTED DINNER

WINE
Luigi Bigi-Nobile di Montepulciano

Tortelli della vigilia (see page 169)

Anitra in porchetta (see below)

Insalata verde (see page 387)

Fragole al vino rosso (see page 496)

———◆———

Anitra in Porchetta
(Duck in the Style of Suckling Pig)   (SERVES 6)

Duck as well as chicken is prepared filled with the *pancetta* and generously seasoned stuffing typical of *porchetta*, or suckling pig. This treatment is, if possible, even better than the chicken version, as the duck retains something of the weightiness of pork meat. American duck from Long Island are so good, probably better than Italian ones, that one is inspired to use them often in a variety of treatments.

  1 sweet sausage (about 4 ounces)
  3 ounces *pancetta* or an additional 3 ounces sausage
  1 large bay leaf
  1 heaping tablespoon rosemary leaves
24 or 25 leaves sage, fresh or under salt (see page 14)
  4 large cloves garlic
20 whole black peppercorns
     Salt and freshly ground black pepper
  1 duck (about 5 pounds)
  2 tablespoons olive oil

Remove the skin from sausage and place the meat in a bowl.

Coarsely chop the *pancetta*, bay leaf, rosemary leaves, 20 of the sage leaves, and garlic, then add to the bowl with the sausage. Add the peppercorns, 4 teaspoons salt, and 1½ teaspoons freshly ground pepper and mix very well with a wooden spoon.

Wash duck very well and dry it with paper towels. Remove the liver and set aside for another purpose, but do not remove any fat. Stuff the duck with the sausage mixture, then sew up the lower opening with needle and thread. Place the remaining 4 or 5 sage leaves in the neck opening and sew it up as well.

Preheat the oven to 375°.

Remove the grill from a roasting pan and spread the olive oil over bottom of the pan. Put in the duck, sprinkle with salt and pepper, then roast in the preheated oven for 2 hours, turning the duck over twice.

Remove the pan from the oven, take out the duck, and pour off all the fat. Replace the grill in the pan and put the duck on the grill. Return to the oven, still at 375°, for 30 minutes more.

Remove the pan from the oven and transfer the duck to a board. Allow it to cool for 10 to 15 minutes before cutting, then cut in half lengthwise and then each half into 4 pieces.

Place the stuffing in the center of a serving dish and the duck pieces around the stuffing. To each diner, serve a piece of duck with a tablespoon of stuffing.

Note: This is a dish that is best accompanied by green or mixed salad.

A SUGGESTED DINNER

WINE
Frescobaldi-Pomino

Pasta e fagioli (see page 127)

Coniglio ripieno con carciofi (see below)

Carciofi fritti (see page 398)

Cenci (see page 457)

Coniglio Ripieno con Carciofi
(Tarragon Rabbit Stuffed with Artichokes)   (S E R V E S 4)

Here the whole rabbit is cleaned and soaked in wine vinegar to remove any gaminess, stuffed with artichokes and seasonings, including tarragon, and then cooked almost covered with white wine. The wine-tarragon perfume of the rabbit cooking is not easily forgotten. A really delicious dish, this should be the centerpiece of a countrified dinner, and the ideal vegetable to accompany it is artichokes, to go with the artichoke stuffing.

Rabbit is eaten a great deal in Italy and France. Once the most economical of meats, it is now quite expensive in these countries, so that dishes which were once rustic country dishes are now plates for *buongustai*. Rabbits, however, are plentiful in America, and are available at many markets, certainly Italian meat markets. Buy the rabbit fresh with the pelt still on and have the butcher skin it for you. The meat is often compared to chicken, but of course it has its own individual, sweet flavor. The meat is light, unlike that of the wild hare, which is dark and gamy.

This recipe is from the until-recently marshy area of Etruscan country in Tuscany, the Maremma, a hunter's paradise.

1 whole rabbit (about 3½ pounds with skin and head removed)
1 cup wine vinegar
1 lemon
3 large artichokes
2 large cloves garlic
¼ pound *pancetta* (or 2 ounces salt pork plus 2 ounces boiled ham), plus 4 long strips *pancetta* or salt pork
   Salt and freshly ground pepper
1 tablespoon fresh tarragon or 1½ teaspoons dried
5 tablespoons olive oil
2½ cups dry white wine, approximately

Wash the whole rabbit very carefully and discard the liver, then place the rabbit in a large bowl containing 4 cups of cold water and the wine vinegar. Soak for 1 hour to remove the gamy flavor.

Meanwhile, cut the lemon in half and put in a bowl of cold water.

Soak the whole artichokes in this for 20 minutes, then clean (see page 394) and cut into small pieces, using both body and stems. Place the artichoke pieces in a second bowl.

Chop the garlic and ¼ pound *pancetta* (or salt pork and boiled ham) coarsely and add to the bowl with the artichokes. Add salt, pepper, and tarragon and mix well.

Preheat the oven to 375°.

When the rabbit has soaked for 1 hour, wash it in cold running water, making sure all the cavities are clean, then dry with paper towels. Stuff the large cavity of the stomach with the artichoke mixture, then sew up completely with a needle and thread. With a larding needle, lard each leg with a strip of *pancetta* (or salt pork).

Pour the olive oil into a rectangular Pyrex baking dish (13½ x 8¾ inches), then put in the rabbit. Sprinkle generously with salt and pepper, then pour in the wine; the wine should cover almost two-thirds of the rabbit. Place the baking dish in the preheated oven and bake for 1 to 1½ hours, until all the wine has evaporated. During this time, turn rabbit over twice.

Take the baking dish out of the oven and remove the thread from the rabbit before transferring to a serving dish. Serve immediately.

Note: Only white wine should be drunk with this dish.

A SUGGESTED DINNER

WINE
Corvo di Salaparuta-Rosso

Riso forte (see page 86)

Coniglio in agro-dolce (see below)

Insalata composta (see page 388)

Crema zabaione (see page 435)

Coniglio in Agro-Dolce
(Rabbit in Sweet and Sour Sauce)   (SERVES 6)

Here the rabbit is cut up and cooked in an elaborate sweet and sour sauce made with *odori* (aromatic vegetables), red wine, wine vinegar, raisins, pignoli, peppercorns, and a little sugar. This sweet and sour rabbit is made all over Italy.

    1 rabbit (about 3½ pounds with skin and head removed)
    2 cups dry red wine
    2 red onions
    1 large bay leaf
    4 or 5 whole black peppercorns
    ¼ cup wine vinegar
    1 cup all-purpose flour
    5 tablespoons of olive oil
       Salt and freshly ground pepper to taste
    2 ounces raisins
    1 heaping tablespoon granulated sugar
    2 ounces pignoli (pine nuts)

Wash the rabbit well and dry it with paper towels, then cut it into 12 pieces and place them in a large bowl.

Heat the wine, 1 whole onion, bay leaf, peppercorns, and 1 table-spoon of the wine vinegar in a saucepan. When the mixture reaches the boiling point, immediately remove the saucepan from the flame and pour the contents into the bowl with the rabbit. Let the rabbit marinate for 2 hours.

After marinating, remove the rabbit pieces from the bowl and dry them with paper towels, then place in a large plastic bag, along with the flour. Gently shape the plastic bag until the pieces are evenly floured. Strain the marinade into a bowl and save it.

Chop the remaining onion coarsely and place it in a large flameproof casserole, preferably terra-cotta, along with the olive oil. Place the casserole on the heat and sauté the onion for 4 or 5 minutes, then add the rabbit pieces and sauté them gently until golden brown all over (about 15 minutes). Sprinkle with salt and pepper and continue to sauté gently for about 25 minutes more, adding the reserved marinade little by little, stirring often. During this time, turn over rabbit pieces two or three times.

Meanwhile, soak the raisins in a small bowl of lukewarm water for 20 minutes.

Heat the remaining wine vinegar and the sugar in a small saucepan. When the vinegar is hot and the sugar dissolved, add the soaked raisins and the pignoli and remove from the flame. Cover and let stand until needed. Preheat oven to 375°.

After sautéing for 25 minutes, when the rabbit has absorbed all the wine and is almost cooked, remove the casserole from the flame. Pour in the contents of the small saucepan and stir with a wooden spoon. Cover the casserole and place it in the preheated oven for 15 to 20 minutes. Serve hot.

Funghi Broiler

Serving Platter
 Olio
 Ail
 Thyme
 Prezzemolo (Garnish)

Rissoto

Vino
Olio
Burro
Prezzemolo (Garnish)
 Ognuno
  Riso
  Brodo
  FROMAGGIO
Gamberetti

 Ail
 Prezzemolo
 gamberetti
 ~~Garnish~~
 Burro
 Vino
 Olio   Caffè

PANNE / BURRO

Veal and Beef

A SUGGESTED DINNER

WINE
Fontana Candida-Frascati Superiore

Cannelloni della vigilia (see page 184)

Involtini di vitella (see below)

Bietole saltate (see page 423)

Bomboloni (see page 454)

Involtini di Vitella
(Stuffed Little Veal "Bundles")   (S E R V E S   4)

The boneless veal cutlets are pounded very thin, so they can be easily rolled up, and are stuffed with a mozzarella-prosciutto-parsley mixture. The little "bundles" are then tied and sautéed in olive oil and white wine.

Try to find the youngest, whitest veal for this dish, which is suitable for a wide range of occasions, from an ambitious family dinner to a formal entertainment.

33 1

  4 thin slices of veal
  2 ounces mozzarella
  2 ounces very fat prosciutto or salt pork
  5 or 6 sprigs Italian parsley
  ¼ cup freshly grated Parmigiano cheese
     Salt and freshly ground black pepper
  ¼ cup all-purpose flour
  2 tablespoons olive oil
  ½ cup dry white wine

If the butcher has not already done so, pound the veal slices thin. (Use an Italian *batticarne*, with the veal between two pieces of wet wax paper.) Coarsely chop the mozzarella, prosciutto, and parsley. Place the veal slices on a board and place one-fourth of the mixture on top of each slice of veal. Sprinkle with Parmigiano and, if necessary, salt and pepper. (In Italy, mozzarella is unsalted, but in America it is sometimes salted. If the cheese is unsalted, then use the salt and pepper.) Roll each slice of veal and tie with thread.

Spread the flour on a sheet of aluminum foil. Roll the *involtini* in the flour to coat them very lightly.

Heat the olive oil in a flameproof casserole. When the oil is warm, place the *involtini* in the casserole and sauté until golden brown (about 15 minutes). Sprinkle the veal rolls with a little salt and pepper, then add the wine and let it evaporate very slowly (about 10 to 12 minutes), stirring frequently with a wooden spoon.

Remove the casserole from the heat and allow to rest for 5 minutes, then remove the thread with scissors and transfer the *involtini* to a serving dish, pouring a little sauce from the casserole over the top of each one. Serve hot.

———◆———

A SUGGESTED DINNER

WINE
Chianti Classico Villa Antinori

Lasagne (see page 189)

Bistecca alla fiorentina (see below)

Insalata mista (see page 387) or *Insalata composta* (see page 388)

Crostata di frutta (see page 444)

———◆———

Bistecca alla Fiorentina
(Beefsteak, Florentine Style)

One doesn't ordinarily think of a good, thick charcoal-broiled steak as an Italian dish, but nonetheless, centuries before the Alamo and Texas, *bistecca alla fiorentina* was already an established specialty of Florence. A real *fiorentina* requires the special Chianina breed of beef found in the valley of the Chiana near Florence (and justly admired by cattle breeders the world over). However, the Val di Chiana beef is so scarce that it is not available except in Florence, and is becoming less available even there. And so, in Italy, the only place you can get a real *fiorentina* is in Florence.

There is another aspect as well—the cutting of the meat. Like most steaks, this cut comes from the loin (*costata*). It is the same cut as the American T-bone or Porterhouse, except that only the fillet and contrafillet (also called "shell," "strip," "New York steak," and "entre-côte") are used. The tail is cut off and used for *bollito* (see page 268). For some reason, in Italy only the Florentines cut the meat so that both the fillet and contrafillet are part of the same piece. In the rest of Italy, they are separated.

And so, though Chianina beef is not available here, we can more easily get a cut similar to the *fiorentina* than one can in Italy outside of Florence.

Though the preparation is a simple one, the rules must be very strictly observed to get an authentic *fiorentina*.

Buying and Preparing the Steak

Ask your butcher for a T-bone or Porterhouse cut, and ask him to cut off the "tail" third. You may have to buy that piece also. If so, use it for boiling or to make stock.

Have the steaks cut so that each one weighs about 1¾ pounds after the tail has been removed. Each of the 1¾-pound steaks serves 2 people. Absolutely do not have the steaks cut smaller in order to have individual servings. The meat must be of this size and thickness when cooked.

Before using, the meat should be well aged. (Italians say it should be aged for at least six days after the animal is slaughtered. It is difficult to know what that means nowadays, with shipping in refrigeration and freezer units.) In any event, if the meat seems too fresh to you, or if it was frozen immediately after slaughter, allow it to age in your own refrigerator until it is soft. (If you happen to live in a cattle-raising area, you can also eat the meat just a few hours after slaughtering, and it is marvelous. But once past that point, it must be well aged.)

Do not wash the steaks at any point; do not marinate the meat or pour any fat over it. And since the correct amount of salt and pepper is just what clings to the steak when it is turned, do not rub the steak with peppercorns or with salt. These will be sprinkled on at a later stage.

Finally, be sure the steaks are at room temperature when it is time to cook them.

Cooking the Steak

Prepare the fire with wood or charcoal. Wait until the fire is completely burned out and only hot ash remains; there should be no flames.

Place the grill in fireplace or on barbeque well before the steaks (the grill must be very hot before the steaks are placed on it), then place the steaks on the grill with your hands or a spatula, *not* a fork. Do not puncture the meat with a fork at any point while cooking.

After 4 or 5 minutes, when the steak is brown and has formed what is almost a crust, turn it with a spatula. Without touching the steak, sprinkle it with salt; do not try to push the salt into the meat. Cook the second side for 4 or 5 minutes and then turn it again with a spatula. Some salt will fall off, and what clings is the right amount for a *fiorentina*.

Cook the first side for 4 or 5 minutes more and immediately re-move the steak from the grill and place it on a serving dish. *A real fiorentina is always rare inside.* Sprinkle lightly with pepper (a *fioren-tina* should not be very peppery) and do not add any oil.

Serve with lemon wedges. (These are not only a garnish, but some people squeeze lemon juice onto the steak. This is optional, according to taste.) Since each steak serves two, cut the steaks into at least 4 pieces each, so that everyone gets some *filetto* and some *controfiletto*.

Enjoy your *fiorentina!*

A SUGGESTED DINNER

WINE
Chianti Classico Riecine

Passato di fagioli (see page 119)

Polpette di bistecca in umido (see below)

Finocchi al burro (see page 414)

Pesche ripiene di mandorle (see page 493)

Polpette di Bistecca in Umido
(Fresh Steak "Sausages" in Sauce)   (SERVES 4)

These are sausage-shaped *polpette* of coarsely chopped steak, lightly floured, sautéed in olive oil and then lightly in tomatoes. A simple but quite elegant family dish.

The meat must be of top quality and coarsely ground. If you have a food processor, the coarseness of chopping can be controlled. With a meat grinder, pass the meat through only once. Already ground supermarket meat should be a last resort.

　1 pound coarsely ground round or sirloin
　½ cup plus 2 tablespoons olive oil
　3 tablespoons freshly grated Parmigiano cheese
　Salt and freshly ground pepper to taste
　½ cup all-purpose flour, approximately
　3 or 4 leaves sage, fresh or under salt
　1 cup canned tomatoes
　1 clove garlic, peeled but left whole
　Chicken or meat broth, if necessary

Place the ground meat in a bowl with the 2 tablespoons olive oil, Parmigiano, and salt and pepper to taste. Mix very thoroughly with a wooden spoon, then divide the mixture into 8 parts and roll each into the shape of a sausage. Lightly flour each "sausage." Heat the ½ cup olive oil in a flameproof casserole, preferably terra-cotta, along with the sage leaves. When the oil is hot, add the "sausages" and brown gently, on a medium flame, on all sides. Add the tomatoes and the whole garlic clove, then cover and simmer on a low flame for 10 minutes. Taste for salt and pepper.

At this point, check the consistency of the sauce. If the tomatoes contain very little liquid, you may need to add a little broth. Be careful, however, not to add too much liquid. There should be very little sauce left unabsorbed at the end. Simmer for 15 minutes more, with the lid on, adding broth as needed.

Remove the garlic clove and serve hot.

◆

A SUGGESTED DINNER

WINE
Chianti Classico Straccali

Topini di patate (see page 232)

Manzo ripieno (see below)

Peperonata (see page 419)

Pan di ramerino (see page 40)

◆

Manzo Ripieno
(Rolled Stuffed Sirloin)   (S E R V E S 4 T O 6)

Have your butcher butterfly a large, thick tender slice of sirloin. This is flattened into a very large *braciola*, which is stuffed with a spinach, *pancetta*, egg, and Parmigiano mixture and closed up into one large roll. It is then sautéed. When served, always cold, it is sliced through like a jelly roll, which it does very easily and nicely.

Another dish for a family dinner.

> 2 pounds fresh spinach (or 2 10-ounce packages frozen)
> 3 eggs
> 1 medium-sized clove garlic
> 5 or 6 sprigs Italian parsley
> 2 ounces *pancetta* or salt pork
> 1 large, thick slice of tender sirloin (about ¾ pound), butter-
>   flied (see page 317)
>   Salt and freshly ground pepper to taste
> 2 tablespoons freshly grated Parmigiano cheese
> 4 tablespoons (½ stick) butter
> 2 tablespoons olive oil
> ½ cup dry red wine

Remove the stems from the spinach and rinse the leaves very well. Heat a large quantity of salted water in a stockpot. When the water is boiling, put in the spinach and cook it for about 15 minutes, then drain and cool under cold running water. For frozen spinach, follow package directions. Squeeze the spinach very dry and chop it fine, then set aside in a bowl until needed.

Fill a saucepan with salted water and set on the heat; when the water reaches the boiling point, add the eggs and let them cook for 10 to 12 minutes, until hard-boiled. Remove the eggs and cool under cold running water, then peel and set aside until needed.

Chop the garlic and parsley fine; cut the *pancetta* (or salt pork) into small pieces.

Place the butterflied slice of meat between two damp sheets of wax paper. Flatten it with a meat pounder (*batticarne*), then place on a board.

Cover the slice of meat with the chopped spinach. On top of the spinach, arrange the *pancetta* pieces and sprinkle with chopped garlic and parsley. Cut the eggs lengthwise into quarters and place them lengthwise on top of the other ingredients. Sprinkle with a little salt, pepper and Parmigiano.

Pick up one end of meat with both hands and roll it up. Tie up the roll with thread (see page 349).

Heat the butter and olive oil in a large flameproof casserole. When the butter is melted, put in the meat roll and sauté very gently, turning it often with a wooden spoon. Cook for about 15 minutes, until golden brown all over, then add the wine and season with salt and pepper. Cover the casserole and simmer for 15 minutes more, turning the meat roll two or three times. When the wine has evaporated, the meat is ready.

Remove the casserole from flame and let cool for about 2 hours, then transfer the meat to a board and cut it into ½-inch slices. Arrange the slices on a serving dish and serve.

Note: Before serving, you may heat the remaining gravy in casserole and pour it over the slices.

◆

A SUGGESTED DINNER

WINE
Chianti Classico Poggio al Sole

Zuppa di porri (see page 115)

Braciole ripiene (see below)

Fagioli al forno (see page 403)

Bombe (see page 443)

◆

Braciole Ripiene
(Stuffed Meat Slices)   (SERVES 4)

Braciola refers to the thin slice of meat itself. The word is used in America generally to refer to what is properly called *braciola ripiena*, or stuffed *braciola*. This filling of artichoke and a thin omelet is one of the classic ways to stuff a *braciola*.

2 small artichokes or 1 large one
1 lemon
2 eggs
2 tablespoons freshly grated Parmigiano cheese
2½ tablespoons olive oil
4 *bracioline* (very thin meat slices) of boneless sirloin
5 or 6 sprigs Italian parsley
1 medium-sized clove garlic
2 ounces *pancetta* or salt pork
Salt and freshly ground pepper to taste
½ cup dry red wine
½ cup meat or chicken broth

Soak the whole artichokes in a large bowl of cold water, along with the lemon cut into halves, for 20 minutes.

Meanwhile, break the eggs into a small bowl and beat them slightly, then mix in the Parmigiano and a pinch of salt. Heat the ½ tablespoon of oil in an omelet pan and make a thin omelet from the egg-Parmigiano mixture; place it on a dish to cool.

Remove the outside fat from each meat slice and flatten them between 2 pieces of damp wax paper with a meat pounder (*batticarne*).

Chop the parsley, garlic, and *pancetta* (or salt pork) and place in a bowl.

Remove the outer leaves and inside "choke" from the artichokes, then cut both the bodies and stems into small pieces (see page 394) and add them to the bowl. Mix with the other ingredients and season with salt and pepper.

Cut the cooled omelet into quarters and place one piece on each meat slice. Place one-quarter of the artichoke mixture on top of each piece of omelet. Roll each *braciola* and tie it with thread (see page 349).

Heat the olive oil in a flameproof casserole and then put in the *braciole*. Sprinkle with salt and pepper and let sauté very slowly until golden brown (10 to 15 minutes), turning the rolls with a wooden spoon. Add the wine, cover, and simmer until the wine has evaporated (about 15 minutes).

When the wine has evaporated, add the broth and simmer until the *braciole* are cooked (about 12 to 14 minutes), then remove the casserole from the heat and allow to rest for 5 minutes.

Remove the thread from the *braciole* and transfer them to a serving dish. Pour the gravy from the casserole over them and serve.

———◆———

A SUGGESTED DINNER

WINE
Chianti Classico Castello di Cacchiano

Taglierini in brodo (see page 109)

Stracotto alla fiorentina (see below)

Boiled potatoes

Budino di ricotta (see page 491)

———◆———

Stracotto alla Fiorentina
(Pot Roast, Florentine Style)   (SERVES 6)

The Italian pot roast is one large piece. The rump is preferred so it can cook a long time (the word *stracotto* means "very well cooked"). Some fat must be left on, and, so the meat remains juicy on the inside, it is larded by drawing strips of *pancetta* through the inside with a larding needle (in Italy, *ago lardellatore*). The carrot drawn through the center also helps to flavor the inside of the meat and is aesthetically pleasing when the meat is sliced.

Stracotto is cooked with the full red wine of the area where it is made. Barolo is used in Piedmont; in Tuscany, one of the fuller Chiantis.

2 medium-sized red onions
3 celery ribs
4 carrots
5 tablespoons olive oil
  Rump roast of beef (about 3½ pounds), with some fat left on
  Salt and freshly ground pepper
4 to 5 long strips of *pancetta* or salt pork
½ cup dry red wine

1 ¼ pounds fresh ripe tomatoes, skin and seeds removed, or 1 can
(20 ounces) tomatoes
1 tablespoon tomato paste
1 to 2 cups hot meat broth

Cut the onions, celery, and 3 of the carrots into ½-inch pieces. Put them in a large flameproof casserole, preferably terra-cotta, along with the olive oil, and set aside until needed.

Put a long, thin knife lengthwise all the way through the meat, in the center. Withdraw the knife and fit the remaining carrot, whole, through the opening made by the knife. Then, with a larding needle, insert 2 4-inch strips of *pancetta* or salt pork at each end, on either side of the carrot. If you have no larding needle, make 2 punctures with a knife on either end of the carrot, 4 inches deep. Enlarge the holes with your finger and insert a strip of *pancetta* (or salt pork) into each puncture.

With thread, tie the meat in the manner of a salami (see page 349), then place in the casserole with the vegetables. Add salt and pepper to taste, then set the casserole on a low flame and sauté very gently, stirring the vegetables and turning the meat, until it is brown on all sides (about 20 to 25 minutes).

Add the wine and simmer until it evaporates, then add the tomatoes and tomato paste. Cover and simmer very slowly for 2½ hours, adding some hot broth when needed and turning the meat several times. Taste for salt and pepper.

Remove the meat from the casserole and place it on a chopping board for 10 to 12 minutes to rest.

Meanwhile, remove the fat from the top of the gravy and reheat.

Cut meat into slices ½ inch thick. Arrange the slices on a platter and serve, accompanied by the gravy in a gravy boat.

This dish should be served with whole peeled, boiled potatoes. Serve the potatoes in a basket, wrapped in cloth napkins.

———◆———

A SUGGESTED DINNER

WINE
Chianti Classico Castello di Meleto

Pappa al pomodoro (see page 230)

Spezzatino alla fiorentina (see below)

Broccoli strascicati (see page 406)

Frittelle di riso (see page 485)

Spezzatino alla Fiorentina
(Florentine Beef Stew in Chianti)   (SERVES 4)

    1 medium-sized red onion
    1 celery rib
    1 carrot
    2 or 3 basil leaves, fresh or under salt
    5 tablespoons olive oil
    2 pounds beef chuck, preferably eye of chuck, cut into large
       cubes
  ½ cup dry red wine
    1 can (12 ounces) tomatoes
       Pinch of hot red pepper flakes
       Salt and freshly ground pepper to taste

Coarsely chop the onion, celery, carrot, and basil leaves.

Heat the oil in a flameproof casserole, preferably terra-cotta, and when it is warm, add the chopped ingredients and sauté on medium heat for 15 to 18 minutes. Add the meat, and let sauté for about 15 minutes, stirring every so often with a wooden spoon so the meat does not stick to the pan. Add the wine and lower the flame, to allow the wine to evaporate slowly (about 15 minutes).

Pass the tomatoes through a food mill into the casserole. Season with salt, pepper, and a pinch of hot pepper flakes, then cover the casserole and simmer very slowly for 2½ hours, adding some cold water if additional liquid is needed.

Taste for salt and pepper and let simmer for 10 to 15 minutes more (at which time the meat should be soft and the sauce rather thick), then remove the casserole from the flame. Transfer the *spezzatino* to a serving dish and serve hot.

Note: In Florence *spezzatino* is served on the same plate with whole boiled potatoes, peeled before serving, or with slices of polenta (see page 367). Sometimes the potatoes are peeled, cut into pieces, and placed in the casserole, about 20 minutes before the *spezzatino* is completely cooked, to allow the potatoes to cook in the meat gravy.

A SUGGESTED DINNER

WINE
Chianti Classico Terciona

Zuppa di porri (see page 115)

Peposo (see below)

Insalata composta (see page 388)

Crema zabaione (see page 435)

Peposo
(Peppery Beef Stew)   (SERVES 4)

Another dish that goes back to the days when freshly ground black pepper was used in some dishes in such quantity that one got beyond the spiciness to the flavor of the pepper itself. The name itself comes from the word for pepper, *pepe.*

The beef shank meat is simmered for a long time in a covered casserole with lots of red wine. There is very little oil and no thickening, but the gelatin from the shank meat itself produces a thick, rich sauce.

Peposo is associated with the little hill town of Impruneta, near Florence, which is famous for making the red tiles that cover the roofs of the city. It is a tradition that, while the tile makers were baking the tiles for Brunelleschi's red dome for the Cathedral, they put the casseroles of *peposo* in the oven to cook at the same time. Michelangelo wrote a little poem when he was departing for Rome to make the dome of St. Peter's, addressed to Brunelleschi's dome: "I go forth to make your sister, larger perhaps, but certainly not more beautiful."

    ¼ cup olive oil
    4 cups red wine
    4 cloves garlic
    2 pounds beef shank, cut into pieces 1 inch square
       Salt to taste
    1 cup canned tomatoes
    1 scant tablespoon freshly ground black pepper
    4 cups cold water

Put the olive oil, wine, garlic, and meat in a large casserole, preferably terra-cotta, then set on medium heat and cover. Simmer very slowly for 1 hour.

Add the tomatoes, cold water, and salt to the casserole and simmer for 2 hours more. Taste for salt and add the freshly ground pepper, then simmer, covered, for 1 hour longer.

Remove the casserole from the flame and let rest for 20 to 25 minutes, covered. Serve from the same casserole.

Note: Serve on the same dish with whole boiled potatoes. In this case the *insalata composta* should not contain potatoes.

Pork and Pork Products

A SUGGESTED DINNER

WINE
Chianti Classico Badia a Coltibuono

Tortelli al gorgonzola (see page 170)

Maiale ubriaco (see below)

Rape saltate in padella (see page 420)

Schiacciata con zibibbo (see page 473)

Maiale Ubriaco
("Inebriated" Pork Chops)   (SERVES 4)

The pork chop in a refreshing treatment, sautéed in wine with fennel seeds among the flavorings. No more difficult or time consuming than any other simple treatment of pork chops, this is a useful dish for a simple family dinner.

  10 sprigs Italian parsley
   1 clove garlic   *(continued)*

2 tablespoons olive oil
Salt and freshly ground pepper to taste
1 teaspoon fennel seeds
4 large pork chops, with some fat on them
1 cup dry red wine

Chop the parsley and garlic fine, then place in a bowl. Add the olive oil, salt, pepper, and fennel seeds to the bowl and mix all the ingredients together.

Transfer the contents of the bowl to a frying pan and place the pork chops on top. Set the pan on the heat and sauté the pork for about 5 minutes on each side, then add the wine, lower the flame and cover the pan. Simmer very slowly for 20 minutes, until the wine is evaporated and the pork cooked.

Serve very hot.

———◆———

A SUGGESTED DINNER

WINE
Chianti Classico Castello di Vicchiomaggio

Cannelloni di ricotta (see page 185)

Braciole di maiale con cavolo nero (see below)

Fresh fruit

———◆———

Braciole di Maiale con Cavolo Nero
(Pork Chops with Kale)   (SERVES 4)

Pork chops cooked together with kale, again flavored with fennel seeds and also with tomato. Kale is, next to rape, the vegetable that weds best with pork.

After the pork chops and kale are cooked separately, each in its own mode, they are then cooked together to absorb each other's flavors.

2 pounds of kale (*cavolo nero*)
Coarse salt
5 tablespoons olive oil
1 large clove garlic, peeled
4 large pork chops
Salt and freshly ground pepper to taste
2 teaspoons fennel seeds
1 cup water
1 tablespoon tomato paste

Remove the large stems from the kale. Cut the remaining kale into 2-inch pieces and place them in a large bowl of cold water for 30 minutes. Put a large quantity of cold water and some coarse salt into a stockpot and set on the heat. When the water reaches the boiling point, add the kale and cook for about 20 minutes.

Meanwhile, heat the olive oil in a large frying pan. When it is warm, add the garlic clove and sauté very gently for 2 or 3 minutes. Add the pork chops and sauté them for 5 minutes on each side, then season with salt, freshly ground pepper, and the fennel seeds.

Heat the 1 cup of water and dissolve the tomato paste in it. Add the watered tomato paste to the frying pan, then cover and let cook for about 30 minutes.

Meanwhile, remove the stockpot containing the kale from the heat. Drain the kale in a colander and cool it under cold running water, then squeeze out excess water and let the kale stand until needed.

Remove the clove of garlic from the pan and transfer the pork chops to a serving dish. Keep warm.

Add the kale to the frying pan and let sauté for about 10 minutes. Taste for salt and pepper, then replace the pork chops in the pan, putting them on top of the kale. Cover the pan and simmer very slowly for 6 or 7 minutes more.

Serve very hot.

◆

A SUGGESTED DINNER

WINE
Chianti Classico Brolio

Tortellini alla panna (see page 176)

Arista (see below)

Rape saltate in padella (see page 420)

Pere al vino (see page 495)
with *Crema zabaione* (see page 435)

———◆———

Arista
(Loin of Pork with Garlic, Rosemary, and Black Pepper)
(SERVES 8 TO 10)

Around 1450 the Turks were at the gates of Constantinople, and
it seemed that the thousand-year-old Eastern Roman Empire would
fall if help did not come from the West. The Emperor and the
Patriarch of the Orthodox Church went to Italy to have a conference
on the union of that church with that of Rome, a precondition for
aid. The Medici were hosts for most of the conference. Benozzo
Gozzoli's famous fresco of the journey of the Magi is supposed to
depict the personages of that historic event. At one of the feasts
(Florence was the culinary center of the West), a roast of pork, a
specialty of Florence, was served. One of the Greek dignataries, in his
own language exclaimed: *Arista!* ("the best"). The Eastern Roman
Empire fell, but *arista* has remained to this day.

    8 to 10 large cloves garlic
    2 heaping tablespoons rosemary leaves
 1½ tablespoons salt
    1 level tablespoon freshly ground black pepper
    4 pounds front part pork loin, boned but untied
  10 to 12 whole black peppercorns
    1 tablespoon olive oil

Preheat the oven to 350° or 375°.

Cut the garlic cloves into 4 to 6 pieces lengthwise, then combine, in
a bowl, with the rosemary leaves, salt, and ground pepper.

Place the loin on a board and open it out flat, with the inside facing
up. Spread half the garlic mixture over the inside surface, then scatter

The famous painting by Gozzoli of the journey of the Magi, showing the personages of the council to unify the churches and save Constantinople. It was at this council that *arista* got its name.

over the whole black peppercorns. Roll the loin and tie with thread, as follows:

Wrap the thread around the meat, starting at one end, and pull tight. Do not break the thread but bring it down lengthwise 2 inches and wrap it around the meat again. Continue this process until the entire length is tied around, at a distance of every 2 inches or so. (This is the usual way of tying salami as well, in Italy.)

When rolled and tied, make about 12 punctures in the outside of the meat with a thin knife, about ½ inch deep. Fill these holes with most of the remainder of the spice mixture, and if any of the spice mixture is left, sprinkle it over the outside surface of the loin.

Put the olive oil in the bottom of a roasting pan, then set the meat in it. Place the pan in the preheated oven for about 25 minutes to the pound. The pork should not be overcooked, and generally in Italy is cooked less than in America; it is advisable to cook the meat completely, but to be careful not to leave it in the oven beyond that point. Not only the weight, but the width of the roll affect cooking time.

After about an hour in the oven, turn the meat over. For the last 5 to 10 minutes, raise the temperature to 400°, to brown the outside.

Remove the pan from the oven and immediately transfer the *arista* from the pan with its drippings. Let cool for 10 minutes before slicing in thin slices and serving.

Note: Arista may be eaten cold for several days following, and many Florentines prefer it that way.

Salsicce
(Tuscan Sausages)   (MAKES ABOUT 15)

Tuscan sausages are of pork meat, the fat of the fresh *pancetta*, and a little veal. Cured with salt, pepper, and whole peppercorns only, they differ from most Italian sausages in that they are not flavored with herbs and spices, nor do they contain preservatives or saltpeter.

Since it is not possible to find them in America, the recipe for making them is given. If you do not have the time to make them, use Italian sausages with the least flavoring added, or even large American breakfast sausages, because they are often pure pork with little flavoring. When in Italy, try the sausages of Siena, which are particularly outstanding.

Making your own sausages is, however, worth the trouble. You can, for one thing, avoid artificial preservatives and flavorings. The main thing to remember is not to grind the meat too fine or you will have an uninteresting texture. And be sure to obtain pork casing, not veal or anything else; good pork stores, such as Italian or Hungarian, usually have it.

When you see your sausages turn reddish on the third day or so, you won't be able to suppress a feeling of pride. Try them.

    2 pounds fresh boneless pork
    1 pound fresh *pancetta*
    2 ounces boneless veal
 1½ tablespoons salt
    2 teaspoons freshly ground black pepper
   20 whole black peppercorns, approximately
    1 pork casing

Cut the different kinds of meat into small pieces, then grind the pieces coarsely, using a grinder or food processor. (With the grinder, grind only once; the pieces should not be too fine.) Add the salt, ground pepper, and peppercorns and mix very thoroughly with a wooden spoon.

Soak the casing in a small bowl of lukewarm water for 10 minutes, then remove from the water and dry with paper towels.

Improvise a syringe by inserting the tube end of a funnel into one end of the casing. Then push the casing up until all of it is rolled onto the funnel tube.

Making sure that your hands are very clean and dry, insert some of the meat into the mouth of the funnel, then, with the handle of a wooden spoon or one of your fingers, push it through the funnel tube into the rolled-up casing, to the end (see photo 1). Gently unroll the casing. The meat pushed through will have opened the entire casing to allow air to rush in. It is now open to stuff.

Salsicce: 1. Pushing the meat through the funnel tube into the casing.

Little by little, push the meat in until the casing is full, being careful not to leave empty pockets of air. Fill it well, but do not overstuff.

When the casing is full, tie a long string to one end. (At this point, move your hands over casing again to be sure that stuffing is evenly distributed.) Now, 3 inches from the end where it is tied, draw the long string around, pass it through, and knot it tight (see photo 2). Every 3 inches, tie the long string around in the same manner, in this way making a long series of sausage links (see photo 3).

2. Making a link in the sausage.

3. Sausage, in links.

Let the sausages hang in a cool room with lots of fresh air. About the third day, they should turn a reddish color. Allow them to hang for another 3 or 4 days; the salt will cure the meat in this period. After 6 or 7 days they may be used or refrigerated.

A SUGGESTED DINNER

WINE
Chianti Classico Cerbaiola

Ribollita (see page 124)

Salsicce con rape (see below)

Frittelle di tondone alla fiorentina (see page 467)

Salsicce con Rape
(Sausages with Rape)   (S E R V E S 4)

This is the classic combination, the pork sausage with its ideal complement, wonderful, slightly bitter green rape.*

    2 pounds rape
       Coarse salt
    4 large sweet sausages
    2 tablespoons olive oil
    1 clove garlic, peeled but left whole
       Salt and freshly ground black pepper to taste
       Lemon wedges

Remove the heavy stalks from the rape, leaving the light stalks and leaves. Cut these into 2-inch pieces and wash them thoroughly under cold running water, then place in a large bowl of cold water and let soak for 1 hour.

Heat 6 cups of cold water and some coarse salt in a large flameproof casserole. When the water reaches the boiling point, add the rape and cook for about 30 minutes, until soft. Remove the casserole from the heat, drain the rape in a colander, and cool it under cold running water. Gently squeeze excess water from the rape and let stand until needed.

Puncture the sausages with a fork in two or three places.

---

* See introduction to *Rape saltata*, page 421.

Heat the olive oil, garlic clove, and sausages in a medium-sized, flameproof casserole, and sauté gently for about 15 minutes.

Remove the garlic clove from the casserole and add the rape. Season with salt and freshly ground pepper and mix thoroughly with wooden spoon, then cover the casserole and let simmer very slowly, stirring every so often, for about 20 minutes.

Remove the casserole from the flame and transfer the sausages and rape to a serving dish. Garnish with lemon wedges and serve immediately.

———◆———

A SUGGESTED DINNER

WINE
Chianti Classico Fattoria Fizzano

Passato di spinaci (see page 118)

Salsicce e fagioli (see below)

Crostata di ricotta (see page 446)

———◆———

Salsicce e Fagioli
(Tuscan Beans with Sausages)   (SERVES 4)

A filling, satisfying dish for a nice winter night. A rustic family dish that can also be shared with good friends on an informal occasion.

    4 large sweet sausages
    3 tablespoons olive oil
    6 or 7 large leaves sage, fresh or under salt (see page 14)
    4 large cloves garlic, unpeeled
    ½ pound very ripe fresh or canned tomatoes
    4 cups boiled cannellini beans (see boiled Tuscan beans, page 400)

Puncture the sausages with a fork in three or four places.

Heat the oil in a flameproof casserole, preferably terra-cotta. When the oil is hot, add the sausages and sauté on a low flame for 15 minutes, turning them over several times. Add the sage and garlic and sauté for 2 or 3 minutes more.

Pass the tomatoes through a food mill into the casserole and simmer for 3 to 5 minutes more. Season with salt and pepper, then add the boiled cannellini beans and simmer very slowly for 15 minutes more, stirring with a wooden spoon.

Remove the casserole from the heat, and serve hot from the same casserole.

———◆———

A SUGGESTED DINNER

WINE
Borgogno-Barbera

Minestra povera di patate (see page 125)
Rospo nel buco (see below)
Fagiolini in umido (see page 405)
Fresh fruit

———◆———

Rospo nel Buco
(Sausages Baked in Batter; "Frogs in the Hole") (SERVES 4)

A more elaborate treatment of the rustic sausage, but still a family dish. The sausage pieces form part of a light batter cake.

8 sweet sausages
1 tablespoon olive oil
6 eggs, separated
1 cup milk
6 tablespoons all-purpose flour
  Salt and freshly ground pepper to taste
1 tablespoon rosemary leaves

Preheat the oven to 400°. Use a 13½ x 8¾ baking dish.

Prick each sausage with fork in two or thrce places, then place in a baking dish with the olive oil. Put the dish in the preheated oven for 20 to 25 minutes, until all fat has rendered out of the sausages.

Meanwhile, prepare a batter by mixing the egg yolks, milk, flour, salt, pepper, and rosemary leaves in a bowl with a wooden spoon. Let the batter stand for 20 minutes in a cool place; do not refrigerate.

When the sausages are ready, take the baking dish from the oven and remove all but 2 tablespoons of fat.

Beat the egg whites until stiff and quickly fold into the batter. Pour the batter over the sausages in the hot baking dish and put back in the oven, still at 400°. Bake for about 35 minutes.

Remove the "frogs in the holes" from the oven, allow to cool for 5 minutes, and serve.

Variety Meats

A SUGGESTED DINNER

WINE
Chianti Classico Castello di Fonterutoli

Pappa al pomodoro (see page 230)

Fegato alla griglia (see below)

Fagioli al fiasco (see page 400)

Ciambella di frutta (see page 487)

Fegato alla Griglia
(Calf's Liver, Grilled Florentine Style)   (SERVES 4)

The simplest of treatments, calf's liver cooked on a *gratella*, the Italian range top grill (see photo, page 291). If the liver is fresh and good, all of its own flavor will emerge. Use very thin slices.

    Salt
 4 large slices calf's liver, ½ inch thick
    Freshly ground black pepper to taste
 2 tablespoons olive oil
    Lemon wedges

Place the grill on the flame and sprinkle it with 2 or 3 teaspoons of salt. (If the grill is well seasoned, it should not be necessary to use any oil.) When the grill is very hot, put on one slice of the liver and cook it for about 45 seconds on each side, then remove it to a serving dish; keep warm. Repeat the procedure with the other 3 slices.

Sprinkle the liver with a little freshly ground black pepper and uncooked oil, then garnish with lemon wedges and serve immediately.

Note: The liver should be light pink inside and very tender and soft. Keep in mind that the longer you cook liver, the tougher it becomes.

A SUGGESTED DINNER

WINE
Venegazzù Rosso

Tortelli della vigilia (see page 169)

Fegato alla toscana (see below)

Fagioli all'uccelletto (see page 402)

Latte alla portoghese (see page 437)

Fegato alla Toscana
(Sautéed Calf's Liver, Tuscan Style)   (SERVES 4)

Another simple treatment, flavored with olive oil, sage, and very lightly with garlic. If the calf's liver is good, it should be cooked as little as possible. The longer it is cooked, the tougher it gets.

   ½ cup all-purpose flour
1 ½ pounds calf's liver, sliced thin
   5 tablespoons olive oil
   5 or 6 leaves sage, fresh or under salt (see page 14)
   1 large clove garlic, unpeeled
     Salt and freshly ground black pepper to taste

Flour the liver slices very lightly.

Put the oil, sage, and unpeeled garlic clove in a large frying pan and set on a medium flame. When the oil is hot, place the liver slices in the pan and sauté very lightly for about 2 minutes on each side, so the liver remains pink inside. Sprinkle with salt and freshly ground black pepper, then remove the pan from flame.

Transfer the liver to a serving dish and serve hot.

A SUGGESTED DINNER

WINE
Chianti Classico Machiavelli Serristori

Pasta e ceci (see page 128)

Fegatelli alla fiorentina (see below)

Rape saltate in padella (see page 420) or *Insalata verde* (see page 387)

Pane co' santi (see page 471)

Fegatelli alla Fiorentina
(Pork Liver, Florentine Style) (SERVES 6)

Fresh pork liver cut into pieces, rolled in a mixture of good bread crumbs, fennel seeds, salt, pepper, and crushed bay leaf and then wrapped in caul fat. Sautéed in olive oil and then simmered in wine, a flavor is achieved that would not be possible with any other kind of liver. The caul fat cooks away, but the liver has absorbed the flavors of all the ingredients. Pork liver is very cheap in America because it is unjustly neglected.

½ pound caul fat
1½ pounds pork liver
¾ cup bread crumbs, preferably homemade (see page 45)
3 tablespoons fennel seeds *(continued)*

Salt and freshly ground pepper to taste
6 medium-sized bay leaves
6 tablespoons olive oil
½ cup red wine

Soak the caul fat in a small bowl of lukewarm water for 10 minutes. Meanwhile, cut the pork liver into 12 pieces and set aside. Combine the bread crumbs, fennel seeds, salt, and pepper in a large bowl and mix well with a wooden spoon.

Carefully open the caul fat and spread it out on a board. Cut the caul fat into 12 pieces.

Put the liver pieces in the large bowl and mix well with the bread crumb mixture, then place each piece of liver on top of a piece of caul fat. Add ½ bay leaf to each piece and wrap the liver and bay leaf completely in fat (see photos 1 and 2). Fasten the caul fat to the liver with a toothpick.

Heat the olive oil in a large frying pan and add all the wrapped liver pieces. Sauté very gently, on a medium flame, for 10 minutes, turning the liver pieces once or twice, then sprinkle with salt and pepper. Add the wine, cover, and simmer for 20 minutes, turning the *fegatelli* once more.

Remove the pan from the flame; the caul fat will have dissolved. Transfer the *fegatelli* to a serving dish, sprinkle over one or two tablespoons of the gravy, and serve immediately.

Fegatelli alla fiorentina: 1. Placing a piece of liver and half a bay leaf on a piece of caul fat.

2. Wrapping the pork liver completely in caul fat.

A SUGGESTED DINNER

WINE
Ricasoli Brolio Bianco

Passato di spinaci (see page 118)

Ciambella con cibreo (see below)

Meringhe alla panna (see page 468)

Ciambella con Cibreo
(Potato-Ricotta Ring with Chicken-Liver Sauce) (**S E R V E S** **4**)

Cibreo sauce should be made not only with chicken livers, but also with the crests and wattles of the rooster. Another touch of a generation ago was to use as well the little yellow eggs that were still inside the hen when slaughtered. These combs and eggs have disappeared from American markets recently enough perhaps to arouse some nostalgia. If you can get them, by all means include them in the recipe.

14 ounces boiling potatoes
14 ounces ricotta, preferably "part skim"
 5 eggs, one of them separated
 3 tablespoons freshly grated Parmigiano cheese
   Salt and freshly ground pepper to taste
½ cup bread crumbs, preferably homemade (see page 45), approximately
   Cibreo sauce (see page 75)

Put the potatoes in a large saucepan of boiling salted water and cook for about 30 minutes, then peel and pass them through a potato ricer into a large bowl.

Add the ricotta to the bowl and mix well with the potatoes. Add the whole eggs, the egg yolk, Parmigiano, salt, and pepper and mix thoroughly, until homogenous.

Butter a ring mold (8½ inches in diameter) and coat it with the bread crumbs; preheat the oven to 400°.

Beat the egg white until stiff, then fold it very gently into the contents of the bowl. Transfer the potato mixture from the bowl to the ring mold and place in the preheated oven for 20 to 25 minutes.

Remove the mold from oven and allow to cool for 15 to 20 minutes before unmolding.

Meanwhile, prepare the *cibreo* sauce according to the directions on page 75, using 1 pound of chicken livers and veal kidneys if the crests and unlaid eggs are not available.

Unmold the ring on a serving dish, then, with a slotted spoon, transfer the solids in the sauce to the center of the ring. Pour remaining sauce from pan into sauceboat. Serve each person a slice of *ciambella*, or ring, with some of the solids and sauce on the side.

————◆————

A SUGGESTED DINNER

WINE
Sella & Mosca Cannonau

Timballo di riso (see page 222)

Torta Manfreda (see below)

Piselli alla fiorentina (see page 415)

Frittura mista di frutta (see page 497)

———◆———

Torta Manfreda
(Antique Chicken Liver Paté)   (SERVES 6)

Here, coarsely chopped chicken livers are sautéed with wine, *pancetta*, and other ingredients. *Mollica* (soaked, crustless bread), eggs, and Parmigiano are added, and then all is transferred to a pie-plate mold, the top coated with bread crumbs, and baked.

A great favorite of the Renaissance, the dish appears in almost all cookbooks of those early centuries.

Usually served hot, it makes a good appetizer or first dish for an important dinner, as well as a good light second dish after a heavier first one, still for a rather formal type of dinner. A very versatile dish indeed.

> 6 ounces *pancetta* or 3 ounces boiled ham plus 3 ounces salt pork
> 2 tablespoons olive oil
> 1 pound chicken livers
> ½ cup dry red wine
> 2 slices white bread, crusts removed
> 4 eggs
> 8 ounces freshly grated Parmigiano cheese
> 5 tablespoons bread crumbs, preferably homemade (see page 45)
> Salt and freshly ground pepper to taste
> 2 tablespoons butter, approximately

Preheat the oven to 375°.

Chop the *pancetta* (or ham and salt pork) coarsely. Set a saucepan containing the olive oil on a low flame. When the oil is hot, add the chopped *pancetta* and sauté gently until lightly golden brown.

Chop the chicken livers coarsely and add them to the saucepan. Sauté gently for 4 or 5 minutes, then add the red wine and let it evaporate.

Remove the pan from the flame, transfer the contents to a board, and chop them fine. Return the chopped ingredients to the saucepan and put the pan back on the flame. Taste for salt and pepper and simmer slowly for 3 or 4 minutes, then remove the pan from the heat again.

Put the crustless bread slices in a crockery bowl. Pour the contents of the saucepan over the bread and let cool, then mix well with a wooden spoon, incorporating the bread into the other ingredients. Stirring constantly, add the eggs, one at a time, then the Parmigiano and 1 tablespoon of the bread crumbs. Taste for salt and pepper.

Coat a Pyrex pie plate with the butter and some of the remaining bread crumbs. Transfer the contents of the bowl to the pie plate, pressing the mixture down well so the top is level. Sprinkle the top with the last of the bread crumbs.

Place the pie plate in the preheated oven and bake for 30 to 35 minutes, then remove from the oven and let cool for 10 to 15 minutes.

Unmold onto a serving dish and serve.

Note: Torta Manfreda can be eaten as an appetizer, in place of pasta as a first course, or as a second course.

———◆———

A SUGGESTED DINNER

WINE
Chianti Classico Villa Cerna

Minestrone alla contadina (see page 122)

Trippa alla fiorentina (see below)

Insalata di peperoni alla griglia (see page 389)

Budino di riso (see page 490)

———◆———

Trippa alla Fiorentina
(Tripe Florentine Style) (SERVES 4)

Tripe, cooked first and then simmered with meat broth, tomatoes, and seasonings. It is cut into thin strips almost resembling pasta, and sprinkled with Parmigiano. A very pleasant introduction to tripe for those who haven't tried it. (There is no strange aftertaste as in *tripes à la môde de Caens*.)

In Florence there are little tripe stands on wheels that sell already cooked tripe without sauce, as well as sandwiches made with the tripe. With sly Tuscan humor, these stands poke fun at the Florentine pride in their long history. Often the wagons have painted on them something like "This house was founded in 1903."

In Italy the tripe is completely precooked, so it has to be cooked only 20 to 35 minutes. In the United States the tripe is precooked for much less time, and generally requires 3 to 4 hours of additional cooking. (Check with your butcher, for occasionally there is tripe that cooks in only 2 hours.)

    2 pounds fresh tripe
    5 or 6 sprigs Italian parsley
    1 large clove garlic
    ¼ cup olive oil
    2 tablespoons tomato paste (or 1½ cups canned tomatoes
      Salt and freshly ground pepper to taste
    1 cup meat broth
    ¼ cup freshly grated Parmigiano cheese

Bring a large amount of salted water to a boil in a stockpot. When it is boiling, add the tripe and simmer for from 2 to 4 hours, depending on the amount of precooking it has undergone.

When the tripe is cooked, slice it into strips ⅓ inch wide.

Chop the parsley and garlic coarsely. Heat the olive oil in a flameproof casserole. When it is hot, add the chopped ingredients and sauté very gently for about 10 minutes. Add the tripe to the casserole and cook for 5 minutes more.

Add the tomato paste or canned tomatoes and broth. Simmer until the broth is almost completely evaporated (about 25 minutes) and the tripe is soft, then taste for salt and pepper and cook for 5 minutes more.

Remove the casserole from the heat. Transfer the tripe to a serving dish and allow it to cool for 2 minutes, then sprinkle with the Parmigiano and serve.

Polenta

POLENTA is made from corn meal, cooked in a special way, and serves as the basis for hundreds of dishes. It is a staple of the diet of the Veneto region and some of the other far northern parts of Italy. There is no doubt that polenta is the descendant of the staple food of the ancient Roman Empire, *puls*. Remember that bread made from wheat flour was only eaten by the rich in those days. The *puls* was not yet made from corn meal, because there were still many centuries to wait before corn was brought to Europe from America. But corn meal replaced other grains, and polenta is still very much with us. Unfortunately, there is only space for a few recipes, those with sausage and with herring, and for a more complicated dish in which the polenta is cooked and cut into strips that serve as the pastry for a *timballo* filled with quails and sauce.

In addition, there is a polenta-like recipe, *gnocchi di farina gialla* (see page 224), that is used as a first course.

The main danger to avoid in cooking polenta is the formation of lumps. For this reason it must be stirred constantly while it cooks on a low flame. The technique of first pouring the meal into the boiling water must also be mastered to avoid the meal's bunching together. Follow the instructions carefully and all will be well.

A little over 2 quarts cold water
1½ teaspoons salt
1 pound yellow corn meal

Heat the water and salt in a stockpot. When the water reaches the boiling point, begin adding corn meal. Pour it in a very slow stream, simultaneously stirring with a wooden spoon or a simple non-rotary rolling pin. (It is important to pour slowly and steadily and to keep stirring because, otherwise, the polenta can easily become lumpy). Stir slowly, without stopping, for about 35 minutes. If some lumps form, push them against the side of the pot to dissolve them.

Prepare a smooth wooden surface (preferably a round board about 18 inches in diameter, or substitute a pasta board) by wetting it with cold water.

When the polenta has cooked for about 35 minutes, leave it on the flame for about 3 minutes more without stirring. Shake the pot a little; in this way, some steam will form under the polenta and it will completely detach from the bottom of the pot. After the 3 minutes are up, quickly reverse the pot of polenta onto the wooden surface.

Polenta is best cut with a string. Fit a string under the polenta layer and draw it through to the top surface (see photo). Continue slicing the polenta this way, then place the slices on individual dishes.

Cover with whichever sauce you have prepared and serve hot.

Slicing polenta with a string.

A SUGGESTED DINNER

WINE
Chianti Classico Verrazzano

Crostini al ginepro (see page 91)
Polenta con salsicce (see below)
Buccellato alle fragole (see page 470)

Polenta con Salsicce
(Polenta with Sausages)   (SERVES 6)

Sausages cooked in a wonderful sauce made with wild mushrooms
and all poured over slices of polenta. It makes one look forward to
the cold weather.

    4 ounces dried *porcini* mushrooms
    6 large sweet sausages
    1 red onion
    5 tablespoons olive oil
    ¼ cup tomato paste
      Salt and freshly ground pepper to taste
    2 cups meat or chicken broth
      Polenta (see page 367)

Soak the dried mushrooms in a bowl of lukewarm water for 20
minutes. Meanwhile, cut the sausages in half; chop the onion fine.
Heat the olive oil in a saucepan on a medium flame. When it is
warm, add the chopped onion and sauté until golden brown (about
12 minutes), stirring with a wooden spoon every so often. Add the
sausage pieces and sauté very lightly for 10 minutes, then add the tomato paste and simmer for 5 minutes more. Add the soaked mushrooms and season with salt and pepper.
In a second saucepan, heat the broth to boiling. When it is hot,

pour it into the saucepan containing the sausages. Let simmer very slowly until a large quantity of broth has evaporated (about 25 minutes).

While the sauce is reducing, make the polenta, with quantities listed according to the directions on page 367. When the polenta is ready and on its round board (or pasta board), cut it into slices with a string.

Pour the sauce into a large sauceboat and serve hot, along with the polenta. Place several slices of polenta on each individual dish and cover it with the sausage sauce.

———◆———

A SUGGESTED DINNER

WINE
Chianti Classico Cantina del Papa

Passato di spinaci (see page 118)

Aringhe e polenta (see below)

Fresh fruit

———◆———

Aringhe e Polenta
(Herring with Polenta)   (SERVES 4)

Perhaps herring does not leap to mind as an Italian dish. But it is widely eaten in the Tuscan Appenines. The salted smoked herring is not soaked, so it remains potently salty. Cooked on the Italian range-top grill, the *gratella* (see photo, page 291), and eaten in a small quantity with polenta, on a cold winter night, it can be a very satisfying, hearty country dinner. Often, as a joke, the friends of a bridegroom would give him a bachelor party in the country the night before his wedding. They would have this dish made, with the humorous intent that the following day the groom would be incapable of opening his mouth to say "I do."

Polenta (see page 367)
2 herrings, with milt or roe
½ cup olive oil
Freshly ground pepper to taste

Prepare the polenta according to the directions on page 367. Place it on wooden surface and cover with a cotton dishtowel to keep warm. Take herrings directly from the barrel. Do not wash, soak, or fillet; leave whole, with the milt or roe.

Heat the *gratella* until very hot; put no fat on it, or salt. Place the herrings on the hot grill and cook them on both sides until quite brown (about 8 minutes each side). Those lucky enough to have a fireplace for cooking should roast them instead over the open fire until each side is brown.

Place the herrings in a large soup bowl and pour over the uncooked olive oil. Sprinkle with freshly ground black pepper.

Slice polenta with string and place several slices on each individual dish. Cut herrings in half widthwise and place a half herring with some of its sauce on each dish.

———◆———

A SUGGESTED DINNER

WINE
Chianti Classico Villa Tizzano

Passato di verdura (see page 117)

Timballo di polenta con quaglie (see below)

Bietole all'agro (see page 423)

Fragole al vino rosso (see page 496)

———◆———

Timballo di Polenta con Quaglie
(Pastry Drum of Polenta Filled with Quails) (S E R V E S 4)

This dish is the ennoblement of polenta. Made into an elegant *timballo* filled with quail, at this point polenta may be served at the fanciest of tables. (Two small squabs may be substituted for the 4 quail, but the result is definitely a compromise.)

Making the *timballo* with polenta is even more difficult than making the normal *timballo*, so practice making it for the family before you try it for an important dinner. The steps that require extreme care are pointed out in the recipe. Be sure that the polenta is extra smooth, with no lumps, before beginning.

For the polenta

>   2 quarts water
>   Salt
>   ¾ pound corn meal

For the filling

>   ¼ pound *pancetta* or 2 ounces boiled ham
>   plus 2 ounces salt pork
>   1 clove garlic
>   7 or 8 leaves sage, fresh or under salt (see page 14)
>   ¼ cup olive oil
>   Salt and freshly ground pepper
>   4 quails or 2 small squab
>   1 tablespoon tomato paste
>   1 cup canned tomatoes
> 1 ½ cups hot chicken or meat broth
>   1 bay leaf
>   2 cups freshly grated Parmigiano cheese
>   3 or 4 pats of butter

To make the polenta, put 2 quarts of water in a stockpot and set on the heat. (The *timballo* polenta requires a larger proportion of water than the classic polenta.) Add salt, and when the water reaches the boiling point, add the corn meal, pouring in a continuous stream and stirring constantly with a wooden spoon. Keep stirring until the polenta is completely cooked (at least 30 minutes).

Stop stirring and let the polenta rest on the flame for about 3 minutes. Shake the pot a little. In this way a little steam will form at the bottom of the pot, which will help to unmold the polenta.

Unmold the polenta onto a wet, smooth surface of marble, wood, or formica, then spread it out with a wet spatula until it is uniformly ¼ inch thick. Let the polenta cool for 2 hours. Meanwhile, begin to make the sauce.

Coarsely chop the *pancetta* (or ham and salt pork), garlic, and sage.

Heat the olive oil in a saucepan, preferably terra-cotta, and when it is hot, add the chopped ingredients and sauté on medium heat until golden brown (about 15 minutes). Put a pinch of salt and pepper inside each quail and add them to the saucepan. Sauté for 5 to 7 minutes. Add the tomato paste and allow 2 or 3 minutes for it to incorporate.

Add the tomatoes and enough hot broth to cover the quails completely (1 to 1½ cups of broth), then taste for salt and pepper and simmer very gently for 20 to 25 minutes. Remove from the flame and let cool for 30 minutes.

Meanwhile, start to put the *timballo* together.

To make the circular top of the *timballo*, place the removable bottom of an 8-inch springform on the polenta layer and cut around it. The circular bottom of the *timballo* must be a little larger than the top. Place the bottom of the springform on the polenta layer again, but this time cut the circle ½ inch larger all around.

Put the springform together and butter it generously, then carefully place the bottom layer of the *timballo* inside. Since it has a larger diameter than the springform, the edges will curl up and overlap the sides.

To make the sides of the *timballo*, cut long strips of polenta as wide as the springform is high (about 2¾ inches). Fit the strips along the inside of the springform, being careful to place them inside the overlap of the circular *timballo* bottom. For the sides, try to use as few separate pieces as possible, and be sure to allow ½ inch overlap in the connection of 2 separate polenta strips.

Remove the quails from the saucepan and place them inside the *timballo*. Sprinkle 2 tablespoons of the Parmigiano and 2 tablespoons of the sauce over them.

Cut the leftover polenta into 1-inch squares; preheat the oven to 400°. Fit polenta squares between and around the quails, filling in empty spaces. Again sprinkle with Parmigiano and sauce.

Using additional polenta squares, completely fill in the *timballo*, using up the remaining Parmigiano and sauce as well. Top with the pats of butter and cover with the *timballo* top.

Place the *timballo* in the preheated oven for 50 minutes, then allow to cool for 15 minutes.

Say a prayer and open the springform. Place the *timballo* on a serving dish and serve hot, cutting through like a cake, being careful to leave the quails whole.

Composite Main Courses

---◆---

A SUGGESTED DINNER

WINE
Chianti Classico Pagliarese

Tortellini alla panna (see page 176)

Budino di carne (see below)

Melanzane alla parmigiana (see page 412)

Pasticcini ripieni (see page 440)

---◆---

Budino di Carne
("Pudding" of Veal, Chicken Breast, and Prosciutto)

(SERVES 6)

This is a light second dish for a more formal dinner, but is easy enough also to do for the family. The *balsamella* is prepared, then the three kinds of meats are ground. These are mixed with the remaining ingredients and slowly baked in a soufflé dish placed in a *bagno maria* (bain-marie). The *budino* is unmolded onto a dish before serving. Cut like a cake, it is served warm. There is an optional sauce often used with it, but I prefer it without.

Balsamella

> 3 tablespoons butter
> ¼ cup all-purpose flour
> 1 cup milk

For the budino

> 2 tablespoons butter
> 4 slices white bread, crusts removed
> 1 cup cold milk
> ¼ pound veal
> 1 small whole chicken breast, boned and skinned
> 6 ounces prosciutto
> 3 eggs
> ¼ cup freshly grated Parmigiano cheese
> Salt, freshly ground pepper, and freshly grated nutmeg to taste
> 5 or 6 sprigs Italian parsley

For the sauce

> 1 chicken liver
> 2 tablespoons olive oil
> 1 cup canned tomatoes
> Salt and freshly ground pepper to taste

Make the *balsamella* according to the directions on page 52, then cover the saucepan and let cool for 1 hour.

Melt the butter in a small saucepan and let it cool for 20 minutes; soak the bread slices in the cold milk for 20 minutes.

Grind the veal, chicken breast, and 4 ounces of the prosciutto in a blender or food processor. Place the meat in a large bowl and add the eggs, Parmigiano, and melted butter. Mix well with a wooden spoon until all the ingredients are well amalgamated.

Squeeze the bread dry and add it to the bowl, along with the *balsamella*, salt, pepper, and nutmeg. Mix thoroughly, then coarsely chop the remaining prosciutto and the parsley and add them to the bowl. Gently mix them in.

Preheat the oven to 400°.

Butter and flour a soufflé dish 8½ inches in diameter, then improvise a *bagno maria* (bain-marie) by placing the soufflé dish in a rectangular Pyrex baking dish (13½ x 8¾ inches) containing 5 cups of cold water. Transfer the mixture from the bowl into the soufflé dish and place the improvised double-boiler in the preheated oven for 55 to 60 minutes.

Remove the soufflé dish and allow to rest for 10 to 15 minutes, then unmold onto a serving dish. Slice the *budino di carne* like a cake and serve, if desired, with the optional sauce, prepared as follows.

Chop the chicken liver fine. Heat the olive oil in a small saucepan, and when the oil is warm, add the chopped liver and sauté gently for 2 minutes. Add the tomatoes, salt, and pepper and simmer for about 20 minutes.

◆

A SUGGESTED DINNER

WINE
Antinori-Rosé di Bolgheri

Ravioli nudi (see page 228)

Sformato di prosciutto (see below)

Cardi dorati (see page 408)

Tartufi di castagne (see page 480)

◆

Sformato di Prosciutto
(Ham "Soufflé") (SERVES 6)

Sformati, meaning literally "unmolded," are, along with certain types of *budini*, the Italian soufflés. (See the discussion of the dessert *budino* on page 489). This *sformato* of ham is a main dish employing the same technique that is used more often for an elaborate vegetable treatment appropriate for a *piatto di mezzo*. It is a very light and delicate second course, useful for a formal light meal, or as a relief to a heavier first course.

For the balsamella

> 6 tablespoons butter (¾ stick)
> ½ cup all-purpose flour
> 2 cups milk
> Pinch of salt

For the sformato

> 10 ounces boiled ham
> ½ cup brandy
> 1 tablespoon butter
> 1 tablespoon all-purpose flour
> 2 tablespoons freshly grated Parmigiano cheese
> 4 eggs, separated
> Salt and freshly ground pepper
> Pinch of freshly grated nutmeg

Make a thick *balsamella*, using the ingredients in the quantities listed, according to the directions on page 52. Transfer the *balsamella* to a bowl, cover, and let cool for about 25 minutes. Cut 6 ounces of the boiled ham into small pieces and marinate in the brandy for 20 to 30 minutes; melt the butter in a small saucepan and let cool for 10 minutes.

When the *balsamella* is cool, very finely chop the remaining 4 ounces of boiled ham and add to the sauce. Mix together well until thoroughly combined, then add the flour, Parmigiano, egg yolks, marinated ham, and melted butter and mix very well. Taste for salt and pepper; add a pinch of nutmeg.

Preheat the oven to 400°.

Beat the 4 egg whites until very stiff and fold them gently into the contents of the bowl. Transfer the contents of the bowl to a buttered 8½-inch soufflé dish.

Place the dish in a large casserole of water, making an improvised *bagno maria* (bain-marie). Place the *bagno maria* in the preheated oven for 30 to 35 minutes, then remove the dish from the oven and allow to cool for 10 minutes.

Unmold the *sformato* onto a serving dish and serve hot.

A SUGGESTED DINNER

WINE
Ruffino-Riserva Ducale

Timballo di tortellini (see page 212)

Arrosto girato alla fiorentina (see below)

Insalata mista (see page 387)

Zuppa inglese (see page 452)

A SUGGESTED DINNER
FOR NEW YEAR'S EVE

WINES
Chianti Classico La Quercia
Chianti Classico Montagliari

Crostini al ginepro (see page 91)

Timballo di tortellini (see page 212)

Gran bollito misto (see page 271)
with *Savore di noci* (see page 61)
and *Maionese* (see page 55)

Arrosto girato alla fiorentina (see below)

Insalata verde (see page 387)

Timballo di pere (see page 449)

Arrosto Girato alla Fiorentina
(Mixed Meat and Fowl Roasted on the Spit) (SERVES 12)

A huge spit over a roaring fire of wood or charcoal is one of the
trademarks of the Italian country villas and even of the country
restaurants. The spit has given its name, *girarrosto*, to a kind of restaurant in which these specialties are served. If you have a charcoal grill
with a spit, you can make these dishes with no problem. But if you
do not, it is possible to get something very close indeed to the
original in your own kitchen. As a matter of fact, this recipe not
only tells you how to prepare a variety of meat and fowl for a mixed
broil on the spit, it tells you how to improvise a spit in your own
kitchen.

This is a wonderful festive, countrified Sunday or holiday dinner,
the kind that can be enjoyed by everyone from *buongustaio* to those
of the simplest tastes.

- 1 chicken (about 3½ pounds)
- 1¾ pounds loin of pork
- 18 to 24 leaves sage, fresh or under salt (see page 14)
  - Salt and freshly ground black pepper to taste
- 12 quails
- 3 squabs
- 12 sweet sausages
- 1 pound pork liver, prepared for cooking as *fegatelli alla fiorentina* (see page 359) (optional)
- 1 pound *pane in bianco* (see note below)
- 12 to 14 bay leaves
- 1 cup olive oil, approximately

Prepare the meat and fowl as follows:

Cut the chicken and pork loin each into 12 pieces; place ½ sage
leaf, salt, and pepper in cavity of each quail; cut the squabs in quarters; puncture the sausages with a fork. If you also want to use pork
liver, prepare it, using caul fat, bread crumbs, and fennel seeds, according to the directions on page 359.

Cut the bread in pieces about 1 inch wide and ½ inch thick.

Before you put the meat on the spit, either start the fire in your
charcoal grill or improvise an open-air grill for your oven by putting 2 cups of cold water in a very large stockpot or casserole, along

with 1 tablespoon olive oil and 1 tablespoon coarse salt; preheat the oven to 375°. You will rest the skewer on the stockpot. In this way the steam coming from the water will keep the meat soft and moist, and the result will be almost the same as open-air cooking; see photo 1.

Arrosto girato alla fiorentina: 1. Improvising an "open air" spit in an oven.

Hold a long spit or skewer vertically and push each piece of meat onto it, drawing the first piece to the other end of the spit to make room for the others. Place the meat on the spit according to the following pattern: *

Chicken piece, ½ bay leaf, bread; pork loin piece, ½ sage leaf, bread; squab quarter, ½ bay leaf, bread; sausage, ½ sage leaf, bread; quail, ½ bay leaf, bread; optional pork liver piece, ½ sage leaf, bread.

Continue this pattern until the spit is full. The bay leaf and sage should alternate, but it doesn't matter which is next to which meat.

When all the ingredients are on the spit, sprinkle freely with salt and pepper, then place the spit either over your charcoal fire (be

---

* With these quantities it is necessary to use several skewers over a nonautomatic grill or the stockpot in the oven. For smaller quantities using a single skewer, the automatic spit could be used.

sure the charcoal is gray and there are no flames) or rest it on the stockpot, which should then be placed in the preheated oven. Cook the *arrosto* very slowly (turning it either electrically or by hand) for about 1 hour (1 hour 15 minutes in the oven), sprinkling the meat every so often with salt and brushing with olive oil (using a feather brush). In oven, turn about every 5 minutes.

Remove the *arrosto* from the spit to serving dish and serve immediately.

Note: The bread commonly used for this dish is a Tuscan bread that is shaped in the form of a very long loaf, 1½ inch thick, and baked only for 35 minutes. Because of its short baking time, the bread does not form a. crust and retains a whitish color, even if the dough is made with whole wheat flour. If you prefer, you can substitute ordinary Tuscan bread (see page 32).

In Italy, under the skewer itself we put a special pan called a *ghiotta*. Potatoes are placed in the *ghiotta* to cook so they can collect the delicious drippings from the meat cooking above on the spit (see photo 2). These *patate alla ghiotta* accompany the dish when made on the open air spit.

2. The pan called *ghiotta*, containing potatoes, which is placed under the spit to catch the drippings.

A SUGGESTED DINNER

WINE
Antinori—Tignanello

Torta Manfreda (see page 363)

Pastello di caccia (see below)

Insalata mista (see page 387) or
Insalata composta (see page 388)

Pesche al vino (see page 496)

Pastello di Caccia
(Great Pie of Quail, Squab, Chicken, Sausage, and Tortelli)
(SERVES 10 TO 12)

A huge pie of many layers, filled with whole quail, chickens, squab, sausages, and *tortelli* of chicken breast. It must be made in a very large casserole with two handles, preferably of tin-lined copper. I usually make it in a large antique copper one, 15 inches in diameter and 6 inches high. This fourteenth-century recipe is reminiscent of "four and twenty blackbirds baked in a pie," and it was indeed such a dish to which the rhyme referred. A fifteenth-century English adaptation of it was called "grete pye." In those days it could be made in a huge cauldron in the big stone fireplace, with dozens of birds and even a whole beast in it.

This recipe will serve about 12 people. In an old pot, when brought in whole, it can make a stunning effect. Each person is served a quail, a squab quarter, some *tortelli*, a sausage and a piece of chicken with some crust. For a large party, naturally it is possible to make more than one, but the pies must be served hot. *Pastello di caccia* is a *piatto unico*, a single dish that includes both first and second course. It should be preceded only by something light, if by anything. Save it for your fanciest party.

For the crust

> 3 cups all-purpose flour
> 1 tablespoon olive oil
> Pinch of salt
> 1 cup very cold water

For the tortelli filling

> 1 tablespoon olive oil
> 2 tablespoons butter
> 1 whole chicken breast
> 1 bay leaf
> Salt and freshly ground pepper to taste
> ¼ pound prosciutto or boiled ham
> 2 egg yolks
> ¼ cup freshly grated Parmigiano cheese
> Freshly grated nutmeg to taste

For the tortelli

> 2 cups all-purpose flour
> 2 "extra-large" eggs
> Pinch of salt
> 2 teaspoons olive or other vegetable oil

For the pastello filling

> 1 chicken (about 3 ½ pounds)
> Salt and freshly ground pepper
> 3 squabs
> 12 quails
> 20 leaves sage, fresh or under salt (see page 14), approximately
> 12 sweet sausages, preferably Tuscan sausages (see page 350)
> 2 tablespoons olive oil
> 12 thin slices *pancetta* or boiled ham
> 1½ bay leaves
> 1 tablespoon rosemary leaves

Plus

> Coarse salt
> Olive oil

Prepare the crust first.

Place the flour on pasta board and make a well in it. Put the olive oil, salt, and water in the well, then incorporate with half of the flour, mixing with a metal fork.

Start kneading, gently but steadily, until all but 3 or 4 tablespoons of the flour is incorporated. From this point knead for 20 minutes more, incorporating 1 more tablespoon of flour.

Wrap the dough in a dampened cotton dishtowel and let rest in a cool place for 3 hours; do not refrigerate.

To make the *tortelli* filling, heat the oil and butter in a small casserole, on a low flame. When the butter is melted, add the chicken breast and bay leaf and sauté on a low flame for 20 minutes, turning the chicken breast over several times. Sprinkle with salt and pepper, then remove the casserole from the flame.

Place the chicken breast on a chopping board, discarding the bay leaf. Skin and bone and chop the chicken coarsely. Add the prosciutto to the chicken meat and continue to chop until quite fine.

Transfer the chopped ingredients to a bowl. Add the egg yolks, Parmigiano, and 1 tablespoon of fat from the casserole. Season with salt, pepper, and nutmeg, then mix thoroughly with a wooden spoon. Cover the bowl with aluminum foil and place in the refrigerator until needed.

Make fresh pasta, using the ingredients in the proportions listed above, according to the directions on page 133, then form into *tortelli* as directed on page 162, using the filling you have just prepared.

Place a stockpot containing a large quantity of cold water and some coarse salt on the heat. While the water is coming to a boil, fill a large bowl full of cold water and add 2 tablespoons of oil; wet a cotton dishtowel with cold water and spread it out on a board.

When the water reaches the boiling point, place 10 *tortelli* at a time in the boiling water and let them cook for 20 seconds. Remove from the stockpot with a strainer-skimmer and place in the bowl of cold water. Let the *tortelli* cool for 3 or 4 minutes, then transfer from the bowl to the wet towel and spread them out.

Repeat the procedure until all the *tortelli* are on the towel, then wet a second cotton dishtowel and place it on top of the *tortelli*. Let stand while you prepare the rest of the *pastello* filling.

Open the chicken, cutting it through the breast, then place it, open side down, between two sheets of wet wax paper and flatten it by pounding it with your fist. Transfer the chicken to a dish, sprinkle with salt and pepper, and let stand until needed.

Wash the squabs and quails very well, removing and discarding the livers. Place a leaf of sage and a pinch of salt and pepper inside each bird.

Puncture the sausages with a fork in two or three places.

Heat the olive oil in a very large casserole, on a medium flame. When the oil is warm, add the sausages, squabs, and quails and sauté gently for about 30 minutes, gently moving the birds around every so often with a wooden spoon.

Remove the casserole from the heat and let cool for 1 hour.

When you are ready to put the *pastello di caccia* together, oil a very large two-handled casserole, preferably of tin-lined copper; preheat the oven to 375°.

Divide the ball of dough in half and roll out one half into a paper-thin sheet, large enough to completely line the casserole. Lower the pastry sheet into the casserole, letting the extra pastry hang out over the sides.

Place the flattened chicken on the bottom of the casserole, then scatter over 3 or 4 leaves of sage and ½ bay leaf cut in pieces. Wrap each quail in a slice of *pancetta* (or boiled ham) and place on top of the chicken. Fill in the cracks with about 15 *tortelli*, then sprinkle with a little salt and pepper.

Make a layer of quail. Place more *tortelli* over them, sprinkle with salt and pepper, and add 1 more bay leaf cut in pieces.

Next make a layer of sausages and the remaining *tortelli*, then make a layer of the remaining *pancetta*. Sprinkle with rosemary leaves.

Roll out the other half of the dough into a sheet about ¼ inch thick. Cover the top of the casserole with this sheet of pastry, pressing the edges of the two pastry layers together all around the casserole. Make sure the edges are closed, then cut off any overlapping pasta with a knife.

With a toothpick, make 3 or 4 holes in the top pastry layer, then place the casserole in the preheated oven for about 45 minutes. Place a sheet of aluminum foil over the casserole and raise the oven temperature to 400° for about 35 minutes more.

Remove the pie from the oven and serve directly from the casserole: break the top layer of pastry and prepare each plate with some *tortelli*, sausage, quail, squab, and crust. (The chicken at the bottom is usually finished by those who return for second helpings.)

Salads

Insalata Verde and *Insalata Mista*
(Green Salad and Mixed Salad)

For a simple salad, Italians use a single green, dressed with olive oil, salt, and wine vinegar or lemon juice. This is referred to as *insalata verde*.

When green salad is the only vegetable for the dinner, generally Italians prefer to have the more elaborate *insalata mista*, which is a mixture of different kinds of greens with the addition of some vegetable, such as carrots, which give a different flavor and color. For this reason, the name "mixed salad."

The greens used in Tuscany are what we call here Boston lettuce and romaine lettuce. (Iceberg lettuce does not exist there; it was developed in America to withstand long voyages, with some sacrifice in flavor and texture.) In addition, there are two kinds of leaf salad, one green and the other red, and called appropriately *radicchio verde e rosso*. There is no counterpart to the red *radicchio* (which comes from Treviso near Venice) in America.

Green *radicchio*, or leaf lettuce, was available in the United States years ago, but it is very perishable and gave way to such things as iceberg. Its taste, however, is well approximated by dandelion leaves, and while the marvelous arugola is not used in Tuscany, nor is watercress, both also make good substitutions here.

The other vegetables that can be used in the salad, in moderation, are carrots, celery, fennel (all in small pieces), and tomato. Italians prefer tomato still a little green for salad.

So an *insalata mista* could consist of any combination of the following: Boston lettuce, romaine lettuce, dandelion, arugola, watercress, carrots, celery, fennel, tomato. The dressing is always olive oil (the best available) and vinegar made from good red wine, preferably Chianti, or lemon juice. Salt is added but no pepper. And Italians never add cheese, croutons, or anything else to a salad.

Dressing the Salad

First pour olive oil into a large spoon that will distribute it evenly over the salad and mix it through. (This coats the leaves so the vinegar or oil will not make them wilt.) Then place salt in the tablespoon and pour vinegar or lemon juice onto it. With a fork, stir hard to dissolve the salt in the vinegar, and as it dissolves, let the vinegar run off the spoon throughout the salad. Finally, with two tablespoons toss the salad lightly but thoroughly to distribute the dressing evenly. Then serve.

Insalata Composta
("Composed" Salad)

Insalata composta, meaning "composed" salad, is made up of several cooked vegetables. Used a lot in summer when fresh vegetables and fresh basil are in season, it is dressed with olive oil like a green salad and garnished with lemon wedges, which may be used or not, according to taste. (Vinegar is not used for *insalata composta*.)

Boil a variety of vegetables which are in season and cook them separately (see methods under individual vegetables). When all the vegetables are cold, place them in a large serving dish in rings or in rows, each vegetable to one ring or row. Freely sprinkle with salt and pepper, and pour on olive oil, then tear several basil leaves into 2 or 3 pieces and place them over vegetables.

Serve cold.

Carote all'Agro
(Marinated Raw Shredded Carrots)   (SERVES 6)

The tender part of the raw carrot, shredded and marinated in olive oil and lemon juice, used both as a salad and as an antipasto, but not as a vegetable to accompany the second course. This classic treatment is widely used.

6 large carrots
  Juice of 2 lemons
  Salt and freshly ground pepper to taste
¼ cup olive oil
6 or 7 sprigs Italian parsley

Wash the carrots, then cut off top and bottom ends. The outer ring of the carrot is darker in color and more tender than the inner core. With a swivel-action peeler, shred only the tender, darker part of the carrot into a bowl; discard the tougher, lighter-colored inner core.

Add the lemon juice to the bowl, along with the salt, pepper, and olive oil. Mix everything together well, then cover the bowl with aluminum foil and place in the refrigerator for at least 1 hour.

When ready to serve, coarsely chop the parsley. Remove the bowl from refrigerator, transfer its contents to a serving dish, sprinkle with the chopped parsley and serve.

Insalata di Peperoni alla Griglia
(Grilled Pepper Salad)   (SERVES 4)

A special technique of roasting peppers right on the flame of a kitchen stove, while keeping the surrounding air moist with steam. The skin is peeled off, and the pepper that remains is still crunchy, with all the flavor of a fresh pepper. The peppers are then cut into strips and dressed as a cold salad. A versatile accompanying vegetable, also useful for buffets.

4 large green peppers
  Salt and freshly ground black pepper to taste
¼ cup olive oil

Heat a large quantity of water in a stockpot, on a high flame. When the water reaches boiling point and a lot of steam is rising, place the peppers, whole, on the burner next to the steaming stockpot, to roast on the high flame (see photo). Turn peppers frequently so the skin will be evenly roasted all over, and keep the stockpot on the flame until the peppers are completely roasted (about 20 minutes), so that while the skin blisters the inside part of the peppers do not dry out.

Remove the peppers from the stove and place them in bowl of cold water. Let them soak for 15 minutes, then peel under cold running water, removing stems and seeds.

Cut the peppers into thin strips and place them in a serving dish. Season with salt, pepper, and oil, mix together well, and serve.

Insalata di peperoni alla griglia: The peppers roasting on the burner, next to a steaming stockpot.

Insalata di Patate alla Fiorentina
(Potato Salad, Florentine Style)   (S E R V E S 4)

A cold potato salad, seasoned with olive oil, anchovies, fresh parsley, and pepper. Lighter than potato salads made with *maionese,* this is a useful dish to accompany lightly flavored main dishes, and for buffets and snacks.

    2 pounds boiling potatoes
       Coarse salt
    4 whole anchovies in salt or 8 anchovy fillets in oil
       Freshly ground black pepper
   ¼ cup olive oil
    1 tablespoon Italian parsley leaves

Put a large quantity of cold water and some coarse salt in a stock-pot and set on the heat. When the water reaches the boiling point, add the potatoes and let them cook for about 25 minutes. (If the potatoes are large, they may require 5 minutes more.) The potatoes should be completely cooked but still firm. Remove the pot from flame, transfer the potatoes to a board, and peel them. Let rest until cold (about 25 minutes).

Meanwhile, if using whole anchovies, clean them under cold running water, removing the bones; if using fillets in oil, drain. Coarsely chop the anchovies.

Cut the potatoes into pieces about 1 inch square and place in a serving bowl. Add the chopped anchovies, olive oil, and freshly ground pepper, then mix all the ingredients together.

Sprinkle parsley leaves over and serve.

Pomodori in Insalata
(Tomato Salad)   (SERVES 4)

Pomodori in insalata is perhaps the summer vegetable course that is most used. I would say that almost every Italian family has its own style of preparing this dish, but the base is always the same: ripe (never overripe) tomatoes, good olive oil, fresh basil, salt, and pepper. Basil is the natural spouse of tomatoes.

4 medium-sized tomatoes, ripe but not overripe
  Salt and freshly ground pepper to taste
¼ cup olive oil
6 or 7 fresh basil leaves

Wash the tomatoes very carefully, then cut them into slices about ⅓ inch thick. Remove the seeds from each slice and place the slices on serving dish, in one layer.

Sprinkle the tomatoes with salt, pepper, and olive oil, then tear the basil leaves into 3 or 4 pieces and sprinkle them freely over the tomato slices.

Note: You can vary the salad by placing half an anchovy fillet and 2 or 3 capers in wine vinegar over each tomato slice.

Pomodori e Capperi
(Tomato and Caper Salad)   (SERVES 4)

A salad of tomato halves, with a dressing of chopped capers in wine vinegar and olive oil.

    4 medium-sized tomatoes, ripe but not overripe
    3 heaping tablespoons capers in wine vinegar
    ¼ cup olive oil
       Salt and freshly ground pepper to taste
    6 or 7 fresh basil leaves

Wash the tomatoes very carefully, then cut them in half horizontally and remove the seeds. Place tomatoes on a serving dish.

Chop the capers fine and place them in small bowl. Add the olive oil, salt, and pepper and mix well with the capers.

Pour some caper mixture on each tomato half, then tear the basil leaves into 3 or 4 pieces and sprinkle over the tomatoes. Serve cold.

Pomodori e Mozzarella
(Tomato and Mozzarella Salad)   (SERVES 4)

A salad of mixed fresh tomato squares and little squares of mozzarella, seasoned with olive oil.

    4 medium-sized tomatoes, ripe but not overripe
    4 ounces mozzarella
    6 or 7 fresh basil leaves
    ¼ cup olive oil
       Salt and freshly ground pepper to taste

Wash the tomatoes very carefully, then cut in half horizontally and remove the seeds. Cut the tomato halves into ½-inch squares and place in a serving dish.

Cut the mozzarella into slightly smaller squares and add pieces to the serving dish, then tear the basil leaves into 2 or 3 pieces and sprinkle them over the tomatoes and mozzarella.

Season with olive oil and pepper (tasting for salt, because frequently American mozzarella is salty), then mix very well and serve cold.

Pomodori e Tonno
(Tomato and Tuna Salad)   (SERVES 4)

Fresh tomato halves covered with chopped tuna and capers in wine vinegar, held together by homemade *maionese*. This may be used both as an antipasto and as a salad, but is not eaten together with the main course.

> *Maionese* (see page 55)
> 4 medium-sized tomatoes, ripe but not overripe
> 1 small can tuna (3 ½ ounces)
> 1 heaping tablespoon capers in wine vinegar
>   Salt and freshly ground pepper to taste
> 8 fresh basil leaves

Make the *maionese* according to the directions on page 55 and set aside until needed.

Wash the tomatoes very carefully, then cut them in half horizontally and remove the seeds. Chop the tuna and capers fine and place in a small bowl. Add 3 tablespoons of the *maionese* to the bowl and mix thoroughly, then fill the tomato halves with the contents of the bowl.

Place the filled tomatoes on a serving dish and spread a layer of *maionese* on each stuffed tomato half. Top each with a whole basil leaf and serve cold.

$\mathscr{V}$egetables

❖

ARTICHOKES

ITALY HAS many celebrated artichoke dishes, some of the best known being from Rome. The season for artichokes in Italy is fall and winter. In the United States they can be found for more of the year because of the variety of growing seasons all over the country.

The larger Italian artichokes are called "*mamme*," or "mothers," and come from Empoli, the famous center of Tuscan glass making. These are usually stuffed as *carciofi ritti* (see page 398). The smaller ones come from all over Italy.

American artichokes are of a slightly different species, and have tough inner leaves and a purple "choke," both of which must be removed. In addition, they are less tender than Italian artichokes. By way of illustration, it is perhaps inconceivable to those who know only American artichokes that in Florence the favorite way of eating artichokes is raw, *in pinzimonio* (see page 83). The small Italian ones are indeed tender enough to be eaten that way.

Cleaning the American Artichoke

Place your whole artichokes in a large bowl of cold water with the juice of 1 lemon. Put the squeezed lemon halves in the bowl as well. Soak the artichokes for 1 hour, then remove one artichoke at a time from the water and rub with half a cut lemon.

Cut off ½ inch from the bottom of the stem (see photo 1). Look at the place where you sliced and see that the stem has a darker outer ring and a lighter inner core. Trim off all of the darker outer ring (photo

394

2). The inner core is not only the tender, nonbitter part, but contains most of the vitamins.

Remove as many rows of the outer leaves as necessary to arrive at those tender inner rows in which you can clearly see leaves that are green at the top but light yellow at the bottom. (Photo 2 shows how many outer leaves have been removed.)

Cleaning artichokes: 1. Cutting off the stem end.

2. Trimming the stem.

At this point, begin to cut off the top green part of each row of leaves with scissors or knife. With each new row, the yellow section will reach higher. You can see in photo 3 that the remaining rows are shorter on the outside and higher on the inside, almost as in a crescendo. It is easy to find the line separating the yellow from the green on each row; that is the place to cut the leaves. (Most Americans are surprised to see that I remove up to one-third of the artichoke leaves for most dishes. But this is necessary, because what remains must be tender enough to eat entirely, and to cook a short enough time to retain the chewy, half-raw quality that Tuscan artichoke dishes require.)

Finally, with a metal spoon, remove the inside hair of the choke completely. Also tear out any little leaves that have red in them, as they are prickly. (Italian artichokes generally do not have the hair and thorny red leaves of the choke, and may be eaten without cleaning the inside. American artichokes work well, however, if the inside is well cleaned and if one has the courage to throw away many more of the outer leaves than would be customary in a dish such as artichokes vinaigrette.)

Rub the inside part of the artichoke with lemon and place it back in the bowl with the cold water and lemon halves.

3. Scooping out the choke. Note the gradation in the trimmed leaves.

Photo 4 shows three different ways of cutting the cleaned artichoke. The whole one at the right would be used for *carciofi ritti*. The middle one is sliced lengthwise for *carciofi fritti* and *carciofi bolliti*. The pieces on the left can also be used for those dishes.

While terra-cotta pots are preferable for cooking artichokes, enameled and stainless steel pots are usable as well. Aluminum must be avoided, because the artichokes will turn black.

4. Showing the cleaned artichoke prepared for different uses— (*l.* and *c.*) boiling and frying, (*r.*) stuffing.

Carciofi Bolliti
(Boiled Artichokes)

Clean the number of artichokes you plan to use as described above. Cut lengthwise into slices about ½ inch thick and place in a bowl of cold water with half a lemon.

Fill a saucepan with cold water, add coarse salt and place on the heat. When the water reaches the boiling point, add the artichoke pieces and a small piece of the lemon and boil for about 30 minutes; at that time they should be soft.

Drain the artichokes, discarding the lemon piece, and place in a dish to cool. They are now ready to be used for such dishes as *carciofi all'agro* (with olive oil and lemon juice) or *sformato di carciofi* (see page 426).

Carciofi Fritti
(Fried Artichokes)   (SERVES 4)

    4 large artichokes
      Juice of 1 lemon
    4 eggs
      Salt to taste
    1 cup flour, approximately
    1 pound solid vegetable shortening
      Lemon wedges

Clean the artichokes according to the directions on pages 394–397 and cut them vertically, including the stem in the central part, into slices about ½ inch thick. Place the artichoke pieces into a large bowl containing the lemon juice and 8 cups of cold water and let stand for about 30 minutes.

Meanwhile, beat the eggs with a pinch of salt in small bowl. Drain the artichoke pieces and dry them with paper towels. In order to flour the pieces, place them in a plastic bag with the flour. Shake them around in the bag and pieces will become lightly floured.

Heat the solid vegetable shortening in a frying pan. When it is hot, dip each artichoke piece in beaten egg and place in the hot shortening, completely filling the pan. Deep-fry the artichoke pieces for about 6 minutes on each side, until golden brown.

Prepare a serving dish by lining it with paper towels. Remove the cooked artichokes from the frying pan with a strainer-skimmer and place them on the serving dish to drain. Repeat the procedure until all artichoke pieces are on the serving dish, then remove the paper towels.

Sprinkle with salt, garnish with lemon wedges, and serve hot.

Carciofi Ritti
(Stuffed Artichokes)   (SERVES 4)

    4 large artichokes
    1 lemon

For the stuffing

    2 medium-sized cloves garlic
    6 or 7 sprigs Italian parsley

¼ pound *pancetta* or 2 ounces salt pork plus 2 ounces boiled ham
Salt and freshly ground pepper to taste

For cooking the artichokes

½ clove garlic
5 or 6 sprigs Italian parsley
2 ounces *pancetta* or 1 ounce salt pork plus 1 ounce boiled ham
2 cups chicken or meat broth
Salt and freshly ground pepper to taste
2 tablespoons olive oil

Soak the artichokes in a large bowl of cold water with the lemon, cut into halves, for 20 minutes.

Clean the artichokes according to the directions on page 394–397, then cut off the stems and save for stuffing. Replace the stemless artichokes in water with lemon and let stand while you make the stuffing.

To make the stuffing, coarsely chop the 2 cloves garlic, 6 or 7 sprigs Italian parsley, and ¼ pound *pancetta* (or salt pork and boiled ham) as well as the artichoke stems. Place in a small bowl, add salt and pepper, and mix well.

Drain the artichokes, dry off the outsides, and stuff them with the mixture in the bowl.

To cook the artichokes, finely chop the ½ clove garlic, 5 or 6 sprigs Italian parsley, and 2 ounces of *pancetta*, then place in a flameproof casserole, preferably terra-cotta, along with the olive oil. Stand artichokes in the casserole, on top of the chopped ingredients and oil, then place the casserole on a medium flame and sauté its contents for 5 minutes, moving the artichokes around slightly so they don't stick.

Add 1 cup of broth to the casserole, cover, and simmer slowly for 15 to 20 minutes, then sprinkle with a little salt and pepper and add the remaining broth. Lower the flame and simmer very slowly for 20 minutes more; the artichokes should become tender but remain whole.

Carefully transfer the whole artichokes to a serving dish. Pour some juice from the casserole over each artichoke and serve either immediately or cold.

BEANS

Fagioli Bolliti
(Boiled Tuscan Beans)

Soak the amount of dried cannellini beans you wish to use in a large bowl of cold water, with 1 tablespoon of flour, overnight.

Rinse the beans in cold water and place beans in large stockpot containing cold water and coarse salt. (The amount of water depends on the quantity of beans. In Italy we say that the amount of cold water should be 6 times the weight of the beans, so, since a quart of water weighs about 2 pounds, 1 pound of beans would require 3 quarts of water.) Add 4 or 5 leaves of sage, fresh (or under salt, see page 14), and about 1 tablespoon of olive oil.

Place the stockpot on a very low flame and simmer very slowly for about 3 hours. (The beans must be cooked very slowly to stay whole and to retain their shape. When beans are used for soups, they may be boiled more quickly.)

Fagioli al Fiasco
(Tuscan Beans Cooked in a Flask)   (SERVES 6 TO 8)

In this, one of the scenic Florentine dishes, white beans are placed inside a wine flask or another flask of thick Italian glass, which in turn is placed in a pan of water. The technique is basically *bagno maria* (bain-marie). Very little liquid is added to the flask, so the beans retain all of their own flavor and that of the *pancetta*, sage, and other seasonings.

The main caution to take to insure that the flask does not crack is to begin with cold water, both inside and outside the flask. Then, if additional water must be added to the pan because of evaporation, be sure that the added water is boiling. In other words, if the temperatures inside and outside the flask are the same, there should be no problem about the glass, so do not be afraid to try it. In any case, the worst that can happen is that a simple crack will appear in the flask, the flask remaining in one piece, so it is not dangerous. But if you follow instructions, there is really very little probability of it cracking. And when it succeeds, the effect is quite attractive when the pan (particularly if it is a beautiful one of antique copper) containing the bean filled flask is brought to the table. The beans may be served with a spoon, or if the mouth of the flask is large enough, with a ladle.

Fagioli al fiasco may be used to accompany a variety of hearty dishes, both simple and more formal, and the leftover beans may be used to make *zuppa lombarda* (see page 129).

> 1 pound dried cannellini beans
> 2 ounces *pancetta*, boiled ham, or prosciutto
> ¼ cup olive oil
> 2 large cloves garlic, peeled but left whole
> 5 or 6 leaves sage, fresh or under salt (see page 14)
>   Salt and freshly ground pepper to taste
> 3 or 4 whole black peppercorns

Soak the beans in a bowl of cold water, with 1 tablespoon of flour, overnight.

The next day, put the drained, soaked beans into the flask you have chosen. (A wine flask is adequate. One of the larger green Italian or Spanish ones with a wide mouth is even better for this purpose, as it takes less time to put the beans into the flask and remove them when cooked.) Add only enough cold water to reach about 1 inch above the beans.

Dice the *pancetta*, then add to the flask, along with the olive oil, whole garlic cloves, and sage. Season with salt, pepper, and peppercorns.

Place the flask in a stockpot or a large, decorative copper pan containing a large quantity of cold water. Set on a medium flame and simmer very slowly for 4 to 5 hours (see photo), with the following precautions:

Keep a saucepan of boiling water ready on a low flame, so you can add boiling water, little by little, to the stockpot when the water evaporates to about half. Do not add cold water to stockpot, otherwise the flask will break. Do not add any liquid to the beans inside the flask while they are cooking.

Remove the stockpot from flame and let cool for 10 minutes, then remove the flask from the stockpot and transfer beans to serving dish. Or, if you have used the flask with large mouth, you can serve from the flask itself.

Fagioli al fiasco: The beans, in their flask, simmering in a water bath.

Fagioli all'Uccelletto
(Tuscan Beans Cooked in the Manner of Little Birds)

(SERVES 4)

Boiled beans simmered in tomatoes, olive oil, sage, and whole un-peeled garlic cloves. The name comes from the manner of cooking *uccelli*, little song birds.

 ¼ cup olive oil
 6 or 7 large leaves sage, fresh or under salt (see page 14)
 4 large cloves garlic, unpeeled and left whole
 ½ pound very ripe fresh or canned tomatoes
  Salt and freshly ground pepper to taste
 4 cups boiled cannellini beans (see page 400)

Heat the olive oil in a flameproof casserole, preferably terra-cotta. Add the sage and unpeeled garlic cloves and sauté, on medium heat, for 4 or 5 minutes.

Pass the tomatoes through a food mill into a bowl, then transfer to the casserole. Taste for salt and pepper and simmer very gently for

5 to 8 minutes. Add the beans to casserole, mix very well with a wooden spoon and simmer for 15 minutes more.

Serve hot.

Fagioli al Forno
(Baked Tuscan Beans) (SERVES 6)

Baked beans, Tuscan style. Again the beans are the white cannellini. They are baked in a closed terracotta casserole, with *pancetta*, whole garlic cloves, sage, and tomatoes and olive oil. A very Mediterranean version, and one you are sure to add to your repertoire.

> 3 cups dried cannellini beans
> ¼ pound *pancetta* or 2 ounces salt pork plus 2 ounces boiled ham
> 2 large cloves garlic, peeled but left whole
> 6 or 7 sage leaves, fresh or under salt (see page 14)
> ¼ cup olive oil
> ½ cup canned tomatoes
> Salt and freshly ground black pepper

Soak the beans overnight in about 6 or 7 cups of cold water. The next day, drain the beans and place them in a casserole, preferably terra cotta.

Preheat the oven to 375°.

Cut the *pancetta* into small pieces, then add to the casserole along with the garlic cloves, sage, olive oil, and tomatoes. Pour in enough fresh cold water to cover the beans completely (about 3 cups), then sprinkle with salt and freshly ground black pepper.

Cover the casserole and place it in the preheated oven for 3½ to 4½ hours. (Cooking time of beans varies because older beans are drier and must cook longer.) Every half hour check the beans and stir gently.

Remove the casserole from the oven and allow to cool, still covered, for 15 minutes. Serve from the same casserole.

STRINGBEANS

ITALIAN STRINGBEANS are used very young, thin, and tender for most dishes. Since American stringbeans are picked when they are more mature and larger, they are not suitable for many Italian recipes. (Can't we prevail upon our growers to let us also have some of the small, young ones?)

The two recipes included here, following the recipe for boiled stringbeans, work well with American stringbeans. The second, *fagiolini in umido,* is often made with the special species of long stringbeans called *"serpenti,"* which incidentally are sometimes found in Chinese and other East Asian markets in America. But American stringbeans are also appropriate for the dish.

Fagiolini in Erba Bolliti
(Boiled Stringbeans)

To boil, remove the ends of the stringbeans as well as the coarse thread that runs along the side. Soak the beans in a bowl of cold water for 1 hour.

Heat a large amount of cold water, with coarse salt added, in a stockpot. When the water reaches the boiling point, add the stringbeans and let them cook for about 25 minutes.

Drain the stringbeans and cool them under cold running water. They are now ready to be used in such dishes as *sformato di fagiolini* (see page 426), *insalata composta* (see page 388), and *fagiolini in fricassea* (see below).

Fagiolini in Fricassea
(Fricassee of Stringbeans)   (SERVES 4 TO 6)

A fricassee of stringbeans, with the usual egg-lemon sauce. It makes a good accompaniment to most main dishes that do not have a sauce of their own.

  2 pounds stringbeans
  4 tablespoons (½ stick) butter
    Salt and freshly ground pepper
  1 lemon
  2 egg yolks

Boil the stringbeans according to the directions above.

When the stringbeans are cooked and cold, heat the butter in a large flameproof casserole. When the butter is hot, add the string-beans. Season with salt and pepper and let the beans sauté very lightly for 4 or 5 minutes.

Meanwhile, squeeze the lemon into a small bowl. Add the egg yolks to the bowl and mix very well until thoroughly combined.

When the stringbeans are ready, remove the casserole from the flame and add the egg-lemon mixture, little by little, mixing thoroughly with a wooden spoon until the egg yolk is homogeneously incorporated. Serve hot.

Fagiolini in Umido
(Stringbeans with Tomatoes and Basil)   (SERVES 4 TO 6)

The *odori* (aromatic vegetables) are lightly sautéed and then the stringbeans are added, along with tomato and basil, and simmered for a long time. The dish may be used with a variety of main dishes, but do not use it with those that already have a tomato sauce.

> 2 pounds stringbeans
> 1 small carrot
> 1 small red onion
> ¼ cup olive oil
> 2 cloves garlic, peeled but left whole
> 2 cups canned tomatoes
> 3 or 4 leaves basil, fresh or under salt (see page 14)
>   Salt and freshly ground pepper to taste

Remove the ends of the stringbeans as well as the coarse thread, then soak the beans in a large bowl of cold water for 1 hour. Chop the carrot and onion coarsely. Heat the olive oil in a casserole, preferably terra-cotta, then add the chopped ingredients and whole garlic cloves. Sauté very gently until lightly golden brown (about 10 minutes), then remove the garlic.

Add the stringbeans to the casserole. Place the tomatoes and basil leaves on top, then season with salt and pepper, cover, and simmer for 1 hour. (No liquid should be needed because stringbeans shed a lot of water.)

Stir the stringbeans well and taste for salt and pepper. Cook for 1 or 2 minutes more, without the lid, and then transfer the stringbeans to a serving dish. Serve very hot.

BROCCOLI

Broccoli Strascicati
("Stir-sautéed" Broccoli)   (SERVES 4)

You might describe making a dish *strascicato* as "stir-sautéing." Here the raw broccoli is cut into small pieces. The toughest parts of the stems are discarded and only the tender parts kept. The stem pieces require more cooking than the flower pieces, so they should be placed on the bottom and then the whole stirred gently, so as not to disturb the arrangement with the stem pieces on the bottom. The broccoli pieces, which should be crunchy and retain the flavor of fresh broccoli, are seasoned very simply, with garlic, olive oil, and a little hot pepper.

    1 bunch broccoli
    5 tablespoons olive oil
    1 large clove garlic, peeled but left whole
       Salt and freshly ground pepper
       Pinch of hot pepper flakes

Remove the large stems from the broccoli and cut the remainder into approximately 1½-inch pieces.

Heat the olive oil in a flameproof casserole, preferably terra-cotta, and add the whole garlic clove. Sauté the garlic very lightly, on medium heat, for 2 minutes, then remove it. Immediately add the broccoli pieces to the casserole. Season with salt, pepper, and a pinch of pepper flakes, then cover and sauté very lightly, stirring with a wooden spoon every so often.

Adding a little bit of cold water if needed, cook the broccoli for about 20 minutes. At that time it should be completely cooked and soft. Serve very hot.

CARDOONS

CARDOONS ARE the stems of the young thistle artichoke plant, picked before the artichokes or flowers themselves appear. The species is slightly different from the artichoke, and its flowers are less interesting than its stems.

Cardi Bolliti
(Boiled Cardoons)

> 1 bunch cardoons (about 2½ pounds)
> 1 lemon
> 2 tablespoons all-purpose flour
> 1 cup cold water

Remove the outer stalks and stringy top part from the cardoon, then cut the remaining stalks into pieces 2 inches long. Rub each piece with half a cut lemon and place it in a large bowl of cold water. Squeeze the remaining half lemon into the water with the cardoons and let soak for 30 minutes.

Dissolve the flour in the 1 cup of cold water and pour into a large stockpot, preferably terra-cotta. Add 8 cups of cold water, coarse salt, and the cardoon pieces to the stockpot, then cover and place on the heat. Simmer very slowly for about 45 minutes.

Remove the stockpot from the flame and let the cardoons cool in the pot for 20 minutes, then remove them from the pot with a strainer-skimmer and dry them on paper towels. They are now ready to be used in such dishes as *cardi trippati* (see below) or *gobbi (cardi) dorati* (see page 408).

Cardi Trippati
(Cardoons Cut in the Form of Tripe)   (S E R V E S 4)

This is one of the most elaborate vegetable dishes in the Italian repertory, used more often as an in-between course, a *piatto di mezzo*, than as an accompanying vegetable. The cardoons are cooked four ways to make the dish, so it is time consuming—but well worth the trouble.

> 1 bunch cardoons (about 2½ pounds)
> 14 ounces (3½ sticks) butter
> 1 clove garlic   (*continued*)

½ small red onion
1 cup freshly grated Parmigiano cheese
1¼ cups bread crumbs, preferably homemade (see page 45),
    approximately

Boil the cardoons as described on page 407.

Chop the garlic and onion coarsely, then place in a large frying pan, along with 8 tablespoons (1 stick) of the butter, and sauté for 5 minutes, until golden brown. Add the cardoon pieces to the pan and sauté for 5 minutes, stirring carefully to avoid breaking up the pieces.

Sprinkle the contents of the pan with ½ cup of the grated Parmigiano. Taste for salt and pepper and sauté for 2 minutes more, stirring to mix in the cheese, then remove the pan from the flame and let the cardoons stand until completely cold (about 1 hour).

Prepare a serving dish by lining it with paper towels; preheat the oven to 375°.

Spread out about 1 cup of the bread crumbs on a sheet of aluminum foil. Remove the cold cardoon pieces from the pan and roll them lightly in the crumbs. Heat 12 tablespoons (1½ sticks) of the butter in another frying pan. When the butter is completely melted and very hot, quickly deep-fry the cardoon pieces until golden brown all over (about 3 minutes), then remove from the frying pan with a strainer-skimmer and place on the prepared serving dish.

When all the cardoons are on the serving dish, butter a baking dish and line the bottom with a layer of cardoons. Sprinkle with some of the remaining grated Parmigiano and dot with 2 or 3 pats of the remaining butter. Then make a second layer of cardoons. Keep alternating layers of cardoon with Parmigiano and butter until you have used up all ingredients; the top layer should be of cardoons.

Sprinkle the top with the remaining ¼ cup bread crumbs, then bake in the preheated oven for 20 minutes. Remove from the oven and serve hot.

Gobbi (Cardi) Dorati
(Deep-fried Cardoons)   (SERVES 4)

A simpler treatment. The cardoons are boiled with flour, then they are lightly floured, dipped in beaten egg, and deep-fried in shortening.

 1 bunch cardoons (about 2 ½ pounds)
1 ½ cups all-purpose flour
 3 eggs
    Salt
 1 pound solid vegetable shortening
    Lemon wedges

Boil the cardoons according to the directions on page 407. Dry on paper towels and let stand until completely cold.

Meanwhile, beat the eggs in small bowl with a pinch of salt; spread the 1 ½ cups flour out on a piece of aluminum foil.

When the cardoons are cold and dry, lightly flour them.

Heat the solid vegetable shortening in a large frying pan. When the shortening is hot, quickly dip the cardoons in the beaten egg and place them in the pan. (Don't put too many cardoons at a time because they must float in the oil.) Deep-fry them for 3 or 4 minutes on each side.

Meanwhile, prepare a serving dish by lining it with paper towels.

When the cardoons are cooked and golden brown all over, remove them with a strainer-skimmer to the prepared serving dish. When all the cardoons are on the serving dish, remove the paper towels. Garnish with lemon wedges and serve very hot.

CARROTS

Carote Bollite
(Boiled Carrots)

Cut off the tips of the carrots on both ends. Do not scrape or peel them; carrots retain more flavor when cooked with their skins. Place the carrots in a large bowl of cold water and let them soak for about 15 minutes.

Heat a large quantity of water, with coarse salt added, in a flame-proof casserole. When the water reaches the boiling point, put the whole carrots into the casserole and let them boil until cooked but still firm (about 20 minutes), then drain and place them in a large bowl of cold water to cool (about 15 minutes).

When cooled, peel the carrots. This is best done by gently pushing off the outer skin; it will come off easily and whole.

At this point, carrots are ready to be used for different dishes, such as *sformato di carote* (see page 426) or *insalata composta* (see page 388).

CAULIFLOWER

Cavolfiore Bollito
(Boiled Cauliflower)

In Italian cooking, the outer leaves of the cauliflower are removed, but often the tender inner ones are left on. The whole cauliflower is soaked for about 30 minutes in abundant cold water to minimize its strong cabbage-family smell. Some Italians go even further and place a teaspoon of white wine vinegar in the water when boiling.

To boil, leave the cauliflower whole. Remove the outer leaves but leave the tender inner leaves on. Soak the cauliflower in a bowl of cold water for 30 minutes. Heat a large quantity of water, with coarse salt added, in a flameproof casserole. When it reaches the boiling point, place the whole cauliflower in the casserole and let boil, covered, for 20 to 30 minutes. (Turn cauliflower over once to be sure that it is evenly cooked, but cook a bit longer right side up, as the bottom is less tender than the top.)

With a large strainer-skimmer, transfer the whole cauliflower to a serving dish. It is now ready to be used for different dishes, such as *cavolfiore all'olio* (see page 411), *sformato di cavolfiore* (see page 426), or *cavolfiore con acciugata* (see page 411).

Note: We do not include *cavolfiore gratinato*, as do some Italian cookbooks in America, as we feel *gratinée* dishes to be completely French.

Cavolfiore Fritto
(Deep-fried Cauliflower)

When all the leaves are removed from the head of cauliflower, turn it bottom side up. You can see that the cauliflower has a solid central piece with a myriad of little "flowers" attached to it each by a delicate stem. Detach the flowers at the stem from the central piece. You should have a large number of pieces, each in the shape of a flower. Leave the smaller flowers whole, not exceeding 1 inch thick and 2 inches long, and cut the larger ones into pieces the same size. Discard the central stalk.

Cauliflower is deep-fried in the same way as artichokes (see page 398), and the cooking time is about the same.

Cavolfiore all'Olio
(Cauliflower with Olive Oil)   (SERVES 4 TO 6)

The simplest of treatments of boiled cauliflower. Leaving the vegetable whole, with a few tender leaves left on, is not only better for the taste, but makes a nicer presentation as well.

    1 head cauliflower
       Freshly ground black pepper
    ¼ cup olive oil, approximately

Boil the cauliflower according to the directions on page 410. Place the boiled whole cauliflower on a serving dish, sprinkle with freshly ground black pepper, and pour the olive oil over. Serve either hot or cold.

Cavolfiore con Acciugata
(Cauliflower with Anchovy Sauce)   (SERVES 4 TO 6)

Boiled whole cauliflower blends extremely well with anchovy sauce. However, because it has a strong flavor, it should be served separately, after the second dish, or perhaps in lieu of the first dish if you want a very light dinner.

    1 cauliflower
       Acciugata (see page 64)

Boil the cauliflower according to the directions on page 410. While it is cooking, prepare the *acciugata*.

Place the whole boiled cauliflower on a serving dish, pour the hot anchovy sauce over, and serve immediately.

EGGPLANT

Melanzane alla Parmigiana
(Eggplant in the Style of Parma)   (SERVES 6)

When selecting eggplants at the market, either large or small ones may be chosen, but feel them to be sure they are firm. If they feel very soft, it means they are full of seeds, which is not desirable.

Italians generally use eggplants unpeeled. The slices should be sprinkled with coarse salt and allowed to stand for 30 minutes to an hour. The eggplants shed some dark liquid, and with it a good bit of the bitterness of the vegetable. Instructions for doing this are included in the recipe.

Here the eggplant slices are first deep-fried without flouring and arranged in layers, alternating with a lightly simmered tomato sauce, coarsely grated mozzarella, and Swiss cheese (groviera) and a sprinkling of Parmigiano with a pat of butter. When baked, this dish should be considerably lighter than many recipes with the same name.

> 6 small or 2 large eggplants
> Coarse salt
> 1 pound very ripe fresh or canned tomatoes
> 1 tablespoon tomato paste
> 1 tablespoon olive oil
> 5 or 6 leaves basil, fresh or under salt (see page 14)
> Salt and freshly ground pepper
> 4 ounces mozzarella
> 4 ounces Swiss cheese
> 1 pound solid vegetable shortening
> 5 or 6 pats of butter
> ¼ cup freshly grated Parmigiano cheese

Cut the eggplants lengthwise into slices ⅓ inch thick; do not peel. Sprinkle the eggplant slices with coarse salt, place them in a dish, and let stand for 30 minutes. Meanwhile, prepare the sauce.

Pass the tomatoes through a food mill into a saucepan. Add the tomato paste, olive oil, and whole basil leaves to the saucepan, then place on the heat. Season with salt and pepper and simmer for 15 minutes.

Coarsely grate the mozzarella and Swiss cheese into a bowl; wash the eggplant slices in cold water and wipe with paper towels; prepare a serving dish by lining it with paper towels.

Heat the solid vegetable shortening in a frying pan. When it is very hot, deep-fry the eggplant slices, a few at a time, until golden brown on both sides (about 3 minutes). Remove the fried slices from the pan and place on the prepared serving dish to drain. When all eggplant slices are transferred to serving dish, sprinkle them with a little salt.

Preheat the oven to 375°.

Spread 1 tablespoon of the sauce over the bottom of a rectangular Pyrex baking dish (13½ x 8½ inches). On top of the sauce put a layer of eggplant slices. Then add a layer of mozzarella and Swiss cheese, sprinkled with Parmigiano. In this and every subsequent layer, also add a pat of butter. Make one more layer of eggplant and on top a layer of sauce. Alternate layers of eggplant and cheese and sauce, finishing with sauce on top.

Bake in the preheated oven for 25 minutes.

Note: This may also be eaten well chilled. If serving hot, let rest for 15 minutes before serving.

FENNEL (Finocchio)

FENNEL, BOTH raw and cooked, is used much more as a vegetable in Italy than in America, though it grows very well here and is easily found at many specialty vegetable markets and Italian markets. It has a light flavor, similar to that of the fennel seeds that are used as a spice.

Of the many ways that fennel is cooked in Italy, we include two recipes here, besides a basic one for boiling.

Finocchi Bolliti
(Boiled Fennel)

If the fennel are medium-sized, cut them into quarters vertically. Cut off the small knob at the bottom and cut out the hard inner part at the bottom, which is a continuation of the knob. Place the fennel quarters in a large bowl of cold water and let them soak for about 15 minutes.

Heat a large quantity of cold water, with coarse salt added, in a flameproof casserole. When the water reaches boiling point, add the fennel and let it boil until cooked but still firm (about 20 minutes, varying a bit depending on size).

Drain the fennel, then place it on paper towels to absorb all excess liquid. The fennel is now ready to be used in such dishes as *sformato di finocchi* (see page 426), *insalata composta* (see page 388), or *finocchi al burro* (see below).

Finocchi al Burro
(Fennel Sautéed in Butter)   (SERVES 4)

The fennel is cut into pieces and then boiled, after which it is sautéed in butter and oil and seasoned with nutmeg and Parmigiano.

> 4 fennel bulbs
> 6 tablespoons butter
> ½ tablespoon olive oil
> Salt, freshly ground pepper, and freshly grated nutmeg to taste
> ¼ cup freshly grated Parmigiano cheese

Boil the fennel as described above. After draining it, let it cool.

Heat the butter and oil in a flameproof casserole. When they are hot, add the fennel. Sprinkle with salt, pepper, and nutmeg, then mix very well and sauté for about 10 minutes. Sprinkle with the Parmigiano and mix thoroughly.

Cook for 5 minutes more, then remove the casserole from the heat. Transfer the fennel to a serving dish and serve hot.

Finocchi in Sugo Finto
(Fennel in Winter Tomato Sauce)   (SERVES 4)

Here the fennel pieces are floured and browned in olive oil, and then simmered in the sauce.

4 medium-sized fennel bulbs
1 cup all-purpose flour, approximately
5 tablespoons olive oil
Salt and freshly ground pepper to taste
1 cup canned tomatoes

Remove the outside leaves from the fennel, then cut the stalks into lengthwise slices, ½ inch thick. Place the slices in a bowl of cold water for about 15 minutes, then remove from the water and dry on paper towels.

Spread out the flour on a piece of aluminum foil and lightly flour the fennel pieces.

Heat the olive oil in a large frying pan. When it is hot, put in the fennel pieces and sauté them, turning them, until golden brown all over (about 4 minutes on each side). Sprinkle with salt and pepper.

Pass the tomatoes through a food mill into the frying pan. Simmer very slowly for 15 minutes, loosening the fennel pieces every so often with a spatula so they do not stick.

Remove the pan from the flame and serve very hot.

PEAS

Piselli alla Fiorentina
(Peas in the Florentine Manner)   (SERVES 4)

The small peas, *piselli novelli*, were developed in Florence in the early sixteenth century. When they arrived in France they were called there *"petits pois."* In this country, "June peas" probably correspond best to these. However, if one uses the larger fresh peas that are found for much of the year in the United States, the peas must be soaked, shelled, in cold water for some hours to tenderize them. Soak them with salt and a bit of flour to cause fermentation. After this, when cooked, they should be as tender as the real *piselli*.

1½ pounds of shelled fresh peas or 2 packages (10 ounces each)
    frozen tiny peas
4 ounces *pancetta* or salt pork   (*continued*)

4 or 5 sprigs Italian parsley
1 large clove garlic
1 ½ tablespoons olive oil
    Salt and freshly ground pepper to taste
¾ cup hot meat broth, approximately
1 ½ tablespoons granulated sugar

If peas are fresh, unless they are "June peas," soak them in a large bowl of cold water with salt and a bit of flour for 2 hours.

Coarsely chop the *pancetta* (or salt pork), parsley, and garlic. Heat the olive oil in a flameproof casserole, then add the chopped ingredients and sauté very gently for about 5 minutes.

Add the peas to the casserole. Season with salt and pepper, then stir the peas thoroughly and add ½ cup of hot broth. Simmer very slowly until broth has evaporated (about 15 minutes). At that time, if the peas are small and tender, they should be cooked; if not, add another ¼ cup of broth and let it evaporate (about 8 minutes). Add the sugar and simmer for 1 minute more, until the sugar has dissolved.

Remove the casserole from the flame, transfer the peas to a serving dish, and serve immediately.

Note: This is the typical *contorno* (accompaniment) for the Easter season.

POTATOES

Patate Saltate alla Salvia
(Potatoes Sautéed with Sage)   (SERVES 6)

Potatoes, cut into small pieces and "stir-sautéed" with olive oil, sage, and the light garlic flavor that comes from using the whole clove with the skin left on. Easy to prepare and a delicious way to make potatoes, one that goes with almost any main dish.

2 pounds potatoes
6 tablespoons olive oil
5 or 6 leaves sage, fresh or under salt (see page 14)
1 clove garlic, unpeeled and left whole
    Salt and freshly ground pepper to taste

Peel the potatoes and cut them into 1-inch pieces.

Heat the olive oil in a flameproof casserole, preferably terra-cotta, then add the sage leaves and unpeeled garlic clove. Sauté very lightly for 2 minutes, then add the potato pieces and stir with a wooden spoon. Cover and cook for 2 minutes on low flame, then stir the potatoes again. Season with salt and cover the casserole again. The potatoes should be stirred about every 2 minutes, but must be kept covered in between. After 20 minutes, they should be cooked.

Remove the clove of garlic and transfer the potatoes to a serving dish. Serve immediately, sprinkling with freshly ground pepper.

Patate alla Contadina
(Country-style Potatoes)   (S E R V E S   3   O R   4)

Boiled potatoes, cut up and flavored with olive oil, coarsely chopped fresh parsley, and garlic. A simple dish of extraordinary flavor, you will use it often once you try it.

    1 pound boiling potatoes
       Pinch of coarse salt
    1 large clove garlic
    10 sprigs Italian parsley
    ¼ cup olive oil
       Salt and freshly ground pepper to taste

Place a flameproof casserole containing the potatoes, about 7 cups of cold water, and coarse salt on a medium flame. Simmer until the potatoes are soft (about 35 minutes).

Meanwhile, finely chop first the garlic, then the parsley. Place them in a serving bowl, along with the olive oil and salt and freshly ground pepper to taste.

When the potatoes are ready, peel them while still very hot and cut them into pieces about 1 inch square. Add the potato pieces to the bowl and mix with the other ingredients, using a wooden spoon.

Serve warm or cold, to accompany boiled meat.

Patate con Pesto
(Potatoes with Pesto)   (S E R V E S   6)

Potatoes have a special affinity for *pesto*. Even when pasta is prepared with this sauce, it is boiled with a potato. Here the potatoes are boiled, cut up, and tossed very gently with a little olive oil. Then the *pesto* is added. This is a very strong-flavored vegetable, which should accompany only dishes that do not have their own sauce.

    Coarse salt
    2 pounds boiling potatoes
    1 tablespoon olive oil
    3 heaping tablespoons *pesto* (see page 77), approximately

Put a large quantity of cold water and some coarse salt in a stock-pot and set on the heat. When the water reaches the boiling point, add the potatoes, whole, in their skins; the potatoes must be completely covered with water. Let the potatoes boil until cooked but firm (about 35 minutes for medium-sized potatoes).

Remove the potatoes from the pot and transfer them to a board, using a strainer-skimmer in order not to puncture them. Peel the potatoes while still very hot, then cut into pieces about 1 inch square.

Place the potatoes in a serving dish, pour the olive oil over, and mix very gently. Let stand until cold.

When the potatoes are cold, place the *pesto* sauce on top and serve.

PEPPERS

Peperoni e Melanzane
(Peppers and Eggplant)   (SERVES 6)

Peppers, eggplant, onions, and tomato all simmered together with just a little olive oil produces the most marvelous vegetable dish. May be used to accompany a large range of main dishes. Do not use it with main dishes that have a tomato sauce.

    4 tablespoons olive oil
    1 medium red onion
    4 peppers (green or yellow)
    2 medium eggplants
    1 cup canned tomatoes
    Salt and freshly ground pepper to taste

First put olive oil in a casserole. Then cut onion into 1-inch pieces and add to the casserole. Remove stems and inside parts of the peppers and cut into rings. Make a layer on top of the onions in the casserole. Cut the eggplants into 1-inch cubes and place on top of the peppers. Add the tomatoes, and sprinkle with salt and pepper. Do not mix.

Cover the casserole with a lid and place it on medium flame. Simmer for 20 minutes without mixing. Then mix thoroughly and taste for salt and pepper.

Simmer for 15 minutes more, without lid, mixing every so often with a wooden spoon. Transfer to serving dish and serve.

This dish may accompany boiled or roasted meat.

Peperonata
(Peppers Sautéed in Tomatoes)   (S E R V E S 4)

Peppers simmered in tomatoes, cooked just long enough to retain some of the crispness of the peppers and keep the sweet, light quality of the tomatoes, without the acidity produced by cooking them too long. The large number of Mediterranean dishes that combine peppers with tomatoes suggests their affinity.

    6 peppers, yellow, orange, red, or green, or mixed
    1 medium red onion
    2 large cloves garlic
    8 very ripe fresh or canned tomatoes
    3 tablespoons olive oil
      Salt and freshly ground pepper to taste

Remove the stems and seeds from the peppers, then cut them into pieces about 2 inches square (see note below). Cut the onion and garlic into small pieces; if the tomatoes are fresh, remove the skins and seeds.

Heat the olive oil in a large casserole, then add the onion and garlic and sauté very gently for 4 minutes. Add the peppers to the casserole and place the tomatoes over them; do not mix. Add salt and pepper.

Cover the casserole and cook for 15 to 20 minutes, then mix the ingredients with wooden spoon. Taste for salt and pepper and cook, uncovered, for 15 minutes more, until the peppers are soft.

Remove the casserole from the heat, transfer the *peperonata* to a serving dish and serve either hot or cold.

Note: In Florence it is not usual to peel the peppers. For those who prefer to do so, each pepper must be held over the flame for about 1 minute, and the skin will then come off easily.

RAPE

Rape Saltate in Padella
(Sautéed Rape)   (SERVES 4)

The pleasantly bitter turnip green called *"rape"* in Italian is sometimes known in America by its southern Italian dialect name, *broccolirab*. Because of its strong flavor, it ideally accompanies roast meats, especially pork (see *arista*, page 348). However, it is quite versatile.

Recipes for rape appear in the first cookbooks of the fourteenth century. Spinach aside, there is probably no vegetable more typically Tuscan. Therefore it is strange that Janet Ross, the Englishwoman of the late nineteenth century, does not even mention it in her well-known Tuscan vegetable cookery book.

    2 pounds rape
      Coarse salt
    1 large clove garlic
    4 tablespoons olive oil
      Salt and freshly ground pepper to taste

Remove the heavy stalks from the rape, leaving the light stalks and leaves. Cut these into 2-inch pieces, then wash them very well in cold running water. Place the cut rape in a large bowl of cold water and let soak for 1 hour.

Heat 6 cups of cold water and 1 tablespoon of coarse salt in a large flameproof casserole. When the water reaches the boiling point, add the rape and cook it for about 30 minutes, until soft. Drain the rape in a colander and cool under cold running water, then gently squeeze out excess water.

Cut the garlic clove coarsely. Place it in a large saucepan, along with the olive oil, and sauté until lightly golden brown (about 5 minutes). Add the rape to the saucepan. Taste for salt and pepper and mix thoroughly with a wooden spoon, then cover the saucepan and let simmer very slowly for about 15 minutes, stirring every so often. (At that time all the liquid should be absorbed and the rape ready to be served.)

Remove the saucepan from the flame, transfer the rape to a serving dish, and serve immediately.

SPINACH

Spinaci Saltati
("Stir-sautéed" Spinach)   (SERVES 4)

Here, boiled spinach is "stir-sautéed" with a little olive oil and garlic. In Florence it is probably the most frequently used accompanying vegetable. Indeed, it can be used to accompany almost anything.

    2 pounds fresh spinach
      Coarse salt
    1 large clove garlic
    3 tablespoons olive oil
      Salt and freshly ground pepper

Clean the spinach well, removing the heavier stems, then boil in a large quantity of salted water for 12 to 15 minutes. Drain, then place under cold running water to cool. When the spinach is cold, squeeze it very dry and chop it coarsely.

Cut the garlic clove into small pieces and place them in a frying pan, along with the olive oil. Place the pan on medium heat and let the garlic sauté very slowly, until golden brown (about 5 minutes).

Add the chopped spinach to pan and season with salt and freshly ground pepper. Mix the spinach thoroughly with the other ingredients, using a fork, then let cook on a medium flame for 5 or 6 minutes.

Transfer the spinach to serving dish and serve hot.

Spinaci alla Fiorentina
(Spinach, Florentine Style)   (SERVES 4 TO 6)

Here, after boiled spinach is "stir-sautéed" with a little olive oil and garlic, it is mixed with *balsamella* with Parmigiano and arranged in a baking dish with a layer of the same sauce on top. After baking, it is served hot. It may be used with a wide variety of main dishes, but avoid those that already have a *balsamella* sauce. It may also be used as a light first course.

> 2 pounds fresh spinach
> 1 clove garlic
> 3 tablespoons olive oil
>   Salt, freshly ground pepper, and nutmeg to taste

For balsamella with Parmigiano

> 3 tablespoons butter
> 3 tablespoons flour
> 2½ cups milk
> 3 tablespoons freshly grated Parmigiano cheese
>   Salt and white pepper to taste
>   Pinch of nutmeg

Make the *balsamella* with Parmigiano according to the directions on page 52, using quantities listed here. Let the sauce cool in the covered pan.

Prepare the spinach as directed in the recipe for *spinaci saltati* (see page 421), up to the point where the chopped spinach is added to the pan with the garlic. Season with salt and pepper and sauté the spinach, stirring constantly, for 10 to 15 minutes. Transfer to a bowl to cool.

Preheat the oven to 375°.

Place half of *balsamella* in the bowl with spinach. Add nutmeg and mix very well, until the *balsamella* is incorporated into the spinach.

Butter the bottom and sides of a baking dish. Place the spinach in the dish, making a smooth, even top surface, then pour on the remaining *balsamella* as a top layer. Put the Pyrex in the preheated oven and bake for about 25 minutes; the top layer should be lightly golden brown.

Serve hot, right from the baking dish.

SWISS CHARD

Bietole all' Agro
(Boiled Swiss Chard with Olive Oil and Lemon) (SERVES 4)

So-called Swiss chard is used in Italy almost as much as spinach, and is sometimes substituted for it or mixed with it. It has a milder, sweeter taste. Boiled Swiss chard dressed *all'agro* may be used to accompany a great many dishes that do not have specific vegetables associated with them. Indeed, Swiss chard is almost always a safe accompanying vegetable.

> 2 pounds fresh Swiss chard
> Coarse salt
> Salt and a pinch of freshly ground pepper
> 3 tablespoons olive oil
> 1 lemon

Clean the Swiss chard very carefully. Remove the stems and place the leaves in a bowl of cold water; let soak for 30 minutes.

Heat with 2 cups of cold water and some coarse salt in a stockpot. When the water reaches the boiling point, add the Swiss chard to the pot, half cover with a lid, and boil very gently until soft (about 15 minutes).

Drain the Swiss chard and cool it under cold running water, then gently squeeze it to remove excess water and chop it very coarsely. Place it in a serving dish.

Sprinkle the Swiss chard with salt and a pinch of pepper and pour over the olive oil. Squeeze half of the lemon over the Swiss chard and garnish with the other lemon half, cut into wedges. Serve cold.

Bietole Saltate
("Stir-sautéed" Swiss Chard)

Follow recipe for *spinaci saltati* (see page 421) substituting 2 pounds of Swiss chard for the spinach.

TOMATOES

Pomodori Fritti
(Deep-fried Green Tomatoes)

Tomatoes are deep-fried in the same way as artichokes (see page 398). The tomatoes, which must still be green, are first cut horizontally into slices ½ inch thick and then dried very carefully with paper towels.

The cooking time is about 3 minutes on each side.

Pomodori al Forno
(Baked Tomatoes)   (SERVES 6)

Fresh tomato halves, lightly baked, with a little basil, parsley, garlic, and olive oil to bring out their flavor. Some bread crumbs are sprinkled over to make a crisp top. This dish may accompany almost anything.

    6 large ripe tomatoes
      Coarse salt
    1 large clove garlic
    1 cup fresh basil leaves
    1 cup Italian parsley leaves
      Salt and freshly ground pepper to taste
    2 tablespoons bread crumbs, preferably homemade (see page 45)
    ¼ cup olive oil

Wash the tomatoes and wipe them with a paper towel, then cut in half horizontally and remove all the seeds. Sprinkle the inside of the tomato halves with coarse salt and leave them to stand for 20 to 25 minutes.

Meanwhile, chop the garlic very fine, then chop the basil and parsley leaves coarsely. Mix the chopped garlic with the chopped basil and parsley and season with salt and pepper.

Preheat the oven to 375° or 400°.

Place the salted tomato halves face down on paper towel for a few minutes, then wipe them off with a paper towel and fill the cavities with the chopped herb mixture. Sprinkle the tops with bread crumbs, then place the stuffed tomatoes in a baking dish containing 2 tablespoons of the olive oil.

Sprinkle remaining olive oil over tomatoes and bake in the preheated oven until the tomato halves are still whole but soft (about 25 to 35 minutes).

Serve hot.

ZUCCHINI

Zucchini Bolliti
(Boiled Zucchini)

In selecting zucchini, try to find them as small and young as possible. The very large zucchini cultivated in America pay a large price in taste for their size. Zucchini should be very firm and the skin light green.

To boil, cut off both ends of the zucchini, top and bottom, and put into a large bowl of cold water for about 30 minutes, then slice lengthwise in quarters. Cut slices into 1-inch pieces.

Soak the zucchini pieces in more cold water for 30 minutes more.

Heat a large quantity of water, with coarse salt, in a large flameproof casserole. When the water reaches the boiling point, put in the zucchini pieces and let them simmer until they are cooked but firm (about 15 minutes). (Cooking time of zucchini varies a lot because it depends on how fresh they are, if they grow in a sunny or shady place, and if they have been in the refrigerator for a long period.)

Drain the zucchini and place in a dish to cool. It is now ready to be used in such dishes as *sformato di zucchini* (see page 426) or *insalata composta* (see page 388).

Fiori di Zucca Fritti
(Fried Zucchini Flowers)   (SERVES 4)

Our friend Todd Hunt, journalist and expert in food and gardening, tells us that zucchini have female and male flowers. The vegetable we eat is the stem of the female flower, and the flowers attached to the female are less good for eating. The male has a thin stem that never grows into the zucchini vegetable but puts all its force into its orange flower, which is delicious when fried with a light batter.

      Batter as for *pollo fritto* (see page 275)
16 zucchini flowers
 1 pound solid vegetable shortening
    Salt

Prepare the batter using the ingredients and directions on page 275. Set aside in a cool place (not the refrigerator) for 2 hours.

Cut off stems of the flowers and remove the pistils from inside. Wash the flowers very gently in cold water and dry them with paper towels.

Heat the solid vegetable shortening in a deep-fat fryer. While it is heating, prepare a serving dish by lining it with paper towels.

Dip each flower into the batter and place in the hot shortening. Cook for about 1 minute on each side, until golden brown, then remove with a strainer-skimmer and place on the prepared serving dish.

Repeat the procedure until all the flowers are cooked and on the serving dish, then remove the paper towels from the serving dish, sprinkle the flowers with a little salt, and serve immediately.

Zucchini Fritti
(Fried Zucchini)

Cut the zucchini into strips 2 inches long by 1½ inches wide and fry in batter as for fried zucchini flowers above.

Sformati di Verdura
(Baked Vegetables in Mold)   (SERVES 6)

This molded dish represents the most elaborate treatment of vegetables. A variety of vegetables may be used, boiled first and then treated in the same manner as *sformati* of meat or pasta or dessert. As usual with Italian *sformati*, the dish is unmolded when served.

Because of the special treatment of the vegetables, the dish is often used as a *piatto di mezzo*, the course in between the *primo piatto* and *secondo piatto*, in an important dinner.

    1 pound of a vegetable such as artichokes, asparagus, carrots, fennel, or cardoons, boiled (see the individual vegetables for procedure on boiling)

  10 tablespoons (1¼ sticks) butter

     Salt and freshly ground pepper to taste

  ½ cup all-purpose flour

   2 cups milk

   4 egg yolks

   3 tablespoons freshly grated Parmigiano cheese

     Freshly grated nutmeg to taste

   3 tablespoons unflavored bread crumbs, preferably homemade (see page 45)

When the boiled vegetable is cool, cut it into small pieces. Heat 4 tablespoons of the butter in a saucepan. When the butter is warm, add vegetables pieces and sauté for about 15 minutes. Taste for salt and pepper, then remove the saucepan from the flame and let the vegetable cool completely (about 30 minutes).

Sformati di verdura: 1. The loaf pan containing the *sformato* mixture, in a *bagno maria.*

Make *balsamella*, using the remaining 6 tablespoons of the butter, the flour, and the milk, according to the directions on page 52. When the *balsamella* is done, cover the saucepan and let the sauce cool completely (about 30 minutes).

Preheat oven to 400°.

When *balsamella* is cold, transfer it to a large bowl. Add the egg yolks and grated Parmigiano to the bowl and mix thoroughly with a wooden spoon. Add the vegetable pieces and salt, pepper, and nutmeg to taste, then gently mix all the ingredients together.

Butter a loaf pan (9 x 5 x 3 inches) and coat it with the bread crumbs, then pour the contents of bowl into the pan.

Prepare a *bagno maria* (bain marie) (see page 27 and photo above) and place it in the preheated oven for about 1 hour 15 minutes. (If during baking the top of the *sformato* begins to darken too much, place a sheet of aluminum foil over it.)

When the *sformato* is done, remove the loaf pan from the oven and let cool for 20 minutes. As the *sformato* cools, it will detach itself from the bottom and sides of the pan. Carefully unmold the *sformato* on a serving dish (see photo 2) and serve immediately.

2. The unmolded *sformato* on a serving dish.

Desserts

—◆—

AT this point it is common knowledge in America that the end of a usual Italian meal is not a dessert in our American sense, but rather fresh fruit. A dessert is served at the end of a family meal about once a week, perhaps on Sunday.

But nonetheless there is an unsurpassed number and variety of Italian desserts. When are they served, besides at that once-a-week family meal? At a formal dinner or when there are guests; on traditional feast days; at the café (in Italy called "bar"); at home for guests that call between meals. The variety of any area of Italian cooking is generally apparent only over the course of the entire year, since many dishes are meant to be made only once a year, for a particular day. This is true of desserts as well.

Italian desserts run the gamut of complicated pastries; creams and custards; sweet breads and *schiacciate*; nut biscuits; specialties with chestnuts and chestnut flour; *crespelle* (crêpes); rice desserts; fruit fried in batter; *budini* (most using the principle that the French called "soufflé" when they adopted it); meringues; fruit in pastry drums; stuffed fruit; special seasonal fruits, such as *fragolini di bosco* (wild strawberries) adorned simply with wine or whipped cream; etc., etc.

In short, the Italians have an enormous repertoire of desserts, and have through the centuries developed the most sophisticated techniques for producing them, but this sophistication is balanced by native good sense, which since the sixteenth century has run side by side with the sophistication, creating a balance to it. The repertoire is there, but rich desserts are not eaten with every meal nor even every day.

CUSTARDS AND CREAMS

Crema
(Cream Custard) (SERVES 4)

Crema is an independent dessert; it is not used to fill anything. Made in a double-boiler, with the same technique as we will see in the pastry creams, it is not difficult if instructions are followed carefully. Watch for the change in color of the eggs; add the milk cold. Then place the mixture over the heat and absolutely do not let it boil.

Crema is nice old-fashioned dessert that was eaten most at teatime at the turn of the century. When served with tea, it was put into cups rather than dessert bowls.

    4 egg yolks
    ⅓ cup granulated sugar
    1 cup cold milk
       Small piece of lemon or orange peel or 2 or 3 drops of vanilla
         extract

Put water in the bottom part of a double-boiler and set on the heat.

Place the egg yolks in a bowl and add the sugar. Stir with a wooden spoon, always in the same direction, until the sugar is completely incorporated and the egg yolks turn a lighter color. Add the cold milk mixing slowly and steadily, then transfer the contents of the bowl to the top part of the double-boiler along with the lemon or orange peel or vanilla.

When the water in the bottom of the double-boiler is boiling, put on the top part. Stir constantly with a wooden spoon, always in the same direction. Just at the moment before it boils, the cream should be thick enough to stick to the wooden spoon. That is the moment it is ready. *Absolutely do not allow it to boil.*

Immediately remove the top part of the double-boiler, and continue to stir the contents for 2 or 3 minutes more. Remove the lemon or orange peel, if present, and transfer the *crema* to individual dessert bowls to cool.

Crema may be eaten at room temperature after 1 hour; it may also

Crema: Stirring the *crema* in the top part of a double-boiler. The double-boiler technique was invented in Florence in the sixteenth century.

be eaten chilled. After reaching room temperature, cover the bowls with aluminum foil and refrigerate until needed.

Note: Crema retains optimum flavor for about 24 hours.

Crema Pasticcera
(Pastry Cream)   (M A K E S   A B O U T   1   C U P)

The techniques of pastry cream and the following chocolate pastry cream are similar to that of *crema* (see above). If the same care is taken in its preparation, it will not be difficult to make.

Crema pasticcera is used to fill cream puffs (see page 440) and *bomboloni* (see page 454) and as a layer on such pastries as *crostata di frutta* (see page 444).

  2 egg yolks
      Scant 3 tablespoons granulated sugar
  1 teaspoon potato starch or all-purpose flour
½ cup cold milk
      Small piece of lemon or orange peel or
  2 drops of vanilla extract

Put water in the bottom part of a double-boiler and set on the flame.

Place the egg yolks in a bowl and add the sugar and potato starch or flour. Stir with wooden spoon, always in the same direction, until the sugar and starch are completely incorporated and the egg yolks turn a lighter color. Add the cold milk slowly, mixing steadily, then transfer the contents of the bowl to the top part of the double-boiler, along with the lemon or orange peel or vanilla.

When the water in the bottom part of the double-boiler is boiling, insert the top part. Stir constantly with a wooden spoon, always in the same direction. Just at the moment before it boils, the cream should be thick enough to stick to the wooden spoon. That is the moment it is ready. *Absolutely do not allow it to boil.*

Immediately remove the top part of the double-boiler from the heat, and continue to stir the contents for 2 or 3 minutes more, then remove the lemon or orange peel, if present, and transfer the *crema pasticcera* to a crockery bowl to cool (about 1 hour).

The *crema* may be used in other recipes after cooling for 1 hour, or may be prepared some hours in advance and kept, covered, in the refrigerator until needed.

Cioccolata Pasticcera
(Chocolate Pastry Cream)　　　(MAKES ABOUT 2 CUPS)

Chocolate pastry cream is exactly like pastry cream, except that the melted chocolate is added when the pastry-cream ingredients in the top of the double-boiler have become warm.

Though chocolate cream and glaze are widely used in Italy, there is no such thing as chocolate cake. (Think of nearby Austria and Germany!) But for the Italians, it would make the cake itself too heavy. They prefer to add the chocolate only as filling or decoration.

(Chocolate as a drink, hot, with whipped cream, is another matter. Florentines are mad about it and make some of the best hot chocolate there is.)

    4 egg yolks
       Scant ⅓ cup plus 1 tablespoon granulated sugar
    2 teaspoons all-purpose flour
    1 cup plus 2 tablespoons cold milk

2 or 3 drops vanilla extract
2 tablespoons unsweetened cocoa powder

Put water in the bottom part of a double-boiler and set on the heat.

Place the egg yolks in a bowl and add the scant ⅓ cup sugar and the flour. Stir with a wooden spoon, always in the same direction, until the sugar is completely incorporated and the egg yolks turn a lighter color. Slowly add the 1 cup of cold milk and drops of vanilla, mixing thoroughly.

In a small saucepan, heat the 2 tablespoons of milk to lukewarm, then dissolve the cocoa powder and the tablespoon of sugar in it. Keep saucepan near the heat but not on flame.

Transfer the contents of the bowl to top of the double-boiler.

When the water in the bottom part of the double-boiler boils, put on the top part. Stir steadily with wooden spoon, without stopping, always in the same direction. When the ingredients in the top of the double-boiler are warm, add the chocolate mixture.

Just at the moment before boiling, the *cioccolata pasticcera* should be thick enough to stick to the wooden spoon. That is the moment it is ready. *Absolutely do not allow it to boil.* Immediately remove the top part of the double-boiler from the heat, and continue to stir the contents for 2 or 3 minutes more.

Transfer the *cioccolata pasticcera* to a crockery bowl. After about 15 minutes, cover the bowl with aluminum foil and allow the cream to cool for about 1 hour more before using.

Zabaione (MAKES ABOUT 1 CUP)

The technique of making *zabaione* is similar to that of pastry cream, except that it uses Marsala wine in place of milk.

Zabaione is used as a filling for sweets or as an accompaniment to fruit and pastry desserts. It is often mixed with whipped cream to make *crema zabaione* (see page 435), and in that form can also be eaten independently. Pure *zabaione* would be overly rich to eat by itself.

Marsala flavoring has come to replace almost all the sweet wines that used to exist in Italy: Malvasia (Malmsey), Greco, the old sweet Vernaccia, and so on. The fine dessert wines that still exist in Tuscany, Vin Santo and Aleatico, are not used in cooking. (They are perfect accompaniments to desserts not made with wine, but are, alas, unavailable in America, simply from lack of interest.)

> 3 egg yolks
> 3 tablespoons granulated sugar
> ½ cup dry Marsala

Put water in the bottom of a double-boiler and set on the heat.

Place the egg yolks in a bowl and add the sugar. Stir with a wooden spoon, always in the same direction, until sugar is completely incorporated and the egg yolks turn a lighter color. Add the Marsala slowly, mixing steadily, then transfer the contents of the bowl to the top part of the double-boiler.

When the water in the bottom part is boiling, insert the top part. Stir constantly with wooden spoon, always in the same direction. Just at the moment before boiling, *zabaione* should be thick enough to stick to the wooden spoon. That is the moment it is ready. *Absolutely do not allow it to boil.*

Immediately remove top part of the double-boiler from the heat, stir the contents for 2 or 3 minutes more, then transfer the *zabaione* to a crockery bowl to cool (about 1 hour).

Panna Montata
(Whipped Cream, Florentine Style)
(MAKES 2 TO 2 ½ CUPS)

The critical condition for making whipped cream is that all utensils and the cream itself must be cold. Also, the fresher the cream, the easier it usually is to whip. Indeed, if the cream is very fresh, it often whips easily without all of the precautions. A crockery bowl is preferred for beating cream. Plastic may be substituted but not aluminum. Prepare by placing the utensils in the refrigerator, then place the cold bowl in ice.

Whipped cream is used a great deal in Italy, especially in Florence. But it is usually the only "rich" ingredient in the dish. It is used to mix with fresh fruit or to fill an otherwise unadorned pastry. You will not find it used to "gild the lily" in an already rich dessert, such as one using *crema* (see page 430) or in *zuppa inglese* (see page 452). It is always part of the dish, not an adornment.

Italian whipped cream is sweetened a little with both granulated and confectioners' sugar.

> 1 cup heavy cream
> 2 tablespoons granulated sugar
> 1 teaspoon confectioners' sugar

Place the heavy cream, beating bowl, and wire whisk in refrigerator for a minimum of an hour.

Improvise a cold double-boiler by placing a crockery bowl in a larger bowl of ice cubes. Pour the heavy cream into the chilled bowl and then, with the whisk, start whipping, with a continuous rotary motion from bottom to top. Continue to whip until cream is no longer liquid (about 1 minute). At this point, to avoid any danger of the heavy cream turning to butter, add 1 teaspoon of the granulated sugar. Then continue whipping until the cream is solid but soft (about 2 minutes for this amount).

When the cream is ready, sprinkle with the remaining granulated sugar and confectioners' sugar and mix gently.

Note: Whipped cream may be kept in the refrigerator, covered, for several hours.

Crema Zabaione
(Whipped Cream with Zabaione)
(SERVES 6 TO ACCOMPANY FRUIT DESSERT)

Crema zabaione is made by mixing whipped cream and *zabaione* to a homogenous texture.

It is used to accompany the stuffed peaches, on page 492 and as an alternative to pastry cream for filling in *pasticcini ripieni* (see page 440) and with *bocca di dama* (see page 450).

It is also served as an independent dessert in small bowls.

> *Zabaione* (see page 433)
> 1 pint heavy cream
> 2 heaping tablespoons granulated sugar
> 1 teaspoon confectioners' sugar

Make the *zabaione* according to the directions on page 433. When it has been transferred to the crockery bowl, cover it with aluminum foil and let stand until completely cold (about 1 hour).

When the *zabaione* is cold, make *panna montata*, using the heavy cream and sugar, according to the directions on page 434. When the whipped cream is ready and very stiff, gently fold in the cold *zabaione*. Mix very carefully but thoroughly with a whisk.

Cover the bowl with aluminum foil and place it in the refrigerator until needed.

Lattaiolo
(Old-fashioned Cinnamon Custard)   (SERVES 6)

An older type of custard dessert, unfortunately disappearing even in its native land. Unlike *latte alla portoghese* (see page 437), it is not made with sugar, but is lightly sprinkled with confectioners' sugar before it is served. Its subtle flavor of cinnamon, nutmeg, and vanilla bean is well worth preserving.

Mixing milk and eggs with a little thickening and then baking it is the main procedure in custard-type dishes. Encased in a bottom crust, this procedure appears in the fourteenth-century Florentine *torta di latte* and is the basis for the category of dishes generally known by the French name "quiches." When sweetened and used without crust, it is the basis of a number of well-known desserts.

> 5 cups milk
> Pinch of salt
> 1 small piece lemon peel
> 1 small piece vanilla bean
> 2 eggs plus 6 egg yolks
> 2 tablespoons all-purpose flour
> Pinch of nutmeg
> ½ teaspoon ground cinnamon
> 1 tablespoon cold butter
> ½ cup confectioners' sugar

Put the milk in a saucepan, along with the salt, lemon peel, and a small piece of vanilla bean, then set the saucepan on a medium flame. When the mixture reaches the boiling point, simmer very slowly for 30 minutes. Keep removing the skin that forms on top of the milk with a wooden spoon.

Remove the saucepan from the flame and let the milk cool for 1 hour.

Preheat the oven to 300°.

Place the eggs and egg yolks in a bowl, then add the flour and mix very well. Add the nutmeg and cinnamon, and then, when the milk is cold, pour it into the bowl and mix thoroughly. Pass the contents of the bowl through a piece of cheesecloth into another bowl.

Butter a loaf pan (9 x 5 x 2¾ inches) and pour in contents of the bowl. Bake in the preheated oven for 40 to 50 minutes, then remove from the oven and let cool for 1 hour.

Wrap the loaf pan in aluminum foil and place in refrigerator for at least 4 hours, then unmold the *lattaiolo* onto serving dish, sift the confectioners' sugar over the top, and serve.

Latte alla Portoghese
(Caramel Custard)   (SERVES 6)

Latte alla portoghese is the same as *crème caramel*. The name suggests an origin in the Iberian peninsula, and perhaps the flan is the original of all these dishes. As previously mentioned, however, the principle is already present in a fourteenth-century Florentine manuscript.

Sugar replaces the cinnamon and nutmeg flavoring of *lattaiolo* (see above); the dish is coated with caramelized sugar, the process for which is explained below.

> 5 cups cold milk
> Pinch of salt
> 1¼ cups granulated sugar
> Small piece vanilla bean
> 2 eggs plus 6 egg yolks

Heat the cold milk in a saucepan, along with salt, the small piece of vanilla bean, and ¼ cup of the sugar. When the mixture reaches the boiling point, simmer very slowly for 30 minutes. Keep removing the skin that forms on top of the milk with a wooden spoon.

Remove the saucepan from the flame and let the milk cool for 1 hour.

Meanwhile, place ¾ cup of the sugar in a small saucepan, preferably of copper, and set on a low flame until the sugar dissolves into a brown syrup. (Italians do not add water to the sugar when caramelizing it and usually melt the sugar in a copper pan, as here, not in the mold itself.) Immediately and completely, coat a loaf pan (9 x 5 x 2¾ inches) with the caramelized sugar by pouring the syrup into the loaf pan and moving it around until the pan is completely lined. Let the loaf pan stand until cool (about 40 minutes).

Preheat the oven to 275°.

Place the eggs, egg yolks, and the remaining ¼ cup of sugar in a large bowl. Stir continuously until eggs become lighter in color, then strain the milk through a piece of cheesecloth into the bowl. Mix very well with a wooden spoon and pour the mixture into the prepared loaf pan.

Place the loaf pan in the preheated oven and bake for 60 to 75 minutes, until firm, then remove the pan from the oven and let rest until cool (about 1 hour).

Wrap the pan with aluminum foil and place it in refrigerator for at least 4 hours, then unmold on a serving dish and slice, as a loaf, to serve.

Note: Latte alla portoghese can also be made in the oven in a *bagno maria* (bain-marie). Cooking time will be about 15 minutes longer.

PASTRY AND PASTRY DESSERTS

IT IS impossible to speak about Italian pastry techniques without discussing the debt of French pastries to Italy. Almost all of the basic types of pastry listed in *Larousse Gastronomique* went to France from Italy.

PASTA SOFFIATA (Cream puff pastry/pâte à chou)

In 1533 Pantanelli, one of the Florentine cooks of the court of Caterina de Medici, brought *pasta soffiata* to France. The name *"pâte à chou"* is supposed to be a corruption of *pâte à chaud*, using a hot technique as opposed to the cold technique of puff pastry. The technique is described on page 440.

PASTA SFOGLIA (Puff pastry/pâte feuilletée)

Larousse has a long discussion, justly refuting the derivation of the name from the pastry cook Feuillet, and taking its history back long before his time. The history of "flaky" pastry without butter need not concern us here, but the early use of puff pastry with butter by the Dukes of Tuscany is well documented* and accepted by *Larousse.* Strangely, *Larousse* does not seem to realize, however, that the name *"pâte feuilletée"* is simply a translation of *"pasta sfoglia."* Its use seems to have become widespread in France under Henry IV, married to Maria de Medici. (It is amusing to think that Henry of Navarre, leader of the Protestant cause, became King of France largely with the financial backing of his in-laws, the Medici, even though two members of the family had recently been pope.)

Although puff pastry plays a big part in many Italian recipes, in "salted" antipasti, snacks, and desserts, I have made the reluctant decision to not include it in this book, since there is not space to deal with it properly.

PASTA FROLLA (short pastry/pâte sucrée)

Again of Italian origin. There are a number of types of *pasta frolla,* but the basic ingredients are flour, shortening (butter, lard, or both), sugar, and eggs, flavored with lemon, orange, or vanilla. All four recipes that we use here (pages 444–450) are slightly different from one another, the variations being in the butter and/or lard, the flavoring, and the proportions of ingredients. The *pasta frolla* used in Genoa, without eggs, is not given here.

BOMBOLONI

Bomboloni pastry is fundamentally the same as brioche pastry, though *bomboloni* are deep-fried rather than baked. The recipe is included on page 454.

---

* The fourteenth-century *torta frescha* used puff pastry.

BOCCA DI DAMA (Italian spongecake/pâte à biscuit Italien)

This light basic cake utilizes the Florentine technique of separating egg whites and yolks, and folding in the stiffly beaten whites. The recipe is given on page 450.

Pasta Soffiata
(Cream Puff Pastry) (MAKES ABOUT 3 ½ CUPS)

1 ½ cups cold water
    Pinch of salt
1 heaping tablespoon granulated sugar
8 tablespoons (1 stick) butter
1 ¼ cups all-purpose flour
4 eggs

Put the water and salt in a saucepan and set on low flame. Add the sugar, and when the water reaches the boiling point add the butter.

When the butter is completely dissolved, remove the pan from the flame and immediately add all the flour at once. Mix very well with a rubber spatula until all flour is well incorporated and the dough is smooth (about 10 minutes).

Place the pan back on the flame and cook for 7 or 8 minutes more, stirring constantly with wooden spoon.

Remove pan from stove. Add one of the eggs to the dough, and working very fast, mix until completely absorbed. (If you do not work fast enough, the egg may cook and curdle.) Repeat the procedure with, one by one, the second, third, and fourth eggs.

When eggs are completely incorporated, the dough should be very smooth and completely detached from the bottom and sides of the pan. It is then ready to be used.

Pasticcini Ripieni (Bignè)
(Cream Puffs) (MAKES ABOUT 24)

Cream puffs filled with *crema zabaione* or whipped cream. The pastry is *pasta soffiata*.

A pastry syringe is necessary to form the pastry puffs. A photo of the pastry syringe and the technique of making the puffs is shown below.

> *Pasta soffiata* (see page 440)
> *Crema pasticcera* (see page 431), *cioccolata pasticcera* (see page 432), *crema zabaione* (see page 435), or *panna montata* (see page 434)

Make the *pasta soffiata* according to the directions on page 440.
Butter a cookie sheet; preheat the oven to 375°.
Fill a pastry syringe with the *pasta soffiata* batter; do not put on a tip. Press down on the end of the syringe, making two circular movements and causing the exiting string of batter to form an outer ring (2 inches in diameter) connected to an inner one on the pastry sheet (see photo 1). Continue until all the batter is used up.

Pasticcini ripieni (bignè): 1. Forming the pastries.

Place the cookie sheet in the preheated oven for about 20 minutes; do not open the oven for at least 15 minutes. Remove the cookie sheet from the oven and let the *pasticcini* cool (about 1 hour).
Meanwhile, prepare the filling you have chosen, following the appropriate recipe for procedure. (If you make *panna montata*, how-

ever, make it when the pastries are already cold). Let the filling stand until cold.

Place the finest tip on your pastry syringe and fill it with the selected filling. Insert the syringe inside each *bignè* and fill it with about 2 teaspoons of the cream. Then, still using the syringe, place a little of the filling on top of the *bignè* (see photos 2–3). (Leave the glazed topping to the commercial pastry shops.)

2. Filling the pastries.

3. Topping the pastries with a little of the filling.

Place all the *pasticcini ripieni* in a serving dish. If you do not plan to serve the pastries immediately, cover the serving dish with aluminum foil and place it in the refrigerator.

4. The finished product.

Bombe
(Deep-fried Pastry "Nuggets") (SERVES 6 TO 8)

Little balls of *pasta soffiata* flavored with orange are deep-fried and then sprinkled with confectioners' sugar.

Pasta soffiata (see page 440)
Grated peel of 1 orange
1 pound solid vegetable shortening
¾ cup confectioners' sugar

Make the *pasta soffiata* according to the directions on page 440. Add the orange peel to the dough, mixing thoroughly.

Heat the solid vegetable shortening in a deep-fat fryer; prepare a serving dish by lining it with paper towels.

When the shortening is hot, make separate little *bombe* by dropping individual tablespoons of dough into the deep-fryer, each one well separated from the others. Leave enough room, because the *bombe* will swell up a lot.

Fry the *bombe* until golden brown all over, then remove with a strainer-skimmer and place on the prepared serving dish.

When all the *bombe* are on serving dish, remove the paper towels and sprinkle the confectioners' sugar over. Serve immediately.

Crostata di Frutta
(Fruit "Shortcake") (SERVES 6)

Pasta frolla, baked and covered with a layer of pastry cream topped by an eye-catching arrangement of fresh fruit. The fruit—which can include half or sliced peaches or apricots, whole strawberries, raspberries, grapes—makes a colorful design in which you can use your own eye and imagination (see photo).

Crostata di frutta: 1. The finished crust. The photo also shows the fruit that is going to be used.

For the pasta frolla

    8 tablespoons (1 stick) butter
    4 tablespoons lard
    3 cups all-purpose flour
    1 lemon or 1 thick-skinned orange

½ cup granulated sugar
1 egg plus 2 egg yolks

Crema pasticcera (see page 431)

For the fresh fruit topping

1½ pounds assorted fresh fruit such as peaches, apricots, strawberries, raspberries, etc. (but not apples or pears)
Juice of 1 lemon
2 tablespoons granulated sugar

First make the *pasta frolla*.
Melt the butter and lard in a saucepan and let stand until cool
(about 20 minutes).
Put the flour on a pasta board in a mound, then make a well in it.
Place sugar in the well. Grate the lemon or orange skin into the well,
then put in the egg, egg yolks, and melted butter and lard. Using a
fork, quickly mix all ingredients in the well together with the flour.
Knead the dough for a very short time, just long enough to form a
large ball, then wrap the *pasta frolla* in a cotton dishtowel and let
rest in cool place for 30 minutes; do not refrigerate. Thoroughly
butter an all-purpose round aluminum pan (12 inches in diameter,
¾ inch high); preheat the oven to 375°.
With a rolling pin, roll out the *pasta frolla* into a circle a little over
12 inches in diameter. Place the prepared pan over the pastry and cut
all around with pastry wheel to make a perfect circle 12 inches in
diameter. Place the pastry circle very carefully in the pan, then bake
in the preheated oven for about 30 minutes. Remove the pan from the
oven and let stand until cold (about 1 hour).
Meanwhile, make the *crema pasticcera* according to the directions
on page 431. Cover the pan and let stand until cold (about 40 minutes).
Wash the fruit you have selected for the topping very carefully,
removing possible pits and stems. If using large strawberries, cut
them in half lengthwise; for large grapes, cut in half lengthwise and
remove the seeds; for peaches or apricots, halve them, remove the pits,
and then cut them in slices less than ¼ inch thick.
Sprinkle the lemon juice and sugar over the fruit and set aside until
needed.
Carefully remove the pastry from the pan and place it on a large

serving dish. Place the *crema pasticcera* on top and spread it out evenly with a long spatula, then arrange the fruit pieces in whatever design you like (see photos), and serve.

Note: Generally I arrange fruit in rings of contrasting colors and place a whole large strawberry or half a peach or apricot in the center. Some place a glaze over the fruit, but I dislike it because it detracts from the naturalness of the fruit.

2. The finished dish, with the fruit arranged in a design.

Crostata di Ricotta
(Italian Cheesecake)   (SERVES 6)

This is close to what is known in America as "Italian cheesecake." The crust of *pasta frolla* covers the bottom and sides. The ricotta is mixed with eggs and flavored with ground almonds held together with egg white, and glacéed fruit and raisins soaked in rum. Part-skim ricotta as well as the eggs make the cheese filling quite light, and the crisscross of pastry strips on top is attractive and traditional.

For the crust

    1½ cups all-purpose flour
    ⅓ cup granulated sugar

    6 tablespoons (¾ stick) butter
    1 egg plus 1 egg yolk

For the filling

    2 ounces mixed glacéed fruit
    2 ounces raisins
    ½ cup rum
    2 ounces almonds, most blanched, with 2 or 3 almonds un-
        blanched
    3 eggs
   15 ounces ricotta, preferably part-skim
      Grated peel of ½ lemon
      Grated peel of ½ orange
    7 tablespoons granulated sugar
    3 tablespoons all-purpose flour

Make the dough for the crust, using the ingredients in the proportions listed, according to the directions on page 445. While the dough is resting, make the filling.

Put the glacéed fruit, raisins, and rum in a small bowl and let soak 20 to 25 minutes. Meanwhile, grind the almonds very fine with mortar and pestle or blender. Separate one of the eggs and add the egg white to the almonds, mixing thoroughly.

Drain the ricotta in a piece of cheesecloth, then place it in a large bowl, along with the eggs and the egg yolk, and mix very well with a wooden spoon. Add the orange and lemon peel to the ricotta mixture, then add the glacéed fruit and raisins in rum, the almond and egg white mixture, and the sugar. Mix thoroughly.

When the mixture is homogenous, add the flour and keep stirring until it is uniformly incorporated. Set aside until needed.

Butter a 9-inch layer cake pan with a removable bottom; preheat the oven to 375°.

With a rolling pin, roll the dough out to a sheet ⅜ inch thick. Place the sheet of dough over the prepared layer cake pan and gently fit it to the shape of the pan, letting the excess dough hang over the sides.

Transfer the filling from the bowl to the dough-lined pan and distribute it evenly with a wooden spoon. Cut around the perimeter of the pan top to remove excess dough, and use the leftover dough to make ½-inch strips; place these crisscross on top.

Bake in the preheated oven for 40 minutes. Let the *crostata* cool for about ½ hour before removing it from the pan. The *crostata* may be eaten warm or cold.

Torta di Ricotta
(Ricotta "Torte")   (SERVES 6)

Another Italian cheesecake, but flavored with anisette, topped with a layer of ground almonds, and then covered with meringue and baked a second time.

The pastry is again *pasta frolla*.

For the crust

> 1 ½ cups all-purpose flour
> ⅓ cup granulated sugar
> 6 tablespoons (¾ stick) butter
> 1 egg plus 1 egg yolk
>   Pinch of salt
> 1 drop vanilla extract
>   Grated peel of 1 orange or lemon

For the filling

> 3 ounces glacéed mixed fruit
> 2 ounces glacéed cherries
> 1 cup lukewarm milk
> 15 ounces ricotta, preferably part-skim
> 4 egg yolks
> 4 ounces chocolate chips
> ⅔ cup granulated sugar
> 2 tablespoons anisette liqueur
> 3 ounces blanched almonds

For the meringue

> 2 egg whites
> 2 tablespoons granulated sugar

Make the dough for the crust, using the ingredients in the proportions listed, according to the directions on page 445, adding salt and vanilla with the eggs. While the dough is resting, make the filling.

Soak the glacéed fruit in a bowl containing the lukewarm milk for 20 minutes.

Meanwhile, drain the ricotta in a piece of cheesecloth and place it in a bowl, along with the egg yolks, chocolate chips, sugar, and anisette. Mix very well with a wooden spoon, then drain the glacéed fruit and add to the bowl. Combine thoroughly and let rest for 10 to 15 minutes in a cool place; do not refrigerate.

Butter a 9-inch cake pan with removable bottom; preheat the oven to 375° or 400°.

With a rolling pin, roll out a sheet of dough ⅜ inch thick. Place the sheet of dough over the prepared layer cake pan and gently fit it to the shape of the pan, letting the excess dough hang over the sides.

Transfer the filling from the bowl to the dough-lined pan and distribute it evenly with a wooden spoon. Cut around the perimeter of the pan top to remove excess dough, then bake in the preheated oven for 45 to 50 minutes. Let cool for 10 minutes.

Meanwhile, grind the almonds, then sprinkle them over the cooked ricotta layer.

Whip the 2 egg whites very stiff with the 2 tablespoons of sugar. Spread the egg whites over the *torta*, making sure you touch the crust all around, then replace the *torta* in the oven for 12 minutes more. Let *torta* cool for about ½ hour before removing it from the pan. Remove and serve, or wait and serve cold.

Timballo di Pere
(Whole Poached Pears in a Pastry Drum)   (S E R V E S 6)

A combination of elegance and simplicity, whole pears are poached in good Chianti and port and then placed in a pastry drum made of *pasta frolla*. Whipped cream is spooned into the spaces between the pears, and the pastry lid sits lightly on it like a little hat.

The whole ensemble, sitting on a large serving dish, is brought in. Each serving should consist of a whole, wine-colored pear with some sauce spooned over and some whipped cream on the side. The *timballo*, or pastry drum, is supposed to be for presentation. But the temptation is always too great, and everyone ends up by eating some of it. And why not? But the little game is always played first.

It is particularly important for presentation that the pears used have nice full stems. This is a dish for special occasions.

> 9 ounces (2¼ sticks) butter
> 4 cups all-purpose flour
> 1 egg plus 4 egg yolks
> 1 cup plus 2 tablespoons sugar
>   Pinch of salt
> ¼ cup dry white wine or dry Marsala, if necessary
>   *Pere al vino* (see page 495)
>   *Panna montata* (see page 434)

To make the pastry, melt butter in a small saucepan and let cool for about 30 minutes.

Put the flour in a mound on a pasta board and make a well in it. Put the melted butter, egg, egg yolks, sugar, and salt into the well and mix well with a metal fork, then incorporate the adjacent flour until only 3 or 4 tablespoons of flour remain.

Knead for only about 1 minute, just enough to make dough into a ball, then place the dough in a floured cotton dishtowel and let rest in a cool place for 2 hours; do not refrigerate.

This sweet dough for *timballo* is unpredictable. Sometimes after resting, especially when it is hot and dry, the dough becomes tough and impossible to roll properly. If so, after the dough has rested, add ¼ cup of dry white wine or dry Marsala to make it elastic. Flour the dough again and knead for 1 minute more. Roll out dough, make lid, line springform, and bake according to procedure on pages 207–210.

Prepare *pere al vino* according to the directions on page 495, up to the point where the sauce is refrigerated.

Open the springform and place the baked *timballo* on a serving dish. Remove the pears from refrigerator and place them in *timballo*, then sprinkle cold sauce over them.

Prepare the whipped cream, according to the directions on page 434, then spoon into the spaces between the pears.

Put the *timballo* lid in place for presentation and serve immediately.

Bocca di Dama
(Italian Spongecake)   (MAKES 1 TEN-INCH CAKE)

This is the basic Italian cake, which is never eaten as is but is used to make many other desserts. It is a light cake, flavored with a bit of lemon or orange rind. Cake, as a matter of fact, is never made in a heavier form in Italy. It would not be mixed with chocolate, ground nuts, or the other ingredients that make for the many varieties of heavier cake with which we are familiar in America. It is not even really sweet enough to satisfy our idea of cake. As in *zuppa inglese*, which follows this recipe, the *bocca di dama* is adorned and made into a complete dessert.

In Italy, *bocca di dama* can often be bought commercially made and used to make the dessert. This, of course, produces a result inferior to that which comes from making your own fresh cake.

The French call it *"biscuit italiens"* and use it in the same way as the Italians. Its "spongy" quality comes from separation of whites and yolks of egg, the whites then beaten stiff and folded into the batter, causing the dough to rise a little when baked and to be very light and full of air. This is the same principle used to make the soufflé type dishes, such as *budini* and *sformati*. The French adoption of *biscuits italiens* is proof that this technique went from Florence to France, and not vice versa.

6 eggs, separated
6 ounces granulated sugar
1½ cups all-purpose flour
Grated peel of 1 lemon or 1 orange

Place the egg yolks in a large bowl, along with the sugar, and stir continuously with wooden spoon for about 20 minutes, until the sugar is completely incorporated and the color of the egg yolks lightens. Pour in the flour, little by little, in a light shower, mixing continuously with the wooden spoon. Finally, add the lemon or orange peel.

Butter a 10-inch tube pan; preheat the oven to 375°.

Beat the egg whites until stiff, then fold them gently into the egg yolk mixture.

Pour the contents of the bowl into the tube pan and bake in the preheated oven for 45 minutes; do not open the oven for 30 minutes after you put in the pan.

Remove the tube-pan from oven and let cool for 2 hours, then remove the *bocca di dama* from the pan and place on a serving dish. Use as needed.

Zuppa Inglese
(The Original Italian Rum Cake)   (S E R V E S   8)

Zuppa inglese, meaning, literally, "English soup," is a dessert made with Italian spongecake (*bocca di dama*) and pastry cream and is the authentic original for the type of Italo-American pastry called "Italian rum cake." However, though some rum is used in *zuppa inglese*, the critical ingredient is another liqueur called *Alkermes di Firenze*. The name of the dessert is sometimes said to derive from its supposed relation to the English trifle. This is incorrect. The name derives instead from the color of the Alkermes, which is the same red used in the British flag (and which, incidentally, is made from cochineal, a substance produced by an insect).

Because it has become very difficult to find Alkermes even in Italy nowadays, the true *zuppa inglese* is disappearing. Of Florentine origin, it was a favorite *dolce* all over Italy, copied in Bologna and Ferrara as well as the south. See the recipe for Alkermes on page 453, as it is not possible to buy it in this country at all, and be sure to have it ready several days in advance of making the *zuppa inglese*.

> *Bocca di dama* (see page 450)
> 8 egg yolks
> ¾ cup granulated sugar
> 4 teaspoons potato starch or all-purpose flour
> 2 cups cold milk
> 2 small pieces orange peel
>
> 1 ½ cups rum
> 1 cup Alkermes (see page 453)
> 1 tablespoon butter

Prepare the *bocca di dama* according to the directions on page 450, then let cool for at least 3 hours. (It would be much better if the *bocca di dama* could be done one day in advance.)

Using the egg yolks, sugar, potato starch or flour, milk, and orange peel, make a *crema pasticcera* according to the directions on page 431. When it is done, transfer from the top part of the double-boiler to a bowl. Cover and let cool for 30 minutes, then place the bowl in the refrigerator until completely cold.

Cut the *bocca di dama* into slices ¼ inch thick and set out two large serving dishes; lay half of the slices flat on one serving dish and the other half on the second. Soak the *bocca di dama* slices on the first serving dish with 1 cup of the rum and those on the other with the Alkermes.

Butter a loaf pan (9 x 5 x 2¾ inches) and place it in refrigerator for about 10 minutes; meanwhile, preheat the oven to 375°.

Remove the loaf pan from the refrigerator and line it completely, bottom and sides, with soaked slices of *bocca di dama*, alternating rum slices with Alkermes slices. Make a thin layer of *crema pasticcera* over the cake lining the bottom of pan, then make another layer of cake slices and cover it with *crema pasticcera*. Repeat the procedure until the pan is completely filled; the top layer must be of cake slices.

Cover the top of the pan with aluminum foil and place in preheated oven for 25 minutes. Remove from the oven and let cool for 30 minutes, then place in the refrigerator until completely cold (about 3 hours).

Remove the pan from the refrigerator and unmold the *zuppa inglese* onto a large serving dish. Pour the remaining ½ cup rum over and serve, slicing it like a loaf of bread.

Alkermes di Firenze

The red liqueur Alkermes is essential for a genuine *zuppa inglese*. Not only is its taste important to the dish, but also the particular red color, which contributes to the alternating yellow and red of the outer layer of *bocca di dama*.

Alkermes di Firenze (of Florence) was long a secret formula of the Medici family, and was also called "Elixir of the Medici." (Maria de Medici and her alchemist Ruggieri took it to France, where it was called "Liquore de'Medici").

Since pure grain alcohol is not sold freely here as it is in Italy, substitute an American 80 proof vodka, which is all but tasteless and gives just about the same result as pure grain alcohol. If you cannot obtain cochineal, there is an essence of Alkermes sold by Milan Laboratories on Spring Street in New York City.

    12 grams cinnamon (about 2 tablespoons)
    10 grams coriander seeds (about 2 scant tablespoons)
     7 grams cochineal (about 1 heaping tablespoon)
     3 grams mace (about ½ tablespoon)   (*continued*)

2.5　grams cloves (about a scant ½ tablespoon)
  5　grams dried orange peel (about 1 scant tablespoon)
  3　grams aniseed (about ½ tablespoon)
 10　pods cardamom
 ½　vanilla bean
  3　cups unflavored 80 proof American vodka
3½　cups cold water
1¾　pounds granulated sugar
 ½　cup rose water

Put all the spices except the vanilla bean in a spice grinder or a mortar and grind them very well with the pestle; cut the vanilla bean into 4 or 5 pieces.

Place the ground spices and vanilla pieces in a 2-quart jar with a screw top. Add the vodka and 1½ cups of the cold water, then close the jar and let it stand for 1 week, shaking the jar once a day.

After a week, dissolve the sugar in the remaining 2 cups of cold water. Add the water with the dissolved sugar to the jar and let it rest for 1 more day, shaking the jar twice during this time.

Strain the contents of the jar through a paper filter into a large bowl. Add the rose water to bowl, then transfer the contents to 2 bottles. Close the bottles and let it rest for 1 day more. Then it is ready to use.

Note: Left in closed bottles, Alkermes will last indefinitely. Use it as needed.

Bomboloni
(Florentine Custard Doughnuts)　　(MAKES ABOUT 14)

Bomboloni are made with a yeast dough, which is cut out in circles and filled with pastry cream and deep-fried rather than baked.

As a variant, *bomboloni* are sometimes filled with fruit preserves or a combination of pastry cream and preserves.

Crema pasticcera (see page 431)

For the "sponge"

1　ounce (2 cakes) compressed fresh yeast or 2 packages active dry yeast

½ cup of lukewarm or hot milk, depending on the yeast
½ cup all-purpose flour
   Pinch of salt

For the dough

8 tablespoons (1 stick) butter
3 egg yolks
1½ tablespoons granulated sugar
½ cup warm milk
2¾ cups all-purpose flour

Plus

1 pound solid vegetable shortening
8 tablespoons lard
½ cup granulated sugar

Make the pastry cream according to the directions on page 431. Let stand until needed.

To make the "sponge," dissolve the yeast in ½ cup lukewarm or hot milk. Place the flour in bowl and make a small well in it, then put in the dissolved yeast and a pinch of salt. Keep mixing with wooden spoon until all the flour is incorporated, then cover the bowl with a cotton dishtowel and let stand in a warm place, out of drafts, until doubled in size (about 60 minutes).

Improvise an oversized double-boiler by bringing a large quantity of water to boil in a stockpot and placing a large metal bowl over it. Put the butter into the metal bowl and let melt very slowly, then remove the bowl from the stockpot and let butter cool in the bowl (about 15 to 20 minutes). Be sure butter is cool, then add egg yolks, one at a time, incorporating them into the butter with a wooden spoon.

When the "sponge" is ready, place it in the bowl with the butter and eggs. Mix very well, with a rotary motion for 10 to 15 minutes, then add the sugar and warm milk, stirring continuously. When all the ingredients are well amalgamated, add 2¼ cups of the flour, a little at a time, stirring continuously.

When all the flour is incorporated, keep stirring for 20 minutes more, until the dough is completely detached from bowl, then cover with a cotton dishtowel and let stand in a warm place until doubled in size (about 1 to 1½ hours).

Sprinkle the remaining ½ cup of flour over a pasta board and place the dough on it. Roll out gently with rolling pin to make a sheet about ¼ inch high, then cut out 28 circles with a circular 2-inch cookie cutter.

Bomboloni: 1. Forming the *bomboloni*. In the background is the deep-fat fryer.

On each of 14 circles, place 1 heaping teaspoon of the *crema pasticcera*. Moisten the edges of the circles with a finger dipped in a glass of water, then cover with the other 14 circles. Press the edges to be sure they are sealed.

Cover the *bomboloni* with a cotton dishtowel and let rest for about 1 hour, until doubled in size.

Heat the solid vegetable shortening and lard in a deep-fryer; prepare a serving dish by lining it with paper towels. When the shortening and lard are melted and hot, carefully transfer 4 *bomboloni* to the deep-fryer with a spatula. Let fry for about 30 seconds on each side, turning them with a strainer-skimmer. (In that time they should rise and become a golden brown color.) With the strainer-skimmer, transfer the fried *bomboloni* to the prepared serving dish.

Repeat the procedure until all are cooked, then remove the paper towels from the bottom of the serving dish, sprinkle the *bomboloni* with the sugar, and serve hot.

Note: Cioccolata pasticcera (see page 432) or jam may be substituted for the pastry cream.

2. The finished pastry. The photo includes the Moka type of espresso maker.

Cenci
("Rags," Deep-fried Pastry Snacks)   (SERVES 6)

The dough for *cenci* is fundamentally like that for making pasta, except that it is flavored with rum. After resting an hour, the little squares of pasta are deep-fried and sprinkled with sugar. These little snack cookies are eaten widely.

> 3 cups all-purpose flour
> 2 eggs
> 3 tablespoons olive oil
> 2 tablespoons rum
>   Pinch of salt

(*continued*)

½ cup granulated sugar
1 pound solid vegetable shortening
½ cup confectioners' sugar

Place the flour in a mound on a pasta board and make a well in it. Put the eggs, oil, rum, salt, and sugar in the well, then mix the ingredients in the well together with a fork, working outward little by little to absorb almost all the flour.

Knead the dough until very smooth (15 to 20 minutes), then cover with a cotton dishtowel for 1 hour.

With a rolling pin, roll the dough out to a sheet ⅛ inch thick, then cut into rectangles, 1 inch wide and 2 inches long, with a pastry wheel.

Melt the solid vegetable shortening in a deep-fryer; prepare a serving dish by lining it with paper towels.

When the shortening is very hot, place the rectangles, a few at a time, in it to fry. When golden brown on both sides (about 1 minute), place them on the prepared serving dish to drain.

When all the *cenci* are cooked and placed on the dish, remove the paper towel and sprinkle confectioners' sugar over generously. Serve hot.

Tortelli Dolci
(Dessert Tortelli)   (SERVES 6)

Like *cenci* (see page 457), *tortelli dolci* are made with pasta dough and deep-fried. They are now eaten as a dessert, but centuries ago, before the distinction was made between "salted" and "sweet" dishes, many kinds of pasta, even lasagne, were eaten sweet, first with honey, later with sugar. Many so-called "sweet and sour" dishes are holdovers from that time.

These are real *tortelli*, filled with a ricotta sweetened and flavored with rum. They are flamed, again with rum, and lightly sprinkled with sugar.

For the filling

1½ ounces raisins
½ cup rum
7 ounces ricotta

> 2 egg yolks
> 1 ½ tablespoons granulated sugar

For the pasta

> 2 cups all-purpose flour, preferably unbleached
> 2 "extra-large" eggs
> 2 teaspoons olive or other vegetable oil
> Pinch of salt

Plus

> 1 pound solid vegetable shortening
> ½ cup sugar
> ¼ cup rum

Make the filling first. In a small bowl, soak the raisins in the rum for 20 minutes.

Meanwhile, place the ricotta in a large bowl and add the egg yolks and sugar. Mix thoroughly with a wooden spoon, then add the soaked raisins to the ricotta and combine thoroughly.

Make fresh pasta, using the ingredients in the quantities listed, according to the directions on page 133, then form into *tortelli* as directed on page 162, using the stuffing you have just made.

Heat the solid vegetable shortening in a deep-fat fryer; prepare a serving dish by lining it with paper towels.

When the shortening is hot, put in the *tortelli*, a few at a time, and cook until golden brown on both sides (about 1 minute a side), then remove the *tortelli* with a strainer-skimmer and place them on the prepared serving dish to drain.

Repeat the procedure until all the *tortelli* are cooked and on the dish, then remove the paper towels from the bottom of the dish and sprinkle the *tortelli* with the additional sugar.

In small saucepan, warm the ¼ cup rum on a very low flame for 30 seconds. Pour over the *tortelli*, flame immediately, and serve.

Brigidini
(Stamped Pastries)   (M A K E S   A B O U T   2 0)

The traditional Florentine fairs are held in the great piazzas. Each piazza has its own fair once a year, called by such picturesque names as "fair of the jealous ones," "fair of those in love," "fair of the birds," and so on. The stands that are set up sell many things, among them always the wafers called "*brigidini*," made with a *schiaccia*, a type of waffle iron. The villagers of a little place called Lamporecchio make the most celebrated *brigidini*, and they set up stands at every fair to sell them. See photo on page 502.

Brigidini: 1. Placing the ball of dough in the center of the *schiaccia*.

The *schiaccia* must be well seasoned with oil, and after use, oiled again and wiped clean with paper towels. It may be placed on an ordinary stove for cooking. Directions are also given for preparing *brigidini* without the *schiaccia*.

    3 teaspoons aniseed
    1 tablespoon olive oil
    2 cups all-purpose flour
    2 eggs
   10 tablespoons sugar
      Pinch of salt

Grind the aniseed coarsely with mortar and pestle or blender. If the blender requires liquid, put in the olive oil now and be careful not to grind the aniseed too fine.

Place the flour in a mound on a pasta board and make a well in it, then place in it the eggs, sugar, salt, ground aniseeds, and oil if not already used. Using a wooden spoon, mix all ingredients together with the flour until they are completely amalgamated.

Knead the dough for 2 or 3 minutes, then divide into balls of about ½ inch in diameter.

Place the *schiaccia* on the flame for 5 minutes. Then open the *schiaccia*, place one ball of dough in the center (see photo 1), and close tightly.

Place the *schiaccia*, with the piece of dough inside, on the flame and let stand for about 30 seconds on each side, then remove the *schiaccia* from the flame, open it (see photo 2), and remove the *brigidino*. Put the wafer into a bowl or serving dish.

2. Opening the *schiaccia* to reveal the finished *brigidini*.

Repeat the procedure for all the balls of dough.

If you don't have a *schiaccia*, roll out each ball of dough into a thin layer with rolling pin. Cut out the dough, using a cookie cutter of any desired shape. Oil an aluminum cookie sheet; preheat the oven to 375°. Place the cookie shapes on the cookie sheet and place it in the preheated oven for about 15 minutes, until golden brown and crisp, then remove from oven and transfer the *brigidini* into bowl or serving dish. Let them cool for about 2 hours.

Note: If kept in a closed jar, *brigidini* may last as long as two weeks without losing any flavor.

Biscotti di Prato
(Little Almond Cookies)   (SERVES 8 TO 10)

The favorite "cookie" of Tuscany, and very well known through-out Italy. It is an almond cookie, with the nuts both ground up in the dough and left in large pieces throughout. The best ones are made in the lively commercial town of Prato, ten miles from Florence. It was Prato's Datini who is reputed to have invented the invoice in the fourteenth century. His letters also reveal him to have been a great *buongustaio* (gourmet).

Biscotti di prato are almost always served with one of the two sweet wines of Tuscany, Vin Santo or Aleatico. They are most often dipped into the wine (see photo, page 464). This combination may be dessert after a very rustic meal, but is most often served to guests who come in the afternoon or after dinner.

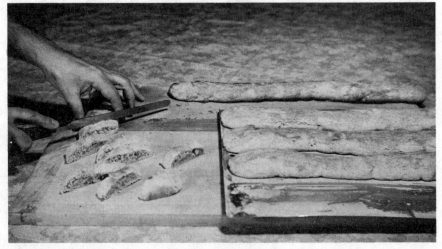

Biscotti di prato: 1. Cutting the baked almond rolls, at a 45-degree angle, into cookies.

2 ounces blanched almonds
6 ounces unblanched almonds
4 cups all-purpose flour
2 cups granulated sugar
4 eggs
  Pinch of salt
  Pinch of saffron
  Scant teaspoon baking soda
1 egg white

Preheat the oven to 375°.

Place both the blanched and unblanched almonds on an aluminum cookie sheet and toast in the preheated oven for 15 minutes, until lightly golden brown.

Grind 2 ounces of mixed blanched and unblanched toasted almonds very fine, then cut the remaining toasted almonds in two or three pieces.

Place the flour on a pasta board in a mound and make a well in the center. Put the sugar and eggs in the well. Mix together well, then add the salt, saffron, and baking soda. Mix thoroughly and when all the ingredients in the well are well integrated, incorporate the flour little by little, until all but about 2 tablespoons is incorporated. Set the leftover flour aside.

Knead the dough for 10 to 15 minutes, then add the very finely ground almonds and the almond pieces. Knead for 2 or 3 minutes more, incorporating the remaining flour.

Preheat the oven to 375°.

Divide the dough into 8 pieces. With your hands, shape each piece into a long, thin roll about ¾ inch in diameter, then place, widely apart, on a buttered and floured cookie sheet. Beat the egg white slightly in a small bowl and lightly coat the tops of the 8 rolls with it, using a pastry brush, then put the baking sheet in the preheated oven for 18 to 20 minutes.

Remove the rolls from oven (they will have expanded in size sideways) and cut with a long slicing knife at a 45 degree angle every ¾ inch (see photo 1) to get the shape required for this type of little cookie, or *biscotto*. Place the *biscotto* back in the oven, this time at 275°, for 35 to 40 minutes. They will be very dry.

Remove from the oven and let cool.

Note: These cookies are much better eaten after 2 or 3 days, when they have softened a little; keep them in a paper bag. If you wish to keep them indefinitely, transfer after a week to a jar or can.

2. The usual way of eating them, dipped in a Tuscan dessert wine such as Aleatico or Vin Santo.

Amaretti
(Bitter Almond Cookies)   (MAKES ABOUT 30)

Already packaged *amaretti* are widely available, imported from Italy; the Lazzaroni brand is particularly good. However, any packaged commercial product cannot be as authentic as the real thing, freshly made at home. Try to find bitter almonds (see page 21; you will probably have the best luck at a Hungarian store); a very small quantity goes a long way. And try these homemade *amaretti*, made almost totally from ground almonds, both sweet and bitter, and then you will know the difference.

        10 ounces sweet almonds
         1 ounce bitter almonds
      1½ cups granulated sugar
         1 heaping tablespoon confectioners' sugar
         5 egg whites

Mix the sweet and bitter almonds together; preheat the oven to 375°.

Place a saucepan containing 2½ cups of cold water on the heat. When the water reaches the boiling point, put the almonds into the saucepan and let them cook for 30 seconds. Quickly drain the almonds in a wire strainer, then cool them under cold running water.

Peel the almonds by pulling skin off between two fingers, then dry with paper towels and transfer onto a sheet of aluminum foil. Place the foil containing the almonds in preheated oven for 2 minutes, then remove from the oven and let cool for about 15 minutes.

Place the almonds, 1¼ cups granulated sugar, and confectioners' sugar in a mortar (or blender or food processor) and grind everything very fine, then transfer to bowl. Add the egg whites to the bowl and mix very well with a wooden spoon until a homogenous paste results.

Lightly oil and flour a cookie sheet.

Fill a pastry bag with the paste, and by pushing the end of the funnel, make balls, 1 inch in diameter, on the cookie sheet. Sprinkle a little of the remaining sugar on top of each ball and place the cookie sheet in the 375° oven for 20 minutes.

Remove the sheet from the oven and carefully detach the *amaretti*. Place the *amaretti* in a bowl and let them cool completely (about 1 hour).

Note: Amaretti can keep for months in a closed jar. However, do not place them in the jar until they are completely cold.

Ritortelli Pieni alla Fiorentina
(Renaissance Egg Crespelle)   (M A K E S   1 0)

Crespelle or *crespe* appear in Renaissance cookbooks in many forms. Some batters use more flour, others more eggs. This favorite type of the sixteenth century uses mainly eggs and is flavored with orange, like the later French crêpes Suzettes. Italians are not as fond of cooking with distilled liqueurs as the French, though in the period of this recipe no one was doing it yet. Instead the dried grapes are soaked in an orange sauce, which thickens naturally. After the *ritortelli* are stuffed, the orange sauce is put over them and they are briefly baked.

Crêpes have their counterpart in a number of countries. Whether the French ones did indeed come from the simple folk of Brittany or whether their court imported them from Italy, we leave for you to ponder.

4 sweet oranges
4 ounces raisins
¼ cup granulated sugar
1 scant teaspoon ground cinnamon
4 tablespoons (½ stick) butter
4 "extra-large" eggs
2 tablespoons milk
Pinch of salt
1 tablespoon all-purpose flour

Squeeze the oranges into a bowl. Add the raisins to the juice, along with the sugar and cinnamon, and let soak for 40 to 50 minutes. Meanwhile, melt the butter in a saucepan and remove it from the flame.

Place eggs, milk, and salt in a second bowl and beat well with fork. Mix in the flour slowly, being careful to prevent lumps from forming. Let rest for 10 to 15 minutes in a cool place.

Lay out a sheet of aluminum foil; preheat the oven to 375°.

When you are ready to make the *crespelle*, brush an omelet pan 8½ inches in diameter with melted butter and prepare to work quickly.

Place the pan on a low flame. Put about 3 tablespoons of the batter in a ladle, and when the pan is hot, pour batter into the pan and very quickly swirl it around until the bottom of the pan is covered. As the batter sets, shake the pan vigorously to keep the bottom of the *crespella* detached from the pan. All this happens very quickly, and after 40 seconds it should be firm enough to turn. Shake the *crespella* over the edge of the pan so, with finger and thumb of both hands, you can quickly turn it over. Cook other side for only 5 seconds, then slip the *crespella* out onto the aluminum foil.

In a similar manner, make the remaining 9 *crespelle* and stack them on top of the first.

Butter a rectangular Pyrex baking dish (13½ x 8¾ inches). Place one *crespella* on a plate. At one end put a tablespoon of the orange-raisin mixture, then roll the *crespella* up around the filling and put it in the baking dish. Repeat the procedure until all the *crespelle* are in baking dish.

Pour the remaining orange-raisin mixture over the *crespelle* and place the dish in the preheated oven for about 18 minutes. Remove the dish from the oven and serve immediately from the same dish.

Frittelle di Tondone alla Fiorentina
(Pancake Fritters) (SERVES 6)

Unusual "fritters" made by first cooking a large pancake, and then making a batter by crushing the cooked pancake. The *frittelle* that result are light and fluffy on the inside and really very good.

        6 ounces raisins
    1 ½ cups all-purpose flour
        1 cup of cold water
          Pinch of salt
        2 tablespoons butter
          Grated peel of 1 lemon
        7 eggs
        1 pound solid vegetable shortening
        1 cup granulated sugar

Soak the raisins in lukewarm water for 20 minutes.

Meanwhile, make a batter by placing the flour in a bowl and making a well in it. Pour in the cold water little by little, stirring constantly with a wooden spoon, then stir until the batter is smooth, without lumps. Add a pinch of salt.

Melt the butter in a 12½-inch omelet pan on a medium flame. When the melted butter is hot, pour in the batter all at once. A high pancake will form; turn it over when still a very light color and cook other side only for 30 seconds.

Place the pancake (*tondone*) in a mortar (or electric mixer) and break it up until it becomes a soft and homogeneous dough. Remove the dough from the mortar (or electric mixer) and place it in a large bowl.

Sprinkle the lemon peel over the dough in the bowl, then add 2 of the eggs and mix them in very well with a wooden spoon, until they are completely incorporated. Drain the raisins and dry them with paper towels. Add them to the bowl and mix them into the dough, then let the dough rest for 15 to 20 minutes.

Separate the remaining 5 eggs. Place the egg yolks over the dough and put the egg whites in another bowl and beat them stiff. With a wooden spoon, incorporate the egg yolks very carefully into the dough; then, very gently, fold in the egg whites.

Heat the solid vegetable shortening in a deep-fat fryer; prepare a serving dish by lining it with paper towels to absorb excess grease. When the shortening is hot, make separate little *frittelle* by placing a tablespoon at a time of dough in the pan, each one well separated from the others. Cook the *frittelle* until golden brown on both sides, then remove to the prepared serving dish to drain.

When all *frittelle* are cooked and transferred to the serving dish, remove the paper towels. Sprinkle the *frittelle* with sugar and serve hot.

Meringhe alla Panna
(Meringues with Whipped Cream)   (SERVES 6)

Meringues appear in the fourteenth century dish *pinocchiati*, in which they are baked, flavored with a few pignoli and orange or lemon. The principle is almost certainly a Florentine discovery.

In this more modern dish, the baked meringues are filled with a light whipped cream. A versatile dessert, and easier to make than the finished product might seem.

    3 very fresh egg whites, at room temperature
    7 tablespoons granulated sugar
    1 cup heavy cream
    3 tablespoons confectioners' sugar

Beat the egg whites with a whisk until stiff, preferably in an unlined copper bowl. Add 5 tablespoons of the sugar and keep beating until very firm.

Butter and flour a baking sheet; preheat the oven to 375°.

Place the whipped egg whites in a pastry bag. Squeeze at the top to form 12 to 14 individual half-balls, 2 inches in diameter, on the baking sheet. Sprinkle over 1 more tablespoon of sugar and let rest for 10 or 12 minutes. Place the baking sheet in the preheated oven for 4 or 5 minutes, then lower the oven heat to minimum and leave meringues in for 20 or 25 minutes more.

Remove the baking sheet from the oven and carefully detach the meringues with a spatula. Replace the baking sheet with the meringues detached in the oven at minimum heat for about 15 minutes more, until very crisp. Remove the meringues from the oven and let them cool (about 20 minutes).

Whip the cream with a whisk, adding the remaining tablespoon sugar and the confectioners' sugar (as directed on page 434).

When the meringues are cold, fit 2 half-balls together to make a ball. Put some whipped cream in the center between the halves, then place on a serving dish. Continue until all the meringues and whipped cream are used up, then serve.

Ricotta Fritta
(Fried Ricotta)   (SERVES 8)

Ricotta, sweetened and orange flavored, formed into little balls held together with a few egg yolks and deep-fried. Unusual, imaginative, and very good. Not difficult to make if you are sure to squeeze out the excess water from the ricotta so they don't fall apart.

15 ounces ricotta
 2 eggs plus 3 egg yolks
 2 cups all-purpose flour, approximately
 1 orange
 1 pound solid vegetable shortening
 1 cup granulated sugar, approximately

Drain ricotta very well in cheesecloth to remove all excess water. Place the drained ricotta in a bowl, along with the egg yolks and 3 tablespoons of the flour. Grate the orange peel into the bowl and mix all ingredients well with wooden spoon.

Spread the remaining flour on a sheet of aluminum foil. On the floured foil, roll the ricotta into balls 1 inch in diameter. In rolling, lightly coat the balls with flour.

In a second bowl, beat the eggs with a pinch of salt; prepare a serving dish by lining it with paper towels.

Heat the solid vegetable shortening in a deep-fat fryer. When it is hot, quickly dip the balls in the beaten eggs and then drop them into the fryer. Cook the balls until lightly golden brown all over (about 2 minutes), then remove from the fryer with a strainer-skimmer and place them on the prepared serving dish.

When all the balls are cooked and on the serving dish, remove the paper towels and sprinkle with the sugar. Serve hot.

BREAD AND CAKE DESSERTS

Buccellato alle Fragole
(Buccellato with Strawberries)

(SERVES FROM 8 TO 10)

This recipe is not simply a way of using leftover *buccellato* in Lucca. It is such an important dessert in that town that often the *buccellato* is made just in order to make this dessert. Try it, the combination is preordained.

A different fruit would never be substituted, since this is the one that blends ideally—an aspect of the Tuscan point of view that is perhaps the most difficult for Americans to understand.

See discussion of the Luccan *buccellato* on page 42.

> *Buccellato* (see page 42)
> 1½ pounds fresh strawberries
> 6 heaping tablespoons granulated sugar
> 5 cups red wine

Make the *buccellato* according to the directions on page 42. When it is ready and cold (and it is better made a day in advance), cut it into ¼ inch slices. Let the slices stand until needed.

Carefully clean the strawberries, then place them in a large bowl, along with the sugar. Mash the strawberries with a fork, amalgamating them with the sugar, then add the wine to strawberry-sugar mixture and combine thoroughly. Place the bowl in the refrigerator and let stand for 2 hours.

Make a layer of *buccellato* slices on the bottom of a large tureen, then pour over some of the strawberry mixture. Alternate layers of *buccellato* slices and strawberries until the last slice of *buccellato* is used; the top layer should be of strawberries.

Cover the tureen with a lid or aluminum foil, allow to stand for a minimum of 2 hours. Serve carefully with a spatula, keeping slices whole.

Pane co' Santi
(Sweet Bread for All Saints' Day)   (MAKES 1 LOAF)

The sweet version of the nut bread. See the discussion of bread for All Saints' Day on page 44.

For the "sponge"

> 2 ounces (4 cakes) compressed fresh yeast or 4 packages active dry yeast
> 1 cup lukewarm or hot water, depending on the yeast
> 1½ cups all-purpose flour

For the dough

> 4 ounces raisins
> 4 ounces shelled, blanched walnuts
> 1 cup olive oil
> 2 tablespoons lard
> 2 ounces blanched almonds
> 6 cups all-purpose flour
> Pinch of salt
> ½ cup granulated sugar
> Grated peel of 1 lemon
> Grated peel of ½ orange
> 1 teaspoon aniseed
> 1 teaspoon freshly ground black pepper
> ¾ cup lukewarm water

To make the "sponge," dissolve the yeast in the lukewarm or hot water. Place the flour in a bowl and make a well in center. Pour in the well-dissolved yeast and stir very well with a wooden spoon to incorporate all the flour. Cover the bowl with a cotton dishtowel and place it in a warm place, away from drafts. Let rise until doubled in size (almost 1 hour). Meanwhile, soak the raisins in lukewarm water for 20 minutes; chop the blanched walnuts coarsely.

Heat the olive oil and lard in a saucepan, on a low flame. Add the chopped walnuts and sauté very gently, then remove the pan from the flame and add the soaked raisins. Allow to cool for 10 minutes. While it is cooling, chop the blanched almonds coarsely.

When the "sponge" is ready, place the 6 cups of flour on a pasta board. Make a well in the center and place the sponge in it. To the sponge, add the lukewarm walnut-raisin mixture and stir carefully with a wooden spoon, in order to integrate the yeast and olive oil. Then mix into the sponge one by one: a pinch of salt, the sugar, grated lemon and orange peel, aniseed, coarsely chopped almonds, and pepper. Add the ¾ cup lukewarm water and incorporate it with the other ingredients in the well.

Start kneading, little by little absorbing all the flour. After the flour is absorbed, keep kneading until the dough is elastic and smooth (about 15 to 20 minutes). Place dough on a buttered and floured aluminum baking sheet. Cover the dough with a cotton dishtowel and move the baking sheet and dough to a warm place, without drafts, to rise.

Preheat the oven to 400°.

When the dough has doubled in size (1 to 2 hours), place it in the preheated oven for 50 to 55 minutes.

Remove from the oven and allow to cool for about 2 hours before eating.

Schiacciata Unta di Berlingaccio
(Sweet Carnival Schiacciata)　　　　　　　　(SERVES 6)

Low like a *schiacciata*, this dessert pastry has shortening (lard) and is flavored with orange, vanilla, nutmeg, and saffron. It is this last, combined with the lard shortening, that gives it its antique flavor. A dessert for the Carnival season, it takes the name of one of the Commedia dell'Arte masks, *Berlingaccio*. It is also eaten at the big parties given on Thursday of Easter week.

> 1 ounce (2 cakes) compressed fresh yeast or 2 packages active dry yeast
> 1 cup lukewarm or hot water, depending on the yeast
> 2 cups plus 5 tablespoons all-purpose flour
> Pinch of salt
> 1 large, thick-skinned orange
> 1 teaspoon saffron
> 2 or 3 drops vanilla extract
> Pinch of freshly grated nutmeg
> 2 eggs
> ⅔ cup sugar
> 6 ounces lard

In a small bowl, dissolve the yeast in the lukewarm or hot water. Put the 2 cups of flour in a large bowl. Make a well in the center and put in the dissolved yeast, along with a pinch of salt. Stir the yeast mixture with a wooden spoon, gradually incorporating half of the surrounding flour.

Cover the bowl with a cotton dishtowel and let rest in a warm place, until the "sponge" is doubled in size (about 1 hour). While the sponge is rising, grate the orange peel into another small bowl. Add the saffron, vanilla, nutmeg, eggs, and sugar and mix very well with a wooden spoon.

Melt all but 1 tablespoon of the lard in a saucepan, then remove from the flame and let stand for 10 to 12 minutes, until lukewarm.

When the sponge has risen, add the orange-peel–saffron mixture to it and stir with a wooden spoon until well amalgamated. Add the lukewarm lard and keep stirring, using a motion pushing up from the bottom rather than a rotary one. Incorporate all the flour remaining in the bowl.

Add the 5 tablespoons of additional flour, one by one, incorporating each before adding the next. Continue to mix, using the motion described above, for 10 minutes more. The "dough" will have the consistency of a very thick batter.

Grease a jelly-roll pan with remaining tablespoon of lard. Pour the dough into the pan, cover with a cotton dishtowel and let rise until almost doubled in size (about 1 hour).

Preheat the oven to 400°.

When the dough has risen, place the pan in preheated oven for 35 to 40 minutes, then remove from the oven and allow to cool. Sprinkle with confectioners' sugar and serve.

Schiacciata con Zibibbo
(Schiacciata with Raisins) (SERVES 6 TO 8)

This is a winter version of the *schiacciata* made with the fresh grapes of the Chianti harvest. I have not succeeded in finding wine grapes in America that have a flavor close enough to reproduce the dish successfully. However, the large Muscat raisin from California is close enough to the *zibibbo*, the raisin made from a type of large grape in Italy, to successfully reproduce this winter version.

It is also like a distant dessert relative of *pan di ramerino* (see page 40), because of the olive oil and rosemary.

> 6 ounces seedless raisins, large ones if possible
> 1 ounce (2 cakes) compressed fresh yeast or 2 packages active dry yeast
> ½ cup lukewarm or hot water, depending on the yeast
> 3½ cups all-purpose flour
> ½ cup olive oil
> 4 tablespoons lard
> 2 tablespoons rosemary leaves
> ⅔ cup granulated sugar
> 1 egg

Soak the raisins in lukewarm water for 20 minutes. Meanwhile, dissolve the yeast in the ½ cup lukewarm or hot water.

Place the flour in a large bowl and make a well in it. Pour the dissolved yeast into the well and mix with a wooden spoon until about one-third of the flour is incorporated into the yeast mixture. Cover the bowl with a cotton dishtowel and let stand until the "sponge" has doubled in size (about 1 hour).

Meanwhile, drain the raisins and pat them dry with paper towels. Place the olive oil and lard in a saucepan, along with the rosemary leaves, and sauté very gently for 8 or 9 minutes, then remove the pan from the heat and let cool for 10 or 12 minutes.

When the sponge is doubled in size, pour half the contents of the saucepan, still lukewarm, over the sponge then add ⅓ cup of the sugar, the egg, and all of the raisins. Stir everything into the sponge with a wooden spoon, then incorporate all the flour but 2 or 3 tablespoons.

Transfer the dough to a pasta board and knead until the remaining flour is incorporated and the dough is smooth (about 15 minutes).

Oil a jelly-roll pan (17⅞ x 12⅞ inches). Place the dough on pan and spread it out with your fingers to cover the surface. Pour the remaining contents of the saucepan over dough and sprinkle with the remaining sugar.

Cover the pan with a cotton dishtowel and let rest until the dough has doubled in size (about 1½ hours).

Preheat the oven to 400°.

When the dough has risen, bake in the preheated oven for 35 or 40 minutes, until the top is golden brown.

Remove from oven and serve, hot or cold, from the same jelly-roll pan.

Torta di Mele
(Apple Cake)   (SERVES 6)

An apple cake, with half of the apples incorporated into the dough and the other half thinly sliced and arranged on top, a cake for family occasions, not very difficult to make. (A more complicated version, with pastry, called *crostata di mele* is served on more formal occasions.)

Generally in Italy, Delicious– and Golden Delicious–type apples are used. However, I have tried this with American Macintosh, which do not exist in Italy, and find the result outstanding, even better than the original.

½   cup raisins
4   tablespoons lard
5   medium-sized Macintosh apples
     Juice of ½ lemon
1½ cups all-purpose flour
1   ounce (2 cakes) compressed fresh yeast or 2 packages active dry yeast
¼   cup lukewarm or hot water, depending on the yeast
⅔   cup granulated sugar
     Grated rind of 1 lemon
2   eggs

Soak raisins in lukewarm water for 20 minutes; melt the lard in a saucepan and let cool.

Cut the apples in quarters and remove the cores and skin, then cut them into thin slices. Place the apple slices in a bowl and sprinkle the lemon juice over them.

Place 1 cup of the flour in a bowl and make a well in it. Dissolve the yeast in the ¼ cup of lukewarm or hot water and pour it into the well; stir with a wooden spoon. Add the sugar, melted lard, grated lemon peel, and eggs, and when these ingredients are all well incorporated, sprinkle the remaining ½ cup of flour over. Stir very well until dough is homogeneous and very soft, then add the soaked raisins and half of the apple slices to the dough, incorporating them well.

Oil a cake mold or 12-inch springform. Place the dough in the mold and arrange the remaining apple slices on top. Cover with a cotton dishtowel and leave to rise until the dough is almost doubled in size.

Preheat the oven to 400°.

When the dough has risen, place the mold in the preheated oven for 35 to 40 minutes, until the top is golden brown. Let cool for 30 minutes, then unmold and serve.

Dolce di Polenta
(Corn-meal Cake)   (SERVES 6)

A sweet cake of corn meal, lightly flavored with saffron and white wine, the outside covered with confectioners' sugar. It has the shape of a long, serrated jelly mold. Appropriate for the cooler season.

    8 tablespoons (1 stick) butter
    1 cup all-purpose flour
    ¾ cup corn meal (*farina gialla*)
    ½ cup granulated sugar
    1 egg yolk
      Pinch of saffron
    1 cup dry white wine
    ½ cup bread crumbs, preferably homemade (see page 45)
    ½ cup confectioners' sugar

Melt 6 tablespoons of the butter in a saucepan and let cool for 10 to 12 minutes.

Mix the flour and corn meal in a bowl with a wooden spoon. Make a well in the center, then place the sugar and melted butter in it and stir very well, incorporating the sugar into the butter but not the flour mixture. Add the egg yolk and saffron to the sugar and butter, then begin incorporating the flour mixture little by little, at the same time adding the wine, a little at a time.

When all the ingredients are well combined, stir for 10 to 12 minutes more in order to have a very soft dough.

Coat a serrated jelly mold (4 x 7 x 2½ inches) with the remaining butter and the bread crumbs; preheat the oven to 375°. Pour the dough mixture in the prepared mold and bake in the preheated oven for about 1 hour 20 minutes. (If the top of the cake appears to be browning too quickly, place a piece of aluminum foil over the top.) Remove from the oven, let rest for 10 minutes, then unmold on a serving dish.

Sprinkle the confectioners' sugar over the cake and let it rest until completely cold.

Note: This cake is even better eaten the following day.

CHESTNUT AND CHESTNUT-FLOUR DESSERTS

ITALY IS a great land for chestnuts. Indeed, many of the chestnuts we find in America are imported from there. Even the particular excellence of the wild mushrooms found in Tuscany comes from their growing under chestnut trees. The mountainous area known as Garfagnana uses the flour of chestnuts for many dishes, including those which would ordinarily use polenta and other flours. Naturally, many chestnut and chestnut-flour desserts come from Tuscany and the Garfagnana.

The fall is the best period for chestnuts, and that is when they are imported from Italy. The shipment of chestnut flour arrives in the Italian markets in America a little before the Christmas holidays. There is usually only one shipment a year, so it is best to buy enough for the entire winter and spring. The flour keeps until the summer.

The desserts made from chestnuts or chestnut flour (*farina dolce*) are hearty ones, and are most appropriate to cooler weather.

Following are recipes for flamed roasted chestnuts, a low cake of chestnut flour, chestnut "truffles," and *crespelle*, or crêpes, of chestnut flour.

Note: Be sure to obtain Italian flour, made from fresh chestnuts. Some countries, such as Hungary, make flour from dried chestnuts, and the result is very different.

Bruciate Ubriache
(Burned, Drunken Chestnuts)   (SERVES 4)

Bruciate ubriache, "burned, drunken chestnuts," describes the dish with Tuscan humor. The chestnuts are roasted in a special pan (see photo), then peeled and flamed with sugar and rum. They

Bruciate ubriache: The pan used for roasting chestnuts.

could be served as dessert for a hearty dinner, either simple or elegant. They would go well after a good roast.

    1 pound fresh chestnuts
    ¼ cup granulated sugar
    ½ cup rum

Make a small cut, lengthwise, on each individual chestnut, then place them in a perforated pan. Set the pan on a low flame (charcoal or gas), and shaking the pan frequently by the handle, roast the chestnuts. This will take about 40 minutes; the chestnuts should be soft inside and the outside shell lightly burned all over.

Remove the shells from chestnuts and place them in an ovenproof serving dish. Add the sugar to the chestnuts and mix together. (If you do not use them immediately, cover the chestnuts with a cotton dishtowel and a woolen cloth—in Italy, a piece of bedspread is used—to keep the chestnuts warm. This will prevent them from drying out.)

At the moment you are ready to serve the *bruciate*, warm rum for 30 seconds on low flame. Remove the cover from the chestnuts and bring the serving dish to the table.

Pour the rum over the chestnuts and flame it. While the rum is

burning, stir the chestnuts so that all the sugar is flamed, and as soon
as the flame burns out, serve immediately.

Castagnaccio or *Migliaccio*
(Flat Chestnut Cake) (SERVES 6)

A low cake made of chestnut flour, this most typical Florentine
sweet is found in the earliest cookbooks, those of the fourteenth century. Flavored with olive oil, rosemary, raisins, and nuts, it makes a
perfect hearty snack or the ending to a rustic meal. To this day it is
one of the most widely appreciated Florentine specialties. Until recently, *castagnaccio* slices were sold on street corners, from a large
copper pan.

    3 tablespoons raisins
    ½ cup lukewarm milk
    2 cups plus 2 tablespoons chestnut flour
    1 tablespoon granulated sugar
      Pinch of salt
    2 tablespoons pignoli (pine nuts) or walnuts
    2 cups cold milk
    3 tablespoons olive oil
    1 tablespoon rosemary leaves

In small bowl, soak the raisins in the lukewarm milk for 20 minutes.
Sift all but 1 tablespoon of the chestnut flour into a large bowl. Add
the sugar, a pinch of salt, and the pignoli or walnuts. (If you use walnuts, cut them into pieces.) Mix very well with a wooden spoon, then
add the 2 cups of milk little by little, stirring constantly and being
careful to avoid lumps.

Drain the raisins and flour them with 1 tablespoon chestnut flour.
Add the raisins to bowl, along with 1 tablespoon of the olive oil, and
mix very well until smooth.

Oil a round baking pan, preferably tin-lined copper, 9½ inches
in diameter and 3 inches high, with the entire second tablespoon of
olive oil (do not remove the excess oil from the pan); preheat the
oven to 425°.

Pour the contents of the bowl into the prepared pan and sprinkle
the remaining tablespoon of olive oil and the rosemary leaves over.

Place the pan in the preheated oven for 40 to 50 minutes. (If you are not using a copper pan, the cooking time will be about 10 minutes less.)

Remove the cake from the oven and let rest for 15 to 20 minutes before serving. Serve from the same pan, sliced in the manner of a pie.

Note: Castagnaccio can also be eaten cold, but do not keep it in the refrigerator.

Tartufi di Castagne
(Chestnut "Truffles")   (SERVES 12)

A dessert of much fantasy, useful also for a dinner of some elegance. The chestnuts are cooked and then made into a shape resembling a truffle. When rolled in chocolate powder, the resemblance is intensified. These may also be eaten as a snack.

        Pinch of salt
    2   pounds fresh chestnuts
    5   tablespoons rum
    1   cup plus 2 tablespoons unsweetened cocoa powder
    ¼   cup granulated sugar
    2   tablespoons confectioners' sugar
    4   tablespoons (½ stick) butter
    ½   cup cold milk, approximately

Place a stockpot three-quarters full of cold water on the heat. Add a pinch of salt. When the water is boiling, add the unshelled chestnuts and let boil for about 1½ hours, or until soft.

Remove the pot from the flame. Take the chestnuts out of the hot water, a few at a time, and peel them, making sure you remove both shell and inner skin.

When all the chestnuts are shelled, pass them through the ricer (or mash them in a blender) and transfer to a crockery bowl. Add the rum, 2 tablespoons cocoa powder, granulated sugar, and confectioners' sugar and mix very well.

Melt the butter and add it, hot, to the mashed chestnuts. Mix very well until all the ingredients are well incorporated. The consistency should be firm, but smooth. If not smooth enough, add some cold milk—the quantity necessary may vary from 2 tablespoons to ½ cup —and mix very well.

Spread the 1 cup of cocoa powder in a thin layer on a sheet of aluminum foil. Take 1 tablespoon at a time of mashed chestnuts and roll it into a ball on the cocoa powder. The outer coating of cocoa powder and the shape will suggest the form of a truffle.

Place "truffles" in a serving dish and let them rest for 1 hour before serving.

Crespelle di Farina Dolce
(Chestnut-Flour Crêpes) (MAKES 18)

Crespelle, or crêpes, made from chestnut flour are very good indeed, and may be served filled with a ricotta-rum filling or, for extra lightness, with just whipped cream (see note below).

> 4 ounces raisins
> ½ cup rum
>
> 2 cups plus 1 tablespoon chestnut flour
> 2 eggs plus 1 egg yolk
> Pinch of salt
> 2½ cups cold milk
>
> 15 ounces ricotta
> 4 ounces chocolate chips, preferably bittersweet
> 3 tablespoons granulated sugar
> 4 tablespoons (½ stick) butter

In a small bowl, soak the raisins in the rum for about 30 minutes.

Meanwhile, sift the flour into a bowl and make a well in it. Place the eggs and egg yolk in the well and start mixing with a wooden spoon very slowly, incorporating a little bit of flour. (Be sure that no lumps form, because it is very difficult to remove them afterward.) Add a pinch of salt and then, still mixing continuously, add the cold milk, little by little, until all the milk and flour is incorporated.

Let the batter stand for 30 minutes in a cool place; do not refrigerate.

Place the ricotta in a large bowl and add the chocolate chips and sugar. Mix very well with a wooden spoon until thoroughly combined, then drain the raisins and add them to the ricotta mixture. Mix gently until the raisins are well distributed.

Cover the bowl with aluminum foil and place it in the refrigerator until needed.

Melt the butter in a small saucepan, then remove from the heat.

Using the batter and the melted butter, make the *crespelle*, according to the directions on page 466. Place the *crespelle* on aluminum foil, stacked one on top of the other to cool. (You can prepare *crespelle* even one day in advance, keeping them in the refrigerator.) After cooling, they should be wrapped completely with aluminum foil.

Butter 2 rectangular Pyrex baking dishes (13½ x 8¾); preheat the oven to 375°.

Place 2 tablespoons of the ricotta mixture on each *crespella*, then roll it up and place it in one of the baking dishes. Repeat the procedure with all the *crespelle*.

Place the baking dishes in the preheated oven for about 10 minutes, then remove and serve immediately.

Note: You can substitute a whipped-cream and chocolate-chip filling for the ricotta mixture. In this case, do not place them in oven.

Using 1 pint heavy cream, ¼ cup granulated sugar, and 2 teaspoons confectioners' sugar, make *panna montata* as described on page 434, then mix 4 ounces chocolate chips, preferably bittersweet, throughout the whipped cream. Place 2 heaping tablespoons of the whipped cream mixture on each *crespella* and roll it up. Do not heat, but place the filled *crespelle* on a serving dish and serve.

RICE DESSERTS

WE BEGIN with the two simpler, but extremely characteristic rice desserts, *frittelle*, or rice fritters, and *budini*, or little rice cakes. The large rice custard cake is appropriate for an elaborate dinner and the *ciambella*, the large rice ring stuffed with fruit and covered with a fruit-wine sauce, is even more so. Among the soufflé-type dishes, you will also find a type of rice soufflé, the *budino di riso* (see page 490).

Recipe from an early fourteenth-century Florentine manuscript, for *crespelle* or *crespe* (crêpes). There were many kinds of early Florentine crêpes. Included in this book are recipes for *crespelle* of chestnut flour and egg *crespe* flavored with orange, called *ritortelli alla fiorentina*.

Budini di Riso
(Rice Cakes)   (MAKES 16 TO 18)

Little baked rice cakes, eaten mainly for breakfast or the eleven o'clock morning coffee break. In the cafés, they are delivered still warm, as that is the best way to eat them. At home, they would go very well for a brunch or ambitious breakfast, made shortly in advance so that they remain warm but not hot. Florentines I know who are resident abroad miss most, along with Brunelleschi's dome of the Cathedral and the many bells of Florence, the *budini di riso*.

When in Florence, have a *cappuccino* with *budini* at Donnini's café in the central Piazza della Repubblica.

    3 cups milk
    ½ cup raw rice, preferably Italian Arborio
       Pinch of salt
       Scant ½ cup sugar
    4 tablespoons (½ stick) butter
    ½ cup mixed glacéed fruit
    1 thick-skinned orange or 1 lemon
    2 eggs, separated
    2 tablespoons rum
    1 cup bread crumbs, preferably homemade
    ½ cup confectioners' sugar

Heat the milk to the boiling point in a flameproof casserole. Add the rice and salt and stir with a wooden spoon until the milk reaches boiling point again. Simmer for about 10 minutes, then add the sugar and butter and let simmer until the rice is almost cooked (about 7 or 8 minutes more). Add the glacéed fruit and simmer for 1 minute longer, stirring with a wooden spoon.

Remove the casserole from the flame and transfer the rice to a bowl with a strainer-skimmer. Allow the rice to cool for 1 hour. When the rice is cool, grate the orange or lemon peel into the bowl. Add the egg yolks and rum and mix very well.

Butter a 12-muffin pan (10 x 7½ inches) and coat it with the bread crumbs; preheat the oven to 375°.

Beat egg whites until stiff, then gently fold them into the rice mixture. Place a heaping tablespoon of mixture in each cup of the muffin pan, then place the muffin pan in the preheated oven for about 25 or

30 minutes. Remove the muffin pan from the oven, allow to cool for 10 minutes, then gently uncup the *budini* with a knife.

Transfer the *budini* to a serving dish, sprinkle the tops with the confectioners' sugar, and serve hot.

Frittelle di Riso
(Rice Fritters) (SERVES 6)

On March 19, the feast of San Giuseppe, every family in Florence makes *frittelle di riso*, these characteristic rice fritters. Every family has its own slight variation, and it is the custom for families to exchange their *frittelle* with others. My aunt used to exchange *frittelle* with twenty to twenty-five families and ate nothing else for all of the day of San Giuseppe. In my family, they fold in egg whites to make the *frittelle* lighter, and flavor with orange and vanilla.

For the first stage

    3 cups milk
    1 cup water
    1 cup raw rice, preferably Italian Arborio
      Pinch of salt
    2 tablespoons butter
    2 or 3 drops vanilla extract
      Scant ½ cup granulated sugar

For the second stage (*next morning or 5 or 6 hours later*)

    4 egg yolks
    1 thick-skinned orange
    2 egg whites
    2 pounds solid vegetable shortening
    ¾ cup confectioners' sugar

Put the milk and water in a flameproof casserole. Add the rice and salt and set the casserole on the heat. Stir continuously with a wooden spoon until the contents reach the boiling point, then add the butter, vanilla, and sugar. Let simmer very slowly, until the rice is soft and has absorbed almost all the liquid.

Remove the casserole from flame and let rest for 10 to 15 minutes, then transfer the contents of the casserole to a colander and let stand overnight (or a minimum of 5 to 6 hours) to drain completely and to thicken.

The next day (or 5 to 6 hours later), transfer the rice to large bowl, add the egg yolks, and mix very well. Grate the orange peel into the bowl and mix thoroughly, then beat the egg whites until stiff and fold into the rice. Prepare a serving dish by lining it with paper towels.

Heat the solid vegetable shortening in a deep-fryer.

When the shortening is hot, make separate little *frittelle* by placing heaping tablespoons of the rice mixture in the pan, each one well separated from the others. Cook the *frittelle* until golden brown on both sides, then remove with a strainer-skimmer to the prepared serving dish to drain.

When all the *frittelle* are cooked and on the serving dish, remove the paper towels and sprinkle over with the confectioners' sugar. Serve hot.

Torta di Riso uso Garfagnana
(Rice Custard Cake)   (SERVES 6 TO 8)

One of the ambitious rice desserts. A large rice cake, incorporating the technique for *latte alla portoghese* (see page 437) and flavored with Marsala. It is a specialty of the area of the marble quarries near Carrara, where white marble has been quarried since Roman times, scarcely making a dent in the huge marble mountains. These white mountains are among the great sights of Italy; the stone of Michelangelo's sculpture comes from there. Did Michelangelo eat this dessert while he was collecting stone for the monument of Julius II?

> 1 scant cup raw rice, preferably Italian Arborio
>   Pinch of salt
> 5 eggs
> 9 tablespoons plus 1 cup granulated sugar
> ½ cup dry Marsala
> 1 tablespoon confectioners' sugar
> 1½ cups cold milk
>   Grated peel of a medium-sized orange or lemon
> 3 or 4 drops vanilla extract

Put the rice in a saucepan containing 6 cups of cold water and a pinch of salt. Place the pan on a medium flame and keep stirring with a wooden spoon until the water reaches the boiling point, then stop stirring and let the rice half cook (about 10 or 12 minutes). Remove the saucepan from the flame, drain the rice, and cool it under cold running water. Leave the rice in the colander.

Place the eggs in a bowl with the 9 tablespoons sugar and beat with a wooden spoon. When the eggs change color, turning almost white, add the Marsala, confectioners' sugar, cold milk, grated orange or lemon peel, and vanilla. Stir very well until all ingredients are well combined.

Put the 1 cup sugar in a heavy saucepan and place on a very low flame. Let the sugar caramelize very slowly. (See pages 437–8 for procedure.) When golden brown, quickly pour it into a loaf pan (9 x 5 x 2¾ inches) and move it around so the pan is lined completely. Let rest until cold (about 15 minutes).

Preheat the oven to 350°.

Transfer the rice from the colander to the bowl containing the other ingredients. Mix thoroughly, then pour all the contents of the bowl into the prepared pan. Place pan in the preheated oven for 1½ hours.

Remove the pan from the oven and let rest until cool (about 1 hour), then cover the pan completely with aluminum foil and place it in the refrigerator for at least 5 hours.

Unmold on a serving dish and serve.

Ciambella di Frutta
(Rice Ring Stuffed with Fruit)   (S E R V E S   8)

A beautiful presentation with its rice crust, the sauce making a rich color, the drama of flaming when serving it. It is also a versatile dish, because with fresh fruit it is a fine dish for summer, and with dried fruit it works well for winter.

It is also useful as a strong dessert course for dinners that have elaborate but light first and second courses.

For the rice ring
    3 cups milk
    1 cup raw rice, preferably Italian Arborio   (*continued*)

    1 small piece vanilla bean
    Pinch of salt
    1 tablespoon butter
    1 large, thick-skinned orange
    2 eggs plus 1 egg yolk
    3 tablespoons granulated sugar

For the filling

    6 medium-sized ripe plums
    3 ripe peaches
    2 ounces raisins
    4 tablespoons granulated sugar
    4 or 5 small pieces lemon peel
    ¼ cup red wine
    1 medium-sized orange

Plus

    ¼ cup granulated sugar
    ¼ cup of rum

Put the milk and rice in a flameproof casserole, along with the vanilla bean and salt. Place the casserole on a medium flame and stir with wooden spoon until it reaches the boiling point. Add the butter, stir for 1 minute more, and then simmer very slowly until the rice is half cooked (about 10 or 12 minutes). Remove the casserole from flame, let rest for 10 minutes, then drain rice in a colander. Leave rice in colander until cold (about 30 to 35 minutes).

Start the stuffing. Remove the stones from the plums and peaches and cut them into quarters. Place the fruit pieces in a second flameproof casserole with the raisins, sugar, lemon peel, and wine. Place the casserole on medium heat and simmer very gently for 15 minutes.

Cut the orange into very thin slices (with the peel) and add to the casserole. Simmer for 15 minutes more, then remove the casserole from the flame and let rest until cool (about 20 minutes).

Butter a tube pan and coat it with about ¼ cup sugar; preheat the oven to 400°.

Transfer the rice to a large bowl, removing the vanilla bean. Grate the orange peel into the bowl, then add the eggs, egg yolk, and sugar. Mix very well with a wooden spoon until all ingredients are well amalgamated, then arrange three-quarters of the rice mixture around the bottom and sides of the prepared tube pan. Fill the cavity with fruit, but no juice.

Cover the fruit completely with the remaining rice and smooth with a small spatula. Sprinkle with a little sugar, then place the tube pan in a large roasting pan. Pour 4 or 5 cups of cold water into the roasting pan in order to improvise an oversized *bagno maria* (bain-marie).

Place the *bagno maria* in the preheated oven for 45 to 50 minutes, then remove the tube pan from the *bagno maria* and let cool for 15 minutes. Unmold on a large ovenproof serving dish.

Warm the rum in a small saucepan (for 30 seconds on a low flame) and pour over the *ciambella*. Flame it and serve immediately, with the leftover fruit juice in a sauceboat.

Note: The stuffing for this *ciambella* can be done with dried fruit in winter. The technique will be the same.

Ingredients for the dried fruit stuffing:

   6 dried peach halves
  10 dried apricots
   2 ounces raisins
   4 or 5 small pieces lemon peel
   4 tablespoons granulated sugar
1½ cups red wine
   2 fresh oranges

Soak the dried fruit in lukewarm water for 20 minutes, then place in a flameproof casserole with the raisins, lemon peel, sugar, and wine. Simmer very slowly for 25 to 35 minutes. Cut the oranges into thin slices (with peel), place them in casserole and simmer for 10 minutes more.

Then proceed with the rest of the recipe.

THE DESSERT BUDINO

THESE *budini* share with *sformati* the soufflé-like principle of folding in egg whites to make the mixture rise when baked. They are, of course, extremely light. Both types are completely Italian, and evidence points to this principle having traveled from Italy to France and not vice versa. Unlike the French, however, the Italians often prefer to unmold these *budini* and *sformati*, causing them to fall slightly. If you are careful, they do not fall very much. Or, if you prefer, serve them in the baking dish.

(Though the word *budino* probably derives from the same root word as the English "pudding," it usually does not connote a similar dish.)

Budino di Riso
(Rice Cake with Amaretti)   (SERVES 6 TO 8)

This is related to the *budino di ricotta*, and should not be confused with the little pastries called *budini di riso*.

The rice is cooked in milk and flavored with orange and the bitter almond taste of *amaretti*. Stiffly beaten egg whites are folded in, and when baked the dessert rises to a fine lightness.

    2½ cups milk
        Pinch of salt
    ¾   cup raw rice, preferably Italian Arborio
    1   tablespoon butter
    10 *amaretti* cookies, imported or homemade (see page 464)
    1   orange
    4   eggs, separated
    4½ tablespoons plus ¼ cup granulated sugar
    3   tablespoons all-purpose flour

Heat the milk to the boiling point in a saucepan. Add the salt and rice and stir continuously for 3 or 4 minutes with a wooden spoon. Let simmer until the rice is half cooked (10 to 12 minutes), then, stirring continuously, add the butter and let simmer until all the milk is absorbed by the rice. Place the contents of the saucepan in a large bowl and let cool (about 1 hour).

Grind the *amaretti* into crumbs in the blender and place them in a small bowl. Grate in the orange peel and mix through.

When the rice is cold, add the *amaretti* and orange peel to the rice; then mix in the egg yolks and 4½ tablespoons of sugar and stir until all ingredients are very well amalgamated. Add the flour, little by little, stirring constantly for 10 minutes.

Take a soufflé dish 8½ inches in diameter and coat it with butter and the ¼ cup sugar; preheat the oven to 400°.

Beat the egg whites until stiff and fold them very gently into the rice mixture. Pour the rice mixture into the prepared soufflé dish and bake in the preheated oven for 35 to 40 minutes.

Remove from the oven, allow to cool for 10 minutes, then unmold onto a serving dish. Serve hot or cold.

Budino di Ricotta
(Ricotta Soufflé)   (SERVES 6)

The egg whites folded into the ricotta make this dish beautifully light. If unmolded, the *budino* may remain for several days, gradually falling a bit when cold, but turning into one of the lightest of cheesecakes.

   3 tablespoons mixed glacéed fruit
   1 cup lukewarm milk
 15 ounces ricotta
   1 orange
   4 eggs
   2 tablespoons all-purpose flour
 11 tablespoons granulated sugar

Soak the glacéed fruit in a bowl containing the lukewarm milk for 20 minutes. Drain the ricotta in a piece of cheesecloth to remove excess liquid, then place in a bowl. Grate the orange peel into the ricotta. Separate 3 of the eggs and add the yolks and the remaining whole egg and mix thoroughly. When the mixture is homogenous, add the flour, 7 tablespoons of the sugar, and the drained glacéed fruit. Mix very well with a wooden spoon for 3 to 4 minutes.

Butter a soufflé dish 8½ inches in diameter, and coat it with the ¼ cup sugar; preheat the oven to 375°.

Beat the egg whites with a whisk until stiff, then very gently fold into the ricotta mixture. Pour the mixture into the prepared dish and place in the preheated oven for 45 minutes.

Remove from the oven, unmold onto a serving dish, and serve hot.

FRUIT DESSERTS

Two VERY elaborate treatments of fruit for dessert have already been given: *timballo* of pears poached in wine with whipped cream and *ciambella di frutta*, the rice ring stuffed with fruit and covered with a wine sauce. These two are for the most elaborate, most formal dinners.

A second stage, less elaborate, but still fancy is represented by the next three recipes: peaches filled with an *amaretti* stuffing, accompanied by *crema zabaione* or whipped cream; peaches filled with a stuffing of *savoiardi* (crushed, toasted ladyfingers), almonds, and bitter almonds, also possibly accompanied by one of the two creams mentioned above; pears poached in wine, preferably Chianti with a little port (this time without the *timballo*), possibly accompanied by one of the two creams.

Thirdly, we have fresh fruit in some special treatment: strawberries in red wine, preferably Chianti; fresh peaches in red wine; raspberries with whipped cream. These are probably the most favored treatments of these fruits.

In its own category is the Florentine favorite fruit dipped in batter and deep-fried. The recipe included suggests apples, pears, and strawberries. Deep-fried apple slices is another Florentine specialty adopted by the French as *beignet des pommes*.

And finally, though there is no recipe necessary, let us not forget that the most frequent way to complete a meal in Italy is with simple unadorned fresh fruit of the season. Though this would not be served at a formal dinner, it is very frequently served to family and close friends.

Pesche Ripiene
(Stuffed Peaches)   (SERVES 6)

The peaches are baked just enough so they don't lose their fresh taste. The natural flavor is also enhanced by the stuffing, which has an apricot flavor, complementing the peach taste without covering it.

> 6 large freestone peaches, ripe but not overripe
> 3 ounces *amaretti* cookies, imported or homemade (see page 464)

  6 pats butter
  ¼ cup granulated sugar
  ¼ cup brandy

Preheat the oven to 375°.

Divide the peaches in half and remove the pits. (To halve a peach and remove the pit without breaking the peach, find the line that girdles the peach and follow it in cutting through with a knife. Place each hand firmly on each of the peach halves. To loosen both halves from the pit, gently turn the two halves in opposite directions until they are free of the pit.) With a teaspoon, enlarge the holes left by the pit a little.

Butter a rectangular Pyrex baking dish (13½ x 8¾ inches) and place all 12 peach halves in it. Crush the *amaretti* into crumbs with mortar and pestle or blender, then fill the peach holes with the *amaretti* crumbs. Put half a pat of butter, then a teaspoon of sugar over each peach half.

Place the baking dish in the preheated oven for 20 minutes, then remove the dish from oven, add 1 teaspoon of brandy to each peach half, and bake for 15 to 20 minutes more.

Remove the dish from the oven and transfer the peaches to a serving dish. Let stand until completely cold; do not refrigerate.

Note: The dish may be eaten as is or with *panna montata* (see page 434) or *crema zabaione* (see page 435) or *crema pasticcera* (see page 431).

Pesche Ripiene con Mandorle
(Peaches Stuffed with Almonds)   (S E R V E S   6)

Similar to the previous treatment but with a more elaborate stuffing. Almonds and bitter almonds work extremely well in complementing the still-fresh taste of the peaches.

  ⅔ cup mixed glacéed fruit
  1 cup dry white wine
  6 large freestone peaches, ripe but not overripe
  1 lemon
 18 *savoiardi* (ladyfingers)
  4 ounces sweet almonds   (*continued*)

   1 ounce bitter almonds
  10 tablespoons granulated sugar
   1 egg yolk

Preheat the oven to 375°.

In a small bowl, soak the glacéed fruit in the wine for 1 hour; place the peaches in a large bowl of cold water with the lemon, cut into halves, and let soak until needed.

Toast the ladyfingers on aluminum foil in the preheated oven for about 15 minutes. (Italian ladyfingers are crisp. When the American ones are toasted, they have a similar texture.) Meanwhile, mix the sweet and bitter almonds together and blanch them, according to the directions on page 465.

Remove the ladyfingers from oven and let them cool (about ½ hour). While they cool, place the blanched almonds in the 375° oven, on aluminum foil, to toast for about 15 minutes. Remove the almonds from the oven and let them cool (about 15 minutes).

Place the ladyfingers in a mortar (or food processor) and grind them very fine. Transfer them to a large bowl.

Place the cooled toasted almonds in the mortar (or food processor) and grind them very fine as well. Add the ground almonds to the bowl with the ladyfingers.

Add 6 tablespoons of the sugar, glacéed fruit and its wine to the bowl, then mix all the ingredients together with a wooden spoon. Add the egg yolk to the bowl and mix thoroughly.

Remove the peaches from the water and dry with paper towels. Cut the peaches in half, removing the pits, then enlarge the holes left by the pits slightly with a teaspoon. Fill each peach half with some of the mixture in the bowl, then place the peaches in a buttered rectangular Pyrex baking dish (13½ x 8¾ inches). Sprinkle each peach half with 1 teaspoon of the remaining sugar.

Place the baking dish in the 375° oven for 35 to 40 minutes, then remove the baking dish from oven and let the peaches cool for 30 minutes.

Transfer them to serving dish to cool completely. Serve at room temperature; do not refrigerate.

Note: This dish may be accompanied by *panna montata* (see page 434) or *crema zabaione* (see page 435).

Pere al Vino
(Pears Poached in Wine)   (s e r v e s   6)

These whole pears, carefully peeled and with their long stems intact, if cooked according to the directions given will acquire a beautiful wine-red color. They make a fine presentation, simply accompanied by whipped cream or *crema zabaione* or as the contents of an elaborate *timballo* (see page 449). They should be cooked in a typically Italian wine, the finer the quality, the better. A good Chianti or Chianti Riserva will produce a really fine result.

> 6 large, firm pears, preferably Bosc, with stems
> 4 cups good-quality dry red wine
> 1 cup tawny port
> 1 cup cold water
> ½ lemon
> 6 tablespoons granulated sugar

Peel the pears with a peeler rather than a knife, then flatten the bottoms by cutting off a thin slice. Stand the pears up in a large metal casserole. (The casserole should be large enough to fit pears closely together without crowding, but not large enough to allow them to fall over.)

Add the wine, port, and water to the pears. Squeeze the half lemon and cut off a slice of peel. Add the juice and peel to the casserole, then sprinkle over with 4 tablespoons of the sugar.

Cover the casserole tightly and let simmer slowly for about 25 minutes. Test with a toothpick to be sure the pears are well cooked before removing from the flame, then leave the cooked pears in the casserole for 10 to 15 minutes to cool.

Stand cooled pears up on a serving dish. Cover the dish with aluminum foil, being careful not to bruise the pears. Place the dish in the refrigerator for an hour.

Remove the lemon peel from the casserole and transfer the sauce to a small saucepan. Add the remaining sugar and simmer again until the sauce is reduced to the consistency of a light syrup (30 to 40 minutes). Let the sauce cool for 20 to 30 minutes, then remove the pears from the refrigerator and pour the sauce over. Return the pears to the refrigerator for at least 3 hours more before serving.

Fragole al Vino Rosso
(Strawberries in Chianti Wine)   (SERVES 4)

Italians choose a "setting" for a special fruit that will best bring out the quality of that fruit. Good red wine is made for strawberries. Good Chiantis generally absorb the fragrance of flower or fruit growing nearby. Perhaps that is why they wed so well with strawberries.

    1 pound strawberries
    1 lemon
    4 cups good-quality red wine, preferably Chianti
    ½ cup granulated sugar

Clean the strawberries and wash them carefully, then dry with paper towels. Cutting the large strawberries in half, place the strawberries in a large bowl.

Squeeze the lemon over the strawberries, then add the wine and sugar to the bowl. Mix the contents of bowl very well and let rest, covered, in the refrigerator for several hours.

Serve a portion of strawberries with some of the wine in each individual bowl.

Pesche al Vino
(Peaches in Chianti Wine)   (SERVES 6)'

Of the nonberry fruits, it is fragrant fresh peaches that respond best to wine. The peaches should not be overly ripe, and should be allowed to live with the wine for some hours, to wed with it.

    6 peaches, ripe but not overripe
    1 lemon
    6 heaping tablespoons granulated sugar
    3 cups good-quality red wine, preferably Chianti

Carefully wash the peaches; do not peel them. Cut the peaches in half, removing the pits, then cut the peach halves into 6 square pieces.

Place the pieces in a plastic container. Squeeze the lemon into the container, over the peaches, then sprinkle on the sugar.

Add the wine to the container, cover, and place in the refrigerator for at least 4 hours.

Remove the container from the refrigerator, mix the contents well, and transfer them to a serving bowl. (Generally, the bowl is then placed in an improvised oversized *bagno maria* (bain-marie) prepared with ice, because *pesche al vino* should be served very cold.)

Lamponi alla Panna
(Raspberries with Whipped Cream)   (S E R V E S 4)

In Italy, June is the chief month for the incomparable wild strawberries, *fragolini di bosco*, and for soft, sweet raspberries. These delicacies should be accompanied by the soft unobtrusiveness of a light whipped cream. Wild strawberries are not given the attention they deserve in America, though very good ones grow here. But, fortunately, raspberries are available for this dessert.

    1 pound raspberries
¼ cup granulated sugar
      Panna montata (see page 434)

Clean and wash the raspberries very carefully, then dry with paper towels and let them stand on some more paper towels. Sprinkle the raspberries with a little sugar.

Make the *panna montata* according to the directions on page 434. When the whipped cream is ready, transfer it to a serving bowl. Add the raspberries a few at a time, mixing very gently. Serve immediately.

Note: You can prepare this dessert in advance, but combine the *panna montata* and raspberries only at the very last moment before serving.

Frittura Mista di Frutta
(Deep-fried Fruit in Batter)   (S E R V E S 8)

The fruit is used absolutely natural and fresh, and not marinated. It is dipped in a batter similar to that used for deep frying chicken, except that brandy replaces the wine. The folded-in egg whites lighten the batter, and keep it full of air when fried. But the nicest aspect of the dish is that the fruit tastes almost fresh after cooking. The apple version is best known, but pears are equally good. The strawberries work marvelously, and usually create a little sensation.

1½ cups all-purpose flour
      Pinch of salt
1½ tablespoons olive oil
  2 eggs, separated
  ¾ cup cold water
  2 tablespoons brandy

  2 large Delicious apples, ripe but firm
  2 large Bosc pears, ripe but firm
      Lemon juice
16 large strawberries

  2 pounds solid vegetable shortening
  1 cup granulated sugar

First prepare the batter.

Place the flour in large bowl; add the salt and mix thoroughly. Make a well in the flour and put in the oil and egg yolks, then begin stirring, adding the cold water little by little and incorporating the flour. When all the water is added and the flour incorporated, put in the brandy and stir very well for 10 minutes more.

Let the batter rest for at least 2 hours in a cool place; do not refrigerate.

Meanwhile, prepare the fruit.

Core apples and pears with an apple corer, then peel carefully and cut horizontally into slices almost ½ inch thick. Place the slices of fruit on a dish. (If you do not use fruit immediately sprinkle it with some lemon juice to keep it from turning brown.)

Remove the stems from the strawberries and wash very carefully. Dry with paper towels and let stand on the towel until needed.

When the batter is ready (after at least 2 hours of resting), beat the egg whites until stiff. Gently fold the beaten egg whites into the batter and mix carefully. Heat the solid vegetable shortening in a deep-fat fryer; prepare a large serving dish by lining it with paper towels.

When the shortening is hot, dip each piece of fruit in the batter, making sure that the fruit is completely coated with batter but that excess is removed. Place the coated fruit pieces in the pan and fry until golden brown all over (about 1 minute on each side for apples and pears and 1 minute in all for strawberries). Remove the fruit from the pan with a strainer-skimmer and place it on the prepared serving dish.

Place the sugar in a small dish. When all the fruit is cooked and placed on the serving dish, remove the paper towels and then coat the fruit pieces on both sides with sugar. Arrange them on the serving dish in the shape of a ring and serve very hot.

COFFEE

COFFEE IS always served at the end of a dinner in Italy, and it is always served black. In the north of Italy it is not accompanied by lemon peel. As previously mentioned, it is served in another room, not at the dinner table.

Anyone who has traveled in Italy has probably noticed that there is a great difference in the taste of the coffee there and what is called "espresso" in America. This has to do with both the kind of bean used and the way of roasting it.

The chief bean used in Italy is from the species called *coffea robusta,* and it is found in Africa, Madagascar, India, Southeast Asia, and Java. It is roasted very slowly, at temperatures even less than that used for ordinary American coffee. It acquires a color and flavor very different from what is called "Italian roast" in America. It is brown rather than black in color. From the taste I would guess that it is roasted both longer and at lower temperatures than the American "Italian roast," and is a mixture of beans of different origin. Certainly it should not have the bitterness one often finds in espresso in America.

If you have access to a store that sells a variety of coffee beans, I would suggest a mixture of 50 percent Java beans and 50 percent another bean, brown rather than black roast.*

The best espresso is made with a large machine that has strong

* An authentically Italian commercial coffee in cans has begun to be imported recently, produced by Motta.

A mixture of two kinds of coffee beans (see page 499). In the background is a pan used for roasting green coffee beans at home.

steam pressure, so that the water passing through the coffee always remains boiling. The closest home machine to this is the Moka type of pot (see photo, page 457) because it also uses the same technique. The reason I do not recommend the Neopolitan type of pot is because when it is turned, though the first water passing through is boiling, it cools down considerably by the time the last water passes through. And it is only boiling water that can draw the essence, the *crema*, out of the coffee to produce the best possible flavor.

Coffee originated in Ethiopia, where it grows wild at high altitudes. It was introduced into Europe by the Venetians in the fifteenth century and into South America, where it is not native, in 1723. It was in the eighteenth century that the real coffee rage started; the first café in Paris was founded around 1700 by the Florentine, Procopio.

Making Coffee with the Moka Machine

Fill the detachable bottom half with cold water up to the level of what looks like a little screw on the outside of the pot.

After the beans have been freshly ground, fill the coffee holder loosely without pressing down on the coffee.

From the very beginning, keep the pot on a low flame. The pressure will force the water up through the coffee into the upper half. Because the water must travel up, it requires a consistently high temperature to produce the pressure, keeping the water boiling hot even at the end. When the machine begins to gurgle, all the water has passed through and the coffee is ready.

The instructions that come with the machine give some additional tips.

A little sugar brings out the flavor of the coffee. Do not drink the coffee too hot, or you will not taste it.

My thanks to Dr. Massimo Schiavi, whose knowledge of coffee has made his shop one of the best in Florence.

The Renaissance piazza of Santissima Annunziata in Florence with country
people setting up for a fair. Brigidini (page 459) are sold at all of these fairs.
Foto Torrini, Florence

Afterword:
The Aesthetic of
Florentine Cooking

---◆---

At the center remains the Renaissance concept of balance and linearity. One should be able to taste all ingredients. It is the correct proportions of a few ingredients that yields the oft-mentioned "sum greater than the parts."

The simplicity of Florentine cooking is the conscious simplification of very complex cooking. Waverley Root* has written "[it is] subtle in its deliberate eschewing of sophistication, which is perhaps the highest sophistication of all."

The reverberations of this simplicity go on and on.

* Waverley Root, *The Food of Italy*, Atheneum, New York, 1971.

Measurements Used in This Book

————— ⟨◆⟩ —————

Cup measurements are based on U.S. standard measuring cups such as Foley.

Conversion to Metric System

1 cup all-purpose flour (do not sift) =   about 112 grams
   about 4 ounces

1 cup granulated sugar = about 8 ounces about 224 grams

16 tablespoons = 1 cup

3 teaspoons = 1 tablespoon

1 ounce (solid)   about 28 grams

1 pound (solid)   about 448 grams
                                (1 kilogram = 1000 grams)

4 cups = 2 pints = 1 quart (liquid)   almost 1 liter

Recipes That Can Be Prepared in an Hour

Recipes that can be prepared in an hour or less are marked in the index*. The following recipes can be made quickly if you have one basic ingredient already prepared:

Broth
Leek soup
Modern Tuscan onion soup
Pasta in broth
Renaissance cinnamon broth

Leftover Tuscan bread
Tuscan garlic bread

Breadcrumbs
Spaghetti with bread crumb sauce

Leftover Tuscan beans
Bean soup for the Lombards
Tuscan puréed bean soup

Leftover polenta
Crostini with anchovy butter

Recipes that can be prepared in advance and served later are marked in the index†.

Index

* Recipes that can be prepared in an hour
† Recipes that can be prepared in advance

Acciuga, pasticcetti con, 89
Acciugata, 64
  braciole fritte con, 282 note
  cavolfiore con, 411
Agliata, 81
Agnello, cotoletta di, 283
Agresto, 59
Agresto sauce, 59
Alkermes di Firenze, 453
Alloro, 15
Almonds, 20
  bitter, 21
  blanching, 465
Amaretti, homemade, 464
Anchovies, 21
Anchovy
  pastries, 89
  sauce, 64
  sauce, spaghetti with, 159
Anitra
  all'arancio, 323
  in porchetta, 325
Anonimo Toscano c.1300, 4
Antipasti, 83–103
  in 16th century Florentine dinner, 8
  carote all'agro, 388
  crostini al ginepro, 91
  crostini con burro e acciughe, 92
  fagioli, tonno e cipolle, 102
  fettunta, 101
  foglie di salvia ripiene, 87
  frittate, 96–99
    al basilico, 98
    di pomodori verdi, 98
    di porri, 97

  insalata di riso, 85
  melanzane marinate, 90
  mozzarella in carrozza, 88
  panzanella, 92
  pasticetti con acciuga, 89
  peperoni ripieni, 94
  polenta fritta, 84
  pomodori e tonno, 393
  porrata, 99
  riso forte o pasticcio di riso amaro,
    86
  sedano, finocchi, carciofi in
    pinzimonio, 83
  uova ripiene, 94
Apicius, 3
Appetizers, 83–103
  *anchovy pastries, 89
  bread salad, 92, *menu*, 301
  canapes of liver paste and juniper
    berries, 91, *menus*, 369, 379
  †crostini with anchovy butter, 92
  fried polenta appetizer, 84
  *frittate, 96–99
    with basil, 98
    of green tomatoes, 98
    of leeks, 97, *menu*, 252
  †leek pie, 99
  †marinated eggplant, 90, *menus*, 272,
    302
  †marinated raw shredded carrots,
    388
  *mozzarella in a carriage, 88
  peppery rice pasticcio, 86, *menu*,
    328

Appetizers (cont.)
  *raw celery, fennel, and artichoke in
      pinzimonio, 83
  rice salad, 85, *menu,* 302
  sage "sandwiches," 87
  †stuffed eggs, 94
  †stuffed peppers, 94
  tomato halves with tuna, capers,
      and *maionese,* 393
  †Tuscan beans, tuna, and fresh
      onions, 102
  Tuscan garlic bread, 101
Apple
  cake, 475
  deep fried in batter, 496
Aringhe e polenta, 370
Arista, 347
Arrosto girato alla fiorentina, 380
Artichokes, 394–399
  introduction, 394
  baked in mold, 426, *menu,* 256
  boiled, 397
  cleaning the American, 394
  fried, 398, *menu,* 283
  Jerusalem, xiv
  raw in pinzimonio, 83
  stuffed, 398, *menu,* 326
Artusi, Pellegrino, xi, xiii
Asparagi
  alla fiorentina, 288
  sformato di, 426
Asparagus
  baked in mold, 426
  boil, how to, 288
  Florentine style, 288
  sautéed, with eggs (Florentine
      style), 288
Aspic (Gelatina), 107–9
  clarifying, 108
  coloring, 108–9
  straining and clarifying, 109
  stuffed whole fish in, 263
  unmolding, 109

Baccalà, 238
  alla fiorentina, 254
Bagno maria (bain-marie), 27, *photo,*
      427
Balsamella (béchamel), 52
  con parmigiano, 76
Basil, 14
  preserving in salt, 14

Basil sauce (pesto), 77–81
  historical background, 77–79
  with blender or food processor, 81
  with mezzaluna, 80
  with mortar and pestle, 79–80
Basilico, 14
Batter
  deep-fried fruit in, 497
  for deep-frying chicken, zucchini,
      zucchini flowers, 276
  for deep-frying fruit, 497
Battuto alla genovese (pesto), 77–81
Bay leaves, 15
Beans (white cannellini or Tuscan)
  historical note, 5
  preparation for cooking, *note,* 119,
      400
  soups with:
    for the Lombards, 129
    minestrone country-style,
        Tuscan, 122
    minestrone with kale and, 124
    pasta and, 127
    reboiled, Tuscan, 124
    with rice, 121
  sausages and, 354
  used as vegetable
    baked 403, *menu,* 338
    boiled, 400
    cooked in a flask, 400, *menu,* 307,
        357
    cooked in the manner of little
        birds, 402, *menu,* 298, 358
Béchamel, *see Balsamella*
Beef
  boiled, 268
  leftover boiled, with leeks, 72
  meat slices, stuffed, 338
  pot roast, Florentine style, 340
  †sirloin, rolled, stuffed, 337
  *steak, Florentine style, 333–5
    buying and preparing, 334
    cooking, 334–5
  *steak "sausages," fresh, in sauce, 335
  stew in Chianti, Florentine, 342
  stew, peppery, 343
  veal or, deep-fried cutlets, 281
    with anchovy sauce, *note,* 282
Bietole all'agro, 423
  saltate, 423
Bignè (pasticcini ripieni), 440

Biscotti
  Amaretti, 464
  di Prato, 462
Bistecca alla fiorentina, 333
Bitter almonds, 21
  cookies, 464
Bocca di dama, 450
Boiled course, 266–273
  beef, 268
  beef, leftover, with leeks, 272
  calf's foot, 271
    head, cheek of, 271
    tail, 271
  cotechino, 269–70, 271
  fowl, 267–8, 271
    capon, 267–8, 271
    chicken, 267–8, 271
    hen, 267–8, 271
    turkey, 267–8, 271
  "grand" mixed boiled dinner, 271
  historical background, 266
  in 16th century Florentine dinner, 8
  veal tongue, 269, 271
  zampone, 269–70, 271
Bollito misto, Gran, 271
Bomba con salsicce, 222
Bombe, 443
Bomboloni, 454
Braciole di maiale con cavolo nero,
    346
Braciole fritte, 281
  con acciugata, note, 282
  ripiene, 338
Brains, calf's, fried, 277
Bread, 29–46
  basic technique, *see* Tuscan bread,
    32–37
  brick oven, improvising, for, 32
  croutons, Italian, 46
  crumbs, homemade, 45
  flour and wheat for, 31
  Luccan sweet, 42
  nut, for All Saints' Day, 44
  rosemary, 40
  sausage, 39
  sweet, for All Saints' Day, 471
  Tuscan country, 32
  Tuscan dark, 37
  Tuscan whole-wheat, 38
  with olives, 40
  yeast for, 30
Bread crumbs, homemade, 45

Bread crumb sauce, 82
  spaghetti with, 158
Bread salad, 92
Bread soup, 230
Briciolata, 82
Brick oven, improvising, 32
Brigidini, 459
Brillat-Savarin, 7
Brioche pastry, *see* bomboloni
  pastry, 439, 454
Broccolirab, *see* rape
*Broccoli, "stir-sautéed," 406, *menu*,
    278, 342
Broccoli strascicati, 406
Brodo, 104
  ristretto, see consommé
Broth
  clarifying, 106
  coloring, 106
  meat, 105
Broth and consommé, 104–105
Bruciate ubriache, 477
Bruschetta, see fettunta
Buccellato, 42
  alle fragole, 470
Buccellato with strawberries, 470
Budini di riso, 484
Budino
  di carne, 375
  di ricotta, 491
  di riso, 490
Buffet, menu for, 302
Butter, 16

Cabbage
  "black" (cavolo nero), *see* kale
  red, xiv
Cacciucco, 256
Caffé, see coffee
Cake
  apple, 475
  cheese, Italian, 446
  corn meal, 476
  rice, 484
  rice custard, 486
  rice with Amaretti, 490
Calamari, 246–253
  e gamberi, fritto di, 249
  ripieni, 252
  in zimino, 251
Calf's brains, fried, 277

Calf's foot, boiled, 271
  see also Gelatina
Calf's head, cheek of, 271
Calf's tail, boiled, 271
Canapes of liver paste and juniper
      berries, 91
Cannellini, see beans
Cannelloni alla sorpresa, 187
Cannelloni con carne, 178
Cannelloni con ricotta, 185
Cannelloni della vigilia, 184
Cannelloni verdi di ricotta, 186
Caper sauce, 68
Capers, tomato and, salad, 392
Capon, boiled, 267
Capperi e pomodori, 392
Carabaccia, 113
Caramel custard, 437
Carbonara, spaghetti alla, 155
Carciofi bolliti, 397
Carciofi fritti, 398
Carciofi in pinzimonio, 83
Carciofi ritti, 398
Carciofi, sformato di, 426
Cardi bolliti, 407
Cardi (gobbi) dorati, 408
Cardi, sformato di, 426
Cardi trippati, 407
Cardoons
  baked, in mold, 426
  boiled, 407
  cut in the form of tripe, 407
  deep-fried 408, menu, 244, 377
Caréme, 4
Carote all'agro, 388
Carote bollite, 409
Carote, sformato di, 426
Carrots
  baked in mold 426, menu, 315
  *boiled, 409
  marinated, raw shredded salad, 388
Castagnaccio or migliaccio, 479
Castagne (marroni)
  tartufi di, 480
  see also chestnuts and chestnut flour
Caul fat, 359
Cauliflower
  *with anchovy sauce, 411
  *boiled, 410
  *fried, 410
  gratinée, note, 410
  *with olive oil, 411

Cavolfiore all'olio, 411
Cavolfiore bollito, 410
Cavolfiore con acciugata, 411
Cavolfiore fritto, 410
Cavolo nero, see kale
Ceci, pasta e, 128
Cefalo or muggine, 238
Celery, in pinzimonio, 83
Cenci, 457
Cernia, 238
Cervello fritto, 277
Cheese
  for cooking, 22
  course in formal dinner, 12
  gorgonzola, 23
    stuffing, tortelli with, 170
  groviera (Swiss cheese), 23
  mozzarella, 23
  parmigiano, 22
  pecorino (sheep's cheese), 22
  ricotta, see ricotta
Cheese cake, Italian, 446
Chestnuts
  burned, drunken, 477
  cake, flat, 479
  "truffles," 480
Chestnut flour, crépes, 481
Chicken, see also Poultry
Chicken, boiled, 267
Chicken breast, pudding of veal, and
      prosciutto, 375
Chicken, deep-fried in batter, 275
Chicken, great pie of quail, squab,
      sausage, tortelli, 383
Chicken liver paté, antique, 363
  as first dish, menu, 383
Chicken liver sauce with tagliatelle,
      149
Chicken liver sauce, 77
Chicken or meat croquettes, deep-
      fried, 278
Chick peas
  pasta and, 128
  tart of red, 9
Chiocciole con salsa di tonno, 160
Chocolate pastry cream, 432
Chopping, 28
Christmas, menu for, see note, 271
Ciambella con cibreo, 361
Ciambella di frutta, 487
Cibreo, 75
Cibreo sauce, 75

potato-ricotta ring with, 361
tagliatelle with, 148
Cinnamon custard, old fashioned, 436
Cioccolata pasticcera, 432
Cipollata, 114
Clams, 238, 257
Cod
  boiling time, 240
  dried salted, 238
  Florentine style, 254
  fresh, 238
Coffee, 499–501
  history, 500
  making, with Moka-machine, 500
  selecting beans, 499
Coniglio in agro-dolce, 329
Coniglio ripieno con carciofi, 326
Consommé, 106
Cookies
  bitter almond, 464
  little almond, 462
Corn meal
  cake, 476
  gnocchi, 224
  see also polenta, 367
Corrado, 130
Cotechino, 269, 270, 271
Cotoletta alla milanese, see *braciole
    fritte*, 281
Cotolette d'agnello, 283
Crabs, 238, 257
Cream
  chocolate pastry, 432
  custard, 430
  pastry, 431
  whipped, Florentine style, 434
  whipped with zabaione, 435
Cream puffs, 440
Creamed spinach soup, 118
Crema, 430
Crema pasticcera, 431
Crema zabaione, 435
Crème caramel, see *latte alla
    portoghese*
Crêpes, see *crespelle*
Crespelle
  (crêpes) chestnut flour, 481
  Renaissance egg, 465
Crespelle di farina dolce, 481
Croquettes, chicken or meat, deep-
    fried, 278
Crostata di frutta, 444

Crostata di ricotta, 446
Crostini al ginepro, 91
Crostini con burro di acciughe, 92
Crostini with anchovy butter, 92
Croutons, Italian, 46
Custard
  cake, 486
  caramel, 437
  cream, 430
  old fashioned cinnamon, 436

Desserts, 429–499
  bread
    †buccellato with strawberries 470,
      menu, 369
    rosemary, 40, *menu*, 336
    †schiacciata, sweet carnival, 472,
      menu, 281
      †with raisins, 473, *menus*, 292,
        345
    †sweet for All Saints' Day, 471,
      menu, 359
  budino (soufflé)
    introduction, 489
    rice, *see* rice cake with amaretti,
      490, *menu*, 364
    ricotta, 490, *menus*, 244, 340
  cake
    apple, 475, *menus*, 290, 295
    corn-meal, 476, *menu*, 294
    rice custard, 486, *menu*, 307
    rice with amaretti, 490, *menu*, 364
  cakes, rice, 484
  chestnuts and chestnut flour, 477–82
    introduction, 477
    burned, drunken, 477, *menu*, 257
    †cake, flat, 479, *menus*, 272, 319
    crêpes, 481, *menu*, 275
    †truffles, 480, *menus*, 316, 377
  cookies
    †almond, little, 462, *menu*, 249
    †bitter almond, 464
  cream
    †chocolate pastry, 432
    custard, 430
    †pastry, 431
    whipped
      †Florentine style, 434
      †meringues with, 468, *menus*,
        242, 361
      †with raspberries, 497, *menu*,
        288

Desserts (cont.)
    †with zabaione, 435, *menus*, 308, 328, 343, 348
    crêpes, chestnut flour, 481, *menu*, 275
    crespelle, Renaissance egg, 465, *menu*, 270
†custard, cream, 430
    cake, rice, 486, *menu*, 307
    †caramel, 437, *menu*, 358
    †old fashioned cinnamon, 436, *menu*, 304
    fritters, pancake, 467, *menu*, 353
    fruit
      deep-fried in batter, 497, *menus*, 245, 363
      peaches
        †in Chianti wine, 496, *menus*, 280, 301, 383
        †stuffed, 492, *menus*, 252, 323
        †stuffed with almonds, 493, *menus*, 278, 302, 335
      pears
        deep-fried in batter, 497, *menus*, 245, 363
        †poached in wine, 495, *menus*, 283, 348
        †whole poached, in pastry drum, 499, *menu*, 259
    †raspberries with whipped cream, 497, *menu*, 288
    rice ring stuffed with, 487, *menus*, 263, 315, 357
    "shortcake," 444, *menus*, 300, 333
    strawberries
      buccellato with, 470, *menu*, 369
      deep-fried in batter, 497, *menus*, 245, 363
      †in Chianti wine, 496, *menus*, 255, 267, 325, 371
    in 16th century Florentine dinner, 9
    meringues with whipped cream, 468, *menus*, 242, 361
*pancake fritters, 467, *menu*, 353
pastry, 440–462
    bomboloni, 454, *menu*, 331
    †cream puffs, 440, *menu*, 375
    *deep-fried nuggets, 443, *menus*, 297, 338
    deep-fried snacks ("rags"), 457, *menu*, 326

dessert tortelli, 458, *menu*, 277
drum, sweet, 449
    whole poached pears in a, 449, *menu*, 259
†fruit "shortcake," 444, *menus*, 300, 333
†Italian cheesecake, 446
†rum cake, the original Italian, 452, *menu*, 379
†spongecake, Italian, 450
stamped, 459
see also pastry
rice, 482–489, 490–491
    cakes, 484
    †cake with amaretti, 490, *menu*, 364
    †cake, custard, 486, *menu*, 307
    fritters, 485, *menus*, 287, 342
    ring stuffed with fruit, 487, *menus*, 263, 315, 357
    soufflé 490, *menu*, 364
*ricotta, fried, 469
    *soufflé, 490, *menu*, 244, 340
    torte, 448, *menu*, 240
    see also Italian cheesecake
†zabaione, 433
Dolci
    amaretti, 464
    biscotti di Prato, 462
    bocca di dama, 450
    bombe, 443
    bomboloni, 454
    brigidini, 459
    bruciate ubriache, 477
    buccellato alle fragole, 470
    budino di ricotta, 490
      di riso, 490
    budini di riso, 484
    castagnaccio, 477
    cenci, 457
    ciambella di frutta, 487
    cioccolata pasticcera, 432
    crema, 430
    crema pasticcera, 431
    crema zabaione, 435
    crespelle di farina dolce, 481
    crostata di frutta, 444
    crostata di ricotta, 446
    dolce di polenta, 476
    fragole al vino rosso, 496
    frittelle di riso, 485

frittelle di tondone alla fiorentina, 467
frittura mista di frutta (fragole, mele, pere), 497
lamponi alla panna, 497
lattaiolo, 436
latte alla portogese, 437
meringhe alla panna, 468
pane co'Santi (dolce), 471
panna montata, 434
pasticcini ripieni (bignè), 440
pere al vino, 495
pesche al vino, 496
pesche ripiene, 492
   con mandorle, 493
ricotta fritta, 469
ritortelli pieni alla fiorentina, 465
schiacciata con zibibbo, 473
   unta di Berlingaccio, 472
tartufi di castagne, 480
timballo di pere, 449
torta di mele, 475
   di ricotta, 448
   di riso uso Garfagnana, 486
tortelli dolci, 458
zabaione, 433
zuppa inglese, 452
Double-boiler, 27, *photo,* 431
Dragoncello, 15
Duck in orange sauce, 323
   in the style of suckling pig, 325

Easter torta, 234
Egg crespelle, Renaissance, 465
Eggs
   with asparagus, 288
   Florentine, 287
   *fried, Florentine style, 288
   frittate, 96–99
     with basil, 98
     of green tomatoes, 98
     of leeks, 97
   *poached in tomatoes, 285
   stuffed, 94
Eggplant
   introduction, 412
   in the style of Parma, 412, *menu,* 375
   marinated, 90
   peppers and, 418
Escoffier, 6

Fagioli
   al fiasco, 400
   al forno, 403
   all'uccelletto, 402
   bolliti, 400
   minestre e minestroni con
     alla contadina, 122
     di riso, 121
     incavolata, 124
     passato di, 119
     pasta e, 127
     ribollita, 124
     zuppa lombarda, 129
   salsicce e, 354
   tonno e cipolle, 102
Fagiolini in erba bolliti, 404
Fagiolini in fricassea, 404
Fagiolini in umido, 405
   sformato di, 426
Farina dolce (di castagne), see chestnut flour
Farina dolce, crespelle di, 481
Farina gialla, see polenta
Fegatelli alla fiorentina, 359
Fegato alla griglia, 356
Fegato alla toscana, 358
Fennel
   introduction, 413
   baked in mold, 426, *menu,* 300
   *boiled, 413
   raw *in pinzimonio,* 83
   *sautéed in butter, 414, *menu,* 335
   in winter tomato sauce, 414, *menu,* 252
Fettuccine, see *tagliatelle*
"*Fettuccine Alfredo,*" see *tagliatelle alla panna,* 147
Fettunta, 101
Finocchi
   al burro, 414
   bolliti, 413
   in pinzimonio, 83
   in sugo finto, 414
   sformato di, 426
Fiori di zucca fritti, 425
First courses, miscellaneous, 224–236
   †bread soup, 230, *menu,* 342, 357
   †Easter torta, 234
   gnocchi, corn meal, 224
     fish, 228, *menus,* 240, 300
     potato, 232, *menu,* 336
     semolina, 231, *menu,* 251

First courses (cont.)
  nude ravioli, 228, *menus*, 307, 377
  nude ravioli, fish 228, *menu*, 300
  tomatoes, stuffed, 225, *menu*, 249
Fish, 237–265
  introduction, 237
  bass, sea, 237, boiling time, 240
  bass, striped, 237, 244, 246, 257,
      260, 264, boiling time, 240
  bluefish, 238
  boning, 260
  boned whole, baked in a crust, 259
  buying and handling, 238
  clams, 238, 257
  cod
    fresh, 238, 257, boiling time, 240
    dried salted, 238, boiling time, 240
    dried salted, Florentine style, 254
  comparison, Mediterranean and
      Atlantic, 237
  *cooked in a paper bag, 245
  crabs, 238, 257
  frying, methods of, 250, 274–275
  gnocchi of, 226
  haddock, 257, boiling time, 240
  hake, 238, boiling time, 240
  mullet
    red, 238, boiling time, 240
    striped or grey, 238, 244, boiling
      time, 240
  mussels, 238, 257
  *poached or boiled, fresh water and
      sea, 239
  porgy, 238
  ravioli, naked, of, 228
  *roasted, 244
  sardines, fresh, 238
  shrimp, 257
    maionese, 65
    sauce, 66
    stuffing for whole fish in aspic,
      264
  smelts, 238, 257
  sole, 238, boiling time, 240
    *Livorno style, 255
  soup, Tuscan Livorno style, 257
  spotted grouper, 238, 244
  squid, 246–253
    how to clean, 246
    and shrimp, deep-fried, 249
    stuffed, 252
    with spinach, 251

†stuffed whole in aspic, 264
swordfish, 238, boiling time, 240
trout, 240–243
  *boiled with mayonnaise, 240
  *cooked on plate, 242
  how to bone, 242
tuna, fresh, 238
  flavor, turkey with, 319
  sauce, 74
  sauce, shells with, 160
  tomatoes and, salad, 393
  Tuscan beans, and fresh onions,
      102
whiting, 238, boiling time, 240
Flour and wheat, 31
  dark, 31
  white, 31
Foglie di salvia ripiene, 87
Foie gras, *photo*, 10
Formal dinner, in Italy, 9
Fowl, *see* poultry and game
Fragole
  buccellato con, 470
  al vino rosso, 496
Fragoline di bosco, 429
Fresh tomato sauce, 69
Fricassea di pollo, 295
Fricassea, fagiolini in, 404
Fricassee
  historical reference, 5
  chicken, 295
  of stringbeans, 404
Fried course, 274–284
  in 16th century Florentine dinner, 8
  beef, veal or, cutlets, 281
  calves brains, 277
  chicken in batter, 275
  chicken or meat croquettes, 278
  lamb chop, Florentine style, 283
  mixed fry, Florentine style, 280
Frying, methods of, 274–5
  chicken and vegetables, batter for,
      275
Fried polenta appetizer, 84
Frittata
  with basil, 98
  of green tomatoes, 98
  of leeks, 97
Frittata
  al basilico, 98
  di pomodori verdi, 98
  di porri, 97

Frittate, introduction, 96
Frittelle di riso, 485
Frittelle di tondone alla fiorentina, 467
Fritters
   pancake, 467
   rice, 485
Fritto misto alla fiorentina, 280
Frittura mista di frutta, 497
Fruit, *note,* 6
   course in 16th century dinner, 9
   deep-fried in batter, 497
   desserts, 429
   peaches in Chianti wine, 496
      stuffed, 492
      stuffed with almonds, 493
   pears deep-fried in batter, 497
      poached in wine, 495
      whole poached, in pastry drum,
         449
   raspberries with whipped cream,
      497
   "shortcake," 444
   strawberries, buccellato with, 470
      deep-fried in batter, 497
      in Chianti wine, 496
Frutta di mare, 7

Gamberi, calamari e, fritto di, 249
Game, *see* poultry and game
Garlic sauce, 81
Gelatina, 107
Ghiotta, potatoes made in a, 382
Ginestrata, 112
Gnocchi
   potato, 232
   semolina, 231
Gnocchi alla romana, 231
Gnocchi di farina gialla, 224
Gnocchi di pesce, 226
Gnocchi di semolino, 231
Gobbi (cardi) dorati, 408
Gorgonzola, 23
   stuffing, tortelli with, 170
Gran bollito misto, 271
"Grand" mixed boiled dinner, 271
Grantinée note, 410
Green pasta, fresh, 143
Green sauce, 57
Green sauce with walnuts, 58
Groviera (Swiss cheese), 23
Guancia, 271

Ham
   soufflé, 377
   see also prosciutto
Hare sauce, pappardelle with, 151
Healthy, good, cooking, xi, 6
Hen, boiled, 267
Herbs and spices, 13–15
   basil, 14, preserving in salt, 14
   bay leaves, 15
   parsley, Italian, 14
   rosemary, 13
   sage, 14, preserving in salt, 14
   tarragon, 15
Herring with polenta, 370
Historical background, 3–9
History
   sixteenth-century Florentine
      dinner, 7

In-between course
   in formal dinner, 11
   see also:
   baked vegetables in mold, 426
   cardoons cut in form of tripe, 407
Incavolata, 124
Insalata
   composta, 388
   di patate alla fiorentina, 390
   di peperoni alla griglia, 389
   di riso, 85
   mista, 387
   pomodori in, 391
   verde, 387
Involtini di vitella, 331

Jerusalem artichokes, xiv

Kale and bean soup, 124
Kale, pork chop with, 246

Lamb chop, Florentine style, 283
Lamponi alla panna, 497
Larousse Gastronomique, 4, 161, 439
Lasagne al forno, 189
Lasagne all'anitra all'aretina, 195
Lattaiolo, 436
Latte alla portoghese, 437
La Varenne, de, 5, 7, 295
Leek pie, 99
Leeks
   boiled beef, leftover, with, 272
   frittata of, 97

Leeks (cont.)
pie, 99
soup, 115
Leek soup, 115
Lesso rifatto con porri, 272
Liqueur, *Alkermes di Firenze,* 453
Liver
calves
grilled Florentine style, 357
sautéed, Tuscan style, 358
chicken
canapes of liver paste and juniper
berries, 91
cibreo sauce, 75
potato, ricotta ring with, 361
tagliatelle, with, 148
paté, antique, 363
sauce, 77
sauce with tagliatelle, 149
sauce (optional) for pudding of
veal, chicken breast, and
prosciutto, 376
pork, Florentine style, 359
Luccan sweet bread, 42

Maiale
arista, 347
con cavolo nero, braciole di, 346
fegatelli alla fiorentina, 359
polenta e salsicce, 369
rospo nel buco, 355
salsicce, 350
salsicce con rape, 353
salsicce e fagioli, 354
ubriaco, 345
Maionese, 55
al prezzemolo, 65
con gamberetti, 65
Manuscripts of early Italian cookbooks xii, *photos* 10, 54, 167,
113, 273, 483
Manzo
bistecca alla fiorentina, 333
braciole ripiene, 338
lesso rifatto con porri, 272
peposo, 343
polpette di bisteccatalla fiorentina,
335
ripieno, 337
spezzatino alla fiorentina, 342
stracotto alla fiorentina, 340

Marco Polo, 130
Marroni, see chestnuts and chestnut
flour
Martino, Maestro, 4
Mayonnaise, 55
Meat, chicken or, croquettes, deep-
fried, 278
Meat sauce, 72
Meat sauce with tagliatelle, 146
Meat slices, stuffed, 338
Medici, de
Caterina 53, 74, *note,* 274, 323, 438
Elixir de (liquore de), 453
family, 5, 40, 237, 348
Maria, 439, 453
Melanzane alla parmigiana, 412
Melanzane e peperoni, 418
Melanzane marinate, 90
Menus, suggested, 240–383, *see also*
separate listings; *notes,* 240,
236
for buffet, 302
for Christmas, *note,* 271
for New Year's Eve, 379
for Thanksgiving, 316
Meringhe alla panna, 468
Mezzaluna, 28, *photo,* 50
Migliaccio or *castagnaccio,* 479
Minestra "povera" di patate, 125
Minestroni e minestre, 120–129
incavolata, 124
minestra "povera" di patate, 125
minestrone alla contadina, 122
minestrone di riso, 121
pasta e ceci, 128
pasta e fagioli, 127
ribollita, 124
zuppa lombarda, 129
Mixed fry, Florentine style, 280
Modern Tuscan onion soup, 114
Mollica, 59
Mortadella, 78
of Bologna, 17
Mortar and pestle, *photo,* 28, 78
Mozzarella, 23
Mozzarella e pomodori, 392
Mozzarella in carrozza, 88
Mozzarella "in a carriage," 88
Mozzarella, tomato and, salad, 392
Mushrooms, 19
Mushrooms, filled puffs, little in
broth, 110

Mushroom sauce, 68
Mussels, 238, 257

Nasello or merluzzo, 238
New Year's Eve, menu for, 379
Nut bread for All Saints Day, 44

Odori e spezie, 13–15
  alloro, 15
  basilico, 14
    sotto sale, 14
  dragoncello, 15
  prezzemolo, 14
  ramerino, 13
  salvia, 14
    sotto sale, 14
Oil
  cooking oil, 16
  olive oil, 15

Palline ripiene in brodo, 110
Pancetta, 18
Pane e Pizze, 29–50
  Pane, 23–46
    buccellato, 42
    con olive, 40
    con salsicce, 39
    co'Santi, 44
    co' Santi (dolce), 471
    pan di ramerino, 40
    integrale, 38
    pangrattato, 45
    piccoli crostini fritti, 46
    scuro, 33
    toscano, 32
  Pizze, 46–50
    pizza alla napoletana, 46
    con cipolle, 48
    "*special*," 48
    schiacciata con ramerino, 49
Panna, lamponi alla, 497
  meringhe alla, 468
  tagliatelle alla, 147
  tortellini alla, 176
Panna montata, 434
  (crema)-zabaione, 435
Pantanelli, 53, 438
Panzanella, 92
Pappa al pomodoro, 230
Pappardelle sulla lepre, 151
Pappardelle with hare sauce, 151

Parmentier, *note*, 5
Parmigiano, 22
Parsley, Italian, 14
Parsley mayonnaise, 65
Passati, 116–120
  passato di fagioli, 119
    di spinaci, 118
    di verdura, 117
Pasta, 130–212
  introduction, 130
  dried, 155–161
    introduction, 155
    macaroni, squab with, in a
      pastry drum, 206
    *shells with tuna sauce, 160
    *spaghetti, coachman's style, 156,
      menu, 267
      with anchovy sauce, 159
    *with bread crumb sauce, 158,
      menu, 286
      with chicken giblet sauce, 157,
      menu, 315
    *with egg-pancetta sauce, 155
    with a sauce of uncooked
      tomatoes and herbs, 159
  fresh, 131–154
    cutting, by hand, 140–143, by
      machine, 138–139
    farfalle or fiocchi, cutting and
      shaping, 142
    making, by hand, 198–201, by
      machine, 133–138
    pappardelle, cutting, 141
    pappardelle with hare sauce, 151
    tagliatelle, fresh ("fettuccine"),
      146–150
      with chicken liver sauce, 149
      with cibreo sauce, 148, *menu*,
        283
    *in cream sauce, 147, *menu*, 259
      green, soufflé of, 150, *menu*,
        292
      with meat sauce, 146, *menu*,
        288
    *taglierini, fresh, with fresh tomato
      sauce, 145, *menu*, 303
    trenette with basil sauce (pesto),
      153
  fresh green, 143
    tagliatelle, soufflé of, 150, *menu*,
      292
  fresh red, 144

Pasta (cont.)
  fresh stuffed, 161–205
    introduction, 161
    tortelli, 162–178
      great pie of quail, squab,
        chicken, sausage and, 383
      making, 162–164
      of pumpkin, Modena style, 174,
        menu, 316
      in rabbit sauce, 172
      with fresh mint, 168, *menu*, 218
      with gorgonzola stuffing, 171,
        menu, 345
    tortelli, half-moon
      making, 164–165
      alla panna in green cannelloni,
        187
      stuffed with spinach and
        ricotta, 169, *menus*, 325, 358
    tortellini, making, 165–167
      in butter and cream sauce, 176,
        menus, 348, 375
      in meat sauce, 177
      in a pastry drum, 212, *menu*,
        379
  Fresh stuffed, large, 178–205
    cannelloni, 178–189
      green, stuffed with tortelli
        alla panna, 187
      green, with ricotta filling, 186
      how to make, 178–184
      stuffed with ricotta, 185, *menu*,
        346
      stuffed with spinach and
        ricotta, 184, *menu*, 331
      with meat, 178
    lasagne, 189–197
      baked, northern Italian style,
        189, *menus*, 290, 332
      how to make, 191–195
      Ferrara style, *see* baked,
        northern Italian style with
        duck, in the style of Arezzo,
        195, *menu*, 277
    stuffed pasta roll, 198, *menu*, 275
Pasta, 130–212
  cannelloni, alla sorpresa, 187
  con carne, 178
  con ricotta, 185
  della vigilia, 184
  verdi di ricotta, 186
  chiocciole con salsa di tonno, 160

lasagne
  al forno, 189
  all'anitra all'aretina, 195
  pappardelle sulla lepre, 151
  alla puttanesca, 159
  fresca ("fresh pasta"), 131
  rossa, 144
  rotolo di pasta ripieno, 198
spaghetti
  all'acciugata, 159
  alla carbonara, 155
  alla fiaccheraia, 156
  al sugo di "cipolle," 157
  con briciolata, 158
tagliatelle, alla panna, 147
  al sugo di carne, 146
  al sugo di fegatini, 146
  con cibreo, 148
  verdi, sformato di, 150
taglierini al pomodoro fresco, 145
timballo di piccioni (*macaroni*),
  206
tortelli, al coniglio, 172
  al gorgonzola, 170
  alla menta, 168
  della vigilia, 169
  di zucca alla modenese, 174
tortellini, alla panna, 176
  al sugo di carne, 177
  timballo di, 212
trenette al pesto, 153
verde, 143
Pasta and bean soup, 127, *menu*, 326
Pasta and chick peas, 128, *menu*, 359
Pasta e ceci, 128
Pasta e fagioli, 127
Pasta in broth, 109
Pasta sfoglia, 439
Pasta soffiata, 440
Pastella per frittura:
  pollo, zucchini e fiori di zucca, 276
  frutta, 497
Pastello di caccia, 383
Pastello di pesce, 259
Pasticcini ripieni (*bignè*), 440
Pasticcetti con acciuga, 89
Pastries, anchovy, 89
Pastry (and pastry desserts)
  bomboloni, 439, 454
  brioche, 439
  cream puff, 438, 440
  "nuggets," deep fried, 443

puffs, little mushroom-filled, in
  broth, 110
Genoese, *see* Easter torte
puff, 439
short, 439, 444–450
  fruit "shortcake," 444
  drum of, whole poached pears
    in, 449
  Italian cheesecake, 446
  ricotta "torte," 448
short, unsweetened, *see* pastry
  drums
snacks, deep-fried, "rags," 457
spongecake, Italian, 450
  rum cake, the original Italian, 452
stamped, 459
tortelli, dessert, 458
Pastry cream, 431
  chocolate, 432
Pastry drums, 206–212, 449–450
  introduction, 206
  how to make, 207
    squab with macaroni in, 206
    tortellini in, 212
  sweet, 449–450
  whole poached pears in, 449
Patate alla contadina, 417
Patate alla fiorentina, insalata di, 390
Patate alla ghiotta, 382
Patate con pesto, 417
Patate saltate alla salvia, 416
*Pâte à biscuit Italien, see bocca di
  dama*
Pâte à chou, see pasta soffiata
Pâte feuilletée, see pasta sfoglia
Pâte sucrée, see pasta frolla
Peaches
  in Chianti wine, 496
  stuffed, 492
  stuffed with almonds, 493
Pears
  deep-fried in batter, 497
  poached in wine, 495
  whole poached, in pastry drum, 449
Peas in the Florentine manner, 415,
  menu, 363
Pecorino (sheep's cheese), 22
Peperonata, 419
Peperoni alla griglia, insalata di, 389
Peperoni e melanzane, 418
Peperoni ripieni, 94
Peposo, 343

Peppers
  *and eggplant, 418
  *grilled, salad, 389, *menu*, 364
  *sautéed in tomato, 419, *menu*, 336
  stuffed, 94
Peppery rice *Pasticcio*, 86
Pere al vino, 495
Pere, timballo di, 449
Pesce, 237–265
  al cartoccio, 245
  arrosto, 244
  baccala, 238
    alla fiorentina, 254
  bollito, 239
  cacciucco, 256
  calamari e gamberi, fritto di, 249
  calamari in zimino, 251
  calamari ripieni, 252
  cefalo or muggine, 238
  cernia, 238
  cozze, 238
  dentice, 238
  nasello or merluzzo, 238
  ombrina, 238
  pastello di, 259
  ripieno in gelatina, 263
  sarde fresche, 238
  sogliola alla livornese, 255
  spada, 238
  spigola or branzino, 237
  tonno fresco, 238
  triglia, 238
  trota al piatto, 242
  trota bollita con maionese, 240
  vongole, 238, 257
Pesche al vino, 496
Pesche ripiene, 492
Pesche ripiene con mandorle, 493
Pesto, 77
Pesto, patate con, 417
Pesto with trenette, 153
Petti di pollo alla fiorentina, 292
Petto di tacchino arrocchiato, 315
Piatti di mezzo, 11, see also *cardi
  trippati, sformati di verdura*
Piccoli crostini fritti, 46
Pie, great, of quail, squab, chicken,
  sausage and tortelli, 383
Pinzimonio, sedano, finocchi, carciofi
  in, 83
Piselli alla fiorentina, 415
Pizzas, *see* breads and pizzas

Pizza, see *Pane e pizze*
Platina, 4
Poached fish, sea and fresh water, 239
Polenta, 367–374
  appetizer, fried, 84
  basic procedure, 367
  gnocchi, 224
  herring with, 370
  pastry drum of, with quails, 371
  with sausages, 369
  see also corn meal cake
Polenta
  aringhe e, 370
  con salsicce, 369
  dolce di, 476
  fritta, 84
  timballo di, con quaglie, 317
Pollastrino alla griglia, 290
Polpette alla fiorentina, 278
Polpette di bistecca in umido, 335
Polpettone di tacchino al tonno, 319
Pollo affinocchiato, 300
Pollo alla cacciatora, 297
Pollo alle olive, 294
Pollo disossato ripieno, 307
Pollo forte, 302
Pollo, fricassea di, 295
Pollo fritto, 275
Pollo in pane, 303
Pollo in porchetta, 299
Pommarola, 70
Pomodori
  al forno, 424
  e capperi, 392
  e mozzarella, 392
  e tonno, 393
  fritti, 424
  in insalata, 391
  ripieni, 225
  see also tomatoes
Pomodoro, uova al, 286
Porcini, *see* mushrooms
Pork
  *chops, "inebriated," 345
  chops with kale, 346
  liver, Florentine style, 359
  loin of, with garlic, rosemary and
    black pepper, 348
  sausages, Tuscan, 350
  *sausages baked in batter, 355
  sausages with polenta, 369
  sausages with *rape,* 353

  sausages with Tuscan bean, 354
Porrata, 99
Porri, lesso rifatto con, 272
Porri, zuppa di, 115
Potatoes
  *country style, 417
  gnocchi (*topini*), 232
  made in a *ghiotta,* 382
  with pesto, 417
  potato-ricotta ring with cibreo
    sauce, 361
  salad, Florentine style, 390
  *sautéed with sage, 416, *menus,* 285,
    316
  topini (gnocchi) of, and chicken
    breast in broth, 111
Pot roast, Florentine style, 340
Pots, seasoning
  iron, 27
  terra-cotta, 26
Poultry and game, 290–330
  chicken, 290–315
    †appetizer, spicy, 302
    †boned, whole stuffed, 307
    boning, 309–312
    breast, Florentine style, 292
    †fenneled, 300
    fricassee, Florentine, 295
    great pie of quail, squab, sausage,
      tortelli, 383
    hunter style, 297
    liver, *see* chicken liver
    made in the manner of suckling
      pig, 299
    *squab, grilled, 290
    whole, baked in bread, 303
    *with black olives, 294
  duck
    in orange sauce, 323
    in the style of suckling pig, 325
  quail
    great pie of, squab, chicken,
      sausage, tortelli, 383
    pastry drum of polenta filled
      with, 371
  rabbit
    in sweet and sour sauce, 329
    tarragon, stuffed with artichokes,
      326
  squab
    with macaroni in pastry drum,
      206

great pie of chicken, quail, sausage, tortelli, 383
turkey
†breast, rolled stuffed, 315
†loaf with tuna flavor, 319
Prezzemolo, 14
Prosciutto, 17
"ham" soufflé, 377
pudding of veal, chicken breast and, 375
rind (*cotenna*), 127
sformato di, 377
Puff pastry, 439
Puffs, little mushrooms filled, in broth, 110
Pumpkin, tortelli of, Modena style, 174
Puree, origins, 99
Pureed vegetable soup, 117

Quail, great pie of, squab, chicken, sausage, tortelli, 383
Quail, pastry drum of polenta filled with, 371
Quiches, 436, *photo*, 273
Quinquinelle (quenelles), 4, *photo*, 273

Rabbit in sweet and sour sauce, 329
Rabbit, tarragon, stuffed with artichokes, 326
Ramerino, 13
Rape saltate in padella, 420
Rape, sautéed, 420, *menu*, 345, 348, 359
Ravioli, naked, 228
Ravioli alla fiorentina, 228
Ravioli nudi, 228
Ravioli nudi di pesce, 228
Raw celery, fennel, and artichoke in *pinzimonio*, 83
"Reboiled" Tuscan minestrone, 124
Red pasta, fresh, 144
Red sauce, 59
Renaissance cinnamon broth, 112
Renaissance onion soup, 113
Ribollita, 124
Rice
introduction, 213
desserts
cakes, 484
cake with Amaretti, 490
cake, custard, 486

fritters, 485
ring stuffed with fruit, 487
soufflé (cake with Amaretti), 490
salad, 85
timballo stuffed with sausages, 222, as first dish, *menu*, 363
Ricotta, 23
desserts
fried, 469
soufflé, 491
torte, 448
see also Italian cheesecake, 446
and spinach stuffings, 169, 184, 198
stuffings, 168, 185, 186, 171
Ricotta
budino di, 491
crostata di, 446
fritta, 469
torta di, 448
Riso, budini di, 484, 490
Riso forte or *pasticcio di riso amaro*, 86
Riso, frittelle di, 485
Riso, torta di, uso Garfagnana, 486
Risotti, 213–222
introduction, 213
*risotto, 214, *menu*, 297
*with artichokes, 216, *menu*, 255
with cacciucco broth, 221, *menu*, 244
*with dried mushrooms, 215, *menu*, 280, 295
with fish broth, 220, *menu*, 244
*with garlic sauce, 214, *menu*, 245
with meat sauce, 217, *menu*, 254
*with sausage, 218, *menu*, 285
*with shrimp, 219, *menu*, 241
Risotto
alla marinara, 220
alla toscana, 217
con carciofi, 216
con funghi, 215
con gamberetti in bianco, 219
con salsicce, 218
di mare, 221
in bianco, 214
in bianco con agliata, 214
Ritortelli pieni alla fiorentina, 465
Root, Waverley, 503
Rosemary, 13
Rosemary bread, 40

Rospo nel buco, 355
Ross, Janet, xiii–xiv, 420
Rotolo di pasta ripieno, 198
Roux, 53, *photo*, 54
Ruggieri, 453

Sage, 14
  preserving in salt, 14
  "sandwiches," 87
Salads, 387–93
  bread, 92
  †carrot, 388
  *composed, 388, *menus*, 294, 297, 301,
    328, 333, 343, 383
  dressing, 388
  *grilled peppers, 389
  *green, 387, *menus*, 280, 283, 325,
    359, 379
  *mixed, 38, *menus*, 281, 290, 294, 333,
    379, 383
  *potato, Florentine style, 390
  rice, 85
  *tomato, 391
  *tomato and capers, 392
  *tomato and mozzarella, 392
  *tomato and tuna, 393
Salami
  Genoese, 17
  Milanese, 17
  Mortadella of Bologna, 17
  Tuscan, 18
Salsa
  al dragoncello, 63
  bianca, 52
  d'agresto, 59
  di capperi, 68
  di fegatini, 77
  di funghi, 68
  di tonno, 74
  primavera di magro, 62
  rossa del Chianti, 59
  rossa forte, 61
  verde, 57
  verde del Chianti, 58
Salse, 51–82
Salse di base, 52–56
  balsamella, 52
  maionese, 55
  salsa bianca, 53
Salse per carne o pollame, 57–64
  acciugata, 64
  al dragoncello, 63

  d'agresto, 59
  maionese, 55
  primavera di magro, 62
  rossa del Chianti, 59
  rossa forte, 61
  savore di noci, 61
  verde, 57
  verde del Chianti, 58
Salse per pasta, riso e minestre, 69–82
  agliata, 81
  balsamella con parmigiano, 76
  briciolata, 82
  cibreo, 75
  di fegatini, 77
  di tonno, 74
  pesto, 77
  pommarola, 70
  sugo di carne, 72
  sugo di "cipolle," 73
  sugo di pomodoro fresco, 69
  sugo scappato o di magro, 71
Salse per pesce, 65–69
  di capperi, 68
  di funghi, 68
  maionese, 55
    al prezzemolo, 65
    con gamberetti, 65
  savore di gamberi, 66
Salsicce, 350
  con rape, 353
  e fagioli, 354
Salt, coarse, 19
Salvia, 14
Sauces, 51–82
  introduction and historical back-
    ground, 51
  basic sauces, 52–56
    béchamel (balsamella), 52
    mayonnaise, 55
    white sauce, 53
  for chicken or meat, 57–64
    agresto sauce, 59
    anchovy sauce, 64
    green sauce, 57
    green sauce with walnuts, 58
    red sauce, 59
    spicy red sauce, 61
    spring vegetable sauce, 62
    tarragon sauce from Siena, 63
    walnut sauce, 61
  for fish, 65–69
    caper sauce, 68

mayonnaise, 55
mushroom sauce, 68
parsley mayonnaise, 65
shrimp mayonnaise, 65
shrimp sauce, 66
for pasta, rice and soups, 69–82
   basil sauce (pesto) 77
   béchamel with Parmigiano
      cheese, 76
   bread crumb sauce, 82
   chicken liver sauce, 77
   cream sauce, *see* tagliatelle con
   egg pancetta (carbonara), *see*
      spaghetti with
   garlic sauce, 81
   hare sauce, *see* pappardelle with
   meat sauce, 72
   sauce of chicken gizzards, 73
   sauce of chicken livers, crests and
      wattles (*cibreo*), 75
   summer tomato sauce, 70
   tuna sauce, 74
   winter tomato sauce, 71
Sausage bread, 39
Sausages
   baked in batter, 355
   rice timballo, stuffed with, 222
   Tuscan, 350
   with polenta, 369
   with rape, 353
   with Tuscan beans, 354
Savore di gamberi, 66
Savore di noci, 61
Schiacciata con ramerino, 49
Schiacciata con zibibbo, 473
Schiacciata, sweet carnival, 472
Schiacciata unta di Berlingaccio, 472
Schiacciata with raisins, 473
Sedano in pinzimonio, 83
Semolina gnocchi, 231
Sformati di verdura, 426
Sformato di prosciutto, 377
Sformato di tagliatelle verdi, 150
Sheep's cheese (*pecorino*), 22
Shells with tuna sauce, 160
Shrimp, 257
Shrimp mayonnaise, 65
Shrimp sauce, 66
Shrimp, squid and, deep-fried, 249
Shrimp stuffing for whole fish in
   aspic, 263
Simple potato soup, 125

Sirloin, rolled stuffed, 337
Sogliola alla livornese, 255
Sole Livorno style, 255
Soufflé
   dessert budini
      introduction, 489–490
      rice cake with amaretti, 490
      ricotta soufflé, 491
   sformati:
      baked vegetables in mold, 426
      green pasta "soufflé," 150
      ham "soufflé," 377
Soups, 104–129
   broth and consommé, 104
   †broth, meat, 105
   †consommé, 106
   leek soup, 115, *menus*, 338, 343
   little mushroom-filled puffs in
      broth, 110, *menu*, 270
   minestroni and *minestre*, 120–129
      bean soup for the Lombards, 129
      kale and bean soup, 124, *menu*,
         278
      pasta and bean soup, 127, *menu*,
         326
      pasta and chick peas, 128, *menu*,
         359
      †reboiled Tuscan minestrone, 124,
         menu, 353
      simple potato soup, 125, *menu*,
         355
      Tuscan minestrone country
         style, 122, *menu*, 364
      †Tuscan minestrone with rice,
         121, *menu*, 319
      Tuscan onion soup, modern, 114,
         menu, 298
   passati, 116–120
      creamed spinach soup, 118,
         menus, 354, 361, 370
      puréed vegetable soup, 117, *menu*,
         371
      †Tuscan puréed bean soup, 119,
         menu, 335
   pasta in broth, 109, *menu*, 340
   Renaissance cinnamon broth, 112,
      menu, 323
   Renaissance onion soup, 113,
      menu, 294
   stock, 107
   topini of potato and chicken breast
      in broth, 111

Spaghetti
  coachman's style, 156
  with anchovy sauce, 159
  with bread crumb sauce, 158
  with chicken giblet sauce, 157
  with egg-pancetta sauce, 155
Spaghetti all'acciugata, 159
Spaghetti alla carbonara, 155
Spaghetti alla fiaccheraia, 156
Spaghetti al sugo di "cipolle," 157
Spaghetti con briciolata, 158
Spezzatino alla fiorentina, 342
Spices, *see* herbs and spices, *see also*
      3, 66, 259, 453
Spicy red sauce, 61
Spigola or branzino, 237
Spinach
  and cheese stuffing, 169, 170, 198,
      204
  eggs with, *see* eggs florentine
  Florentine style, 422, *menu*, 259
  squid with, 251
  *"stir-sautéed," 421, *menu*, 240, 323
  with béchamel, *see* Florentine style
  see also naked ravioli, 228
Spinaci alla fiorentina, 422
Spinaci saltati, 421
Spit, mixed meat and fowl roasted on,
      380
  on open air grill, 380–381
  on open air grill improvised in
      oven, 380–1
Spotted grouper, 238, 244
Spring vegetable sauce, 62
Squab, great pie of quail, chicken,
      sausage, tortelli, 383
Squab with macaroni in pastry drum,
      206–211
Squid, 246–253
  how to clean, 246–249
  and shrimp, deep-fried, 249
  with spinach, 251
  stuffed, 252
Steak "sausages" in sauce, fresh, 335
Stock, 107
Stracotto alla fiorentina, 340
Strawberries
  buccellato with, 470
  in Chianti wine, 496
  deep-fried in batter, 497
  wild, 429

Stringbeans, 403–405
  introduction, 403–404
  baked in mold, 426, *menu*, 295
  *boiled, 404
  * fricassee of, 404, *menus*, 245, 319
  *with tomatoes and basil, 405, *menu*,
      355
Stuffed eggs, 94
Stuffed peppers, 94
Stuffed tomatoes, 25
Stuffings and forcemeats, *see:*
  beef, pork, ham, for boned chicken
  chicken breast for tortelli, tortellini
  ricotta for ravioli
  sausages, Tuscan
  spinach and ricotta, for *ravioli,
      della vigilia, rotolo di pasta
      ripieno*
  see also "pudding" of veal, chicken
      breast, and prosciutto
Sugo di carne, 72
Sugo di "cipolle," 73
Sugo di "cipolle" with spaghetti, 157
Sugo di pomodoro fresco, 69
Sugo scappato o di magro, 71
Summer tomato sauce, 70
Swiss chard
  *boiled with olive oil and lemon,
      423, *menus*, 269, 371
  *"stir sautéed," 423, *menus*, 263, 331
Swiss cheese (groviera), 23

Tagliatelle, fresh
  in cream sauce, 147
  with chicken liver sauce, 149
  with cibreo sauce, 148
  with meat sauce, 146
Tagliatelle al sugo di carne, 146
Tagliatelle al sugo di fegatini, 149
Tagliatelle alla panna, 147
Tagliatelle con cibreo, 148
Taglierini al pomodoro fresco, 145
Taglierini in brodo, 109
Taglierini with fresh tomato sauce,
      145
Taillevent, 4
Tarragon, 15
Tarragon sauce from Siena, 63
Tartufi di castagne, 480
Thanksgiving, *menu*, 316
Timballo di pere, 449
Timballo di piccioni, 206

Timballo di polenta con quaglie, 371
Timballo di riso, 222
Timballo di tortellini, 212
Tomato(es)
  history, 5, 24
  baked, 424, *menu*, 242
  and caper, salad, 392
  green
    *deep-fried, 424
    frittata with, 98
  halves with tuna capers and
      maionese, 393
  and mozzarella salad, 392
  paste, 25
  salad, 391, *menu*, 251
  sauces
    fresh, 69, with taglierini, 145
    summer, 70
    winter, 71
  stuffed, 225
Tonno e pomodori, 393
Topini di patate, 232
*Topini di patate con petto di pollo in
    brodo*, 111
Topini of potato and chicken breast
    in broth, 111
Torta di mele, 475
Torta di ricotta, 448
Torta di riso uso Garfagnana, 486
Torta Manfreda, 363
Torta Pasqualina, 234
Tortelli, dessert, 458
Tortelli dolci, 458
Tortelli with fresh mint, 168
Tortelli with Gorgonzola stuffing, 171
Tortelli, great pie of quail, squab,
    chicken, sausage and, 383
Tortelli, half-moon, stuffed with
    spinach and ricotta, 169
Tortelli, pumpkin, Modena style, 174
Tortelli in rabbit sauce, 172
Tortelli al coniglio, 172
Tortelli al gorgonzola, 171
Tortelli alla menta, 168
Tortelli della vigilia, 169
Tortelli di zucca alla modenese, 174
Tortelli dolci, 458
Tortelli, see also *pastello di caccia*
Tortellini in butter and cream
    sauce, 176
Tortellini in meat sauce, 177
Tortellini in a pastry drum, 212

Tortellini al sugo di carne, 177
Tortellini alla panna, 176
Tortellini, timballo di, 212
Trenette with basil sauce (pesto), 153
Trenette al pesto, 153
Triglia, 238
Trippa alla fiorentina, 365
Tripe, Florentine style, 365
Trota al piatto, 242
Trota bollita con maionese, 240
Truffles, 19
Tuna
  fresh, 238
  canned
    flavor, turkey with, 319
    sauce, 74
    sauce, shells with, 160
    tomatoes, and salad, 393
    Tuscan beans, and fresh onions,
        102
Turkey
  history note, 5
  boiled, 267
  breast, rolled, stuffed, 315
  loaf with tuna flavor, 319
Turnip greens, see *Rape*
Tuscan beans, tuna and fresh onions,
    102
Tuscan country bread, 32
Tuscan dark bread, 37
Tuscan garlic bread, 101
Tuscan minestrone, country style,
    122
Tuscan minestrone with rice, 121
Tuscan pureed bean soup, 119
Tuscan whole-wheat bread, 38

Uova
  al pomodoro, 286
  alla fiorentina, 286
  in padella, 288
  ripiene, 94

Veal
  beef cutlets deep-fried, 281
    with anchovy sauce, *note*, 282
  *brains, fried, 277
  foot, boiled, 271, see also gelatina
  head, cheek of, 271
  kidneys, see cibreo sauce
  liver, grilled Florentine style, 357
  liver, sautéed, Tuscan style, 358

Veal (cont.)
  pudding of veal, chicken breast,
    and prosciutto, 375
  *stuffed little, bundles, 331
  tail, boiled, 271
  tongue, boiled, 269
Vegetable, baked, in mold, 426,
    menu, 277
  see also individual vegetables
Verdura, sformati di, 426
Vitella
  braciole fritte, 281
    con acciugata, note, 282
  cervello fritto, 277
  coda, 271
  fegato alla griglia, 357
  fegato alla toscana, 358
  guancia, 271
  involtini di, 331
  lingua di, 269
  zampa, 271

Walnut sauce, 61
Whipped cream
  Florentine style, 434
  meringues with, 468
  with raspberries, 497
  with zabaione, 435

White sauce, 52
Wine
  for cooking, 18
  with menus, *see menus,* 240–386
Wine vinegar, 18
  how to make, 18
Winter tomato sauce, 71

Yeast, 30
Yellow pasta, *see* pasta, fresh

Zabaglione, *see* zabaione
Zabaione, 433
Zabaione, crema, 435
Zampa, 271
Zampone, 269–270, 271
Zucchini
  *boiled, 425
  flowers, fried, 425, *menus,* 275, 281
  fried, 426, *menus,* 249, 275
  selecting, *see* boiled
Zucca (zucchini), *fiori di, fritti,* 425
Zucchini
  bolliti, 425
  fritti, 426
Zuppa di porri, 115
Zuppa inglese, 452
Zuppa lombarda, 129